J. B. Lindsley

Steamboat Pacific
New Orleans to Louisville
Ap. 26. 1859

From

New York to Delhi,

By way of

Rio de Janeiro, Auſtralia and China.

By

Robert B. Minturn, Jr.

SECOND EDITION.

New York:
D. Appleton & Co., 346 & 348 Broadway.
London: 16 Little Britain.
1858.

PREFACE.

THE following work has grown out of a six months' tour in India, just before the outbreak of the recent mutiny. The materials were principally derived from letters intended only for the perusal of my family. I have been induced to give my observations a more permanent form and a wider circulation, both on account of the interest which has been excited in the subject by the events of the last year, and because, considering the size and population of the Indian peninsula, its immense capabilities of production, and the important position that it may hereafter hold in the economy and commerce of the world, it certainly has not hitherto attracted in this country its due share of attention.

The policy and administration of the East India Company's government are so generally misunderstood, and so hopelessly unpopular, that it seems a thankless task to say a word in its favour. I have stated, however, only what I believe to be the truth, after the most careful investigation which I could give. I do not hold, with some, that the East India Company was the only perfect government in modern times; but, on the other hand, I believe that posterity, if not the present generation, will admire and wonder at the sagacity and wisdom of a policy which has enabled fifty thousand men (for, until the late difficulties, there have never been more Englishmen in India) to conquer so vast a country, and hold in subjection myriads of men, of most opposite national character, generally civilized, often warlike, and defended, in more than one instance, by the science and skill of the art of war as practised in Europe.

I am aware that many things which I have stated with regard to the character of the natives of India may appear improbable or incredible. All I can say is, that no European can ever comprehend an Asiastic, and that the more their peculiarities are studied, the more inconsistent they appear. How can Englishmen or Americans ever rightly appreciate people who have no expression in any of their languages for "India," the country in which they live; no equivalent for "thank-you," and no word for "patriotism," and many such ideas.

The last five chapters in the book contain statistical and other information, which would perhaps be most valuable, if perused before the description of the country itself.

Since this work has been written, the East India Company has ceased to exist as a government. One of the Queen's ministers is now in name, as he has long been in fact, the supreme authority in Indian affairs. The very slight modifications introduced into the system of government by the new act is the best possible testimony to the excellence of the old organization, an excellence which can only be found in a system which is based solely upon the conclusions of common sense, and has grown up from the results of practical experience.

The difficulties consequent upon the revolt still continue, but the war is now purely defensive on the part of the rebels, and their fate is certain unless they can find new allies among the native princes or feudal lords. The great heat of the present season, the small number of English troops, and the superiority of the natives in rapid marching, all tend to delay the restoration of order; though they do not seem to strengthen the rebellion, which appears to possess neither unity nor organic vitality enough to spread or become aggressive. Disturbances are now confined to a comparatively small extent of country, and do not affect the peace and security of the peninsula at large.

It now only remains that I should acknowledge the very valuable assistance that I have derived from many previous writers on this subject, especially Colonel Sleeman and M. de Valbezen, whose very words I have, in several instances, followed. The facts and figures which I give I have endeavoured to make as accurate as possible by a careful collation of different authorities, and a reference to official documents, whenever practicable.

New York, *August* 14, 1858.

CONTENTS.

CHAP. I.—RIO DE JANEIRO.

PAGE

Cause of visiting Rio—Entrance of the Harbour—Repairing Vessels at Rio—Porters—European Appearance of the City—Architecture—Priests and Religion—Slaves—Villas in the Country—Tejuca—Substantial Houses—Business—Politeness—Opera—Government—Departure from Rio 13

CHAP. II.—AUSTRALIA.

First View of Australia—Sydney Harbour—The Town and its Climate—Passage to Melbourne—Public Land System—The Road to Ballaarat—Colonial Milestones—Bushrangers 20

CHAP. III.—AUSTRALIA, CONTINUED.

First View of Ballaarat—Description of the Place—Gold Digging—A *Colonial* Theatre—Socialism at the Antipodes—Geelong—Melbourne—Paramatta—Republicanism in Australia—Government and Education—Emigration and probable Future of Australia 27

CHAP. IV.—NORTH CHINA.

The Passage from Australia—Making the Chinese Coast—The Yang-tze-kiang—The Foreign Settlement—Dress and Life of the Resident Europeans—Chinese Soldiers—Natural Characteristics in Northern and Southern China—Native Town of Shanghae—Streets—Pawnbrokers—Public Buildings—Temples, and Worship—Phonographic Writing—State Visit of the Taootai—A Chinese Café—Romish Mission—Executions and Torture—Indifference to Pain shown by Orientals—Captain Marryatt's Story—The "Battle of Shanghae" 37

CHAP. V.—A TRIP INLAND.

Leave Shanghae for a Trip up the Canals—Our Boat—Swimming—Banks of the Canal—Military Stations—Temples—Graves—Villages—Dress of Chinese—Town of Kwunsan—Grain Junks—Comparison of Chinese and American Governments—This part of China once Submerged—Cormorants—Approach to Soo-Chow—The City—"Foreign Devils"—Grand Canal—Heat—Hills near Soo-Chow—View of Ty-hao—Mandarin's Tomb—Ty-hao—Chinese River Thieves—Their Honesty. 50

CHAP. VI.—A TRIP INLAND, CONTINUED.

Ascend Toong-toong-ting-shan—The View—The Great Lake of China—A Beautiful Canal—Villages—Return to Soo-chow—Grand Canal—A Customs' Barrier—A Chinese Fort—Ping-bong—Chinzà—Nan-zing—Effect of Drought on Rice Fields—Our Examination by Mandarins—Preparations for the Rebels—Hoo-chow—Pretty Girls—Are compelled to return to Shanghae—Bridge at Yang-kow-shin—Kahing—Troops—Mandarin's House in Lake—Arrive again at Shanghae—Charity in China 61

Contents.

Chap. VII.—Southern China.

PAGE

Leave Shanghae—The Peninsular and Oriental Company—Hong Kong—Foreign Settlement of Canton—The Chinese Suburbs—Ceremonies at Ming-qua's House —Making Tea—Opium Smoking—The OpiumTrade—Temple of a Hundred Gods —Beggars Dying of Starvation—Interior of a House—A Chinese Restaurant—Chop-sticks—Rat Grills and Dog Stew—Public Opium Shops—The Boat Population of Canton—Indifference to Life—Lepers—How-qua's Garden—Unique Method of Hatching Eggs—Monasteries of Honan—Boodhist Services—Sacred Hogs—Gambling—Macao—A Protective Policy—The Portuguese—Effect of the War on the Commercial Importance of Canton.............................. 72

Chap. VIII.—To Calcutta.

The "Lancefield"—Entomology—Singapore—First View of Orientals—The Parsees —Malays—Gárrhees—Proas—Black Water—Torture—Crew of a Ship in the Indian Seas—Jolly Tars—An Indian Watering-place—The Hoogly—Bores—First View of Natives—Hubble-bubble—Fattening Shell-fish for Market............. 85

Chap. IX.—Calcutta.

Palkees—Buggies—The City of Calcutta—Government House—Tanks—Bazárs—The largest Mint in the World—Supreme Court—Conflict of Laws—Missions and Schools—Spence's Hotel—Servants—Expenses of Living in India—Civil Servants—Their Salaries—The Language of the Camp—A People without a Country, and a Country without a Name.................................... 96

Chap. X.—Calcutta, continued.

Roasting Human Bodies—Adjutants in Calcutta—Unpaid Scavengers—Early Rising —The Morning Drive—"The Strand"—Clothing—Country around Calcutta—"Stations"—Dum-Dum—Artillery Mess—An Ameer of Sind—Barrackpoor—The Sepoys—Too much Petted—Some Causes of the Mutiny........................ 105

Chap. XI.—Calcutta, concluded.

Life in Calcutta—My Friends there—The India Trade—Skill of the Natives in Commerce—Conduct of American Residents during the Revolt—Travelling in India—The Palanquin—"Marching"—Steamboats on the Ganges—Gárrhee-dâk—The Mail-cart.. 116

Chap. XII.—To Benares.

Railway to Raneegunj—Indian Railways—Coal—A Dâk-Gárrhee—Dâk Companies—The Rights of Horses—Leopards and Jackals—Dâk-Bungalows—Scenery—Comparison between Natives of India and China—Land-Tenure—Nullahs—People on the Road—Sahussuram—Two fine Tombs—A Dancing Cow—The Village Zĕmindar—"Taking Leave"—Unsympathetic Character of the Natives—Country between Sahussuram and Bĕnarĕs—Sĕroor.................................... 121

Chap. XIII.—The Holy City of India.

The Sacred Apes—The City from the River—The Observatory—Oriental Science—The Golden Temple—Sacred Bulls—The Great Devil—Hindooism—The Goddess of the Skull-Chaplet—Poojah—The Holy Well—Self-Torture—Caste—Brahmunical Regeneration—Supremacy of the Sacred Caste............................ 136

Chap. XIV.—Benares, concluded.

PAGE

Religious Ablutions—Aurungzeeb's Mosque—View from Minâr—Burning Ghât—Market Place—Hindoo College—"Native Gentlemen"—European Manners and Morals in India—Ruins of a Boodhist Monastery—Gold Brocade—Opium....... 147

Chap. XV.—Allahabad—"The City of God."

Arrival at Allahabad—Zubburdustee—Seekhs—Hindoostanees—Fort at Allahabad—An Invisible River—Sooltan Khooshroo's Surai—Hindoostanee Wells—Allahabad to Cawnpoor—Bullock Trains—Elephantiasis.................................. 154

Chap. XVI.—Cawnpoor to Lucknow.

The Station of Cawnpoor—Disorder in Oude—Cawnpoor to Lucknow—Elephants—Kaorees—Lucknow—Making Ice—The Weather—The Generosity of the Sovereign Company—My Man Brown—First View of Lucknow—A Moral—The Gate of Rome—The Taza—The Imambara—A Fine Coup-d'œil—Situation of Oude—Splendour of the Court—Indian Misgovernment—Indian Gentlemen—Extortion and Tortures—Lord Canning's Confiscation—Brutal Degradation of the Court—Relations of the East India Company to the King of Oude—Violated Faith..... 160

Chap. XVII.—Lucknow, concluded.

A Morning Surprise—Salâm—Native Polish—Hindoo Manners—Parade—Red Coat—Character of Sepoys—An Army of Priests and Kings—Caste Misunderstood—Pariahs—India Conquered for the English by Natives—Bullock Artillery—"Hathee pur Howdah" or Elephant Riding—Rich Dresses—Chokeedârs—Fukheers—A Coat of Paint—Royal Palace—Vanity—The Social Evil—A Modern Sodom—Defence of the Lucknow Residency—The Massacre of Cawnpoor....... 178

Chap. XVIII.—To Meeruth.

Appearance of Country—Bishop Heber—Christian Missions—Colonel Tucker—Country between Futtehghur and Meeruth—Ganges Canal—An Indian "Station"—Sirdhâna—Dyce Sombre's Tomb—Free Lances of India—An Ingenious Process for Collecting Money—A Female General—Success of the Bégoom—To Mozuffurnuggur—Dhoolee Travelling—Persian Inscription—Natural History.. 192

Chap. XIX.—The Himalayas.

A Night in a Dhoolee—The Turai Forest—First View of the Snowy Range—Siwalik Hills—Ram! Ram!—The Dhoon Valley—Rajpoor—Ascent of the Himalayas—Puharrees—Munsooree—Indian Hospitality—Landoor—View of Snow-clad Peaks—Hill-stations—An Accident—The Descent—Agriculture in India—Tea Plantation—Chinese Workmen—A Snake Fight............................. 202

Chap. XX.—Return to Meeruth.

Rev. Mr. Woodside's—American Missionaries—Opening of the Ganges Canal—Excitement of Natives—Moral Effect—Missionaries' Opinion of the Company's Government—Its General Effects—Native States—A Seekh Temple—The Gooroo—Farewell to my Countrymen—Last View of Himalayas—Roorkhee—Workshops—Native Workmen—Repugnance between the English and Native Races—The Ganges Canal—Other Buildings—Meeruth Again—Mutiny at Meeruth—Conduct of Officers and their Feelings toward the Sepoys...................... 213

CHAP. XXI.—THE IMPERIAL CITY OF DELHI.

PAGE

First View of Delhi—Entrance to the City—The Palace—The Houses Low—The Arsenal—Col. Skinner's—The Church—The Square of Death—The Signal Tower—Drive to Kootub—Ruins—Old Delhi—An Imperial Whim—Sufdur Jung's Tomb—The Kootub—Indian Sam Patches—The Observatory—Chandee Chok, the Broadway of Delhi—Dandy Moosulmans—The Mosque of Slaughter.. 224

CHAP. XXII.—DELHI, CONTINUED.

A Juggler—Poses Plastiques—Entrance to Palace—Dewán Am—Emperor's Throne—Mosaics—Drawing First Blood—A Paradise on Earth—Peacock Throne—A Microcosmic View of the Mogul Empire—Shah Jehan in State—A Hundred Years Later—Native Tact—The Glory has Departed—Maharattas in the Palace—Gholam Kadur, the Rohilla, seated on the Royal Throne—Restoration of the Empire by the British—Their Majesties, and their "Particular Slaves"—The Last Emperor—The Last Tenants of the Dewán Khas—The Pearl Mosque—Palace Gardens—The Jumma Musjeed—View from Minár—Moosulman Worship—Feerooz's Walking Stick—Hoomaioon's Tomb—Chubootras—Peculiarities of Mahommedan Architecture—Capture of the King of Delhi.................... 236

CHAP. XXIII.—DELHI AND UMBALA.

The Saint's Tomb—A Royal Cemetery—A Victim of the English—The Old Fort—A Nach at Mr. Skinner's—The Dinner—The Girls—Their Songs—Dancing Boys—Native Gentlemen—Snakes—The Bazárs of Delhi—The Streets—A Native Wedding—A "Public Night" at the Mess of the 54th—Dâk to Umbala—Sick—A Dandy Servant—"Vengeance is Sweet"—Sepoy Bands—The Native Army—Cashmeer Shawls.. 251

CHAP. XXIV.—RETURN TO DELHI.

Desertion—Life of an Indian Officer—Christmas Evening at Mr. Beresford's—The Mutiny at Delhi—Murder of my Friends—Fate of the Beresfords—The Revolted Emperor's Government—The City while held by the Mutineers—Uniform Defeats of the Mutineers—The Siege and Assault—Taking of the City and Flight of the Mutineers—News of the Taking of Delhi—The City after its Occupation by the English—Wholesale Punishment.. 269

CHAP. XXV.—AGRA.

Arrival at Agra—The Taj—Its Proportions—Mosaics—The "Tribe of the Infidels"—"The Ornament of the Palace"—Cost of the Taj—The Fort—The Pearl Mosque—The Dewán Am—Dewán Khas—A Seat for a Sovereign—A Court of the Zĕnana—The Palace of Mirrors—The Terrace—Sleeping Rooms—Town of Alexander—The Printing Establishment—Akbur's Tomb—Akbur's Character—His Legislative and Administrative Acts—His Religion—An Unexpected Meeting—Dine with my American Friends—"Young Bengal"—Illumination of the Taj—Revisit the Palace—An Indian Oubliette—The Old Hindoo Palace—Hindoo Art—A Great Well—A Pleasant Summer Residence—Presentation of Colours—Commander-in-Chief's Camp—Manly Sports—The Cathedral—Rambagh—Tomb of Aktmud-ood-Dowlah—"The Light of the Harem"—Her Ambition and its Success.. 281

Chap. XXVI.—Agra to Jaipoor.

PAGE

Chowdris—Combination *versus* Competition—Our Retinue—Price of Labour—Commercial Integrity—Leaving Agra—The Departure of "A Warrior Lord"—A Loan to the Sovereign Company—The Royal Pilgrimage—"Seekree, the City of Victory—Tomb of a Wealthy Saint—Bishop Heber's Guide—Human Chessmen —Blind-man's Buff—A Triumph for Religion—"Pointing a Moral" Four Rupees' worth of Picturesque Piety—Bhurtpoor—English Protection and its Fruits—An Indian Sebastopol—Rajah's Palace—Battle of Deeg—Quail Fighting—A Boxing Match—Deer—Bosawur—Breakfast at 3 P. M.—Antelopes—Manpoor—Walled Villages—Naked Sanctity—Buranah—Hills of Jaipoor—Palace of the Rajah—Jaipoor........ 300

Chap. XXVII.—Jaipoor.

Elephants—Beauty of the City—The Zĕnana and Palace—Novel Stairways—View from Roof—A Court—Revenue Department—Dewán Khas—Sitringees—Native Furniture—Curtain-ladies—A Lovely Character—Palace Gardens—His Highness' Toys—"Composite Architecture"—Native College—Marriage Nach—Observatory—Palace in Lake—Palaces of Ummeer—Tiffin in the Reception Court —Bishop Heber's Praises of the Palace—Bazár of Jaipoor—History of Jaipoor... 320

Chap. XXVIII.—Rajpootana—"The Country of Princes."

Bugroo—Peacock Shooting—Thakoor's House—Dhoodoo—Superstition about Wells Jain Temple—Kishinghur—Visit from Baboo—Rajah's Palace—Excitement of the Public—A Dancing Elephant—Road to Ajmeer—Scenery—Dress and Manners of Rajpoots—Fort of Ajmeer—Ruins of a Hindoo Palace—Nusseerabad—Bombay Sepoys—The Shop of a Fire-worshipper—Bunai—Hindoo Cooking—A Native Huntsman—Dáblah—Filial Grief—Bunaira—Remarkable Castle—Road to Ummeerghur—Cheap Meat—The Day of Rest........ 331

Chap. XXIX.—Country of the Maharattas.

Arrival at Chittór—Seven Miles of Ruins—Tank—The Moon Lady—The Great Temple—Hindoo Religious Architecture—The Great Tower—Antiquity of Hindoo Ruins—Religious Pic-nic—Enter the Maharatta Territories—"Zubburdustee"—"The Good Old Rule"—Poppy-fields—Neemuch—Noble Banyan Tree—Irrigation—Mundissoor—A Pleasant Resting-place—Jowra—Nawáb's English Palace —Khachród—New Style of Architecture—The Soobah's Politeness—Oojen—The City—Temple of Kunaia—The God's Carriage—Indian "Punch"—The Maharattas—A Native Government—Professional Robbing—Spread of the Maharatta Power—Nature of their Government—Their Subjugation by the English—Gwalior States—The Police—Indirect Utility of Native Misrule........ 342

Chap. XXX.—To Ellora.

March of Sir R. Hamilton—Indor—The Rajah's Palace—Strike into the Mail-road—Revolt of Kuhárs—Origin of the Present Rajah—Mhow—Goojree—Kurrumpoora—A Stray White Man—Manners of Natives—Sindwar—Fortress in Ruins—Sirpoorah—Peculiar Police Regulation—Old Venetian Coins—Dhoolia—Native Town—Evidences of having entered British Territory—Malligaum—Cantonments—Native Town—Nandgao*n*—Camp in a Grove—Sakigao*n*—Put up in a Temple—Enter the Dĕkkun—Physical Geography—The Nizam—"Might makes Right........ 360

Chap. XXXI.—The Cave Temples of Ellora.

PAGE

General Description of the Temples—Khailas—Fine Sculptures—"The Work of Gods or Devils?"—Other Caves—A Heavenly Carpenter—A Disorderly Household—View from Hill—Saint's Tomb—Roza—Aurungzeeb's Tomb—His Character—Splendour and Power—Decay of the Mogul Empire—A Night in Paradise—Indra Sabha—Sonorous Obelisks—The Doorma Lena—Architectural Ornaments of the Caves—Hindoo Religious Mendicants—Peasantry—Their Complexions 370

Chap. XXXII.—To Bombay.

Road to Dowlutabad—"The City of Riches"—A Stronghold—The "Master of the Plain"—Meet "the Moon-Lady" again—Aurungabad—A Magician—Tomb of Aurungzeeb's Daughter—Another Revolt—Separation of our Forces—Toka—The Godaveri—Brahmuns—A Hungry God—Rope-and-boat Bridge—Imampoor—Ahmudnuggur—Meet our Friends—The Fort—The Kingdom of Ahmudnuggur—The Largest Brass Cannon in the World—Duelling among Natives of India—Chand Beebee again—Death of Aurungzeeb—Bombay Kuhârs—Sĕroor—Kondapoora—The River Kistna—Poonah—Dismiss our Kuhârs—Good-bye to Dhoolee-travelling—Irregular Cavalry 380

Chap. XXXIII.—Bombay.

Khandâla—The Ghât Mountains—Cave Temples—The Railway—Obstacles to its Construction—Situation of Bombay—The Fort—Native Town—Residences of Europeans—Growth of Eastern Cities—Commercial Ability of Natives—Commerce of Bombay and Calcutta—Variety of Nationalities represented in Bombay—Parsees—Their Costume, Religion, and Customs—Sir Jamsetjee Jeejeebhoy—Other Native Inhabitants—Hindooism in Bombay—Bóhoras and Portuguese—Peculiarities of English—Degeneracy of all other Nations in the East—The Hoolee—Nach at the House of Juggurnathjee Sunkurset—Anglomania in India—Old Hindoo Costume—Cave Temple of Elephanta 390

Chap. XXXIV.—Bombay to Cairo.

The "Ganges"—Our Fellow-passengers—The Crew—Life on the Steamer—Aden—Its Appearance—"Hell with the fires put out"—An Original Head-dress—Arabs—The Cantonments—The Fortifications—Importance of the City—Free Trade—A Foot-print of Civilization—The "Gate of Tears"—The Red Sea—Its Heat—Suez—Transit Across the Desert—Its Appearance—The Road—The Pyramids—The "City of Victory"—A Recommendation for Indian Travel 402

Chap. XXXV.—Climate and History of India.

Size of the Country—Not Thickly Settled—Rainy Season—Cold Season—Hot Season—Unfit for a Residence of Europeans—Effect on their Health—Origin of the Present Inhabitants of India—The Hindoo Conquest—Remnants of the Aborigines—The Four Castes—Changes in Them—Arguments in Favour of this Hypothesis—Mahommedan Invasions—Tamerlane—Foundation of Mogul Empire by Babur—Akbur—Shah Jehan—Aurungzeeb—Decay of the Empire—Revolts—Maharattas—Rajpoots—Death of Aurungzeeb—The Seekhs—Utter Disorganization—Nadur Shah's Invasion—Rise of the English—Conduct of the Company toward Conquered Princes—Annexation contrary to the Company's Policy—Character of Native Dynasties—Government of Dependent States.... 410

Chap. XXXVI.—English Government in India.

PAGE

Abolition of Company's Trading Privileges—Board of Control—Government of India Nominally in the Hands of the Directors, but really under the Control of the Ministry—Civil Servants Appointed by Examination—Objections to this System —Unfitness of Natives for Government Employ—Government in India—District Magistrates—Salaries—Character of the Civil Service—Native Employees—Uncovenanted Service—Universal Lying—Instances from Real Life—Rules of Testimony—Civil Law of India—Mild Criminal Code—Thugs—Dukoitee—Religious Murderers and Robbers—Infanticide and other Crimes—Suttee and Human Sacrifices—Poisoners—Peculiarities of Crime in India—Thieves—Stealing a Sheet from under a Man Sleeping—Precautions—Disregard of Capital Punishment—Black Water—Blowing from Guns—Model Prisons—Caste in Jail—Smoking—Licentiousness—Discourteous Manners of English to Native Gentlemen—What is a Gentleman?—Difficulties of Magistrates—Native Police—Their Corruption and Tyranny—Torture in India—Bribery and Corruption—The Remedy—Causes of the Moral Degradation of the Hindoos 425

Chap. XXXVII.—The Army of India.

Its Strength—Different Classes of Troops—English and Native Officers—Enlistment purely Voluntary—Pay—Madras Army—Bombay Army—Low-Caste Men—An Army of Gentlemen—Truckling to Caste—Tame Tigers—Salaries of Officers—Staff-Service 451

Chap. XXXVIII.—Revenue and Wealth of India.

Undeveloped Condition of the Resources of India—Cotton—Obstacles to Development—Small Agriculturalists—Caste—Want of Capital among Agricultural Classes—Inferiority of Native Labour—Want of Roads—Railways—Ganges Canal —Want of European Capital and Energy—Obstacles to the Supply of this—Land-tax under Native Governments—Under the English—Lord Cornwallis's "Settlement"—The Madras System—The "Village System"—Its Advantages—To be made still more Liberal—Revenue and Expenses of the Indian Government—Low Taxation—*India a Poor Country*—Misapprehensions that have prevailed with regard to the Wealth of Oriental Nations 456

Chap. XXXIX.—The Revolt.

Indian Rebellion not a Matter of Surprise—Revolutions and Rebellions common under Native Governments—Rebellion did not originate among the People—Character of the old Native Governments—Nature of the English Conquest, and Character of their Rule—Evidence that the Rebellion was not a Movement of the People—The Rebellion was not in its Origin a Military Mutiny—The real Instigators were the Moosulman Princes—It was the dying Effort of Islamism—Character of the Mahommedan Population of India—Favourable Circumstances for the Rebel Leaders—Abortive Attempts of the Rebels to arouse the Mass of the Population—The Moosulman Character of the Movement evident in its Development—Atrocities—Noble Stand of the English—The Revolt in Oude—Sympathies of the Population of India—The Disaffected Classes—The probable Result of the Rebellion if it had not been restrained 470

ORTHOGRAPHY.

In writing Indian names and words, I have thought best to adopt a uniform system of spelling, choosing the one in common use in India, rather than that system which has been adopted by the Asiatic Society, and which is, perhaps, neater, but has the disadvantage of giving to every vowel a sound different from its common English pronunciation. In the system which I have followed:

a	is pronounced like		*a*	in	*all*
ă	"	"	*a*	in	*bat*
e	"	"	*e*	in	*there*
ĕ	"	"	*e*	in	*met*
i, or *ĭ*	"	"	*i*	in	*bit*
o	"	"	*o*	in	*so*
ŏ	"	"	*o*	in	*rock*
u	"	"	*u*	in	*but*
y, vowel	"	"	*y*	in	*my*
y, consonant	"	"	*y*	in	*young*
ai	"	"	*ai*	in	*aisle*
au, or *aw*	"	"	*au*	in	*author*
ee	"	"	*ee*	in	*see*
oi, or *oy*	"	"	*oi*	in	*noise*
oo	"	"	*oo*	in	*soon*
ou, or *ow*	"	"	*ou*	in	*house*

The consonants are generally pronounced as in English. *G* is always hard. The letters in *th* and *ph* are pronounced separately, as in *out-house* and *uphill*. *N*, in italics, represents the sound of the French nasal *n*. The acute accent does not change the sound of the vowel, but only indicates the syllable on which the stress of the voice is laid. The circumflex accent also does not change the sound of the vowel, and has only been used in a few instances to prevent long vowels from being carelessly pronounced short.

In the case of certain proper names, I have varied from my system in order not to appear pedantic. Thus, I write Hoogly, not Hooglee; Oude, not Owd; Delhi, not Dihli, or Dillee; Aurungzeeb, not Owrung-zeeb; Mahommedans, not Mohummudans. The latter spelling of each of these words would more truly represent its real pronunciation, but would appear uncouth.

CHAPTER I.

RIO DE JANEIRO.

Cause of visiting Rio—Entrance of the Harbour—Repairing Vessels at Rio—Porters—European Appearance of the City—Architecture—Priests and Religion—Slaves—Villas in the Country—Tejuca—Substantial Houses—Business—Politeness—Opera—Government—Departure from Rio.

WE entered the harbour of Rio de Janeiro on the 16th of January, 1856, having made Cape Frio the day before. The ship on which I was a passenger, was bound for Sydney, and thence for China; but a succession of those violent gales, which, in that winter, destroyed so much property and so many lives on our coast, had completed the work begun by a summer's sun in New York, and when about a fortnight out, we found the ship leaking badly, a state of things which finally compelled us to put into Rio and caulk our upper works.

The entrance to Rio harbour surpassed the highest expectations which any of us had formed. The mouth is narrow and bordered by lofty walls of granite, rising steep and sheer for 1,500 or 2,000 feet, while farther back the Pâo d'Assucar, or "Sugar Loaf," towers into the air—the first of a series of sharply-defined, lofty, barren, and isolated peaks surrounding the harbour, and imparting a grandeur to the rich verdure of its immediate shores, which they would not otherwise possess. From the foot of these peaks, the land slopes gradually down to the water's edge, and is covered with beautiful villas, mostly in the Italian style, embowered in that luxuriant foliage and redundant vegetation which we are accustomed to associate with the idea of a tropical climate.

Passing the picturesque fort which guards the entrance to the bay, we sailed up three or four miles, and cast anchor among a crowd of vessels, all with their ensigns set. On our left, situated on a low flat of not more than two miles' breadth to the foot of the hills, lay the city of Rio. The ground on which it is built is all *made*, or, rather, the city is built upon piles, the locality having been formerly a marsh. It is, ot course, low and flat, and drainage is an impossibility, which accounts for its great unhealthiness at certain seasons. There is usually a great deal of shipping in the harbour, as there is considerable trade, and this is a favourite place of repair for vessels which may have become dismasted or otherwise injured on the voyage to India, Australia, or the western coast of America. In this respect Rio has rather a bad reputation, as the repairing of damaged ships has become a regular branch of trade, and is remarkably well understood—many of the ship-carpenters finding themselves in a position to allow a handsome percentage to such ship-masters as will give them a job. I heard of one or two captains who had put in there with disabled vessels, and who were supplied with luxurious country seats, where they were kept in a continuous round of dissipation while their ships were refitting. Of course, they could not afterwards question the charges of those who had provided for them a "home and all its comforts" in a foreign land, and taken all the tedium of business off their hands.

Most of the loading and discharging at Rio is done by lighters—there being but one wharf. The merchandise is conveyed from the lighters to the shore by negroes, who wade up to their middle in the water, carrying the goods on their heads. On shore, these fellows walk in a long procession, singing a monotonous song. They seem to prefer carrying burdens on their heads—transporting the very heaviest articles in this way. I have seen as many as sixteen men carrying a piano forte, locking step as they walked, and all joining in the song, which, in this case, was of real importance as enabling them to keep step. It is said that when the railway to Petropolis was being built, the negroes insisted on carrying the handbarrows, which were furnished to them, on their heads, turning the wheel in front with the hand, in time to their song. The negro porters are fine burly men, and are always slaves. They are, however, only required to bring home to their master a certain sum each day, which amounts to about one half or two thirds of what they can earn. On landing, I was much struck with the *European* appearance of every thing. The buildings are of that substantial character which may be of any age, and which is so different from the prevailing taste in North America. A large plaza with a fountain borders on the quay, and directly in front of the landing, occupying one side of the square, is the Royal Palace, a large, but not a striking building, where, however, the Emperor rarely resides. In front of the palace gate two negro soldiers were keeping guard. The army is entirely composed of free blacks, by whom, also, the navy is manned. How reliable they may be, I did not have an opportunity of learning. The streets of Rio are narrow—a very good peculiarity in a climate where there is much sun. The houses are usually large, and built with walls three or four feet thick. The shops are full of French goods—the taste of the Brazilians being decidedly Gallic. The churches are not fine, though very massive. They are all in that *Jesuitical* style which distinguishes modern Romish churches everywhere. The interior decoration is generally tawdry. The priests are a low, filthy, and dirty set; very immoral, and far from popular, yet they are said to have great control over the Emperor. They have not been able, however, to prevent the toleration of Protestant opinions, and the free circulation of the Scriptures. A very pretty custom prevails here in celebrating the funerals of children. The pall, the liveries of the coachmen and grooms, and all the decorations are scarlet, while the hearse is covered with flowers placed there by friends, and thrown from house windows as the procession passes through the streets. In the case of young people, not children, blue decorations replace the red; black being reserved for those who are grown up or advanced in life.

The streets of Rio are filled with negroes, free and slaves—many of the latter being African born—and known by the tribal mark branded on their foreheads. Slavery exists, however, in Brazil, or, at least, in Rio, in a mitigated form. Any negro may demand a valuation by a magistrate, and, whenever he can make up the sum fixed, may purchase his own freedom. On becoming free, a negro assumes shoes, a luxury not allowed to slaves. The price of slaves is now high on account of the suppression of the slave trade during the last four or five years, and it is to be presumed that planters cannot now afford to indulge often in the amusement of *boiling* a negro, a sight which two Quakers, who wrote a little work on Brazil, were invited to witness. The negroes live principally on a powdered root termed "farinha," black beans, and fruit. Wages are very low. Negro porters, of whom there are a great many, lie about in baskets, like the *lazzaroni* in the streets of Naples. One of these fellows will carry a parcel a mile, and consider himself well paid by two cents.

The country around Rio is very pretty, and filled with villas and suburban residences belonging to the richer inhabitants. The buildings are low (one or two stories), but built at great expense, with walls two feet thick. The exteriors are stuccoed and decorated with arabesque ornaments on a ground of blue or some gaudy colour, the roof being invariably of bright-red tile. One of these houses, in a beautifully kept garden of tropical plants and trees, has an Eden-like effect, which must be seen to be appreciated. I think that some of the larger and better kept of these residences, might well have written over their gates, the celebrated inscription on the Dewan-ee-Khas at Delhi, "If there be a Paradise on Earth, it is here, it is here!"

Tejuca and Petropolis are both summer resorts, within a few hours' ride of the city. I visited the former only. The scenery is, I think, as fine as anything in Switzerland, though of course, in quite a different style. The immense granite masses which border the gorge through which the road passes, and the views of the sea through the narrow valleys are something magnificent. Near Tejuca I saw much coffee growing; it looks like a hardy plant and did not seem to have been carefully cultivated. Banana trees are, of course, to be seen everywhere, being somewhat of a weed among the trees; and I saw, besides, the breadfruit, bamboo, orange, lemon, palm and palm.

While at Rio, I could not help noticing and admiring the substantial character of all the buildings. The streets are paved with square blocks of stone, and lighted with gas; the walls of the dwellings are of great thickness. Durability and comfort seem to have been much more consulted than in the United States, where, in weather occasionally just as hot, we live in wooden houses, not even filled in with brick. The store of M. W. & Co., the consignees of the ship on which I was a passenger, was a model of its kind. An immense building, with solid walls four feet thick, contained the offices, the rooms where the employees lived, a large parlor looking on the bay, a saloon where partners and clerks all dined in common at two o'clock, and warehouses where their goods were stored. I got, from some of the American residents of Rio, a very curious, and well-nigh incredible, account of the way in which business is done there. A sale for *cash* implies a credit of two or three months, within which it is a personal offence to ask for your money; and one is expected to renew a note as often as requested, provided the interest be punctually paid. I say "a note," but the fact is, that even the largest transactions have, as I was told, in general, only a verbal guarantee.

The market of Rio is well supplied with fruit all the year round (and here I may remark, that no one knows the taste of an orange who has not eaten it fresh from the tree); the fish are very fine; the mutton is excellent, but the beef poor. Oxen and horses do not thrive in Brazil for some reason, probably, at least in the case of horses, from not being fed on grain.

The Brazilians are a tame, inoffensive people. A very marked feature in their manners, that strikes a stranger directly, is their great politeness. On entering or leaving an omnibus you uncover and bow to the company, who do the same; and at a *table d'hôte* the same formality is complied with by all who leave before the rest, the whole company rising and bowing. I was sorry that we could not remain for the carnival, which took place a week after we left, and is, I understood, well kept up. The Brazilians are very fond of holidays, and are always ringing the church bells and firing salutes from the fort in honour of one day or another. The ships in the harbour were until lately bound to reply to these salutes, but as they used good powder, while the Brazilian government bought large quantities of damaged stuff for the purpose, they found it rather expensive. The various admirals, therefore, took advantage of a period of sickness among the men, and gave that as an excuse for not replying, alleging that the noise disturbed their sick men. This was three years ago, and I believe that they have not resumed saluting since.

I went to the Opera the last evening that I spent in Rio. The house is a temporary affair, but the singing and music are good; and I had an opportunity of seeing the Emperor and Empress, and the ladies of Rio, who are seldom visible in the street. The Emperor was a fine looking man, about thirty years old when I saw him—the Empress, a great, heavy, Spanish-looking woman, much older than her husband. Of the beauty of those specimens of Brazilian ladies which I saw, I cannot say much. Their majesties came without any state, in a *coupé*, drawn by eight mules. Their arrival produced no commotion in the audience, but I suppose much enthusiasm could hardly have been expected, as the Emperor attends the opera every night. His suite were in court-dress, but himself and the Empress in the simplest evening costume. It seemed to be very common to bring little children to the opera, at least among the occupants of the boxes—but as they and all the *élite* left when the Emperor did, at 10 o'clock, this is perhaps not surprising. His majesty is said to be an intelligent man, fond of, and well read in, the sciences, but not possessing enough strength of character to resist the Jesuitical influence which surrounds him.

The government of Brazil is very liberal, both houses of the Parliament being elected by the people, and the lower house having complete control if there be in it a majority of three-fourths in favor of a measure; since, if the Senate do not agree, the two houses meet in convention, and a plurality of votes passes the law. The Senate can always be outvoted, as its number is small compared to that of the House. The Emperor's veto *suspends* a law for one year, when, if it be again passed by the Legislature, it takes effect. The government is thus a real republic, with a permanent executive deprived of legislative power. There are, however, some ardent young men in the country who desire a republic in name. This would be, as an old American resident once said to me, the worst thing that could happen to Brazil, as it would probably subject her to those periodical *pronunciamentos*, revolutions and upturnings of the whole government, which have ruined all the Spanish-American republics.

On the morning of the 25th we sailed out of Rio harbour, our ship having been made thoroughly tight by caulking the upper works. We again admired the lofty rock-bound coast, the highest peaks of which we did not lose sight of till the afternoon of the following day. The weather had been clear and sultry the whole time of our visit, and the great heat (the thermometer having ranged between 80° and 90°), made it pleasant to get to sea again.

CHAPTER II.

AUSTRALIA.

First View of Australia—Sydney Harbour—The Town and its Climate—Passage to Melbourne—Public Land System—The Road to Ballaarat—Colonial Milestones—Bushrangers.

On the morning of the 8th of April, 1856, I had my first view of the coast of Australia—a long line of low cliffs, with no visible break for the mouth of Sydney harbour, of which, nevertheless, we were nearly abreast. The fact is, the opening is so narrow, and the harbour makes so short a turn (if I may be allowed the expression), that its mouth is almost invisible, except when one is just entering. It is said that, when Captain Cook was in this part of the world, as he sailed down this coast, the man who was stationed at the mast head to look out for harbours and landmarks, hailed the deck and announced that a harbour's mouth was in sight. Before, however, the captain could get on deck, the ship had gone so far that the narrow entrance was quite invisible. The man was, in consequence, reprimanded for giving false alarms, but the circumstance was entered on the ship's log-book, together with the man's name, Jackson. Soon after, the mouth of Botany Bay came in sight, and as there could be no doubt of that being a harbour, it was entered, surveyed and named. When the government sent the first ship load of convicts to Australia, Botany Bay was the place chosen for their disembarkation, but as its shores were found unsuitable for a settlement, the country round was reconnoitred, and Sydney Bay, twelve miles off, chosen for the convict colony. As the new location possessed every advantage, both for the settlement and as regarded the harbour, no more convicts were ever sent to Botany

Bay; and as it was recognized that Jackson had been right, after all, in his discovery, the bay was called after his name, and is now known as Port Jackson or Sydney Harbour. It is one of the finest harbours in the world, and there are few that excel it in beauty. It wants the lofty mountains which give so much grandeur to the harbour of Rio, but the fine slope of its banks, which are studded with country seats (the houses generally of white stone), and the numerous picturesque coves and islands give it a peculiar beauty. As the bay takes a turn immediately inside the heads and runs parallel with the coast, the harbour's mouth is, from most parts, quite invisible. This gives the view a lake-like appearance, that adds much to its effect. The Government House, too, an extensive castellated building, standing on a promontory which forms part of a finely laid out park, "the Domain," as it is called, is visible from all parts of the bay, and has a really fine appearance—the royal standard flying from one of the turrets, giving it a good deal the air of Windsor Castle, though it is of course not so large. The harbour is no less excellent in point of utility, the water being so deep that the largest vessels can enter, while the shores are so abrupt that ships can lie anywhere close to the land, and wharves are almost unnecessary, and the peculiar turn which I have described the bay as making, with the narrowness of the entrance and the height of the surrounding land, protects vessels from all effects of gales.

Sydney itself, is built around one of the coves at the further end of the harbour, and covers also the promontory which divides it from the next cove. It contains now about 85,000 inhabitants, and is an English town in every respect. In some parts you would suppose you were in London, were it not that all the houses are of a bright yellow freestone. This is the cheapest building material, as the woods of the country are too hard for such purposes; they do, however, excellently well for rafters, &c., and are almost fireproof. A great deal of Oregon pine is exported to Australia, for building, but goes mostly to Melbourne, the outskirts of which city resemble New York beyond the fire limits. The inhabitants of Sydney are mostly English, and preserve the old country manners remarkably. Drunkenness is very prevalent, and I more than once saw women drunk on the sidewalk at nine in the morning. In fact, I never saw so much drinking anywhere as in Australia. It is, however, a curious fact, that the "natives," as they call the descendants of Europeans, born in Australia, do not, as a general rule, drink at all. These "natives" are very different in appearance from Englishmen, tall and thin, arriving at puberty earlier than in England, and frequently with an indescribably mild eye and voice. They are said to be much inferior to their parents in energy. When I was in Australia, there had lately been a controversy among the physicians, as to whether the climate is favourable to the European race or not. It was admitted that disease of the heart was more prevalent than elsewhere; and that the teeth go to ruin as rapidly as in America, but in other respects the climate seemed to hold its own against its impugners. Another hundred years will settle the question much more firmly. The weather is oppressively hot, at times. When the "Brickfielders," the north-westerly winds from the interior deserts, blow, the thermometer occasionally rises to 120° in the shade, for a short time, and clouds of dust make it impossible to go out of doors. But the great heat does not last long, and the weather is generally delightful. Frost and snow are sometimes seen in the interior, but never on the coast, and the trees are green all the year round, the old leaves falling only in the spring, when they are forced off by the new.

Sydney has the advantage of a finely kept park, "The Domain," consisting of about 30 acres, running along the shores of the bay, and enclosing a Botanical Garden, in which are the plants of all climates, growing side by side, in the open air. The oak, however, and other northern trees, do not seem to thrive—all the specimens that I saw being puny and stunted.

There are but few fine buildings in Sydney—the cathedral being incomplete. There are, however, several very fair stone churches, and the houses, though none of them are showy, have a well built, comfortable look. The police is excellent, on the plan of that in London—the mounted police, particularly, who patrol the town at night, are as well mounted, and fine looking men, as ever I saw.

MELBOURNE.

After remaining three days in Sydney, I left for Melbourne. There is, as yet, no road between the two places—the only connection being by water. The steamers are fine, iron-built, sea boats, with every comfort, and very gentlemanly captains. And here I must bear my testimony, that as far as my experience is concerned, the class of men who command English steamers, is at least equal to any similar body in our service, while there are some of them who, I think, surpass any that we have, in knowledge of the world, and refinement. With respect to scientific acquirements, the examinations which English masters and mates have to pass before they are entrusted with the care of a vessel, at least ensure a greater amount of *scientific* accuracy than can be found in the American service.

I made the acquaintance, on board the steamer of several "squatters," as the sheep and cattle farmers are called in the colonies, and got a good deal of information from them about the "squatter-system" of disposing of public lands, which is so deservedly unpopular among the miners. It seems that if a man wants a "run," as a sheep farm is called, he may get one in three ways: 1st. By buying one already occupied, in which case he buys the stock also: 2nd, by attending a government land auction, where the land is sold to the highest bidder above £1 the acre: 3d, if he fancies a particular unoccupied run, he gives in his name and a description of the run at the land-office, with proofs that he is able and ready to stock the land directly. After a certain time, if no other applicant presents himself, he receives the land at the upset-price of £1 the acre, but if another applies for the same run, the highest bidder has the preference. This system, of course, throws all the land into the hands of a few large proprietors, and renders it impossible for a poor man to get a few acres to cultivate, at a reasonable price—since, in the vicinity of the coast, all the lands are already taken up as sheep farms, by men who do not wish to have settlers in their midst. And further back, even if the Government could sell lands for other purposes than sheep-raising, the distance from the coast, and the absence of roads, would prevent all profitable cultivation. The squatter system is, then, as before remarked, very unpopular among the miners; and in Victoria, (the colony of which Melbourne is capital,) the squatters are looked on as a sort of landed aristocracy, whose interests are directly opposed to the best interests of the colony. What farming is done, is all on the coast, whence produce can be readily conveyed by coasters to Sydney and Melbourne. Fruit, of all kinds, which can be grown all the year round at Moreton Bay, a place about three hundred miles up the coast from Sydney, is, in Sydney, dearer than I ever saw it elsewhere—pine-apples as expensive as they used to be in London, peaches three to four shillings per dozen, and common cooking apples at the same price.

It is about fifty hours, run (four hundred miles) from Sydney to Melbourne. I arrived in the evening, and after a night in a dirty hotel, where I was nearly eaten up by fleas and mosquitoes, started next morning at six for Ballaarat diggings. We got off at a full gallop—a pace that was kept up, with a few exceptions, the whole way, doing the ninety miles in about eleven hours.

The coaches being under the control of an American, or rather having been started by one, are in the shape of American country "extras," long wagons, uncovered, with half-a-dozen seats facing the same way. The horses seemed to be all fine, fresh, well-groomed animals—as they must have been to sustain the pace for the stages of ten miles. My fellow-travellers were all miners, and had manners of quite *colonial* familiarity. By the way, *colonial* is a term used to explain anything extraordinary you may observe: *e. g.*, I noticed a great many bullocks' skeletons on the road, and enquired how they came there; "Colonial Milestones, Mate!" was the reply—*Mate* being an endearing colonial appellation, constantly given, and indicating a pleasing feeling of equality, and tendency to republican familiarity.

The badness of the roads, generally (though in some parts they were as wide and well made as any in Europe,) compelled a change of horses every ten miles, when everybody went to take a drink. On these occasions it commonly happened that some one man invited the whole company to "drink at his expense,"—no small matter, as each drink cost a shilling sterling, and no one ever declined. After drinking, they would all fill and light their short black *cutties*, and smoke quite contentedly till the next change, or watering of horses, when the same scene was repeated. They were generally good-natured fellows, and not at all surly, though very rough; and I gleaned from their conversation much information with respect to the diggings, and the state of society there.

Every little while we would pass a couple of "mounted police," patrolling. Like the members of the corresponding body at Sydney, they were generally large, fine looking men, on noble horses. Their uniform was blue, and they were armed with a carbine and dragoon sword. Being very well paid, I understood that there were among them many men of good family and education. This corps have done good service, as there were formerly many robberies by the *bush-rangers* (colonial highwaymen)—whereas, when I was there, the road, though mostly through an unpeopled country, was as safe, as in many thickly settled localities. The existence of this force has also spared Australia the horrors of Lynch-law; and it prevents a great deal of bloodshed, by allowing no weapons to be carried. I understood that robbery is unknown at the diggings, though many diggers keep large quantities of gold in their tents. Perhaps this is owing to their being constantly on the alert, and well provided with watch-dogs, of which every man has two or three.

The country between Melbourne and Ballaarat is generally undulating, though there is one level prairie which the road crosses for about ten miles. Most of the land is entirely uncultivated; much of it is not wooded, and much, again, appears as if the wood had been thinned out and the underbrush cleared. There is but little peculiarity in the general appearance of the vegetation, although the trees are all different from those existing in other parts of the world. The "gum-tree," "cherry-tree," and others the names of which I cannot remember, differed very much, even in appearance, from anything I had before seen. A very singular thing is, that the Melbourne "cherry-tree" does not bear any fruit, and does not in the least resemble the European tree of the same name; while what they call the "Australian cherry" in Sydney, is a small fruit with the stone outside, which does not grow on a cherry-tree, and only resembles its European synonym in being red-coloured. The road to Ballaarat, was, as before remarked, in some places very broad, level and finely macadamized; in others, however, we went right through the bush, taking the ground as we found it, and whenever it could be managed, at full gallop. The country was dried up by the hot weather, but I was told that as we were in the month of April, winter weather might soon be expected, when the rains would in a few weeks, make it look green again.

We passed a great many drays carrying goods and luggage to Ballaarat. They were drawn by from eight to sixteen oxen; the driver having a long-lashed whip, which trailed on the ground as he walked by his team, and with which he could touch up any one of them without altering his position.

The expense of conveying goods to Ballaarat makes the necessaries of life very dear, as nothing is produced in the vicinity, and everything has to be brought from the coast on these bullock-drays.

Numerous horsemen passed us on the road, most of them going at full gallop, the horses of Australia not being broken to trot. The occupation of most settlers requiring them to pass the greater portion of their time in the saddle, an equestrian costume is the prevailing fashion outside the towns; and knee-breeches with top-boots or Napoleons are worn by almost every body. A stock-whip completes the equipment. This is shaped like a dog-whip, with a lash six feet long, and an inch and a half thick in the middle—no insignificant weapon, as a well given cut will go right through the hide of a bullock, and make the blood spurt again.

CHAPTER III.

AUSTRALIA

First View of Ballaarat—Description of the Place—Gold Digging—A *Colonial* Theatre—Socialism at the Antipodes—Geelong—Melbourne—Paramatta—Republicanism in Australia—Government and Education—Emigration and probable Future of Australia.

We did not see any diggings, till, about four in the afternoon, Ballaarat burst on the view. I say "burst on the view," for you mount the hill which surrounds the place without seeing any outlying tents or huts, and, all at once, on attaining the summit, come in full view of a valley three or four miles long, by two or three broad, filled throughout its whole extent by white cotton tents—a sea of canvass! The whole view so much exceeded, and differed from my expectations, that I could not help feeling that there was in it a certain sublimity—though I suppose few will understand the application of the term to such a scene.

Tents are almost the only sort of habitation in the place, as there is no soft timber of which, as of our pine, the settler can in a few days build himself a temporary abode.

It is impossible, I believe, for one who has not seen a similar place, to realize the appearance of Ballaarat. The whole valley has been, or is being dug, so that there is not a green bush or blade of grass to be seen from one end of it to the other. The tents are regularly laid out in streets, and just wide enough apart to allow of a shaft being sunk between them.

I went to the United States Hotel—one of the few wooden houses in the places—and having left my carpet-bag, walked out to see the gold-washing. I was not, however, fortunate in witnessing the discovery of any large *nuggets*. The holes are, some of them, from 150 to 200 feet deep. They are always worked by several men who own shares, other parties also, generally shopkeepers in the place, frequently having an interest. Persons who wish to dig must mark out a claim, in the possession of which they will be protected by the police. To secure this protection, however, a gold-digger's license must be obtained, which costs about £1, and does not require renewal. The quantity of land that can be thus secured is limited by the number of the party. If gold is discovered on a squatter's land, he cannot refuse the digger the right of mining, but many demand a certain monthly rent.

The mode of digging gold at Ballaarat is as follows: the shaft is sunk until the workers arrive at a certain pebbly marl which contains the gold. The shaft is generally four feet square, and supported all the way down by a lining of logs, squared and dovetailed into each other. On attaining this depth, or before arriving at it, the shaft is frequently flooded, and months are often spent in freeing it of water, before the digging can be prosecuted. The shaft once dug, and not having more than a foot or two of water in it, the auriferous marl is hoisted out by a hand-windlass, or by horse-power, and *puddled.* Puddling is the first, rough washing, in a large trough, and requires two men with shovels. In the larger establishments, horse-power is applied to this also. The next process, *cradling*, is done by a single man. The sand, &c., taken from the puddling trough, and now much reduced in volume is transferred to a "cradle"—a sort of three-storied tub on rockers. This instrument is kept in motion by the left hand, and water poured on by the right. The sand is thus washed away and the gold, on account of its weight, remains in the cradle. The two lower stages of the cradle, are for the finer grains of gold which are carried off the first stage by the rush of the water, but bring up on the second or third. The refuse of the puddling and cradling processes is bought and worked over by the Chinese, of whom there are several thousands in Ballaarat. They do not however, confine themselves to working over refuse, but have holes of their own—some of them very deep. The Chinese in Australia are a low and abominably degraded set, and as in California, very unpopular. An effort has been made, since I left Australia, to prevent any increase of their numbers, by a prohibitory tax on Chinese immigration. The law, however, has been evaded by landing them up the coast and letting them make their way to the gold diggings overland. They do not bring their women with them, and as soon as they make a little money, return to China to enjoy it.

The description given above of gold-mining is only applicable to what are called "dry diggings." There are also in Australia, as in California, numerous wet diggings, where the bed of the stream is worked for the gold brought down by its waters. The dry diggings are said to pay the best, but are also the most uncertain. No rule can be followed in selecting a claim, no rough test applied to ascertain its probable richness. The shaft has to be sunk as far as the auriferous stratum, and strengthened at great expense and labour, and weeks and months must pass in draining the water before the digger can form even an approximate estimate of the richness of his hole. I saw one man who belonged to a party which had been digging in various places for two years, without getting £100 worth of gold; but they were still persevering, and felt sure of ultimate success. There may be two holes, side by side, out of one of which thousands of pounds worth of gold may be dug, and out of the other, not one ounce. Notwithstanding this well-known fact, no sooner is there a great nugget, or much gold found in any one place, than every one abandons his old claim, if an inferior one, and is off to the new El Dorado. The population of these mining settlements is, consequently very fluctuating; and, a place which contains several thousand inhabitants one week, may not have the same number of hundreds the next. Ballaarat, when I was there, was supposed to contain 60,000 inhabitants. I know not what is the present population.

The diggers generally sell the gold to the shop-keepers at low rates, who send it down to Melbourne once a week, by the government gold escort of cavalry. The shopkeepers and publicans made more money, I was told, than any other class in the place. The bar-room of the hotel I stopped at was full all day long, and till two at night, with men and women drinking; and when I got down stairs next morning about seven, the room was again crowded with drinkers, and one woman was lying drunk on the floor. All drinks cost one shilling, except sherry cobblers, which were two and sixpence on account of the ice used in making them, which came originally from America, and had to be brought up country on ox drays.

There are quite a number of old California gold diggers, at Ballaarat. One or two of them told me that they liked their old quarters much better, on account of the greater quantity of game and other amusement there. In Australia there is no game but kangaroos, and even of them there are but few near the settlements. The gold-yield of Australia is, however, allowed to be greater than that of California, in proportion to the number of diggers.

In the evening I went to one of the two theatres in Ballaarat. Theatres seem an amusement of which the Australians are very fond; as they have several in Sydney, a very fine large one at Melbourne, and at least one in every other place I heard of. The performance at Ballaarat was sufficiently bad to be amusing, none being more fully awake to the absurd incapacity of the company and properties, than the audience in the pit. These gentlemen and ladies kept up a rattling fire of jokes at the players, and even proceeded to the more practical facetiousness of projecting certain missiles, to the discomfiture of the heroes of the buskin. This conduct several times necessitated the interference of the police, the advent of whom was a signal for the suspension of the piece, and for a scene of the most terrific uproar, during which the offender made his escape.

After the play, I returned to the hotel, where there was a public dinner to a Gold Commissioner, or some other official, which did not end till three o'clock, and where every body got so jolly that it was impossible to go to sleep on the floor above.

Before retiring I engaged, and paid for, my place by coach

for the following morning, and settled my hotel bill which is always paid in advance "in the Colonies." I paid for two beds, and was booked as "Mr. Minturn and friend," in order to have a room to myself. At about three the next morning, just as I was falling into a doze, I was wakened by a man undressing himself in my room, and making ready to occupy the spare bed. I told him that I had engaged both and paid for them; but he said that he wanted a bed, and that if I supposed I was in England, where a man could appropriate what was wanted by the public, I would find myself much mistaken. I finally found it necessary to get up, when he left the room. The next morning I found that my little adventure had cost me £4, as the fellow who paid me the visit in the night, was the porter charged to wake me in time for the early coach, who had taken an easy revenge by not calling me.

I left Ballaarat by a different route at eight o'clock, and glad enough I was to get out of it. The inhabitants are the roughest set I have ever seen. The men generally wear the hair and beard long, a red shirt, cord breeches, and long boots. The honest women are commonly very neatly dressed; the others, of whom there was a large number, rigged out in gorgeous satins, with silk bonnets, and all the latest Parisian *modes*. The two bar-keepers at the "United States," had their hands full all day long, and in the evening could hardly manage to wait on the people—the crowd was so great. These bar-keepers were both Americans, and got £10 a week a piece, wages, besides perquisites, which, as they kept the landlord always drunk, must have been considerable.

I left Ballaarat on the morning of the 15th, and arrived at Geelong, a town on the coast west of Melbourne, at three that afternoon. On arriving, I found that the boat for Melbourne had left half an hour before, and that I should have to remain until the next day at the same hour, which brought me to Melbourne an hour too late for the boat of the 16th, to Sydney—a most annoying specimen of Colonial arrangements. Geelong is a fine, stone-built town, of about 15,000 inhabitants. It had formerly a great deal of business with the miners, but they now get most things direct from Melbourne.

The hotel at Geelong is the best in the Colonies. The races had just begun, and the place was crowded with jockeys, betting-men, *et id genus omne.* The coffee-room was crammed all the evening long, by men in top-boots, cut-a-ways, white cravats, etc., making up their books, singing out the odds in a loud voice, and talking horse.

I arrived the next day in Melbourne. In the evening I went to the theatre, an iron building. The performance was good, and the house crowded, as the theatres seem always to be, in Australia.

Melbourne is now almost twice as large as Sydney, the former having about 150,000 inhabitants; the latter, about 85,000. The city is laid out with broad streets, which are generally built up with fine grey freestone houses. The shops are much handsomer than in Sydney, immense plate-glass windows, and other decorations being as much the fashion, as on Broadway.

I called on the Bishop of Melbourne, to whom I had a letter, but found him engaged. He has a fine palace, but his cathedral is a poor affair. In Sydney, the Bishop, though Metropolitan of Australia, lives in a small cottage, while his cathedral will be, when finished, a very fine building. To be sure, it has been in the course of erection for many years, and is only finished as far as the clere-story; but then, they wait for aid from Government, instead of taking up private subscriptions, which would, no doubt, soon complete it.

Melbourne is marked by much more business activity than Sydney, and is, no doubt, destined to be the principal port in Australia. Sydney, however, has great advantages in her harbour; that of Melbourne being exposed, and distant two miles from the city, so that all goods must be lightered nine miles up a winding river, or conveyed to town by railway. The expense of the latter mode of conveyance may be estimated from the fact, that the railroad, although only two miles long, and over a level country, with no bridges or other works to build, is said to have cost £280,000. The principal expense was in the labour, which was hard to obtain at the current rate of £1 a day, when the road was constructed.

SYDNEY AGAIN.

On my return to Sydney, I visited Paramatta, the old capital of New South Wales. It is a small, very English looking country town, with a large Government House in a park, and several handsome rural churches. The latter are of the universal freestone, but the Government House, and most others in the place, are built of brick, which gives them a very un-colonial air. The likeness to an English town is increased by the quantity of English trees, which were planted at the first founding of the place, but are, as elsewhere in this climate, feeble, puny things. A cactus, however, or some other tropical plant, growing by the wayside, undeceives you, and modifies the *home*-air of the place, which constitutes, I believe, the real attraction to the Sydney people, who are always making excursions to Paramatta. We returned from Paramatta by railway, having gone thither in a steamboat. The railway is entirely on the English plan, solidly and expensively constructed, with a double track, stone bridges, servants in livery, three classes of carriages, &c. We did the distance back, 14 miles, in 42 minutes, stopping every mile or two.

I also visited Botany Bay, which is about six miles' ride from Sydney, across a low and sandy country, covered with scrub bushes, &c. The harbour is a large and fine one, but not so good as Port Jackson, while the country about the latter is infinitely superior. There is now at Botany, a hotel to which parties resort on Sundays, and for a drive, from Sydney. A menagerie forms one of the attractions of the place, and contains, beside the standard *lions*, several kangaroos, and some emus, an Australian variety of the ostrich.

I was quite curious to find out whether there were any republican sentiments in the colonies. So far as I could discover, however, there were no such feelings, even at the mines. The sentiments on this subject were emphatically *English*. They knew when they were well off, and preferred to avail themselves of the protection of the mother country; and while

2*

they blustered about the aristocratic feature in the new constitution which confided to the governor the choice of two-thirds of the upper house, no complaints were heard of the gubernatorial office being non-elective, nor of the high salaries which the colony has to pay to crown appointees. The elections for the lower houses were going on while I was in the country, but excited very little interest. A very curious proof of the aristocratic tendency of Australian opinion is found in the fact that before my arrival and during my stay, the subject of an *Australian peerage* was extensively and favourably discussed by the newspapers of Sydney.

The colonies of New South Wales, Victoria, Adelaide, and Swan River, are all entirely independent, each having a governor appointed by the crown, and a legislature chosen by its own inhabitants. A curious proof of their independence was furnished by the fact that sovereigns coined at Sydney, by a royal mint situated at that place, did not pass as currency in Melbourne when I was there, never having been adopted as a legal tender by the colony of Victoria, though they were intrinsically rather more valuable than the English sovereign.

I went into the courts at Sydney. The judges wore the gown and bag-wig, as also the barristers—a costume which must be rather uncomfortable in this climate. The jury consisted of four only—a necessary provision in a country where few have leisure. Either party, however, may demand a full jury, but this is rarely done.

Education and religion are both, in Australia, provided for by government. The schools are of two classes, "denominational" and "national," both of which are aided by government. They are not, however, free, but at the denominational schools a child is rarely refused, even if it cannot pay. The teachers of the denominational schools are appointed by boards chosen by the different sects. There is a regular university at Sydney, which will be a fine institution. A building is now being erected for it, out of town, in a style worthy of a place among the colleges of Oxford.

Salaries are paid by government to the Episcopalian, Roman Catholic and Presbyterian clergy; but of these the

Church of England is much the best provided for. There is, however, no distinction in the legal standing of the various religious societies. The Roman Catholic cathedral will be a fine structure, but the nave is not yet completed. The chancel and transepts are however shut in by a wooden partition, and thus made available for the performance of service. The cathedral is surrounded by a collection of schools, nunneries, &c.

Sydney has two club-houses, both fine buildings. There are several theatres, but none so fine as one of those at Melbourne, which is as large as, and handsomer than, the Metropolitan Theatre on Broadway.

The two Sydney newspapers are well written, well printed, and remarkably good specimens of antipodean journalism. They are the only rival papers I ever heard of that did not abuse one another.

Emigration to Australia had, when I was there, been for sometime very slack, and the want of labour was much felt. Salaries of all kinds were enormously high, and servants hard to get at any wages. While I was in Sydney I sent an umbrella to a tailor's to have a small hole repaired. The tailor sent it back unrepaired, with the message that while he was making half a crown mending my umbrella he might be making a guinea at something more profitable.

On account of the great expense of the passage to Australia, immigrants have usually been assisted by the colonial governments, either gratuitously or else a note was taken for the whole amount of the passage money or a part. The former of these systems has been so badly managed as to bring out to the colonies the refuse male and female population of the large cities—the most undesirable class possible. The following fact, which I had from the American consul, gives a good idea of how this thing was managed. It seems that some one left money, or some money was collected, to bring to New South Wales a number of "destitute Irish orphans." When the "orphans" arrived, the colonists, who had engaged them all as servants, were equally surprised and disgusted at finding them women of thirty or forty years, almost all *enceintes*, and the rakings and scrapings of the worst and most degraded class.

The necessity of emigration is made more urgent by the character of the black race, on whose labours the settlers cannot rely. They will work perhaps steadily for some time, and then leave, without notice, to attend a palaver, or fight with a hostile tribe. If they have no excuse of this kind, they will allege, on their return, that they have been "taking a walk," which means wandering over the country for five or six months.

They are a cheerful, harmless race, but all attempts to civilize them, or permanently improve their condition, have failed. Such has also been the fate of all missionary efforts among them. They are, in fact, rapidly dying away, and disappearing before the white race. The few that I saw were wretched looking objects, begging in the streets of Sydney, but they, I suppose, like the Indians one sees at Saratoga, were not fair specimens. The blacks, however, are not the only beggars in Sydney. I saw some sturdy Irish mendicants, who begged rather than take eight or ten shillings a day, which they considered too low for their services.

Australia, though in time it may become a place of great importance, can never become a rival to America. It is too far from the mercantile portions of the world for its productions to have a ready market, when in competition with what can be produced equally well here. Secondly, access to the interior is difficult, and must continue so, as there are no great navigable rivers, and the mountain chains run in such a way as to be a great obstacle to the construction of railways. Thirdly, it is not by any means certain what may be the effect on the English race of a residence in so warm a climate for several generations, but if we may judge of the ultimate result from what we can now see, it will tend to its deterioration. Fourthly, so long as the present system of land apportionment continues, no considerable and permanent immigration can ever take place. Nearly all the present inhabitants of Australia are only there temporarily, and intend to return home sooner or later; and this will continue to be the case, until immigrants have facilities afforded them for purchasing land to cultivate, and securing a homestead, however small, which shall be their own.

CHAPTER IV.

NORTH CHINA.

The Passage from Australia—Making the Chinese Coast—The Yang-tze-kiang—The Foreign Settlement—Dress and Life of the Resident Europeans—Chinese Soldiers—Natural Characteristics in Northern and Southern China—Native Town of Shanghae—Streets—Pawnbrokers—Public Buildings—Temples, and Worship—Phonographic Writing—State Visit of the Taootai—A Chinese Café—Romish Mission—Executions and Torture—Indifference to Pain shown by Orientals—Captain Marryatt's Story—The "Battle of Shanghae."

We had a delightful passage of about sixty days from Sydney to Shanghae. The sea was so smooth that we might have come in safety in a small boat, and the light winds and fair weather made our long passage seem short by allowing us to amuse ourselves on deck, by reading in the day time, studying astronomy at night, and an occasional game of *shovel-board*, the standard amusement of *ennuyés* on shipboard. Our only excitements were the occasional violent squalls prevalent in that part of the ocean, which, as they give no warning, sometimes caught us with everything set and laid us right over on our side, frequently carrying away something aloft, and always occasioning a fearful disturbance in the steward's department. We had also two adventures; the losing of a boy overboard, and seeing a whale, which remained for a quarter of an hour within a cable's length of the ship. Though both these incidents were exciting, and the first saddening to us at the time, I feel that a description would be out of place. Any one can realize to himself the unfortunate boy, struggling in the water, unable to swim, impeded by his sea-boots and heavy clothing, and finally sinking, in full view of the ship, not two minutes before the arrival at the spot, of the boat despatched to his rescue. The whale is still less difficult to imagine. A black slimy bank, covered with barnacles, visible for a few minutes, and then sinking to appear soon in another direction, is all we saw of the leviathan.

The 25th of June was foggy, and so thick that we dared not run for land, although we saw indications of its proximity in the quantities of cuttle-fish bones on the water, rock-weed, and one yellow water-snake about four feet long. On the 26th we got soundings in thirty-five fathoms, and as it cleared up in the morning, we stood in for land, which we continued doing although the fog soon closed in again. About ten o'clock, just as we had tacked, having given up the attempt to make land, the fog rose just long enough to show us Leuconia on the port beam, and "The Brothers," two rocky islands, on the starboard quarter. We must have passed dangerously near the last. We thus ascertained our position for the first time in two days, and ran with confidence for the Barren Islands, which we made at two o'clock. Thence we steered for the Saddle-rocks, which are at the mouth of the Shanghae river, and anchored within them about eight in the evening. For the last two hours we had a man in the chains, sounding with a hand-lead—a precaution which is necessary in the Yang-tze-kiang, on account of the great shallowness of the river, the numerous banks and mud-flats, and the channel not being marked by any buoys or landmarks. The next morning we found ourselves among three or four other ships at anchor, the land nowhere visible, the water of the colour of coffee and consistency of chocolate—I mean both as prepared for drinking, which the river certainly is not. The weather was thick and unpromising; but as it cleared up early in the day, we made sail, and anchored at Woosung, without adventure, at 4½ P. M. We had taken a Chinese pilot before noon. He boarded us in a two-masted native boat, of about ten tons, which held some twenty-five men, who all talked, screamed, and jabbered at once, and at such a rate that we thought they were in distress. Once delivered of the pilot, however, their noise ceased, and they relieved our ears and olfactories of their noisome presence. The pilot laboured under the disadvantage of not understanding English; his whole attainments consisting in a limited knowledge of the "pigeon-English," the *lingua franca* in which foreigners converse with Chinese shop-keepers and servants. This "pigeon-English" consists of English words, with a few Chinese intermixed. The idiom is Chinese, the nouns having no inflection, the verbs no conjugation. The first question of our captain may serve as a good specimen—"How many piecy Mellikan ship-poo have got top-side that river?" by which he meant, "How many American ships are there up the river?" This pigeon-English is a real language, and it takes a stranger a month or more before he can speak it with fluency. Grammatical English is perfectly unintelligible to the Chinese. They learn this peculiar dialect from native teachers, who make a living by giving instruction to those wishing to enter the establishments of Europeans, or who expect to have business with them as shopkeepers.

The banks of the Yang-tze-kiang are low and level, with no landmarks, and piloting is rather difficult. The fellow we had, however, did very well until we reached the mouth of the Wang-poo river, at the hamlet of Woosung, where we found many foreign ships at anchor. As we turned to go up the Wang-poo, the pilot so mismanaged things as nearly to run us ashore, and then, getting frightened, he jumped into a native boat which was passing under our stern, and we saw no more of him.

We anchored at Woosung, and next morning, leaving the ship in the care of a European pilot, ascended the Wang-poo, in a pilot boat, to Shanghae—twelve miles. The Wang-poo is, in most parts, more than a mile broad, and is navigable for the largest ships. We passed several very large junks, some propelled by sail alone, and some by oars as well. I was surprised by seeing how fast they sailed, and how very manageable was their rig.

At a turn of the river, we came in sight of the foreign settlement, extending for a mile and a half, or more, on the left bank of the river; and a half-mile above it the Chinese city now came into view, with the countless fleet of junks which always lie in the river. Lower down were twenty or thirty European vessels. The houses of the European settlement are always of large size, built commonly of stone, covered with stucco; and as they are not crowded together, but each residence is in a spacious *compound*, or square, which includes the stores and a large garden, the whole effect is very good. Before many of the *hongs*, as the residences of foreigners are termed, rose tall flag-staffs, bearing the flag of the power of which the proprietor of the hong was Consul. The first buildings which we passed were the American Episcopal Mission, a large white building, with a gothic chapel in its compound. This mission, and those of other societies, are separated by a creek from the rest of the settlement. The next house was her Majesty's consulate, which looked quite palatial, with its long row of great columns, and the fine gardens which surround it. Then came the establishments of the important firm of Jardine, Matheson & Co., (perhaps the largest commercial house in the East,) and those of other English business firms, and last, the two large buildings belonging to the great American house of Russell & Co. In the midst was the Chinese Custom House, a regular native wooden building, with two flag-staffs, from which floated pennants of the Imperial yellow. Behind this line of hongs, which front on the *bund*, as the quay is called, are the residences of the other merchants, all on the same magnificent scale.

We landed, and in accordance with the hospitable eastern custom, which welcomes any stranger to take up his residence, without invitation, at the house of any resident with whom he may be, however slightly, acquainted, proceeded at once to the house of B. N. & Co., to whom our ship was consigned.

On the way to the house we met several Europeans, in sedan chairs, each carried by two Chinamen. The costume of the foreigners struck me as delightfully cool and sensible. White canvass shoes, white cotton trowsers and jacket, no waistcoat, and a *sola topee*, forms the universal dress. The *sola topee* is a helmet, or broad-brimmed hat, made of pith, half-an-inch thick. It does not fit to the head, but rests on a frame work which does. It thus allows a constant circulation of air, and the pith is at once so thick and so light, as to prevent the ill-effects of the sun's rays, and not to inconvenience the wearer by its weight. This same dress is worn, even to full dress dinners—a sensible custom, contrasting strikingly with the regulations of society in India, which compel one to put on a full black dress suit when going out for the evening.

On landing in China, every stranger at once provides himself with a Chinese servant, ("boy" as he is called,) who acts as valet, waits on him at table, and accompanies him wherever he may go out to dine. Should he not do this, he will find himself totally unserved, as each foreigner has one boy, and no one of them will wait on anybody but his master.

I spent about two weeks in the foreign settlement, and the description of one day will do for almost any other. I was called by my servant, about 8½ o'clock, who put out clean clothes and got my bath ready in one of those large porcelain bathing tubs that we sometimes see in this country. Conveniencies for full ablutions are always attached to every room in the East. At half-past nine we had breakfast, which most of the company made every day of rice, fish and eggs, mixed into one mess. Breakfast commonly lasted an hour, and the gentlemen then went into the office to business. I should have mentioned before, that all the clerks and subordinates of these establishments, live in the same houses with their principals, and all take their meals together. At half-past two, we had *tiffin*, or lunch, which would be called a dinner in this country, and at which large quantities of "East India Pale Ale," the favourite beverage of the Orient, are commonly consumed. At five, we dressed in flannel, and went out for a drive on the race course, the only road which is passable for carriages; this part of China being entirely cut up by canals, by means of which, or on men's shoulders, all goods are transported. The drive generally lasted an hour and a half, and on our return, we dressed again for dinner, which was on the table by eight. While on the subject of dressing, I should have mentioned, that ladies in the east generally wear low necked dresses all day long, which must, I should think, con duce much to their comfort.

Dinners, in the East, are always on a great scale. It is the event of the day—the consummation, of which the tiffin is the bright foreshadowing. Silver services always deck the board, abundant and numerous courses prolong the entertainment, wine and beer stimulate and aid digestion, while the swinging punkah dissipates the otherwise oppressive heat. There is always a chair and a cover for any friend who may choose to drop in—to provide for which contingency, the eatables are on a liberal scale, which would make an American housewife shudder. The entire care of the household is in the hands of the Chinese servants, who submit to no interference, and make no exceptions to the daily routine. The consequence is, that I have sometimes sat down alone to a dinner which would have been ample for a dozen. This is, perhaps, an appropriate place for describing the punkah, that instrument which is so important a part of the comforts of an eastern climate. It consists of a square frame, two-thirds as long as the room it is hung in, and usually about four feet wide, suspended by cords from the ceiling, so that its lower edge, from which depends a fringe, is about seven feet from the floor. This instrument is kept constantly swinging, by a rope attached to one side of it, and passing out to the verandah, where it is pulled by a servant. It operates as a gigantic fan, and is a delightful alleviation to the intense heat of the climate. In China, punkahs are only used in the dining-rooms, and over the desks of some merchants; but in India, every room has one, and they are pulled all night long in the bed-rooms, by relays of punkah-walas.

During my stay at Shanghae, I made several visits to the native town. It is situated on the banks of the river, about half a mile above the extremity of the foreign settlement. The city is surrounded by massive stone walls, the gateways being strong towers, defended by outworks. At each gateway was a detachment of Chinese soldiers, dirty ragamuffins, whose uniform consisted of a blue cotton shirt, with the Chinese word for "soldier" embroidered on the breast and back. They were mostly armed with long and awkward matchlocks, and seemed to pass their time in smoking opium and gambling.

All the cities in the north of China are accessible to foreigners, who are seldom annoyed by the Chinese. The country, too, is entirely open, and any one can penetrate as far as he pleases. In this, as in other respects, the Northern Chinese present a remarkable contrast to the men of Canton and the south. These latter are a taller and finer race, but marked by an intense hatred of the "Fan-qui" (foreign devil). They will not allow strangers to go into the country even as far as they are permitted by treaty, viz: a day's journey, or to penetrate into any of their towns. At the north, however, the people are a far happier, pleasanter race, detesting the Canton men, and showing rather a liking for foreigners. As before remarked, occidentals can penetrate into the interior as far as they choose, the only risk being that of offending some mandarin, any of whom possesses, by treaty, the power of dispatching all foreign travellers to the sea-coast, where a fine of $400 is imposed.

One Chinese city, as I have been assured by men who had seen many, is precisely like every other. How this may be I do not know, as I have been in the interior of one only; but if they are all like Shanghae, they must be the most uninteresting cities in the world, as soon as the novelty of their common peculiarities has worn off.

Within the walls of Shanghae there is a space left vacant between the town and the ramparts, that the inhabitants may not be in the immediate vicinity of the belligerents in case of an attack. The town itself consists of low two-story houses, with stone partition walls and wooden fronts. They are mostly occupied as shops, in which case the lower story is entirely open. When the house is used as a dwelling exclusively, it is generally situated some distance back from the street, and the view cut off by a wall which entirely separates it from the public thoroughfare. The streets are very narrow, and no wheeled conveyances are ever used. There are no public buildings worth mentioning. The great court of justice is merely an open shed at one end of a large court-yard; and the principal houses of the town, as regards height and size, are certainly the pawnbrokers' shops. Pawnbroking is, in China, a most important business. All Chinese dress well, most of them wearing numerous silk robes and furs in the cold weather. Now as the severe cold only lasts for three months of the year, they deposit their magnificent habiliments at the pawnbrokers' for safe keeping during the other nine. Beside this use these establishments also answer the same purpose as the like establishments elsewhere.

The temples in Shanghae are not very good of their kind. The form is the same as that of others I have seen. A high wall encloses a court within which, at the further extremity, is the statue or painting of the threefold Boodh. In the centre of the court is a bronze urn where scraps of paper and sticks of punk burn in honour of the deity. The idol is also protected by a roof which completely covers the further third of the enclosure. The room thus formed is entirely open towards the court and is usually gaily decorated. Around the wall are frequently arranged the statues of minor gods, in whose honour the joss-stick (punk) defiles the air with its fœtid smoke. The largest temple in Shanghae is connected in some way with the government, and the mandarins go there every week to worship. In it the statue of Boodh is about eighteen feet high, the smaller effigies which surround it being twelve feet in height. I suppose it is generally known, by this time, that educated Chinese have no religion, and the lower classes just as much as they find convenient. So far as I could judge, no worship is ever offered by the laity—the whole form consisting in the chaunting of certain Sanscrit services by the monks. A pious layman propitiates the gods by the simple and compendious process of lighting a few sticks of punk in their honour. The fact of the Boodhist services being in Sanscrit is a remarkable testimony to the Indian origin of that religion. This fact was long overlooked, the Chinese priests being themselves ignorant that the sounds which they sung, and which were represented by Chinese characters, had any meaning in any language. This plan of representing foreign sounds by Chinese characters has been long practised by the Roman Catholic missionaries, who denote in this way, in their Chinese service-books, the Latin words of the Mass. I have heard a Chinese congregation in the Romish cathedral at Shanghae, singing, "Ola pĕlo nobi!" to a Gregorian tune, with as much earnestness as if their language permitted them to represent or pronounce the true Latin sounds of "*Ora pro nobis!*"

One of the most interesting sights in Shanghae is the tea-garden. This is an open space in the middle of the city, arranged on Chinese principles of landscape gardening. There are ponds of green slime, brooks of standing water, artificial rocks which look like nothing in nature, and bridges in the shape of the celebrated structure which we have all admired on the *willow-ware* plates. In this garden are numerous *tea-houses* whither the Chinese resort in the evening to partake of their favourite beverage. The buildings are one or two stories high and open all round. They usually can accommodate from fifty to two hundred persons, seated two by two at small tables, as in a European *café*. No edibles are furnished at these establishments, but the heated wines and spirits of which the Chinese are so fond may be obtained, and it is almost universal for *habitués* to smoke as they drink and converse with their opposite neighbours in the soft-flowing accents of their native land. To a stranger these places seem anything but a delightful resort. All of one's senses are assailed and tortured at once. The breezes which fan the revellers having come first across the town, and having been freshened by the varied odours of the ponds before mentioned, are far from balmy; the smoke of the Chinese tobacco is positively stinking; and the accents of the vernacular, now guttural as Arabic, now nasal as Yankee, and all screamed in those "tones as trumpet loud" which I have only elsewhere heard in the Parisian *bourse*, and certain New York parties, make the visitor indescribably nervous. When you add to this that many of those present, for greater ease, remove all garments but their very short trowsers, that the Chinese have a constitutional aversion to water as a means of ablution, and that the habit of eructation is the recognized exhibition of gastronomic gratification among the most polished oriental society, the picture of this Celestial symposium is complete.

Shanghae is the head quarters of the Romish missions in China. Their establishment is near the river's bank above the Chinese city. They have a large and massive cathedral in the

Italian style, and several other buildings, used as habitations for the priests and as school houses. The whole is under the protection of the French consul, and the imperial tricolour floats from a flag staff in the compound. I visited this mission one Sunday afternoon, arriving during the singing of the "Litany to the Virgin," and was much pleased with the earnestness with which a numerous congregation of Chinese chaunted the responses to a mediæval tune. I suppose, after all, they understood as little of what they were saying as the Boodhist priests do of their Sanscrit liturgy. The priests and acolytes officiating at the altar wore a peculiar and very gay head-dress which I took to be one of those extraordinary *properties* (to use a theatrical term) which the Romish church occasionally permits, to secure the attention of the wavering faithful and attract them to her services by the meretricious fascination of scenic display.

After the service was concluded, I was invited to join the resident missionaries at their afternoon repast. There were about ten at table, all Frenchmen, but dressed in Chinese costume, and wearing the greater part of their heads shaven, with the long cue behind. The collation consisted of rice, fruits, nuts, and wine; and I found my entertainers very pleasant and intelligent men. Only one of the number spoke English, the conversation being chiefly in French. Their custom is to make this mission their head-quarters, and from this point begin their excursions into the country, where they often remain for years, returning again to the sea-coast when they have excited the suspicions of the authorities, or are exhausted by long continued labours, and the want of congenial society. The Romish missionaries have, it is well known, large numbers of Christian disciples in the empire; but I learned from these fathers that they no longer endeavour to make new converts, finding their time fully occupied in taking care of those already under their guidance. These gentlemen had all known M. Huc, the celebrated author of a work on China, and a book of travels in Thibet. They avowed, however, that they had not entire confidence in his narrative;

and thought, that in his writings, he had frequently given way to the temptation of telling *travellers' tales.*

During my stay at Shanghae, I witnessed the state visit of the Taootai (collector), the principal Chinese magistrate of the district, to Mr. Cunningham, the Consul for Sweden. The *cortège* was composed of about 250 civil and military attendants, the whole being preceded by gongs and discordant musical instruments. The great man himself, and one or two others, were mounted on wretched little ponies, but all his followers were on foot. The soldiers had no uniformity in their equipment, some being armed with lances, some with swords, and a few with even more extraordinary weapons. The most remarkable part of the company were some executioners, with whips, swords, and other instruments of punishment and torture, to be used summarily on all who should not treat their master with proper respect. Many of the soldiers had two swords in one scabbard, which were intended to be used in combat, one in each hand.

I saw no executions in China, but they are very frequent, and occasionally very cruel. About a year before I arrived in the country, the town of Shanghae had been occupied by some rebels, and held for a considerable time against the Imperial forces. When the place was taken, about five per cent. of the captives were reserved to be tortured, and all the remainder were executed in a peculiarly Chinese style. Their tails were tied to a bamboo supported above the head, and the neck was then neatly cut through by one stroke of a sword, the body falling to the ground, and the head remaining suspended in a convenient position for subsequent collection. Many thousands of persons were thus disposed of, and their heads packed in baskets, to be exhibited in public situations. I saw two or three over the gates of the city. The Chinese, like other Oriental nations, seem to show great indifference to pain, and even death; whether inflicted by or upon themselves. Suicides are common, from the slightest motives; and the legal punishments are of frightful severity. Another proof of this, to us, inexplicable peculiarity, is the well known fact that vicarious punishment is recognized by the Chinese law, and that substitutes may be hired to undergo every legal penalty, even death itself. An additional fact, corroborating this view, is, that great pirates and robbers have been frequently known to surrender themselves for trial, when a large reward had been offered for their apprehension; in order that their families might be rendered comfortable for life, by the price of their blood. This singular obtuseness to bodily suffering is found, more or less, among all Orientals. The most fearful tortures will rarely extract an avowal of guilt, or the betrayal of a confederate. Captain Marryatt tells a story of a Malay, whom he caught, when on service in the Eastern seas. The Captain was nearly sure that his captive possessed certain information which he wished to obtain, and finding all bribery and gentle means unavailing to make him speak, finally threatened him with death, and ordered a file of marines to be got ready for the purpose. The man was not in the least disturbed, but requested leave to finish a segar which he was smoking; and permission being given, he sat down in a port for the purpose. In a few minutes, however, he threw his segar away, though but half consumed, complaining that it did not draw well, and at once began to make preparations for his own death, by binding up his long hair in a knot, on the top of his head, and unwrapping the *dhotee*, a long cloth worn about the loins. Folding his *dhotee*, and laying it on the deck to catch his blood, he knelt down, and waited with perfect unconcern for the fatal stroke. Captain Marryatt, finding that even this means was ineffectual in overcoming the obstinacy of his prisoner, was unwilling to take life unnecessarily, and had him sent ashore, after giving him some slight presents, in admiration of his *pluck*.

It was in the course of the siege of Shanghae, to which I have alluded above, that the celebrated attack by about two hundred English and Americans on several thousand Chinese, occurred. The Imperial troops had taken up such a position, that the cannon-balls fired by them and the rebels in the town, constantly fell among the houses of the foreign settlement. As this was sufficiently disagreeable and dangerous, notice was given to the Imperial commander, that he had better change his point of attack. He, however, persisted in remaining where he was, and the above number of Anglo-Saxons started one morning, with several small cannon, and a few marines and sailors from the ships, to dislodge him, and the force under his command. They succeeded in effecting their purpose, though at the cost of several lives, and numerous wounds. On taking possession of the Chinese position, it was found that there was an immense piece of artillery, masked, and crammed to the muzzle with all sorts of projectiles, which completely commanded the road up which the American detachment had marched to the attack. Had the Chinese been able to discharge this cannon, they would probably have killed or wounded most of the Americans who were concerned in this *escapade*.

CHAPTER V.

A TRIP INLAND.

Leave Shanghae for a Trip up the Canals—Our Boat—Swimming—Banks of the Canal—Military Stations—Temples—Graves—Villages—Dress of Chinese—Town of Kwunsan—Grain Junks—Comparison of Chinese and American Governments—This part of China once Submerged—Cormorants—Approach to Soo-Chow—The City—"Foreign Devils"—Grand Canal—Heat—Hills near Soo-Chow—View of Ty-hao—Mandarin's Tomb—Tyhao—Chinese River Thieves—Their Honesty.

HAVING spent about two weeks, as above described, in the foreign settlement of Shanghae, I became anxious to see a little more of the country, than I had had the opportunity of observing in the walks and sails which we occasionally took in the afternoon. It fortunately happened that an English gentleman, whose acquaintance I had formed in Shanghae was about to go up the canals, for a ten-day excursion in his boat, and he kindly invited me to bear him company.

We started on the afternoon of the eleventh of July, and proceeded up the canal until about ten o'clock, when we anchored, and all hands turned in except one man, left awake to guard against robbers. Our boat was a regular Chinese junk-shaped craft, square in the bow and stern. Her mast could be lowered when not required, and she sailed remarkably well before the wind, under her one sail of mats; but on the wind, her flat bottom prevented her from doing much. When there was no wind, we put two or three men ashore, and let them tow us by a rope made fast to the mast head. The man who remained on board assisted by sculling with one of those long, heavy, permanent sculls, with which all Chinese canal boats are furnished, and which act at once to propel and to steer the vessel. Our boat's crew consisted of three or four sailors and a mate, who also acted as cook and servant. The length of the boat was about twenty-five feet. Of this, about twelve feet in the waist was occupied by the cabin, which was what is termed half-poop, with windows in the sides. Low lockers which held wine, beer, &c., ran on each side the whole length of the apartment, and served as settees by day and couches by night. The remaining space was occupied by the table. There was, altogether, much more room than one had a right to expect on a boat of the size, and we had in her a most agreeable home during the trip. Of course we had to take wine, beer, coffee, bacon, butter, sugar, and such delicacies with us; but we found, wherever we went, an ample supply of eggs, fowls, fish, and a few other substantials.

On waking on the morning of the second day, we found ourselves, in a flat, but very pretty country, with numerous large trees, and a village on the side of the canal a little way ahead. We at once jumped into the canal, which was tolerably clean, and swam on ahead of the boat, which had been towing slowly since day broke. As we swam past the village before mentioned, the inhabitants espied us, and rushed down in a crowd to the water's edge. They were surprised by three things—*first*, by the sight of our white, and in their eyes, leprous-looking skins, since outside barbarians rarely go up this canal, and still more rarely expose their heads as we were doing, to the full force of the sun's rays; *Secondly*, by the fact of our swimming at all, as the inland Chinese are rarely adepts in the natatory art; *Thirdly*, and this would be the most marvellous feature of the case in a Chinaman's eyes, that we should voluntarily make the exertion to swim, when we could go so much more easily, in our boat. Having astonished the innocent natives, by swimming on our backs, treading water, turning summersaults, and other equally undignified performances, we terminated the exhibition with the fearful *hurrah*, which is so peculiar a characteristic of the foreign white-skinned and red-haired devil, and soon afterwards reëntered our boat for breakfast.

The banks of the canals in China, are mostly so high, that, from a boat like ours, the fields on each side are quite invisible—the view from our cabin windows being generally remarkably similar to that which regales the eyes of railway travellers, when passing through deep cuttings. We used, however, for some hours each day, to go ashore, and walk on the towing path, from which we could see the canal and country round. The features of the country during the first day were remarkably tame, but the large number of boats on the canal, and foot passengers on the tow-path, relieved the monotony. The levée is raised on each side several feet above the general level of the land, and is commonly about two hundred feet broad. It is not cultivated, but covered with graves. Beyond were cultivated fields, generally of rice, and carefully irrigated by water raised from the canal, and conducted in channels, continually subdividing to every inch of soil that required watering. Every quarter of a mile at least, the levée was interrupted to give passage to the waters of a tributary canal; some large and intended for traffic, some small and used only for irrigating purposes. At such points the tow-path is continued by a stone bridge, passing over the subordinate canal; but these bridges, like most other public works which I saw in China, seemed to be generally in bad repair. We also passed frequently, military stations—wooden houses about thirty feet square, and generally out of order and deserted, either from the troops having been called up country to oppose the rebels, or from the military mandarin's finding it profitable to draw the money for their support from the imperial treasury, without going to the expense of keeping them up. Joss-houses, as foreigners call the Boodhist temples, were also of frequent occurrence on the levées, but no care seemed to be taken of them, and, in many instances, they were used either as workshops, or as storehouses for grain or agricultural implements. Their shape and internal arrangements were the same as I have before described, when speaking of similar buildings in Shanghae.

The graves which I have before said cover the levées, seem here to merit a description. When a Chinese dies, his body, protected from offensive decomposition by quick-lime and similar substances, is encased in numerous coffins, the outer one being as magnificent a specimen of the joiner's art as the relatives can afford. Thus encased, the corpse is either kept in the house, or deposited in the open air with a slight arched covering of bamboo and mats. At the end of a year, if the family can bear the expense, the coffin is covered in with stone or stuccoed brick work, or is sometimes buried in the earth, a headstone being erected to mark the spot. The headstone is generally of the shape usual in our cemeteries, or else is a mere square pillar of unhewn granite, with the name roughly carved upon it. In many instances, however, the people are too poor to erect a tomb, however simple, and the coffin with its contents is then allowed to go to decay, the body being generally devoured by rats. When this consummation is complete, the dutiful survivors collect whatever bones and other remnants of mortality can be discovered, and enclosing them in a small earthen vessel, protect them by some permanent covering. These cinerary urns are known among foreigners by the irreverent name of "potted ancestors." The Chinese, like the Hindoos, attach an exaggerated importance to funeral honours, though they do not, like the latter, believe them to have any bearing on their future happiness. M. Huc says, what I understood to be strictly true, that a Chinaman when sick unto death, will often deny himself the expensive luxuries of a physician and medicines, preferring to reserve the money to buy a coffin, and pay for the post-mortem indulgence of a stone tomb.

It often struck me as singular, that so thoroughly utilitarian a people as the Flowery Nation, who are so loath to allow the least waste of any thing that can be turned to account, and tax so unremittingly the productive energies of every inch of soil, should be willing to give up so much good ground to the dead who are of no use to any one; but I suppose that there are none of us poor mortals without our little inconsistencies, and that a contempt for this mortal coil, such as was for many years witnessed in the condition of Washington's last resting place, can only come with a very high degree of civilization.

Every mile or so, along the line of the canal, we passed villages or hamlets, either commercial or agricultural. In the former case, the houses were built in a long row on each bank; in the latter, they were commonly situated a little way back in the country, and frequently sheltered and adorned by fine large trees. The Chinese peasant is generally a free-holder, and allows the shades of no tree to interfere with the patch of ground which has come down to him, diminished in size by continued testamentary subdivision. For this same reason the cultivators live in villages, choosing for their location, a comparatively unproductive spot, and being thus enabled doubly to economize ground, and moreover to enjoy the shade of trees. On the banks of the canal which is nearest a village, there are always several irrigating machines, which raise the water to the level of the embankment, from which it flows in channels to every part of the land owned by the villagers. These machines consist of an endless chain, travelling round a wheel below the level of the water in the canal, and moved by a light windlass on the bank, being the same in principal as the Yankee "chain pump." The ascending part of the chain, passes through a water-tight tube, up which it carries the water, forced into the tube and retained there by projections from the chain like the *box* of a steam-piston. The windlass is generally near the ground, and moved by the feet like a treadmill. Each machine requires one or two men or women to work it, and a slight shed protects the workmen from the sun. The country people seem a hard-working, economical, but light-hearted and cheerful people. Their houses, in the villages, however small, are generally of stone and thatched, and appear comfortable, while the universal order and neatness which everywhere meet the eye, show that however contracted may be their means, there is not among them the same wretchedness as there is among the *ryuts* of India, or the lowest classes in Europe. The dress of those natives, whom we saw working in the fields, consisted of a very broad but short species of trowsers for both sexes, the upper part of the body being covered by a jacket reaching to the middle, but rather longer in the case of women. This is the dress of the lower classes throughout China, in whatever occupation engaged. The material is generally coarse cotton, frequently dyed black. The head is protected during labouring hours in the open fields, by a hat of basket-work, resting on the head, but not fitting to it, and retained in its position by strings. The better classes, in the cities, wear the same trowsers, but of silk, and gathered below into a stocking made of cotton cloth; their coats are long, reaching below the knee, and are of some fine material. Women wear nearly the same dress as the men in both cases. Both sexes frequently remove the shirt or coat when in the shade, retaining only the short trowsers, but in this case, the women always cover the breasts by a short, red boddice, about six inches broad, fastened behind the shoulders. I have often seen girls of ten or twelve with no other covering of any sort, than this narrow waist. The head is generally left uncovered in the case of both sexes, except when on a journey, or during long continued exposure to the sun's rays.

About ten o'clock in the morning, we arrived at Kwun-san, a town of several hundred thousand inhabitants, defended by stone walls about thirty feet high, and a broad ditch formed by the waters of the canals which centre here, and some of which pass completely through the town. It was here that I first saw the grain junks, vessels remarkably similar in their shape to the *Noah's Arks* that children have for toys. They have often a capacity of two or three thousand tons according to our measurement, and were formerly used to convey the tribute of grain from the northern provinces to Pekin, *vià* the Grand Canal. Within ten years, however, the officials have found it cheaper to send the corn in private junks, *vià* the Yang-tze-kiang, so the poor old grain junks are now laid up in ordinary, and are most of them inhabited by a disreputable set of vagabonds, who are supposed to be the crew, and as such draw pay from government. The Chinese government, as at present administered, seems in some respects remarkably like ours. The first great resemblance is, that in theory it is perfect, and in practice works remarkably badly. Secondly, it is a mere machine for collecting taxes, and enriching those who can put themselves into office by bribery or any other means. Thirdly, the officials have no power except when supported by public opinion, and fourthly, the government has lost the respect of the people, who, in case of difficulty, consider a government official the last person to go to for advice or redress.

Soon after passing Kwun-san, we saw on our right the hill of the same name. It is not very high, but is of a conical shape, and becomes a conspicuous object from the general flatness of the country. This hill is owned by the Boodhists, and crowned by a monastery. It is ascended by a winding path, paved with stone and bordered by rows of trees. All this part of China was formerly under water, and records remain of a period when these hills were islands in the ocean.

Leaving Kwun-san we passed into another canal somewhat larger than that upon which we had come thus far. The embankments were now supported by a water-wall of squared stones, which was, however, in many places, in want of repairs. Crowds of boats of all sizes now filled the canal, and frequently compelled us to stop for some minutes before we could obtain a passage. During the afternoon we passed through a lake of considerable size, but shallow. The course of the canal was here marked by a stone causeway, which served as a tow-path and bridge. I saw upon this lake many boats fishing with cormorants. They are filthy looking birds of the vulture kind and about the size of a turkey. When unoccupied, they perch upon the gunwale of the boat, each bird wearing a brass ring round its neck to prevent its swallowing any fish it may catch. At a word from their master they soar over the lake like gulls, and like them dart upon their prey the moment the unwary fish approaches the surface. At another signal, the obedient bird brings the booty to its master, and does not leave the boat a second time until it receives the word of command.

We were now approaching Soo-chow, a city of about two millions of inhabitants, though in China not of the first class. During the afternoon we had passed two *express-boats*, light canoes, holding only a single person, who paddles along at a tremendous pace. These express-boats are dispatched to Shanghae every day, to convey to the Chinese merchants there the price of opium at Soo-chow, which is the great depôt of this drug for the interior. The approach to Soo-chow was marked by a large number of boats and the widening of the canal, which encircles the city in a moat, a quarter of a mile broad. The town is walled, and is about twelve miles in circuit. We passed around two sides of it and then entered and rowed through a part of the city, emerging on a third side. The cities in this part of the country are all like Venice, in being traversed by canals, but unlike that city are also provided with causeways for foot passengers, running along the canals. The general appearance of the streets was similar to that of Shanghae. As it was now approaching evening, and the heat of the day was past, we made our appearance on the outside of our boat, and at once became the cynosure of all eyes. The public followed us in crowds during our progress, saluting us with the oft repeated cry of *Qui-tsa*, *Qui-tse*, *yang-qui-tsa*, terms conveying at once our diabolical character, and the conventional attributes of whiteness and red-hair, which are supposed to mark the outside barbarian. This was the first piece of discourtesy of which we had to complain, and my friend, who had been a good deal inland, and sometimes quite alone, told me that he had seldom had cause to fear violence. Whenever he had been stoned or pelted with mud, he always found that by facing the enemy and stroking his beard, at the same time appealing to that sense of politeness which is so strong in the Chinese, he at once put a stop to all rudeness. He considered his beard a great advantage, as among Chinese, none but a grandfather can wear one, and respect for old age is a most prominent feature in the character of this people. A beard is therefore more of a protection against popular violence in China, than grey hairs would be here. Inside the town the canal is frequently spanned by stone bridges, generally of a single arch and very high. On these bridges there was an immense crowd of *gamins* to see us pass under, but we always disappointed their curiosity by taking refuge in the cabin, my friend having discovered on previous occasions, that the peculiar effects of a dead cat, or rotten egg, when falling or projected from an eminence, are as well understood in China as in the galleries of some theatres. Passing out of Soo-chow from another gate, we found ourselves on a broad piece of water, the *débouchement* of the Grand Canal. There was a great crowd of boats in all directions, but the passage was clear to the Grand Canal, which opened directly in front, and was spanned by one of the largest single-arched bridges I have ever seen. We turned to the right, and passing through the crowded junks soon came to another canal, up which we went. The sides of this canal and the country in every direction around Soo-chow, are completely covered by the suburbs of the great city, which extend for more than two miles in this direction alone. In these suburbs I first saw monumental arches. They consist of four stone columns of from 15 to 25 feet high, surmounted by an entablature decorated with bronze ornaments. They are erected by private individuals in commemoration of some person or event.

After clearing the outskirts of this city, we again anchored for the night. The thermometer had been up to 95° in our cabin during the day, and fell only about ten degrees at night, so that we suffered considerably from the heat. The mosquitoes, too, which abound on this and other canals, troubled us not a little, as our quarters were too contracted to allow of rigging the mosquito nets properly.

The next day found us among a range of hills, perhaps 900 feet high. As soon as we turned out, we determined to ascend them. There was a walk of a mile to the foot of the hills, across rice-fields which had been watered till they were soft mud for six or eight inches deep, and we could only obtain a footing by walking on the narrow banks of the little sluices which conducted the water in different directions. We had a hard climb of an hour to the summit, but when there, the view quite repaid us. On one side, about ten miles off, lay the city of Soo-chow, in a valley, still enveloped by mist, from which emerged its lofty pagodas. On the other, the great lake of China, the Ty-hao, lay spread out before us. The chain on which we stood, stretched thirty or forty miles on each side of us, separating the valley of the lake from that of the city. The rest of the country was a dead level, with the silver network of the canals shining clearly out through the fog, which still lingered on the low ground. We went into a small joss-house, which we found on top of the mountain, and ate a light breakfast: after which we began our descent in a slightly different direction. The side of the hill by which we had ascended was almost bare, with only a few low scrub-bushes here and there. Our path in descending, however, led through a grove of pine-trees, surrounding a mandarin's tomb. The trees afforded us a pleasant protection against the rays of the sun, which had now risen so high as to be uncomfortably warm. The tomb was in an enclosed space of about an acre and a half, surrounded by a stone wall, and planted with cypress and fir-trees. The enclosure was, in shape, a narrow parallellogram, and, as it was situated on the slope of the hill, had been divided into three smaller courts, separated by flights of stone steps to equalize the ascent. In each division was a pond, planted with lotuses, and surrounded by a stone coping; and scattered about each, were uncouth and colossal statues of horses and dogs. At the highest extremity of the upper division was a stone temple, about twenty feet square, which, I suppose, held the body. The entrance was at the lowest extremity of the whole enclosure, the wall on each side being drawn out in a semicircle, broken by an iron gate about fifteen feet wide. Two gigantic stone effigies of watch-dogs acted as janitors. This was the largest private tomb which I saw, but there were several others, on this same hill-side, on a similar plan, but smaller and less elaborately arranged. Subsequently we frequently saw these homes of the dead—the trees which they enclosed lending cheerfulness, and an appearance of nature, to the otherwise monotonous and artificial landscape.

We joined our boat some distance further up the canal, about ten o'clock, and went steadily on all day toward the Ty-hao, keeping under the foot of the hills, round the extremity of which it was necessary to pass to enter the lake. About nightfall, the canal widened into an open bight of water, and we were in an arm of the Ty-hao. We kept on till the inlet was a quarter of a mile broad, from one low bank to the other, and then anchored for the night in three feet of water. The canal through which we had come during the day, was narrower than either of those in which we had been the day before, and after returning from the ascent of the hill, we saw nothing of special interest. The heat was intense all day long, the thermometer standing, for six hours, at 98° in the shade. As nightfall did not bring much alleviation, we sought coolness, and a deliverance from the swarms of mosquitoes, by plunging into the muddy lake, in which we continued for a couple of hours, lying under the water, supported by a short rope from the boat, and occasionally eluding the pursuit of a pertinacious mosquito by plunging wholly under the surface. Before retiring for the night we loaded our revolvers, and fired them off twice, to frighten off any pirates who might be in the vicinity. These canals and lakes are infested by pirates and water thieves, who levy black mail on all the weaker craft. They act, however, with no little moderation—seldom taking more than one third of a boat's cargo. This course commonly prevents a prosecution. Mr. Fortune, who was sent up country by the East India Company to buy tea-plants, was one night robbed, on one of these canals, of a tin box containing all his papers and some silver dollars. The money was to him a matter of importance, but the loss of the papers was irreparable. A hole had been sawn in the side of the boat, and the box taken from under his pillow as he slept. He remained all day at the same place, trying, ineffectually, to discover some trace of the offenders, and had given up all hopes, when, the next night, his boat was hailed from the bank, and a voice informed them that if a man were sent ashore, he would find the box on the tow-path. He accordingly sent ashore and recovered his box, in which not an article had been damaged or removed, except the dollars, which were, of course, all gone. The thieves had, no doubt, surmised, what was actually the case, that the papers were of more importance to Mr. Fortune than the money, and hoped, by returning them, to avoid any further enquiry into the occurrence.

CHAPTER VI.

A TRIP INLAND.—CONTINUED.

Ascend Toong-toong-ting-shan—The View—The Great Lake of China—A Beautiful Canal—Villages—Return to Soo-chow—Grand Canal—A Customs' Barrier—A Chinese Fort—Ping-bong—Chinzà—Nan-zing—Effect of Drought on Rice Fields—Our Examination by Mandarins—Preparations for the Rebels—Hoo-chow—Pretty Girls—Are compelled to return to Shanghae—Bridge at Yang-kow-shin—Kahing—Troops—Mandarin's House in Lake—Arrive again at Shanghae—Charity in China.

At daybreak on the morning of the 13th, we ascended the Toong-toong-ting-shan, a hill about five hundred feet high, which separated the inlet, in which we had passed the night, from the body of the lake. The shape of the hill was irregular, being cut up by deep gullies, around the sides of which wound the long flight of stone steps conducting to the summit. On the top is a Boodhist monastery, of thirty or forty monks, and we passed several minor establishments on the way up. These religious houses, as well as the pathway, were well sheltered by trees. At the highest point, above the large monastery, is a small joss-house, under the shade of which we partook of breakfast. An old woman officiated as *genius loci*, and was terribly frightened by our offering her an empty claret bottle, fearing that it might be in some way connected with a spell, or the Evil Eye. After breakfast, we remained on the summit for a quarter of an hour, enjoying the view. Behind us was the inlet from which we had come, and the low country stretching toward Shanghae; in front another inlet, separated from the first by the hill on which we were; and beyond it another hill, precisely the counterpart of the first, the Si-toong-ting-shan, the summit of which was also occupied by a monastic establishment. On our right stretched the great lake for a hundred miles, bounded by the range of hills behind us, round which we had come on the previous day.

The sun soon became too hot to make a longer exposure to its rays desirable, and we descended to our boat, stopping only to visit the large monastery. This establishment was composed of several quadrangles, surrounded by the cells of monks. At the extremity of the furthest was the temple, in no way remarkable. All the buildings were of stone, and the whole was surrounded by a high stone wall, and shaded by magnificent trees. We saw only a few monks. They were dressed in loose lilac gowns, and had the hair of the head entirely shaven. Many of these Boodhist foundations in China are very rich, and as the monastic vows can be cancelled at will, they afford a sort of asylum to indigent persons who seek a retirement from the troubles of the world in the quiet of the cloister, from which they can emerge at will should better times smile upon them.

On returning to the boat, and consulting with the mate, we found that the lowness of the water in the Ty-hao would prevent our crossing it, which was the nearest route to Hoo-chow, a city which we desired to visit. We, therefore, reluctantly determined to strike into another canal, and proceed to Hoo-chow by a much more round-about route.

The Ty-hao, though the largest lake in China, is never more than six or eight feet deep, and when we visited it was in most places not more than two or three feet deep, while some parts were quite dry. This was owing to the two or three months' drought, which it was feared would cause a famine in all the northern part of China, by lowering the great canals, and drying up their smaller and shallower branches, on which the country depended for irrigation. In the south of China, on the other hand, they had had that year just the opposite trouble, the country being flooded, villages entirely covered by water, and the crops destroyed in consequence of violent and long-continued rains.

The canal which we now entered was a fine one, and apparently well kept up. It was frequently spanned by tall stone bridges, which were in good condition, and some of them actually undergoing repair. The bridges, like those which I had before seen in similar positions, were built with one semicircular arch, the upper line of the bridge rising to a point. No mortar was used in their construction, the structure being held together entirely by the accurate cutting of the stones, and the scientific perfection of the arch. I should have mentioned that the material of all is grey granite.

The country through which we were passing was prettier than on any previous day. The hills on the Ty-hao, and those between that lake and Soo-chow, were all visible, and the fields on each side of the canal were relieved of their monotony by the frequent occurrence of private cemeteries and monasteries. We passed through several very large villages, one of which extended along the canal for more than three miles. When the canal passed through a village, its sides were generally lined with flights of stone steps, ascending to the level of the street, or paved levée. In villages, a large part of the canal was frequently occupied by the buffaloes, who, to get relief from the great heat, stand in the canal when it is shallow enough, with only their eyes and nose above water. We noticed that many of the water-wheels which we passed during this day were turned by very pretty girls, with much clearer complexions than those of the women on the coast. The only drawback to their appearance was that, like all women in the north of China, they had little feet, but even to this one soon gets accustomed, and I am not sure that, after all, it is not a much less unnatural distortion, than the habit which occidental ladies have of compressing the waist.

By evening we again arrived at Soo-chow, to which city we had been compelled to return in order to proceed to Hoo-chow *viâ* the Grand Canal. We had again to pass through the crowded ranks of junks, which I have described as moored about the city, and it was consequently late before we entered the Grand Canal. By nine o'clock we had got clear of the suburbs, and of other boats, and again anchored for the night.

The next morning we had a better view of the great highway to the capital of China—for centuries the largest artificial water-course in the world. It is here more than one hundred and fifty feet in width, but is in some parts of its course narrower, and in some even broader. It is crossed by bridges, similar to those which I had seen on the other canals, but of course longer, and proportionately larger. The embankments on each side were faced with stone, and the tow-path paved with square stone blocks. We continued up the Grand Canal all day. It led us through several lakes, like the Ty-hao, broad but shallow. At a town called Ping-bong we were stopped at a customs' barrier, but as soon as the officials in charge learned who we were, they made no objection to our passing, merely requesting that we would kindly give them some books—a reasonable demand, which my friend hastened to comply with, by presenting to them some of the Chinese publications of a London society. The subjects of these works come under the head of useful knowledge, and it is always customary for foreigners to carry such books on their inland excursions, as they make the best presents to native officials who are disposed to be civil.

The city of Ping-bong is situated in a lake, and all the streets are traversed by canals. The town itself is not walled, but the approaches by the canal, in both directions, are protected by small forts and batteries. In the latter, the guns are of assorted sizes, from two feet to six in length, some mounted, and some lying on the ground. Even in the largest Chinese cannon, the bore is seldom more than four inches in diameter; since, as the celestials buy their guns by weight, it is, of course, the interest of the English manufacturer, to make the calibre as small as possible.

The appearance of Ping-bong, as it were, floating upon the water, is really very pretty, and some wooded islands which surround it, increase the picturesque effect. Many of the bridges which cross the Grand Canal, in its passage through the town, are forty feet high, and the quays are strongly built of stone, descending by stone steps to the water. The city, like all others in the low plain of Northern China, is entirely built on piles. Passing Ping-bong, we proceeded a few miles further along the canal, and again anchored for the night.

The thermometer had stood at 96° during the heat of the day.

Before I awoke next morning, we had got under weigh, and passed Chinza, a considerable town. About ten o'clock we went by Nanzing, a large place, and the *entrepôt* of all the silk which goes to Shanghae, but in appearance similar to the cities already described. We were now entering the silk country, and the plantations of mulberry trees added much to the liveliness of the view. The great drought was here telling severely on the rice, the fields being hard enough to walk on, whereas, they ought, when properly irrigated, to be of the consistence of mud. About noon, we came in sight of the mountains which surround Hoo-chow, and about four o'clock we were stopped at a customs' barrier, and the mandarin sent on board to summon us ashore for examination. Now, it is always the best plan, and saves a great deal of trouble, to treat oriental officials with a high hand, and above all, not to allow them to begin intercourse with an assumption of superiority. It thus became an object with us to cause our dignity to shine upon this little great man, and we answered his messenger that we had prepared and made ready our miserable boat, in the hopes that it would be illumined by his presence. The internuncio soon came back to say, that the press of business would prevent the officials from having the honour of coming on board our magnificent vessel, but that they again ventured to beg us to visit them in the wretched hut where they laboured. This style of communication was kept up for some time, ending in our refusing to go on shore on the ground of illness—a plea which was only diplomatically true. As it became now quite plain, that, come what would, we were not to be enticed ashore, and as these subordinate officials did not dare to let us pass the barrier without examination; and, on the other hand, would not, unsupported, venture on the extreme measure of sending us back to the coast, they determined to visit the boat, and we accordingly drew ashore to enable them to come on board. My friend and I took our seats at the extreme end of the cabin, trying to look as dignified as possible to make up for the simplicity of our attire, which consisted only of night-shirts and loose drawers. The Chinese officers did not make us wait long. Only two came on board, both young men, and simply dressed. My friend, who spoke Chinese, and was well acquainted with their customs, received them with a ceremonious politeness, which set me off into the most indecent fits of laughter. As the Chinamen entered, a sweet smile, expressive of a sort of holy joy, illumined their muddy countenances; changing, as they caught sight of my friend, into a full-blown grin, intended to intimate that they had at length attained to the fruition of perfect bliss, and that all their highest earthly hopes were fulfilled since they were honoured by being permitted to enter into the immediate presence of a chief man of that great nation by whom the extremities of the earth were governed. All this was written on their faces, and spoken in their opening address. My friend also succeeded in moulding his countenance into expressing similar pleasurable emotions, with a skill, which was, to me, a subject of admiring mirth. Both parties *chin-chined*, or saluted, in the Chinese fashion, by clasping both fists, placing them in juxtaposition on the breast, and giving them a prolonged tremulous shake, at the same time uttering the words *tsin-tsin* (hail! hail!) several times. After the first elaborate greetings were over, it was some time before we could so far overcome the modest scruples of our visitors as to induce them to sit down. They remained only a few minutes, which they occupied by questioning my friend about our destination, and then took an elaborate leave, after having accepted the present of a few books.

We found out, afterwards, that these extra precautions (it not being usual to stop foreigners at this barrier) were owing to the vicinity of the rebels, who were, at the time, only 36 miles off, but were prevented from advancing by the lowness of the canals. Hoo-chow was, however, strongly fortified, in preparation for their arrival. The walls were in thorough repair, the outworks on the canal had been put in order, all the cannon were mounted, and we saw a great many of the forty thousand soldiers who had been collected and quartered in and about the city. The gate of the city was more rigidly guarded than even the barrier, and we found it impossible to enter on any pretext.

In size and exterior appearance, Hoo-chow very much resembles Soo-chow. It is surrounded on three sides by hills, the highest of which are about 1,000 feet high, and are covered with monasteries, one of which is well worth seeing. We could not, however, ascend these hills, as the canal leading to their foot was too low to give our boat a passage. We passed through the suburbs of Hoo-chow, which, though not so extensive as those of Soo-chow, seemed to have a larger number of houses inhabited by the wealthier classes, whose dwellings can always be distinguished by the high wall that surrounds them. This city is in the heart of the silk country, and we admired very much the gay costume of the pretty Hoo-chow girls, who are in the habit of wearing bright scarlet silk trowsers, whereas, lower down the country, the women generally wear no colour but black. We put these young ladies very much out of countenance by eyeing them through lorgnettes.

Our appearance caused great excitement here, as in the other towns, and our boat was followed, as before, by shouting crowds of ragamuffins: but, on this occasion, in addition to calling us names, they paid us the more tangible attention of aiming at us mud and stones, from which we had to take refuge in our cabin.

By eight o'clock, we had got clear of the outskirts of the city, and anchored for the night. This was the hottest day of the whole trip, the thermometer in the shade, touching 100° at noon, and remaining above 90° all night. We took a swim in the canal before turning in, but passed an unpleasant night, being tormented by mosquitoes, and by that unpleasant eruption called prickly heat, which attacks nearly all Europeans, in China and India.

From Hoo-chow we had intended to go on to the provincial city of Hang-chow, where are some remarkable temples, and colossal stone representations of Boodh, forty feet high. The lowness of the canals, however, forced us to give up this plan, and on the morning of the 16th, we turned our faces again toward Shanghae.

For the first day, we returned on the same branch of the Grand Canal, by which we had come to Hoo-chow. We again passed through Nanzing, Chinza, and other towns and villages "too numerous to mention." The shopmen were still sitting at the open front of their stores, exposing their sleek, broad bellies to the admiring gaze of passers-by; the buffaloes were still cooling themselves in the canal; the ceaseless activity which is the most characteristic peculiarity of a Chinese community, still went on; and our appearance again excited the curiosity, and called forth the vocal energies of the mob.

By evening, we had passed Ping-bong, near which town we stopped for the night.

The next morning, when I awoke, I found that we had come into another canal, and were opposite the town of Yang-kow-shin, which boasts the finest bridge that I saw in China. The material is granite, the upper lines being straight, and making a very obtuse angle where they meet, at the middle point of the bridge. There are three arches, resting on two piers, with the abutments. The upper curve of all three is a semicircle, slightly returning below to an oval. The centre arch has about forty feet span, and the two side arches over thirty. The breadth of the bridge is at least twenty feet, and its whole length about 175.

During the day, we passed the city of Ka-hing, in the moat of which we found many large junks anchored. One of the largest had, over one end of its house on deck, an extended umbrella, the official signal of the Mandarin, who was on board, and who, we learned, was in command of a body of troops, with which the other boats were loaded. They were going up the canal, in the direction of Hoo-chow. Ka-hing is a city of about a million of inhabitants, and has large suburbs, which we were nearly three hours in passing through. There are several large lakes, which come quite up to the walls, though they do not, as in the case of Ping-bong, entirely surround the city. In one of these lakes, we saw the country-seat of a mandarin, a large building on a low island, nicely shaded by trees. The lake, in front of the house, was preserved for fish, many acres being inclosed in a line of subaquatic hedges, the tops of which just appeared above the surface of the water. This practice is very common in China, and we saw such preserves in several other lakes, though I have not before mentioned them.

The fortifications of Ka-hing had evidently been prepared to resist an expected attack of the rebels, and we saw large numbers of soldiers, as at Hoo-chow. I do not know whether these warriors meant fight or not, but they certainly did not look it.

For the next twenty-four hours, we passed through the prettiest country that I saw on the trip. The trees were not confined to the vicinity of villages, or cemeteries; the canal passed frequently through small lakes; and the merits of the locality seemed to have been appreciated by wealthy Chinese, whose country-houses were visible on all sides. The water-wall and bridges, too, were in good repair, and the latter were frequently covered by creeping vines.

Towards the afternoon of the next day, the country lost its interest, and I saw nothing else worthy of detail here. We arrived at Shanghae on the evening of the nineteenth of July, having been absent just eight days.

Though we had not accomplished as much as we wished or intended, and had at no time been more than 120 miles from Shanghae, and though we had seen and learned less than we could have done in any other country in the same time; yet I could not but feel it a great advantage to be able to see what I did. Although we only, as it were, entered and passed the boundary of the country, yet very few, except the missionaries, have done more; and this feeling of seeing something out of the common track, is what gives the greatest interest to our travels.

After my return to Shanghae I saw more of the American missionaries than when I was first there. In company with one of these gentlemen I visited an establishment in the Chinese town known as the "Institute of Universal Benevolence." It consists of a large room furnished with small tables, at each of which is seated an *employé*, either a physician, lawyer, or visitor of the poor. Here any poor man may receive gratuitous medical advice, legal assistance, or relief in the shape of food, clothing, and money. This institution has been in existence at least a hundred years—I believe more, but have forgotten. It was founded by private Chinese benevolence, and has, since its foundation, received so many bequests that it is now quite wealthy. The system was very complete, and the amount of good effected very large, but its operations were entirely suspended and deranged by the rebellion in the city, and when I visited it, it had not again returned to perfect and harmonious action. The number of applicants who crowded the hall was however considerable. It is very pleasant to see such evidences of charity in a heathen country, and to know that similar institutions exist in many other cities of the empire. Benevolence is one of the most attractive features of the Chinese character, and one that our preconceived ideas find it hard to reconcile with infanticide and other cruelties which disgrace this and all heathen nations. I was told that during a recent famine in the north of China, a single merchant offered to board and lodge, at his own expense, all children from the city of Shanghae who should be entrusted to his care. Several thousands profited by the benevolent offer, and were comfortably sheltered and furnished with food for several months, while men and women were dying, hundreds in a day, in the streets of the city, of starvation and exposure.

In connection with this it should be remembered that the Chinese and other oriental governments do nothing for the relief of paupers—a state of things that always calls out private sympathy to its fullest extent; but still the systematic beneficence of the Chinese, shown in the foundation of such institutions as I have described, and in the custom which allows no beggar to leave a house without an alms, stands in bright contrast with the conduct of all other pagan peoples. In India, for example, though there are asylums for all brute animals, even fleas and lice, established by the Boodhists and Brahmuns, I did not hear of a single foundation for the benefit of the human species, nor of one such act of munificent charity as that of the Chinese merchant at Shanghae. To this remark I must except the case of the Parsee baronet, Sir Jamsetjee Jeejeebhoy, the princely liberality of whose charities has been the theme of admiration throughout the world. It should be remembered, however, that Sir Jamsetjee had the advantage of living at Bombay, among a numerous Christian community, and that he is alone among natives in the distinguished benevolence of his course. In ancient Greece and Rome we hear of no charitable establishments, and I believe that nowhere but in China have they arisen except from the teaching of the Christian religion. Should any one think hardly of the Chinese character, let him remember that they have spontaneously acted upon those principles of benevolence which elsewhere required the teaching of an incarnate God to give them practical force, and that in a heathen land one of the highest virtues of the Christian is practised without the Christian's hope of an immortal reward. My companion, being of Calvinistic views, feelingly regretted that so many good works should not redound to the advantage of the doers, since, being done before justification, and not having as a motive the love of Christ, they would, in the language of the Articles, "partake of the nature of sin." I could only hope that such good intentions might be appreciated by Him in whose eyes the alms of the unconverted Cornelius were pleasing, and that some benighted Chinaman might hereafter find that in doing good, without hope of reward, to one of the least of his brethren, he had done it unawares to that great Elder Brother who is able and willing to reward beyond either our desires or deserts.

CHAPTER VII.

SOUTHERN CHINA.

Leave Shanghae—The Peninsular and Oriental Company—Hong Kong—Foreign Settlement of Canton—The Chinese Suburbs—Ceremonies at Ming-qua's House—Making Tea—Opium Smoking—The Opium Trade—Temple of a Hundred Gods—Beggars Dying of Starvation—Interior of a House—A Chinese Restaurant—Chop-sticks—Rat Grills and Dog Stew—Public Opium Shops—The Boat Population of Canton—Indifference to Life—Lepers—How-qua's Garden—Unique Method of Hatching Eggs—Monasteries of Honan—Boodhist Services—Sacred Hogs—Gambling—Macao—A Protective Policy—The Portuguese—Effect of the War on the Commercial Importance of Canton.

On the last day of July I left Shanghae for Hong Kong, on board the steamer Erin, belonging to the Peninsular and Oriental Steam Navigation Company, or, as they are called for short, the P. and O. Company. This is the largest steamship company in the world, owning, two years ago, thirty-eight steamers, aggregating fifty thousand tons, English measurement. They had, at the time of which I speak, the undisputed monopoly of steam conveyance in the Eastern seas; and even now their only rival is the Australian Steamship Company, to which they lend boats and officers, so that it must be, in fact, either the same parties under a different name, or some good friends of theirs.

The Peninsular and Oriental Company take advantage of their monopoly to charge an enormous price for the passage to Hong Kong. The distance is only about 800 miles, and the fare $120, which, when I paid my passage, was equal to £45 sterling.

The "P. and O." boats are all admirably fitted up, and the whole service is, I suppose, by far the finest private service in the world. The table is as good as circumstances will allow, and beer, wines and liquors are furnished without extra charge.

Our course was close to the shore, and we were always in

sight of, and often close to, the steep and barren hills which form the coast of the Flowery Kingdom; at least, after passing the low alluvial plain of Northern China, which is scarcely raised above the level of the ocean.

On the fourth day we arrived at Hong Kong, which is situated on the sides of a high barren hill, an island in one of the many inlets which receive the waters of the Canton river. The whole island is in the possession of the English, and is a colony by the name of Victoria. The residences of Europeans are built on the side of the hill, and are similar in form to the hongs at Shanghae, except that they are not uniformly so large, and that they are rarely enclosed in compounds. The lower part of the hill, next the water, is occupied partly by the houses and offices of foreigners, and partly by the native town which has grown up since the possession of the island by the English.

I remained only a few hours in Hong Kong, and took, in the evening, the mail-boat to Canton. The distance up the river is about forty miles, and we arrived at Canton about eight o'clock next morning. The branch of the river through which we went, winds among high and steep hills, by which the city of Canton itself is entirely surrounded. The foreign factories were situated outside the walls of Canton and further down the river. They consisted of a compact block of stone houses, four stories high, and each about sixty feet front. Between them and the river was a garden, about a quarter of a mile long and 200 feet broad. This formed the only walk of the foreign residents, and was consequently very prettily laid out. At the upper end of the garden was a building containing a subscription library, and two club billiard rooms. The lower part of this structure was arched and unenclosed, and served as a shelter to the light "out-riggers" in which the younger members of the Canton European community took aquatic exercise.

The whole space occupied by the foreign community at Canton, was not more than eight or ten acres, and was, therefore, very closely built up. The buildings had no enclosures surrounding them as at Shanghae, but were all crammed into a compact block, consisting of five or six rows of houses, one behind the other; each row being divided from the other by only a narrow space, and the whole being connected by tunnelled passages running completely through. It may be easily imagined that Canton was not so pleasant a residence as Shanghae. In fact, the feeling to a stranger was that of a prison.

No strangers are allowed within the walls of Canton, although a free ingress is secured by treaty. The suburbs are, however, very extensive, and through these I made an excursion with Mr. Gray, H. B. M. Chaplain at Canton.

Almost all the wealthy Chinese reside in the suburbs, and we were kindly invited to enter the house of Mingqua, a Chinese merchant of eminence. Like all private residences, this was surrounded by a wall, shutting off all connection from the street. It contained several courts surrounded by buildings. The space between the first and second courts was covered in, and contained a large private temple, similar in its arrangement to all public joss-houses which I saw. During our visit we had the opportunity of witnessing a service performed by some Boodhist monks, to celebrate the recovery from sickness of Mingqua's mother. The ceremony consisted wholly of chaunting and singing to the accompaniment of several discordant instruments; among them a shrill fife, which "carried the air." The ladies of the establishment were present, but in the back-ground, and we enjoyed an opportunity rarely afforded, of seeing Chinese women of the higher classes. They were four or five in number, and dressed in black or blue satin. The face and neck were both painted with admirable art, and the hair drawn back from the forehead into a large knot behind, and retained by gold ornaments. They had all small feet, which, in this part of China, is a mark of high rank; the lower classes allowing their feet to attain the size of nature, which is, after all, very small and pretty.

When the ceremony was concluded, we adjourned with the males of the family to a small room where tea was served. The floor of this room, as of all rooms in these houses, was of marble blocks; the furniture consisted of little tables with marble tops, and marble-seated chairs, placed around the sides of the room, and the walls were entirely bare. At one end of the room was a divan, covered with matting, and furnished with two small hard Chinese pillows and a little lamp. The divan was for opium smoking, and the arrangement was precisely that of the similar divans which exist in every shop in Canton. After partaking of some delightful tea, I was asked to try a pipe of opium, an offer which I was glad to accept, as I wished to make a trial of the fascinations of this drug. I shall first describe the Chinese manner of making tea, and then the opium smoking.

The tea is put into a shallow cup, and boiling water poured on. The saucer, which is not nearly so broad as ours, but deeper, is then put as a cover over the cup, and the tea is allowed to "draw." When the decoction is strong enough, the cup is raised to the lips and the saucer slightly tilted on the edge, so as to retain the tea leaves, but allow the pure tea to pass into the mouth. Sometimes the tea is made in a pot, but what I have described is considered the best plan. In no case, however, is the pot, or cup, ever filled the second time with water, and a Chinese would shudder at the idea of letting the tea "simmer" on the fire.

Opium is not generally indulged in by a man alone. The effect of the drug is to excite the imagination and spirits to such an extent, that a companion is a sort of necessity to perfect enjoyment. The two companions who propose to indulge in a pipe, recline on a divan, supporting the body on the elbow, and resting the legs on a stool. Between them is a lamp, and two little pots of a decoction of opium, as thick as molasses. The opium pipe is generally made of some reed, and is a hollow tube about eighteen inches long with a bore of an inch or more. At one end is an ivory mouth-piece, and the other end is closed. Two thirds of the way down it, is a hole in which fits a hollow earthen bulb, with an interior capacity of about a cubic inch. There is a small aperture of the size of a pin's head in the top of this bulb. The opium smoker, thus reclining, and turned toward his companion, dips a steel instrument, like a square knitting-needle in the solution of opium. A drop adheres to the needle, and is then held in the flame of the lamp, where it effervesces and shrinks into a pasty coating. The needle is then again dipped into the opium, and the process repeated until a small pill is formed on the end of the needle, which is then passed through the little hole on the earthen bulb, and withdrawn with a twist, leaving the pill on the surface of the bulb, over the aperture. The pill is now held in the flame of the lamp, the smoker at the same time inhaling the fumes, which pass into the bulb, and thence into the body of the pipe and the lungs. Each opium pill will furnish three or four full inspirations, and the smoke is retained in the lungs as long as possible. The preparation of the pill takes three or four minutes, and the smoking not more than one or two. It is said that an habitual smoker finds the quantity of opium necessary to intoxicate him, continually increasing up to a certain point; after which the necessary amount becomes less and less until, in some cases, where the system has become very much debilitated by continual indulgence in this habit, a single pipe will produce full intoxication. A European, too, is much less easily affected than a Chinese. I smoked on this occasion, five or six pipes, which did not produce the least mental effect; they entirely removed, however, the great fatigue and exhaustion which I had felt from my long walk in the sun. From what I heard in China, I should imagine that opium smoking does not produce those universally deleterious effects which are commonly attributed to it here and in Europe. Like alcoholic beverages, or any other stimulant, it is very susceptible of abuse; but I should fancy that the victims of over-indulgence in this drug, are not relatively more numerous than drunkards are among those nations where habitual stimulants are of an alcoholic nature. The opium is all smuggled into the country by foreigners, who keep three or four opium store-ships at a place called Cum-Sing-Moon, on a branch of the Canton River, which leads to Macao. When the drug has been once introduced into the Empire, it is conveyed throughout the country with the knowledge of the officials, to whom it pays black mail at at every customs' station.

A class of very fast boats is employed to run the drug from the store ships to Canton. These boats are numerously manned by desperate fellows to whom high pay is given. Their great speed generally enables them to avoid the imperial revenue boats and the pirates, but they are sometimes overtaken and fearful fights and loss of life are the result.

We passed about half an hour at Mingqua's after the conclusion of the religious ceremony. My friend conversing in Chinese with our entertainer. In the course of conversation, he happened to remark that he was a Master of Arts, and I, a Bachelor, upon hearing which the whole company arose, and made us a respectful salutation. It is well known that the Chinese have similar academic degrees, which are conferred on all who can pass the government examinations. The graduates form the body from which mandarins are chosen, and are looked upon in China with great respect.

On our way back to the factories we stopped at a temple which contained, in a vast chamber, over a hundred idols, about four feet high, made of stone and gilded. They were arranged on a shelf along the wall, and no two of them had the same dress or expression.

After leaving the temple of a hundred gods we passed through what is known as the beggars' square, where those mendicants who become too old or infirm to exercise their profession, are taken by their friends to die. They are generally laid on a piece of matting, and protected from the sun by a temporary shelter. They perish of starvation, if not by disease. There were three or four wretched beings there, when I visited the square. They seemed more than half dead, and one man, to whom I threw a quarter of a dollar, did not pick it up.

We stopped, before reaching home, at another private house, the general arrangement of which was like that of Mingqua's establishment. The family, however, had, in this case, gone into the country, and we were shewn all over the house by the children's tutor, a skinny old graduate, with immense horn spectacles. The rooms were all small, bare and cheerless; the only exceptions being the women's quarters, which were smaller, barer, and more cheerless. One or two apartments had been arranged as a kind of green-house, with artificial rocks, stunted trees, growing bushes trained to form bird-cages for canaries, and others of those distortions of nature in which the Chinese take so much pleasure.

I made one or two other excursions among the suburbs of Canton, with Mr. Gray, who was well acquainted with all that there was to see, and very kindly acted as pilot.

On one occasion, we went into a Chinese eating-house, a dirty, noisy hole, but we were very hungry and thirsty, and ventured on a pomegranate and some tea. The establishment was crowded with guests, who removed their shirts for greater coolness, as the Chinese do in the house. We found the smell of the Chinese dishes, which are cooked with rancid oil, by no means appetising. Of course this afforded a splendid opportunity for witnessing the practical management of chopsticks. The method of using these puzzling substitutes for knives and forks is, after all, very simple, but can hardly be described in writing. Both sticks are held by one hand, and the dextrous Chinaman rapidly picks out, by their means, the choice morsels of meat which are brought to him already cut up, and mostly made into ragouts. When dining with a friend, if disposed to be very polite, he will, with his own sticks, extract a choice morsel from the dish, and place it in the mouth of his companion.

Besides this large chow-chow (eating) house, we went into several smaller establishments, where the usual bill of fare was increased by the addition of rat-grills and dog-stew. In the back division of one of these latter restaurants I saw a dozen or two puppies in little coops, being fattened for the table.

I visited several public opium shops. They were mostly dirty rooms up-stairs, *very* dirty, and the resort of the lower classes only. The higher classes prefer to enjoy this luxury, in a room set apart for the purpose, in their own houses. The atmosphere of these places was foul and heavy with opium smoke. It is a strange peculiarity of opium that its taste and smell are disagreeable to all, and the smell of its smoke particularly offensive, and yet the taste of the latter is delightful, and no harsher to the delicate air-passages of the lungs than the purest air. These public opium-shops have a room up-stairs, whither their customers are conveyed when dead-drunk, and left to lie, closely packed on the floor, until they have slept off the effects of the drug.

I went one day with Mr. Gray to visit the Gardens of Howqua, situated a few miles up the river. We went in a large boat. The river off Canton is completely filled with craft of all sorts, leaving only a very narrow passage. In this channel the tide very often runs with prodigious force, and, as collisions often take place, it frequently happens that a small boat goes to pieces. I have several times seen such accidents, the boat breaking completely up, and the passengers floating in the water. Dozens of boats would at once put off from the shore, and pick up every stick of the boat, but it rarely happened that they attempted to save life, until they had got all they could of the wreck. It is really incredible how little attention is paid in these countries to human life. I have seen several people drowned from such accidents as I have described above, and I have heard a ship-captain say, that he had seen a boat row by a drowning man, within an oar's length, without stopping to render him assistance.

Most persons know that there is an immense population living in boats, moored off the city of Canton. These boats are not often more than twenty feet long, and generally about six feet wide. They are entirely covered by a house, in which the whole family sleep and live, taking their meals on the little deck at the bow of the boat. At the stern of these, as of all Chinese boats, there is an idol, which is propitiated by burning joss-sticks. The Chinese boats which were used by foreigners for going off to the shipping, or down the river, were usually of larger size, and propelled by oars. A woman was generally the commander, and worked the large scull at the stern. It was in one of these latter boats that we went up the river to Howqua's Garden. On the way, we passed several flat, unsheltered scows, floating in the stream, and containing lepers. These miserable beings are, in this country, compelled to live in this way, after their disease has made a certain progress. The skin assumes a tint, the colour of an infant's flesh, instead of the putty colour, which is the natural complexion of a Chinaman. They linger miserably on their boats for a few years, never being allowed to go ashore, and having a little food thrown to them, when they pass the craft on the river. Doubtless many of them die from exposure and the want of the necessaries of life, as those I saw had no clothing, and their boats were quite unprotected by any cabin.

Howqua's Gardens, as well as those of another merchant, which we saw, cover several acres, and are laid out with a good deal of taste, in the extravagant and artificial Chinese style. They do not, however, merit a more particular description.

On our return from the Gardens, we stopped at an egg-hatching establishment. This was a large, wooden, barn-shaped building, on the river's bank. The eggs are purchased out of the produce boats that come down the river, and are here artificially hatched. The process employed is singular, as using only the natural heat of the egg, and is as follows. Large baskets, each twice the size of an ordinary barrel, and thickly lined with hay to prevent the loss of heat, are filled with the eggs, and then carefully closed with a closely-fitting cover of twisted straw. The eggs are now left for three days; after which, they are removed from the basket, and replaced in different order—those eggs which were before on the surface being now on the lowest tier. At the end of three days more, the position of the eggs is again altered, and so on, for fifteen days; after which time the eggs are taken out of the basket and placed on a shelf in another apartment, and covered with bran. In the course of a day or two, the chicken bursts its shell, and makes its way out of the bran; being at once taken charge of by an attendant, who is always on the watch. The whole secret of this process is in the fact, that the animal heat of the whole mass of eggs being retained by the basket, which is formed of materials which do not *conduct* caloric, is sufficient to support the animal life of any one particular egg, and to foster its development. This is the only egg-hatching process I ever heard of, which did not require artificial heat. I should think it might be practised in America, in summer.

During my stay at Canton, I visited Honan, an island opposite the factories, belonging to a community of Boodhist monks, and covered by a large monastic establishment. There were several hundred monks in residence at the time of my visit. They occupied rooms around a court, containing two or three acres of ground, nicely sodded, and shaded by fine old trees. At the upper end of this court was a large temple, of the usual form; and behind the temple, another court, precisely like the first. Besides these two open quadrangles, there were several other smaller courts, generally paved, and without trees, around which were the residences of the abbot, and other functionaries. Beyond the buildings was the garden, covering five or six acres, where the monks were at work. At the further end of the garden was a little stone building, within which, upon shelves, were earthen urns containing the ashes of those priests who die at the monastery. Outside the little building was a stone furnace to burn the body. I could not learn whether this practice of incremation was peculiar to this establishment, or prevailed at other conventual institutions. After seeing the garden, we were invited by the abbot into his private parlour, which was elegantly furnished. He entertained us with a cup of tea, and then proposed our witnessing the afternoon service, which was about being performed. He accordingly returned to the temple, where about a hundred monks had assembled, all in their ordinary slate-coloured robes, except two or three, who knelt in front, and acted as leaders. These latter were enveloped in ample scarfs, of yellow satin. The service consisted principally in a monotonous nasal chaunt, alternating between the priests in the yellow scarfs, and the remaining monks, who stood around the wall. Occasionally they would walk in procession around the figure of Boodh, saluting it as they passed. The chaunting was accompanied by a fife and bell. The service lasted about twenty minutes. After the prayers, we visited the printing-press of the monastery, at which all the sacred books for the whole of China are printed. Moveable types are not used, but the characters are cut on blocks of box-wood. There were three or four presses, similar in form to our old-fashioned hand-presses. We also saw the asylum for animals, where several pigs and other beasts are supported at the expense of the monastery, to avert the wrath of Heaven from the Chinese generally, on account of their slaughter of these animals. This convent at Honan is one of the largest and wealthiest in China, and covers, with all its buildings and gardens, about twenty acres.

Gambling forms one of the most prominent amusements of the Chinese, and may be described as their ruling passion. Whenever they have a moment's leisure, they will sit down at some game, and government officials, as having nothing to do, seem to pass most of their time at this employment and opium smoking. There are gambling houses in every street in Canton, all perfectly open and public. The game is generally conducted fairly; and the profits of the establishment do not come, as with us, from an advantage in the game, but from a discount on all sums won by players.

During all the three weeks that I remained at Canton, the river was very high, on account of the long-continued rains, which had caused as much distress in the southern part of China as the drought had in the north. The gardens, in front of the foreign factories, were, for several days, overflowed, and people had to go from one hong to another in boats.

The weather was very warm, all the time, which, added to the damp season, produced much fever and ague. They had an excellent plan to shelter the factories from the greatest heat of the sun. A bamboo scaffolding was built along the whole front of the line of hongs. Upon this scaffold, and upon supports resting on the roofs of the houses, there was a roof of thick matting, which acted like a gigantic umbrella, breaking the force of the sun's rays, and shading the windows of the hongs, and the street in front. Many of the merchants at Canton took their only exercise on the tops of the hongs in the evening. The roofs being flat, and covered with tiles, made a very pleasant, though not very spacious walk. The young men commonly walked in the garden, which was considered somewhat too plebeian a resort for the "tai-pâns," as the partners in commercial houses are called.

I spent about two weeks, very pleasantly, at Macao, which was a sort of watering place of Canton. Most European merchants owned a house at Macao, as well as at Canton, going down to the former when they were exhausted by the hot air and imprisonment of the factories. Macao is a very pretty place, built on the side of a gently sloping hill, which bends around its bay in a semicircle. The hills in its vicinity are very picturesque, and, in the offing, are numerous lofty islands, which act as a great protection to shipping in the bay. The harbour, which is a cove, running around behind the town, is, naturally, I believe, as good as that of Hong Kong, and had the Portuguese government been liberal enough, they might, during the English war with China, have attracted to Macao, and retained there, much of the trade which afterwards centred in the British colony of Hong Kong. But they would not alter their old system of high duties, which were imposed even on the importation of bullion, and would do nothing for the improvement of the harbour. When Hong Kong began to reap the advantages of an opposite policy, the Portuguese saw their error, and endeavoured to repair the mistake by throwing Macao open as a free port, but they were too late, as trade had become firmly settled in the direction of Hong Kong, and Macao can never, in all probability, be anything more than a pleasant residence for foreigners during their weeks of leisure. The native Portuguese population, who once inhabited the vast palace-like residences that abound in Macao, and who once formed the most flourishing and wealthy colony of Portugal, are now miserably degraded by intermixture with Chinese. They speak a corrupt jargon, half Chinese, half their ancestral language; and are most of them miserably poor and ignorant. They are an idle race, and generally live on the remains of their property. Some families manage to exist, in their native fashion, on as little as $80 per annum. Degraded and brutalized as this Portuguese population is in all other respects, they still retain the Christian religion; and the churches, in size and general appearance, remind one of those in Europe. Macao has good sea-bathing, very pretty walks, a good road for a drive, and a pleasant society, composed of such English and American families as live there constantly, (at least the ladies and children,) for the benefit of pure air; and of a continuous stream of transitory visitors from Canton and Hong Kong.

I left Hong Kong for Calcutta about the middle of September. Soon after that time, the disturbances between the English and the Chinese began—among the earliest results of which was the destruction of the foreign factories, and the flight of the merchants to Hong Kong and Macao. This will, probably, be a heavy blow to the foreign trade of Canton, already diminished by the rivalry of Shanghae and Foo-Chow, ports which are much more favourably situated for communication with the tea and silk districts.

CHAPTER VIII.

TO CALCUTTA.

The "Lancefield"—Entomology—Singapore—First View of Orientals—The Parsees—Malays—Garrhees—Proas—Black Water—Torture—Crew of a Ship in the Indian Sea—Jolly Tars—An Indian Watering-place—The Hoogly—Bores—First View of Natives—Hubble-bubble—Fattening Shell-fish for Market.

THE steamer in which I made the passage from China to India was called the "Lancefield," and formed, with the "Fiery Cross," a sister ship, a monthly connection between Calcutta and Hong Kong. Both these boats belonged to an eminent English firm, and their great employment was carrying opium to China, for which purpose they had entirely supplanted the opium sailing clippers, formerly so numerous in the Eastern waters. They had, at that time, and, I suppose, have still, almost a monopoly of this most lucrative traffic. Their cargoes of opium were principally on account of the owners. The "Lancefield" and "Fiery Cross" were iron ships, of the best clipper models, fitted with screws, and most of the wood work was of teak. The cabin accommodations were exceedingly comfortable, the only drawback being the great quantities of centipedes and cock-roaches, which infest all ships in the India trade, but especially those which carry opium. These centipedes are insects, from three to seven inches in length, and shaped a little like the earwig. Their sting is very poisonous, and sometimes causes the loss of a limb—always fever and pain. The cock-roaches look much like the ordinary animal of that name, but are from an inch and a half to three inches long, and have the power of flying. Besides these specimens of the entomological kingdom, to which I had got somewhat accustomed in China, we had, on the "Lancefield," some remarkably fine varieties of monster spiders. One of the hardest things for an Occidental to endure in the East, is the superabundance of animal life, particularly in the lower grades; and it was a long time before I got used to seeing two or three-inch cock-roaches walking calmly across the table, during dinner, as they do frequently, both in China and India. The annoyance of these beasts on the "Lancefield," was, however, intolerable. If I came down into the cabin, during the evening, it was quite impossible to go from the companion-way to my state-room, without crushing several cock-roaches under foot, and they flew in my face, caught in my hair, and walked up my trowsers during supper, until I was fairly disgusted. I only tried one night to sleep in the cabin. On that occasion, I awoke about midnight, and found a cock-roach on my face, several others about the bed, one or two on the wall, and an immense spider on my pillow. I jumped out of my bunk, dressed myself, and slept that night, and the rest of the passage, on deck. I found the deck cooler than below, and not a much harder bed than the mattrasses of bamboo chips which are mostly used in China. The only trouble was the rain, of which we had more or less the whole passage.

We arrived at Singapore, after a week's passage, on the 5th of October, and remained there twenty-four hours to coal.

Singapore is built on an island, the general surface of which is almost perfectly level, but a little way behind the town the ground rises in hillocks, on the tops of which the merchants have built their country houses or bungalows. The sloping grounds around the bungalows are frequently covered with nutmeg trees.

Singapore consists of three divisions. The first has the greatest resemblance to a city, consisting of large solid houses formerly inhabited by Europeans, and numerous streets of houses in the Indian style. This part of the town is mostly inhabited by Hindoos, Parsees, Malays, &c. There is, besides, the Chinese quarter, built and arranged like a Chinese town, and peopled by several thousand of this enterprising and industrious nation. The residences of the English merchants are in a line along the coast of the bay. They are generally large, square, unarchitectural buildings, in roomy compounds, shaded by fine trees. As in China and Calcutta, these buildings were generally of brick stuccoed.

The hotel where we stayed was a very large establishment, consisting of three main buildings, and many outhouses in a great compound. We took our meals under a sort of shed in the open air. The servants were all Chinese, who make, I think, the best servants in the world. The house itself was uncomfortable, as are almost all houses in the East, even the best private ones, to people with European ideas. The great size of the apartments, the bare floors of the bed-rooms, the paucity and poverty of the furniture, with the fact that neither the doors nor the windows will close tightly, give a stranger anything but a feeling of comfort. All large houses in the East, are built with an open hall in the centre, to admit of a free passage of air. The rooms open on this hall, the doors of the sleeping apartments not being closed at night, but a curtain being drawn across the lower part instead.

Having been well seasoned by a summer in China, we did not find the heat oppressive at Singapore although it is nearly on the line.

It was at Singapore that I first saw something of oriental as distinguished from Chinese life. The population is, to be sure, one-half composed of Chinese emigrants, but most of the lower classes are Malays, who wear the graceful *sarong*, and this city is the temporary residence of traders from all parts of the East, Parsees, Jews, Armenians, Turks, Arabs, Indian Moosulmans, and representatives of other nationalities, the picturesqueness and variety of whose costume pleased and surprised me, as I had supposed that most of that show in dress, which we read about and see in pictures, had disappeared. None of these natives appeared to be at all Europeanized, except the Parsees, some of whom wore European trowsers and shoes.

The Parsees are the descendants of the old fire-worshippers of Persia, who were driven from their homes by the Mahommedan conquest, and took refuge in India a thousand years ago. They still follow the religion of Zerdoosht, and the everlasting fire, brought with them from Persia, still burns at Bombay, and wherever else they are settled. Their sacred language is still the Zend, and is the tongue in which their prayers are recited. But few, however, even of their priests, understand the liturgy, which, in truth, is very much mutilated, the largest part of it having been lost in their hurried flight from their Moosulman conquerors. Bombay is the chief settlement of this ancient people, and was their first place of refuge, but in late years their commercial enterprise has led them to settle in all the principal oriental ports. They always, however, look upon Bombay as their home, since it is the residence of their women, whom they do not take with them abroad, on account of the unavoidable publicity of travelling in public conveyances. The opium trade is now getting largely into the hands of the Parsees, of whom there are several, both in Shanghae and Canton. Their dress is a long, plain cassock of white cotton in summer, of black cloth in winter. They wear the loose Eastern pa*n*jama, or trowser, and a high circular turban, resembling a mitre in shape. They delight in imitating Occidentals in equipage, &c., and generally speak good English. They do not bury their dead, but expose them in towers, on hill tops, to be devoured by birds.

The Malays are a fine athletic race of men, with dark flashing eyes, clothed generally in nothing but an ample skirt which is tucked up behind, and thus made into a kind of trowser.

In all oriental countries some sort of conveyance is always employed, in going about, both on account of the heat and as a protection against the coup de soleil, which is supposed to arise from peculiar properties in the sun's rays quite separate from their heat. In China, I have said that people go about in sedan-chairs; in Singapore, they use, as a substitute, a little four-wheeled carriage, with room in the interior for two only, sitting facing one another. These little traps are called *pálkee gárrhees*, (the Hindoostanee word for a carriage being gárrhee) and are commonly drawn by one horse, the groom running by his side, as there is generally no box seat for a driver.

The Malay *proas* deserve the reputation they enjoy for beauty of model and speed. They are generally propelled by oars, but the largest ones by sails. The evening before we left Singapore two other passengers and myself took one of these proas to go round by water to our steamer, which lay five or six miles from the hotel, and were caught in a tropical storm, which wet us through, and drove us among the coral reefs, where we nearly went to pieces. After escaping from the reefs, we got among the nets and fishing-stakes, which were almost as dangerous, as it continued to blow a gale, and our boat ran half way on the tops of the nets, and being very crank, came near being capsized several times. We got back after a couple of hours, and were heartily thankful to put our feet on *terra firma* again, although we had to walk six miles, by land, around to the ship, which started at six the next morning.

Singapore is a British settlement, and has only become a place of importance since the British occupation. It is under the jurisdiction of the East India Company, and is used by them as a convict settlement. I saw several chain-gangs of Indian convicts working on the roads. Transportation is in India a favourite penalty, since it is regarded by the natives as the most terrible of all punishments. By the religion of the Hindoos, all caste is lost by leaving India. The high caste Sepoys of the Bengal army have on several occasions mutinied rather than break through this rule of their religion, which forbids their leaving India—a rule the infringement of which is punished, according to their belief, by the perdition of the offender and of his ancestors and descendants for seven generations. For this and other reasons, "kala pánee" (black water), as the natives call transportation across the leaden sea, is looked upon as the last misfortune, and a calamity to which death is infinitely preferable.

During my stay in Singapore I went into the Court of Justice, and saw the judge in the same hot scarlet robe which is worn in England. He looked as if etiquette would be the death of him. In Australia, the judges wear the wig, and not the gown; in India, they wear the close robe and no wig: which of the two is the more oppressive, I suppose no one but the sufferers themselves can tell.

We arrived without further adventure at the "Sandheads," which mark the mouth of the Hoogly river, on the 13th of October. I had had a most pleasant passage, having been much pleased with the captain and my fellow-passengers. The only drawback was the cock-roaches and spiders. The crew on the *Lancefield*, like those on the P. & O. Company's steamers, was composed of all sorts of nationalities, each of which had its appropriate work. First, the captain and mates were Scotch—that being a nation which has many representatives among the British in the East, particularly in the mercantile classes. Secondly, the quartermasters and secunnies (helmsmen) were from Manilla and China, and wore the naval costume of duck-trowsers, and a shirt with a broad blue collar. Thirdly, the crew of the captain's gig were Chinamen, who make the best rowers in the East. Fourthly, the firemen and stokers were great burly negroes from Africa, known as seedipoys. Fifthly, the cabin servants, to pull the punkahs, were Sooratee Moosulmans. Sixthly, the khitmutgras, who waited at table, were Calcutta Moosulmans. These two last classes wore the *chupkun*, or double-breasted cassock, which forms one of the most common dresses in India. On their heads they had narrow flat turbans. The negroes had no clothing but a cloth around the waist, and a low basket-work cap, with a rude turban twisted around it. This cap was also worn by the cabin boys from Soorat. The mariners were Lascars, or, as they are more properly called from the name of their caste, Kulăssees. They are a low caste of Moosulmans, coming from the Malabar coast, and a more spiritless, miserable looking set of men I never saw. Hindoos never become sailors, as their caste forbids their leaving India, and they would not probably be much inclined to a seafaring life even if this obstacle did not stand in the way. In shipping a Lascar crew, three times as many are always taken as if they were white sailors, and this gives about the correct ratio of their relative strength and activity. It is not usual to provide any shelter for the Lascars at night, but they stow themselves away on deck in the snuggest place they can find, and are allowed to select the softest planks as a bed. They never take more than two suits of clothes on board with them, and keep one of these suits for muster-days, so that our fellows wore the same wet clothes day and night from Hong Kong to Singapore. The Lascars are under the immediate direction of natives called *tyndals*, answering to our boatswain's mates. Each *tyndal* ships the men whom he commands, they having either voluntarily adopted him for their master on shore, or being so much in his debt as to be in his power—so that a *tyndal* is in some respect like a sailors' boarding-house keeper with us. Above the tyndals is the *sĕrang*, answering to our boatswain. The European officers very seldom attempt to work or discipline the men, leaving all that in the hands of the sĕrang and his subordinates, to whom they give the orders. The men are not divided into watches, but when they are not wanted drop off to sleep on deck. When some hands are called to do any piece of work, the tyndals go about the deck, dragging their trembling men out of the hiding places to which they betake themselves, and awaking them to a sense of the realities of life by mild applications of the *colt* (which is said to be so called from its "helping you along"). The food of the Lascars is rice and salt fish, made into a curry, of which they partake squatted on the deck around large kids. The only good point of these Kulăssees is their agility, which far exceeds that of European sailors. They ascend the rigging without the help of the ratlins, by inserting the shrouds between the toes, at the same time grasping them above with the hands. In this way they will *walk* up any large rope as quickly as a monkey. They will also, in the same way, walk out a try-sail gaff, and, in fact, every Lascar is a far better performer than our best *acrobats*. This peculiarity of the native sailors has occasioned the custom of not "rattling down" the rigging in East India ships. Their skill depends principally on the use they make of their toes, which a native uses with almost as much facility as we do our fingers—*e. g.*, if he sees a small object on the ground, he will not take the trouble to stoop down and pick it up, but will take it up with his toes. Nor is it with their toes only that the natives display their remarkable suppleness, as I shall have occasion hereafter to remark when describing the nâch girls and jugglers.

We lay all night at the mouth of the river, in order to give the owners time to profit by the information which we brought, and which we telegraphed to them from Saugor, sending a boat ashore for the purpose.

At the pilot-brig which was anchored outside we were joined by two officers, who had been down there to spend the Doorga Poojah, a two weeks' Hindoo festival, which had just ended. This pilot-brig is rather more comfortable than the light-ship off New York harbour, and that these gentlemen should go there for fresh air and amusement shows how much of each can be obtained in Calcutta.

We began ascending the river on the morning of the 14th of October. The Hoogly, as is well known, is one of the mouths of the Ganges. In its dirty colour, and general features, it resembles the Yang-tze-kiang, Mississippi, and most other great alluvial streams. Like them, its navigation is attended with great danger, from the shifting of the channel and the sudden formation of shoals and banks. In the Hoogly, however, the difficulty and danger are increased by the strength and swiftness of the tides, which, at certain times, come up the river in a wall of water from two to six feet in height, tearing, frequently, even the large ships from their moorings. These tide-waves are called "bores," and are found, more or less developed, wherever the waters are crowded together by a cone-shaped bay like that of Bengal.

The banks of the Hoogly are low and uninteresting, but covered with a luxuriant growth of tropical vegetation, above which rises the spreading banyan, or tall cocoa-nut tree. The river craft are few and ugly, so shaped as to have as small a portion of the boat as possible in the water, the bow and stern being made high and long, and the bottom flat. This enables them to put a great deal of cargo on deck without much resulting depression of the vessel. The natives whom I here saw were, to my surprise, quite black. They were generally nearly naked, having only a narrow cloth twisted around the loins. The hair was commonly shaven off the head, which was unprotected by a turban or other covering. I found afterwards, however, that this description was applicable to all the lower classes in Calcutta. They are certainly a far inferior race to the Chinese. On the boats they may be seen squatted on the high bow smoking the *hubble-bubble*—a position and an occupation which are a Bengalee's ideal of existence. The *hubble-bubble*, as the foreigners call the commonest kind of native *hookah*, from the peculiar noise heard when it is smoked, merits a description, as its use is one of the standard occupations of a native's life; and its awkwardness, with the impossibility of doing any active work while it is in use, are very characteristic. It consists of a cocoa-nut shell, half filled with water, and pierced above with two apertures. Through one of these, which is on top, passes a tube descending into the water. The other hole is for the mouth. The tube is ten inches or a foot long, and is surmounted by the earthen *chillum*, or pipe-bowl. The smoke passes down the tube, through the water, and out of the small hole into the smoker's mouth. The tobacco, as used by the natives, is formed into a soft paste with molasses, and has to be kept alight by the contact of burning charcoal, or balls of dried cow-dung, called *ghools*, which are ignited and laid on the tobacco. When used, the shell is raised to the mouth with both hands, the tube and chillum rising above the head. It has to be held with great steadiness, as any motion will shake off the *ghools*. No more awkward instrument could be devised, and none better calculated to induce inaction in a people whose chief pleasure is smoking, and who are naturally lazy.

But to return to the Hoogly. I have said that it resembled the Yang-tze-kiang, but many things showed that we were not on that river, or in China. First, the small numbers, and awkward build and rig of the native craft, with the laziness of their navigators. Then, again, the river was covered at one place with floating timber, from a lumber vessel which had gone to pieces the day before. In China every stick would have been picked up in an hour. Another most disagreeably distinctive feature was the dead bodies, bloated, blenched, and covered with vultures and crows, which we constantly passed. The regular plan is to burn the dead and throw the *ashes* into the river; but in this observance the will is taken for the deed, and the relatives burn as much of the body as can be consumed by the amount of wood which they can afford. As wood is very dear in Calcutta and most Hindoos very poor, it consequently happens that the body is generally only half burned, or even only singed; and no more disgusting sight can be conceived than such a corpse, swollen by decomposition, half destroyed by the fire and half eaten by the birds, the skin bleached by the weather, affording "shelter and food" to numerous prawns and shrimps, who fatten on such diet for the famous "prawn curry" of Calcutta.

For the last two miles before reaching Calcutta the scenery of the river is so beautiful that it is known as "Garden Reach." On the eastern shore are numerous large houses, the residences of Europeans. The compounds are large, and filled with beautiful trees. A fine road leads down from the city, and is a favourite drive in the evening. On the opposite bank of the river is the Botanical Garden, a very extensive establishment, which the Calcutta people suppose to contain the largest banyan tree in the world.

In a window of one of the houses in Garden Reach we saw the King of Oude. He was sitting in a chair watching the arrival of our steamer. Two servants, with long fans of peacocks' feathers, brushed the flies away from his majesty.

For the last year or so the King has been kept in confinement on account of suspected complicity in the revolt. It is doubtful if the government will be able to prove anything against him in a court of law; though in India every one believes that he and his minister, Ali Nakhi Khan, were aware of the plot from the first, and that they were among the original conspirators. At any rate, his whole offence is confined to concealing from the government what he knew, and abetting the plots of his minister, since the miserable wretch is so utterly exhausted by a life of brutal debauchery as to be quite incapable of devising any great scheme, or taking an active part in it. It is to be hoped that he will not be again released, and permitted to reëstablish such a nest of nameless vices as was his mansion in Garden Reach. In truth, a life spent in confinement would not be an inappropriate termination to the career of one who, in his own person, degraded human nature below the level of the lowest brute.

CHAPTER IX.

CALCUTTA.

Palkees—Buggies—The City of Calcutta—Government House—Tanks—Bazârs—The largest Mint in the World—Supreme Court—Conflict of Laws—Missions and Schools —Spence's Hotel—Servants—Expenses of Living in India—Civil Servants—Their Salaries—The Language of the Camp—A People without a Country, and a Country without a Name.

On landing in Calcutta I was at once surrounded by a crowd of nearly naked "niggers," painted all over the face and breast with red and white streaks, the sign of their having made poojah, *i. e.*, done worship to some idol that morning. These gentlemen crowded me so much with their black, oily bodies, that I found a vigourous beating with my umbrella necessary to keep them at a respectful distance. They offered to convey my luggage to the hotel, and I accepted the services of one fellow, who at once distributed the various articles to about twenty others, one carrying a carpet-bag, another an umbrella, &c. I then inserted myself in a palanquin, or, as they are commonly called in Bengal, *palkee.* This is a black box, seven feet long, three feet high, closed all around, with a sliding door in the side, and furnished inside with a mattrass and bolster. At each end of the palkee, near the top, there is a pole, three feet long, projecting at right angles, which the bearers rest on their shoulders. Four bearers are under the palkee at any one time, and two more run alongside as a relief. To enter the palkee you turn your back toward it and sit down on the mattrass in its bottom, and then, by a dexterous "slew," bring your legs and head inside. You then lie down and are carried along reclining at full length. The palkee-bearers have a peculiar lock-step which prevents the least jolt, and nothing can be more luxurious than this mode of conveyance, at least for short distances.

Palkees were formerly universally used by foreigners in going about the city, but they are now supplanted by garr-hees and buggies; the former, a vehicle which I have described when speaking of Singapore; the latter, a two-wheeled gig, with a top descending very low in front to keep off the sun. Everybody in Calcutta keeps or hires a buggy; even the captains of ships, and some of the mates, have their buggies waiting for them all day on the quay. The necessity of some conveyance arises from the impossibility of walking out exposed to the sun. In the palmy days of palkees, they were richly ornamented, and a single one would often cost as much as 3,000 rupees, or $1,500; and a certain number of palkee-bearers were a necessary part of every gentleman's household.

Calcutta is situated on the eastern branch of the Hoogly, and was the first concession to the British in this part of India. It was, when they obtained it, only a miserable village, known as Kalee-Ghât, of which its present name is a corruption. It is now supposed to have 600,000 inhabitants at least. Below the city of Calcutta, and between it and "Garden Reach," is a broad open plain, of from 100 to 150 acres, running along the water's edge. This is called the "Esplanade," or, as frequently by its Hindoostanee name, *Maidan.* It is the great drive of Calcutta, being divided by fine broad macadamized roads bordered with trees. The space between the roads is plain turf. Along the river's bank runs the largest of these roads, called the "Strand," where is seen in the evening the greatest show of carriages and equipages. Fort William, the principal defence of Calcutta, and one of the strongest fortresses in the world, is on the river's bank, wholly contained within the Maidan. Around the Maidan is built the European portion of Calcutta—fine houses of stuccoed brick, covering much ground, but commonly not over two stories high, and generally without compounds. At the lower extremity of the Maidan, surrounded by fine trees, is the cathedral, a large decorated Gothic building, of no particular merit. The finest building in Calcutta is Government House—the residence of the Governor General. It fronts on the Esplanade, but is surrounded by an open square of its own. It consists of two semicircular galleries, placed back to back, and meeting in a central hall. Rows of columns decorate the exterior, a dome surmounts the central pavilion, the entrance is by a broad and massive flight of stone steps, and the whole is of sufficient size to be imposing, and even majestic. Between Government House and the river is the Town Hall, and Spence's Hotel, where I stopped. The whole vicinity of Government House Square is built up with fine private residences, and streets of shops, which are here on a large scale.

The side of the town toward the river is separated from the water by a broad quay, fronting on which are the stores of the merchants, similar to the private houses in architecture and extent, but much higher. They were formerly occupied by the merchants as residences—a custom which still obtains in China. Behind this line of princely counting-houses, behind that mass of noble residences which surrounds the Maidan and Government House Square, and which have given Calcutta its name, "The City of Palaces," shut out from all view, and light, and air, are the narrow, filthy streets with open sewers, the dark and winding lanes, the low and squalid huts, which form the vast native town, or, as it is commonly called, the "Black Town" of Calcutta.

Calcutta being altogether a modern place, contains no native buildings of interest—the Hindoo temples and Mahommedan mosques being all small and insignificant. The latter are without minarets, which compel the Muezzin to stand at the door when calling the faithful to prayer—a call to which, in Calcutta, they rarely attend, as they are altogether a very spurious and inferior variety of Moosulmans.

The city is supplied with drinking water from wells, but there are beside large tanks, or open reservoirs excavated from the earth. These tanks are commonly 150 or 200 yards long by 100 wide, and thirty or forty feet deep. These become filled in the rainy season, and their water is used for washing, bathing, sprinkling the roads, &c. One of the tanks, much larger than the others, is filled from the Hoogly by a steam pump. These tanks are quite universal in Lower Bengal, about country houses, each house having several.

The bazárs, of which the city is full, are nasty, narrow, native streets, of little low shops. In them you can buy almost anything at ridiculously low rates,by wasting time and patience in chaffering with the natives, who almost stun you as you walk through, with their clamorous entreaties to enter their shops, and the enumeration of their stock, and its excellence. Here, as throughout the East, it is always customary to ask many times as much for a thing as the seller expects to obtain.

The Calcutta mint is the largest establishment of the kind in the world, the next in size being the mints at Bombay and Madras. It is situated in the upper part of the city on the quay. The machinery is of the best kind, and on a much larger scale than at either London or Paris. The coin struck is the Company's rupee, of the value of two shillings sterling, and copper pieces. No gold coin is now struck, gold not being in India a legal tender, or even a recognized currency.

During my stay at Calcutta, I attended the sessions of the Supreme Court, which are held in the Town Hall. The jurisdiction of this tribunal extends to all cases in Calcutta, and over all the inhabitants of the United Kingdom residing in the *Mofussĭl*—a native term used to designate all parts of India, except the three Presidency towns. There is another Supreme Court, the Suddur Dewan-ee-Adawlut, a Company's Court, which hears appeals from the Courts in the Mofussĭl. No Englishman can be tried except in the Presidency town, and before the Suprême Court, with all the privileges of the common law of England. On the other hand, no native can be tried in the Presidency town, for an offence committed in the Mofussĭl, but must be conveyed up country to undergo trial. These regulations are the means of preventing many vexatious prosecutions, as a native possesses to a large extent the common failing of a fondness for law. In the Mofussĭl the criminal proceedings are very simple, the delay short, and the punishment, though mild, certain, except in the case of capital sentences, which must all come before the Suddur Court for approval. In all British India, with its 100,000,000 of inhabitants, there is but one Court in each

Presidency which can, of its own authority, inflict the punishment of death.

The pleadings and legal proceedings in the Supreme Court are in English; in the Suddur Court, as in all the Company's Courts, they are in Persian, the speeches and examinations being in almost any of the numerous tongues spoken in India. The civil proceedings in the Company's Courts are somewhat confused and unsettled, as the Hindoo and Moosulman codes with all the peculiar native usages and customs have been allowed to prevail, almost unchanged. Thus the institutes of Mĕnoo, the Shastras, and Vedas form the only standard of the Hindoo law, while the Koran is the sole guide to the Moosulman code. Again, there are large classes like the converted Christians and half-castes living in the Mofussĭl, who are not properly subjected to either of these codes. It may be imagined that the Company's Judges get rather confused in this "conflict of laws," especially as they are never educated for lawyers—perhaps this last fact is the real secret of their being able to administer at all so confused a system.

Calcutta is the seat of many missionary establishments, one of the largest of which is the schools of the Free Scotch Church. It is situated in the native town near the mint. The buildings are large and suitably arranged, and the benefits of instruction are eagerly sought by the native children. The English language is almost exclusively employed, and the scholars, when their education is complete, generally become Baboos, or native clerks in foreign commercial houses. One of the instructors took great pains in showing me over the establishment. He says the boys are very bright and eager to learn, but the converts are few; instruction seems only to destroy their faith in their own superstitions. In this school the prejudices of caste are entirely disregarded, and the Brahmun sits on the same bench with the Soodra. The teacher told me, however, that the Brahmun boys were often very much delayed on their way to school, being stopped by the common people that they might bless their stock of drinking water by dipping in it their sacred feet. In old times, the touch of one of a lower caste would have defiled a Brahmun for the day. In fact, in Calcutta, among educated natives, (who, it should be remembered, are, after all, only a small class), the prejudices of caste have been very much modified, and many of them will eat or drink with Christians, and even partake of the sacred flesh of a cow, and indulge in the forbidden cup. The latter practice, many of them carry out to its fullest extent, and it may be doubted whether their release from the other prejudices is not dearly purchased at the price of the spreading habit of intoxication. These enfranchised Hindoos continue to celebrate their idolatrous rites and perform all such ceremonies as are necessary to prevent their expulsion from caste, which involved until quite recently by the law of India, *civil death;* but, in heart, they are deists or atheists, and make no scruple of avowing their infidelity. The strict seclusion in which native women are kept, has prevented the formation of girls' schools—but some efforts have been made, with partial success, by the missionaries' wives, for their private instruction.

Spence's hotel, where I stayed, while in Calcutta, is a "furnished apartment" sort of establishment. There is a *table d'hôte*, to be sure, but each man has to keep his own servants, or he will not be waited on at table, and his rooms will not be cleaned. Servants, in Calcutta, are, generally, Moosulmans. Their dress, a tight-fitting, white cotton *chupkun*, loose pa*n*jama, and a flat *pugree* (turban). They speak nothing but Hindoostanee, and the first time I took dinner I got scarcely anything to eat, from not knowing the native words for the edibles. I had the greatest trouble in getting a native servant, who could speak English, to accompany me up country, and finally had to hire an untrained half-caste boy. These half-castes, the descendants of a mixture of the English or Portuguese, and native races, form a large class in India. They dress in a quasi-European costume, and generally speak English, though they are mostly as black as any native. They are supposed to have all the faults of both native and European, with none of their virtues, and are, certainly, a dreadfully proud, lazy, lying set; on account of which qualities Europeans scarcely ever employ them. They are sometimes called by the barbarous name of "Eurasians"—a supposed compound of "Europe" and "Asia."

The wages of servants are very low. A *khitmutgra*, or butler, gets only five or six rupees a month, and the others even less. Out of this, to us small sum, they have to feed, clothe and lodge themselves and family—for all natives are married. But all the necessaries of life are very cheap, and the wages of a working man, which are only three or four rupees a month, ($1.50 or $2,) amply suffice for the support of his household.

The number of servants necessary in India, from the subdivisions of labour, and the prejudices of caste, is enormous. The servant who pours out the water into your basin, will not empty it when dirty; nor would he touch an article of food prepared for your use. Much more display of servants was customary in the "old Indian" times, when the European residents imitated the gorgeous ostentation of the rich natives. Bishop Heber says, that in his time, it was customary for Englishmen of rank, to be preceded in the streets by *sipahees* with spear and buckler, *hurkarus* and *chobdars* bearing massive silver maces, a *chattah-burdar*, carrying a large red umbrella, and many other followers with fans, etc. Now-a-days, all this show is left to the rich natives, who rather despise it, and affect the European style. It is still necessary, however, to keep very large retinues for the ordinary service of the household, and a family of four or five, must, in Calcutta, have twenty or thirty servants, so that their wages, though small for each, will, in the aggregate, amount to more than the pay of the smaller number of domestics who would do the same work in Europe.

The expenses of living in Calcutta, and, indeed, throughout India, are very large, notwithstanding the low price of food. This is owing to several causes. One is the high cost of all European goods, (the price of which is kept up by the universal system of credit, and the consequent number of bad debts,) another is the state which it is customary to maintain, and the extravagant style of living, with the large use of wine and beer, which is universal. House-rent is also very high.

This manner of living prevails all over India, and it is rare, indeed, to find any one living within his means. The consequence is, that nearly all the officers of the army, and most of the civil servants, are deeply in debt to natives; and this, notwithstanding the high pay of the civil servants, (magistrates, judges, &c.,) who receive from 1,000 to 8,000 rupees a month. The Governor-General receives a salary of £25,000 per annum, besides allowances, which make it amount to as much again—but his expenses are very great.

The Governor-General of India resides at Calcutta, and has direction of the general affairs of the whole continent, the Governors of the two other Presidencies of Bombay and Madras being subordinate to him—though not to the same extent, as are the Lieutenant-Governor of Bengal, the Chief Commissioner of Oude, the Lieutenant-Governor of Agra and the North Western Provinces, and the Chief Commissioner of the Punjab, who are directly under his control. The Governor-General, and the Governors of the two other Presidencies, are appointed by the Crown, although under the direction of the Company, which may dismiss them. All other posts in the civil service are, however, now open to competition, those persons being appointed who succeed best at the Company's civil service examination in London. These examinations are open to all British subjects, and several natives have passed high, and received very good appointments.

The language of Bengal, is the Bengalee, a tongue which has much affinity with the Sanscrit; but the common language used by natives to foreigners, both in Calcutta and throughout India, is the Hindoostanee, which is only vernacular in Hindoostan. This Hindoostanee, or, as it is more correctly termed, Oordoo, (the camp dialect) is a sort of *lingua franca*, which arose after the Moosulman conquest, and was invented to facilitate intercourse between the conquerers and the conquered. It contains many Arabic, Persian, and Sanscrit words, the proportions being dissimilar in different parts of the country. The further you go to the north-west, the more does the Perso-Arabic element prevail. It is a very flexible tongue, readily appropriating words from all languages; but has regular declensions and conjugations. Being only used, in the greater part of India, between people who speak different languages, it is, of course, poor in words, and has no literature. I said above, that it was vernacular, in parts of Hindoostan. This expression may be misunderstood, as the term Hindoostan is incorrectly used here, to designate the whole peninsula of India. It, really, only describes the country north of the Nurbudda, west of Běnarěs, and east of the Sutlěj, and is often, if not generally, used in a still more contracted sense—those of the Rajpootana states, which are within these limits, and even the dominions of Scindiah, not being commonly considered a part of Hindoostan. The term Hindoo, also, it should always be remembered, is appropriate to a *religion*, and not to a *race*. The peninsula of India is inhabited, and always has been, by men of various races, different languages, and subject to numerous independent sovereigns. Their only tie is caste, which is at once, a bond connecting together a certain number, and insulating them from all others. There is no approach to a feeling of common nationality among the inhabitants of the various countries into which India is divided, and in none of the native languages is there a word answering to "India," or "an Indian."* I think I am not wrong in saying that there is far less sympathy between a Bengalee, a Hindoostanee, a Punjabee, and a Děkkunee, than between the same number of individuals picked out of the most dissimilar countries in Europe. Were these facts more generally known, they might remove some misconceptions with respect to the recent mutiny in India.

* The word India was formed by the Romans, from the name of the river "Indus"—in the native language "Sĭnd."

CHAPTER X.

CALCUTTA—CONTINUED.

Roasting Human Bodies—Adjutants in Calcutta—Unpaid Scavengers—Early Rising—The Morning Drive—"The Strand"—Clothing—Country around Calcutta—"Stations"—Dum-Dum—Artillery Mess—An Ameer of Sind—Barrackpoor—The Sepoys—Too much Petted—Some Causes of the Mutiny.

ONE of the most remarkable sights in Calcutta, is the "Burning Ghât;" a piece of ground on the river's bank, in the upper part of the city, used for the incremation of the dead. It is about a hundred feet square, surrounded on three sides by brick walls, eighteen or twenty feet high. On the fourth side toward the river it is open. The enclosure is unpaved and slopes to the water's edge, near which the funeral pyres are erected. At the upper end, against the wall, are miserable huts where those sick Hindoos, who can pay for the privilege, come to die near the sacred Gunga—a consummation which must be materially hastened by the stench of the locality, the exposure of lying in wretched hovels made only of mats, and the custom of keeping them on a very light diet indeed. In some very obstinate cases, the relatives shorten the agonies of their dying relations by stuffing the mouth and nostrils with the sacred mud of the Hoogly. The religious rites connected with the burning are in the hands of certain brahmuns, the practical details being intrusted to the members of a peculiar *caste;* both drive a thriving trade. Two bodies were burning and frizzling on miserably insufficient piles of fuel, when I visited the place, and the fetid, deadly, odour of the fumes, the horrid, dissecting-room stench of piles of human bones, half covered with flesh, on which birds of prey were feeding, with the groans and cries of pain from the poor wretches in the sheds, soon sickened me with the place, and made me

5*

glad to leave. I have before mentioned that the bodies are generally only half burned. When all the wood that the relatives have paid for has been consumed, the roasted carcase is thrown into the river, and floats away or not, according to the tide. In either case, it is at once pounced on by the loathsome carrion birds, which sit on the wall of the enclosure, motionless as statues, waiting till their meal be cooked. These birds are called *hurgilas*, but have been nicknamed *adjutants* by the foreigners from the solemnity and stiffness of their carriage. They form quite a feature of Calcutta, standing motionless on the roofs of houses, and even in the streets and squares. They look like a cross between the stork and vulture, stand about three feet high, and measure about eight from tip to tip. They have a disgustingly roomy pouch under the bill, and are altogether horrid looking creatures. Their demeanour is particularly calm and sedate, and they will stand motionless for hours in the most frequented squares, probably reflecting on the possibility of their soon making a meal on the passers-by. They will let you come as near them as you like, having no fear of man, as a city regulation prevents their being molested. This immunity they owe to their being the only scavengers, except the other carrion birds, of which there are great numbers in Calcutta. No such birds are seen in China, where the dead are all buried, and everything else on which they feed is carefully collected, and made into manure, or turned to some useful purpose. The filthy condition of Indian towns and villages contrasts most disadvantageously with Chinese towns; I do not believe that there are any cleaner cities in the world than the latter, if the narrowness of the streets and the absence of drainage be taken into account.

Europeans in India keep very different hours from those in China. Every house in Calcutta is shut up by ten o'clock, and the whole city is asleep. In this respect the habits of foreigners depend very much upon those of the natives. In China, where the Chinese like to sit up late, foreigners conform, and do not go to bed before twelve, getting up very late. In Bengal, however, all the servants leave their master's house by ten, or before, to go to their own homes—and rise very early in the morning, customs which the Europeans are forced to imitate. Up-country, the natives keep later hours, but the requirements of the service compel the officers to rise before day-break, when parade takes place, and in consequence they generally retire to bed by nine o'clock in the evening.

The custom of rising early in Calcutta, enables the residents to get a ride before breakfast—the early morning being the only part of the day, until after sunset, when exercise is possible in the Indian climate. From five till seven in the morning the Maidan is covered with ladies and gentlemen on horseback; but the greatest show is in the evening, from half-past five to seven. Between these hours, every one in Calcutta, who can muster any vehicle, betakes himself to the Strand, which is then as crowded as Hyde Park in the season. The equipages are, some of them, very handsome, but entirely English in style, even when they belong to rich natives. The coachmen are all natives, and generally wear long beards. They drive remarkably well. Each carriage has as many saeeses or grooms, as there are horses. They are Moosulmans of a peculiar caste, and wear a short tight-fitting jacket and flat turban, the lower part of the body being covered by a tightly wound *dhotee* which leaves the legs bare. They carry in their hands the *chouree*, or tail of the Thibet goat, fitted with a short handle; with this, running along side of the horses, they brush away the flies. These saeeses will run for almost any distance with a carriage, or after the horse upon which their master rides, and up-country their endurance is often put to severe tests. In Calcutta, however, as the roads in the Maidan are very crowded, the saeeses are generally allowed to sit on the footboard. Beside the neat turn-outs of the Europeans, one sees on the Strand the equipages of the rich natives, which are also in the English style, but much gayer, each carriage being often accompanied by six or eight servants, including a "silver-stick." The owner of all this splendour will sit alone on the back seat of the carriage, divested of all clothing, if a Bengalee baboo, except a fine linen *dhotee* from the waist downward. These baboos, or native merchants, are often enormously rich, and live in as handsome houses, and in as elegant style, as the most wealthy Europeans. They ape the English customs to a great extent. The native princes, many of whom live at Calcutta on large pensions from the Company, also appear on the drive. Their carriages and attendants are commonly similar to those of the baboos, but with them dress is a great consideration, and their costume is frequently magnificent. Beside these large carriages, there are crowds of buggies, containing officers and gentlemen; and a great many *caranchees*, a miserable, broken-down sort of garrhee, unpainted, unwashed, drawn by a single animated skeleton of a horse, and driven by a naked nigger, who perches on the narrow box-seat, holding the rope-reins with one hand, and with the other plying the whip with unremitting diligence. These caranchees are a sight such as can be seen nowhere else than in Calcutta. They are commonly filled with Bengalee clerks, or a drunken party of sailors from the ships in the harbour. In contrast with these are the Arab horse-dealers, who come to Calcutta with Arab horses for sale, and who take advantage of the evening to show off their steeds, riding them at full speed across the grassy esplanade. They dress in loose and graceful robes of brightly-contrasted colours, their horsemanship is magnificent, and their horses combine every perfection but size, which is the one drawback to an Arab horse.

English horses will not stand the climate of India, and the native animal is a coarse, heavy-boned, big-headed beast, with an ugly temper. Many horses are consequently brought from Arabia, but their price is very high. The best, and cheapest breed is that raised at the Honourable Company's stud stables, from which officers have to buy their chargers. The stud-horses combine the good qualities of the Arab and native breeds, of which they come; being larger, and more bony than the pure Arab, but possessing all his suppleness, speed, and good temper.

Perhaps, no one thing surprised me so much, on first landing in India, as the complexion and features of the natives. I had always supposed them to be of a brownish colour, and to have something like a Caucasian countenance. I found them in Bengal nearly black, and with a very low cast of countenance. Up-country, the features become finer, but even in Hindoostan, the mass of the people are very dark. Towards Bombay, the complexion of the inhabitants is lighter, but they never have the *clear skin*, which is a distinctive mark of the Caucasian race, and which is found even among its darkest variety, the Spaniards, when the blood is unmixed by Moorish, or Negro contamination.

The mass of the people in Bengal wear no clothing, but a narrow cloth around the loins. The women, however, and the men of the better classes, dress in a wide long piece of the finest muslin, which is disposed around the body so as to form a skirt, or loose trowser below (the *dhotee*), and is then brought up over the shoulders, completely covering the whole body, and falling nearly to the ground, in graceful folds. This is a most picturesque costume, especially when seen in the country, but a most unmanageable dress to do any work in.

The country around Calcutta, though very level, is yet pretty, and in some places even beautiful, from the luxuriance of the vegetation. The roads are broad, and finely made, and the trees which border them are of great size. The whole was a scene of exuberant vegetable life, which, perhaps, impressed me the more, because I had become accustomed to the utilitarian neatness of China, where nothing is allowed to go to waste, and not a tree or bush permitted to encumber the ground, except it is directly useful to man. Agriculture in India is quite a different thing from Chinese cultivation, being conducted in the most lazy and careless manner, and the whole of the crops are often pledged to some native banker for sums advanced before the ground was planted. In fact, while I remained in India, I became daily more impressed with the inferiority of the people to the Chinese, and their want of that economy, order, and industry which enables the latter nation to be comfortable, even on the smallest means. The huts of the natives of India are miserable mud hovels, unfit for pigs, wretchedly thatched, and afford a most insufficient protection against the rain; while the houses of the Chinese agriculturists are always solid, in good repair, and comfortable looking, however poor the dwellers in them may be.

The vicinity of Calcutta, for five or six miles around, is a favourite place of residence of the European merchants, and rich natives from the city. All along the roads, one passes large, handsome country-houses, in the Anglo-Indian style, about a quarter of a mile from one another. The compounds are planted with fine large trees, and the lawns covered with turf, which does very well in Bengal, though such a thing is never seen in any other part of India. Many of these suburban residences are occupied by native princes, who have been deposed, and are detained at Calcutta, or who prefer to live at that city. The former class are always in the receipt of large pensions from Government, but they generally contrive to spend all they get, living very expensively, and being an easy prey to horse-jockeys and other sharpers.

I had letters to the officer commanding the artillery stationed at Calcutta. I found him at Dum-Dum, which is the artillery station, as Barrackpoor is the infantry station of the capital. All troops in India are stationed near the cities which they protect, but not in them. The stations consist of a village of mud huts for the soldiers, and lines of bungalows for the officers; each bungalow being separated from the others by a compound, and generally inhabited by two officers, who, unless they are married, prefer to divide the expense of the rent. Every station contains a shop, where all sorts of European stores can be obtained; a bazâr, where the soldiers buy their food and other necessaries, and a mess-house, where the unmarried officers dine in common. In large stations there is also a church, with a chaplain appointed by Government. Where two or more regiments occupy the same station, there is a bazâr for each regiment, and each has its own lines. It will be understood, that when I speak of soldiers, I mean the native sepoys, who, until recently, formed the army of India; and in describing the cantonments, I describe arrangements which are done away with by the revolt of the soldiery, the murder of the officers, or their forced flight, and the burning of the bungalows, stores, and churches.

Dum-Dum was a very large station, but when I was there, had been diminished in importance by the removal of the artillery head-quarters to Meeruth. I found Colonel Mowatt, to whom my letter was directed, living in the largest bungalow, which was about forty feet square, and two stories high. He was a most amiable person, who took the greatest pains to amuse and entertain me during my stay in Calcutta; and when I went up-country, gave me letters to several officers, which I found a great advantage. I dined, by the Colonel's invitation, at the artillery mess-house, which is considered the finest building of the kind in India; it is very spacious, and decorated in front by a broad verandah, with a fine row of columns. The officers were, like all those whom I had the pleasure of meeting in India, a very gentlemanly set of men. Several of them obligingly gave me letters to friends in the interior, and Major Broom, whom I met at the mess, showed me the Company's gun foundry at Cŏssipoor, of which he was the director, and kindly made me a present of some curious native armour. I spent a couple of days at Dum-Dum with Colonel Mowatt, who was unremitting in his attentions. He showed me over the Dum-Dum percussion-cap manufactory, of which he was at the time, the head; took me to an amateur theatrical performance by the officers, and some European soldiers; and got me an invitation to a ball at the mess-house, where most of the great people of Calcutta were present. The Colonel took me also to visit one of the deposed Ameers of Sind, who lives in an elegant residence near Dum-Dum. On the road to the Ameer's, we passed a large country-seat, called "Seven Tanks," belonging to a wealthy native merchant, in the inclosure of which we saw a rhinoceros, standing in a pond of water. Of elephants, I saw several in the roads about Calcutta, but none in the city itself. There are now but few of them used lower down the country than Oude.

On asking for the Ameer, we heard that he was taking his siesta, but, just as we were about driving away, he came out on the verandah and invited us to walk in, having been awakened by the noise of our carriage. He received us in a very large, plain room, with no other furniture than a *pullun* (low native bedstead) in the centre, and a few chairs about the wall. The Ameer seated himself cross-legged on the pullun, over which swung a punkah, and we took chairs near him. He was a little man, of clear olive complexion, and a very Jewish caste of features; not having dressed since his nap, he wore only a fine muslin shirt, and loose pa*n*jama of the same material. We remained nearly an hour, the colonel and the Ameer conversing in Persian, the court language of the East. Of course I could take no direct part in what they said, but the colonel translated to me the most interesting remarks of the prince. Before we left, the Ameer showed us several swords, daggers and other arms, which were heirlooms in his family. These weapons were of the finest Indian steel, which is considered superior to that made in Europe. The hilts, scabbards, belts and buckles of these arms were decorated in the most magnificent manner with diamonds and other jewels. One sword was estimated to be worth £40,000, and one dagger, nearly half that sum. The Ameer also brought out for our inspection a copy of the Koran, which had been in his family for two hundred years. It was written on the finest vellum, and the execution was as perfect as that of any manuscript I have seen. The case which contained it was of velvet, set with jewels, worth many thousand pounds. At the end of the volume were the signatures of the other Ameers, the brothers or cousins of our entertainer, who wrote them there when they swore on this book, to be faithful unto death to him and each other, having done which, with the usual fidelity of natives, they betrayed him to the English the same day. The Ameer's servants were all old followers, dressed like their master in the long muslin shirt, the pa*n*jama, and the low, red cap, with a projecting crown, which form the costume of Sind. They were tall, heavily built men, with long white locks, and magnificent snowy beards, their complexion clear, although rather tawny, their gait and bearing majestic—altogether as fine looking specimens of men as you will easily see. They reminded me a little of the old representations of men in the Nineveh sculptures.

Barrackpoor, the infantry station of Calcutta, and the scene of the premonitory symptoms of the recent general mutiny, is situated about 15 miles from the city; while the distance from the city to Dum-Dum is only 6 miles. There was always a considerable number of troops at Barrackpoor, only two regiments being kept in Fort William. It is also the residence for the greater part of the year of the Governor General, who has here a magnificent mansion, surrounded by gardens and enclosed in a large park, well filled with trees.

It was at Calcutta that I first saw the Sepoys, or more properly *Sipahees*, from *sipah*, the Persian word for a bow. They were a better looking race of men than the Bengalees, being recruited up-country. Their uniform was similar to that of English soldiers, except that their shako had no leather peak, which would be an offence to their caste. The Sepoys always looked better when off duty in their native dress, than when in uniform, as they had not the prominent chest of the European; and the heavy red coat seemed a most inappropriate dress for the climate. However, they were very proud of it, and so much did it take the fancy of the natives, that years ago it was introduced into the armies of all the independent native princes. The Sepoys made good troops generally, and would fight well enough in company with European regiments, of which the Honourable Company had seven, and the Queen generally twenty or more, in India. The English regiments wear, in this hot climate, an undress uniform of white cotton, with a cap of the same, having a white turban wound around it. A turban is found to be the best protection against the effects of the Indian sun, and no European ever goes out without one round his hat.

The great trouble with the Sepoys was that they were always too much petted. Their pay was higher than what they could have earned by any other occupation; and far higher than that of any army in Europe, if the expense of the necessaries of life be taken into account. The lowest wages of a Sepoy were six rupees per month, more than double the ordinary wages of a labouring man, and a sum which would equal $35 to $40 in this country. Their caste was high, and its requirements exacting; they could not pass the limits of India, eat certain food, wear certain clothing, or cook their meals in less than a certain number of hours, which were necessary for the performance of the religious ceremonies which are obligatory in the preparation of all food to be eaten by Hindoos. In all these respects their prejudices were very properly respected; but when they refused to dig in the trenches at Mooltan, and white men did the work, under a broiling sun, while the niggers looked on and sneered at them, it must be acknowledged that the government was rather too complaisant; and when a white soldier could be flogged with five hundred lashes, by order of a regimental court-martial, while a Sepoy could not be touched with the lash, it must be confessed that the regulations of the army were both unjust, and calculated to give the native soldier altogether too high an idea of his own importance—particularly as every native is accustomed to be flogged and kicked from his earliest infancy, and never hesitates to use such discipline on others. The extent to which this system of petting the native soldier was carried on in India is hardly credable. For the last few years it was scarcely possible to punish a Sepoy for any offence, the process of sending the sentence up for approval, being so long and uncertain. The result was that discipline became relaxed, and the men haughty, impertinent, and impatient of the least hardship. It is this state of things which has caused several minor mutinies during the last twenty years, and has at last ended in the recent ferocious outbreak, and grand united effort to step into their masters' shoes. These remarks apply principally to the army in the Bengal Presidency, which was mainly recruited in Oude, from the high caste Rajpoots. In the other Presidencies, and in the Punjab regiments of the Bengal army, the men were of low caste, the requirements of their religion few or none, and the discipline much stricter. The result has been that they have almost without exception remained faithful—the wavering of some of the Bombay regiments being probably attributable to their having been raised in Oude; though, not being Rajpoots, they would probably under ordinary circumstances have made as good soldiers as any others. The natives of India make excellent mercenaries, as they are so split up into nations and castes, that they can be easily played against one another; and have so little patriotism that they will serve whoever pays best. This is one great secret of the wonderful spread of the British power in India, and it was only on account of the negligence of the government, which recruited the Bengal army almost entirely from one caste, that it was possible for the instigators of the recent mutiny, to produce any unanimous and sympathetic action among the various regiments. Had the Bengal army contained men of all castes, and of several different nations, no general rising could ever have been planned, much less carried out, without the government receiving timely warning.

CHAPTER XI.

CALCUTTA.—CONCLUDED.

Life in Calcutta—My Friends there—The India Trade—Skill of the Natives in Commerce—Conduct of American Residents during the Revolt—Travelling in India—The Palanquin—"Marching"—Steamboats on the Ganges—Garrhee-dak—The Mail-cart.

I REMAINED about two weeks in Calcutta, during which I enjoyed myself very much. It is a pleasant place for a stranger during a brief sojourn, is the paradise of the English in the Mofussil, and life in Calcutta represents the extreme of luxurious enjoyment, in the popular imagination of Occidentals; yet, I must confess, that existence in the capital of India is marked by a wearisome monotony, which would be alone a sufficient counterbalance to the luxuries of a large establishment of servants and splendid dinners, even if the climate, the reptiles, and the diseases were all put out of the question. Anything like society is almost impossible, where all the world goes to bed by half-past nine or ten, in other words, immediately after the dinner, which follows the evening drive—and where few will expose themselves to the sun's rays in the daytime, unless some urgent necessity calls them out of doors. There is no theatre, no public amusement of any kind; and the exile cannot even enjoy the pleasures of his family, if a married man, as it is necessary for the health, nay, the very life of his children, that they should be sent to Europe when five or six years old—earlier, if possible. The wearisome sameness of such an existence can scarcely be imagined. It is only surpassed by life in the Mofussil. Many a man who envies the Indian civilian his rich appointments, would gladly renounce all pretensions could he but experience for a month the unenviable life which they lead.

Many kindnesses and unexpected attentions gave me a most favourable impression of those gentlemen in Calcutta, whom it was my good fortune to meet. I was especially indebted to Colonel Mowatt and his amiable wife, and several officers of the artillery, to the mess of which branch of the service I was kindly introduced by Colonel Mowatt. Little did they or I anticipate at the time the fate which has since overtaken many of them. Colonel Mowatt had a high command at the siege of Delhi, and died there—of cholera, it was said, like so many others in prominent positions, including several generals-in-chief. Whether this was the case, and age, with the cares and anxieties of their position, brought on the chiefs the disease, from which the younger, but more exposed, officers entirely escaped, or whether they all perished by one of those subtle native poisons which simulate morbid action so well, will probably never be ascertained. Mrs. Mowatt, who was separated from her husband at the time of the outbreak, had to flee into the jungul, and wander there a week, exposed to every hardship. My friends among the younger officers whom I saw at Dum-Dum were nearly all at Meeruth during the mutiny at that place. Many perished there—many have since died. Of the fate of the ladies, I am ignorant.

I also was shown much kindness by several English and American merchants, to whom I beg here to return my thanks.

The English merchants mostly do business as agents, or on commission. The day for making large and rapid fortunes in the East India trade passed away with the explosion of the colossal houses which took up the Calcutta trade on the abolition of the Company's monopoly. The chances are now the same as in any regular commission business elsewhere Native capital is largely employed by the English houses, and in many instances the natives have gone into the European business in their own names. Their sagacity and shrewdness are far greater than those of Europeans; their resources are often very large, and were their honesty and fidelity in any way commensurate, they would no doubt soon do all the foreign business in India. The natives have no idea of honour or truthfulness, and no regard for character—two defects which have hitherto stood very much in their way. They are, however, daily occupying a position of increasing importance in the commercial world of India.

There are a large number of Americans in Calcutta, and other parts of India, engaged in commercial and other pursuits. They live on terms of perfect friendship and equality with the English, and it would be difficult to find a pleasanter or more hospitable set of men. During the recent disturbances in Bengal, the American residents in Calcutta formed themselves into a military body and offered their services to the Governor-General, which were most gratefully accepted by his lordship. As long as alarm continued, they shared the duty of their English friends, and kept with them alternate watch and watch.

Having seen Calcutta pretty thoroughly, I began my preparations for a trip up-country—a plan which I had formed in China, but as to the feasibility of which I had at first entertained great doubts. Until within a few years there were no great roads opened in India, but since the completion of the Grand Trunk Road, which is fifteen hundred miles in length, from Calcutta to Peshawur, the extreme frontier station in the north-west, travelling has become comparatively rapid and easy. Under the old native rule, the roads were very few and bad. The only available conveyance was the palkee or palanquin, which continued to be employed by Europeans down to quite recent times, and is still used on all the lines of travel except the Trunk Road. Nothing can be more irksome than travelling in a palanquin, the confinement of which is intolerable during the heat of the day, so that the traveller must rest all day, and travel only at night for the greater part of the year. The only other way of travelling in old times was what is called "marching," much slower, but infinitely pleasanter than the palkee. Before the establishment of dâk-bungalows by government, "marching" was the only way of making any considerable journey, and as it is still much employed when a whole family is on the move together, and by the judges and other government officers in their circuits, I will describe the "march" of one of the officials as a specimen of this mode of locomotion. Every official in India has a number of tents, elephants, camels, &c., proportionate to the size of his establishment, always on hand. A day or two before he starts on his circuit, he informs his head servant of his intention, who makes all the necessary preparations. On the morning of the day the magistrate and his family start on elephants at four in the morning, but as soon as it becomes light enough to see the road, they dismount and continue the journey, either on horseback or in a carriage, where the road permits. By half-past seven they have arrived at their resting-place for the day, and the sun is now so hot that they are glad to take shelter in a small "breakfast-tent," which they find ready pitched, where breakfast is served up by the servants, who have preceded them on foot. Meanwhile the house they have left has been entirely stripped. Every article, however bulky, of utility or comfort, has been removed, and brought on by camels or on ox-carts, so that by the time breakfast is finished, and a cheroot or hookah has been smoked, the large tents, which answer in number and size to the rooms of the house, have been furnished, and the travellers have as comfortable a residence for the day as that which they have left. The encampment is generally set up in a tôp or grove, one of which is commonly to be found near the outskirts of every considerable native village. These tôps are generally composed of mango trees, and offer a sufficient shade, even to the traveller who cannot afford the luxury of a tent.

Both these modes of travelling, which, until within a few years, furnished the only means of proceeding up-country, were so slow, that had there been no other conveyances, I should have been obliged to give up my trip; as the steamboats up the Ganges are much slower than even the palanquin, and are, moreover, very uncertain in the length of their passages.

Fortunately, however, I found that companies had been established to run regular carriages along the whole extent of the Grand Trunk Road, or at least, so far as the bridges are completed. Transit by these conveyances I found to be rapid, comfortable, and economical; and the facilities which they offered determined me to go up-country, at least, as far as Delhi.

There is yet one other way of travelling in India, to which I might have had recourse. I mean, the mail-cart, which is allowed to carry one traveller. These mail-carts are a square box, mounted on two wheels, and look very like the English dog-cart. They go along at ten or twelve miles an hour, stopping only to change horses; and for a few minutes, at each post-station. The seat is very hard, there is seldom anything in the way of a shade, only fifteen pounds of baggage can be carried, there is no rest, without waiting over a day; and, what is worst of all, the carts are always breaking down from the imperfection of their construction, the speed at which they are driven, and the viciousness of the post-horses. Altogether, I suppose it is the most uncomfortable mode of travelling yet discovered. Few people ever go by it, unless they are very much pressed for time. As for myself, I think it very unlikely that I should have had the pluck to face the fatigue, hunger, and exposure; and I should probably never have visited the capital of the Moguls, if the mail-cart had been the only conveyance within my reach.

CHAPTER XII.

TO BĔNARĔS.

Railway to Raneegunj—Indian Railways—Coal—A Dâk-Gárrhee—Dâk Companies—The Rights of Horses—Leopards and Jackals—Dâk-Bungalows—Scenery—Comparison between Natives of India and China—Land-Tenure—Nullahs—People on the Road—Sahussuram—Two fine Tombs—A Dancing Cow—The village Zĕmindar—"Taking Leave"—Unsympathetic Character of Natives—Country between Sahussuram and Bĕnarĕs—Sĕroor.

I LEFT Calcutta on the evening of the first of November, 1856. Crossing the Hoogly to Howrah, I took the railway to Raneegunj, a distance of 120 miles, which we accomplished in nine and a half hours. It was dark when we started, and before morning, we had passed the limits of lower Bengal. I have since regretted not taking a train by day, as the country which this road traverses is one of the few parts of India where much cultivation or natural luxuriance of vegetation is to be seen. The carriages were very comfortable, and divided into compartments, on the European plan. I enjoyed a comfortable night's rest, the seats being arranged to draw out, and form a bed.

This railway is to extend to Delhi, and probably in time, to some place on the Indus, as Mooltan. It is to connect at Agra with a proposed road to Bombay, and is one of a great net-work of railways projected to connect all the important points in India. The road had been in construction twelve years, when I was there, and only these 120 miles were completed. Another section was nearly finished, but has been since that time much injured by the mutineers. In the Presidencies of Bombay and Madras, not 200 miles of road altogether had been completed. It is now seen that it was a great error of Government, not to have pushed forward more rapidly the completion of these great highways, since the facility of transporting troops on them would have done much for the prevention or suppression of the recent mutiny. Independently of the use of the railways in a military point of view, they would no doubt have been eminently successful financially, as the navigation of the Ganges is very dangerous, and precarious as regards time; and the transportation of merchandize on camels or ox-carts by the Grand Trunk Road, could never compete with a railway in time or expense. These railroads were the first great public work that the Government of India intrusted to private enterprize, and it was supposed that the advantages presented by the scheme were so great, that private capital would be readily furnished for their completion, especially as Government guaranteed the stockholders a dividend of five per cent. It was found, however, that the rich natives, from whom much of the money was expected, were very backward in contributing to an enterprize of a kind in which they had previously had no experience, and from which any immediate return beyond the five per cent. guaranteed, was doubtful. The idea of any great public work being accomplished by private capital, is something quite opposed to a native's habits of thought—if he has any spare money, he hesitates about investing it permanently in land, or any other way, preferring to retain it in his own hands, and loan it to individuals on short time, and at a high rate of interest. In India, twelve per cent. a year can always be obtained, with the best security, and where the money is loaned to the poor ryuts by the month, at compound interest, and in sums of a few rupees, as is generally the practice of native bankers, the rate amounts to six or seven per cent. a month.

Raneegunj, the present terminus of the railway, is situated at the foot of the Rajmahal hills, a low, irregular range, bounding lower Bengal on the west. It has but few European residents, and they are all connected with the railway, *dâk* companies, or coal mines. The coal obtained is of excellent quality, it is said, and if so, will supply a great want, as the Labuan coal is far from good.

I had engaged at Calcutta my passage to Futtehghur, by the "North Western Dâk Company," one of the three staging companies, (*dâk* being Hindoostanee for "staging,") which conveyed persons and light parcels up-country, along the line of the Grand Trunk Road. As soon as I arrived at Raneegunj, I went to see the vehicle in which I was to proceed to Bĕnarĕs. I found it a square-built, roughly-finished, but strong *gárrhee*, with patent axles, sliding doors, and a row of windows on both sides, shaded by Venetian awnings. The *well*, where, in an ordinary carriage, we put our feet, was covered over, and appropriated to small parcels; and a mattrass extended the whole length of the vehicle. This is a most admirable arrangement for travelling a long time in a carriage, as lying down is, no doubt, the position which can be continued the longest time with the least fatigue; and the convenience for sleeping is a matter of importance, where, as in India, it is customary to travel night and day, and in the hot weather, principally, if not solely, by night.

The Grand Trunk Road is at present the great line of communication between all Northern, and North-Western India, and the coast. It is a broad, macadamized road, as well kept up as any in Europe, stretching in an unbroken line from Calcutta to Peshawur, at least 1,500 miles. The operations of these dâk companies extend along the line of the Trunk Road and its branches, as far to the north-west as Umbala, (the first Punjab station,) beyond which point the bridges are not completed. The branches of the Grand Trunk Road go to Lucknow, Futtehghur, and Moozuffurnuggur, beyond Meeruth. The construction of this great road is entirely the work of the English Government, the Ganges having been previously the only line of communication with the interior.

The dâk companies do not run their gárrhees at any fixed time, but whenever they are engaged. The usual practice is, for one traveller to occupy a gárrhee alone, but the expense and comfort are occasionally shared by two persons, who must be in rather close quarters when they lie down, as the interior of the carriage is not more than four feet wide, if so much. Each gárrhee has a native coachman, who accompanies it for about sixty miles, and a *sáees* or groom, who is changed with the horse, every six miles.

I had heard a great deal about the dâk horses, but the reality far exceeded my expectations. They are the most vicious and untamed set of brutes that it is possible to conceive as being made in any respect useful. The first specimen which I saw, made his appearance with eight or ten sáeeses, tugging at a rope made fast to one of his fore legs; the object of this was to move his leg forward, upon which, he, of his own accord, brought his body up to it. This mode of progression is, as may be imagined, slow, although sure. It took about twenty minutes to get him into the shafts, and when made fast, he planted his fore-legs firmly apart, and again refused to move. The sáeeses renewed their efforts, first trying mild measures, and calling the stubborn beast by every endearing name, among which were the sweet titles of "father," and "mother." As the brute, however, showed himself utterly insensible and unmollified by the attributed honours of paternity; and moreover, seemed determined at least to assume the parental privilege of chastisement by biting and kicking his swarthy and supposititious offspring, the original plan of dragging his foot forward was again resorted to, accompanied and aided by the united efforts of a dozen or more black fellows who pushed the gárrhee behind. These efforts being persisted in for half a mile, and the coachman vigourously applying the *chabook* (whip), our gallant steed at length was wearied with resistance, and, determining to free himself from his persecutors, and give up an unavailing struggle for the rights of horses, rushed off at a ten mile pace, which he kept up the whole stage. The next horse was quieter, but lame. Natives, however, have very little of that quality which "is not strained," and the lame horse did his five or six miles in less time than his predecessor. The above performances, and practical lessons in the art of horse-breaking, are generally repeated at every third or fourth stage. The only variety in the exercises is when you have a particularly pig-headed animal who *lies down*—the remedy for which amiable peculiarity is to light a straw fire under him. These performances are at first amusing, but "familiarity breeds contempt," and their oft repetition causes them to pall. When one is in a hurry, they are particularly annoying, and I have often felt very like shooting some of these beasts, after an hour or so spent in endeavouring, by every gentle and violent means, to terminate an obstinate *baulk.*

It was nine o'clock before I left Raneegunj. Two officers left at the same time in another gárrhee, but as their horse had lamed himself the night before, by falling into a ditch when chased by a leopard, I soon left them behind. India is so thinly populated a country, that there is an enormous number of wild animals, even close to settlements. Everywhere, the jackals make night hideous with their dreary wolf-like howl; and in many parts of the road, even in the day-time, every one you meet, on foot or on horseback, is armed with a sabre, spear or halbert—whether against man or beast, I could not precisely make out, but probably a little for both, and a great deal "dĕkne kee wastee," *i. e.*, "for show"—a phrase that explains more than one thing in India.

The country, after leaving Raneegunj, was an undulating common, but little cultivated or inhabited, and with but few trees. We arrived at two o'clock at Gyra dâk-bungalow, where I stopped for dinner. These dâk-bungalows are buildings for the accommodation of travellers, erected by the liberality of Government, at fixed distances, on all the great roads in India. On the Grand Trunk Road, they are generally ten or twelve miles apart, but on the less frequented routes, the interval between one bungalow and another is often twenty or thirty miles. All dâk-bungalows are of one build, and the size varies but little. They are generally about forty feet square, with walls ten or twelve feet high, a verandah running all around, and covered by a steep thatch or tile roof, the edges of which rest on the verandah wall, the ridge being twenty-five feet or more from the ground. There are in each, two suites of apartments, consisting of a parlour, dressing room and bath room—the latter a great advantage in a hot climate. Each bungalow has about a dozen servants, of whom only two or three are paid by Government—the others being dependent upon the traveller's generosity. Every traveller has a right to occupy one suite of rooms for 24 hours, and as much longer as they are unclaimed by a new arrival. These bungalows are not only a great convenience, but almost a necessity for a dâk traveller in India, where there are no hotels except in the largest stations, and where caste forbids the native to allow a Christian's food to be cooked in his house, or even to give him a drink of water from his cup.

On arriving at the bungalow I was received with low salâms by Khansáhma*n*, Khitmutgrá, and Béras, (*Anglice*, steward, waiter and valets,) and the Khansáhma*n* asked what my honour would be pleased to order. I asked what could be had; and was answered "anything!" On further inquiry, however, I discovered that the only choice was between fowl and duck, of which I preferred the former. A scampering and screaming of the feathered bipeds outside soon told me that my wishes were being carried out, and I made a good meal off curry and rice, and grilled-fowl (commonly called "sudden death"). If there is any one thing that a native can do well, it is cooking; they all seem to be born with a natural talent for the culinary art—a talent practically developed in most cases by the rules of caste, which oblige each man to cook for himself, unless he is rich enough to hire a Brahmun to do so for him. The servants in the dâk-bungalows, except the bearers, are all Moosulmans, as no Hindoo will cook, or have anything to do with the eating of beef or fowls. The bungalow furniture consists of a native cotton floor-cover, a table, bed (with no mattrass), three chairs and a punkah, to each suite of rooms. The bath-room is about ten feet square, with a cement floor, and a ridge to prevent the water flowing into the next room. There is no regular *bath*, but instead, five or six earthen *gurras* of water, each holding about a gallon, which the traveller empties over his head.

The charge for the use of the bungalow for three hours is eight annas (24 cents), for any longer time, one rupee per diem. During the hot weather, it is customary to spend nearly the whole day in the bungalow, travelling only at night, but for three or four months in the year it is quite cool enough to tråvel during the day, especially in a gárrhee, the rapid motion of which alleviates the discomfort of the heat. My habit was to stop twice a day, once in the morning, when I bathed, dressed, and got breakfast, and again in the afternoon, when I took another bath and dined.

I slept very comfortably in the gárrhee, even the first night. The only annoyance was being waked up once or twice to pay toll, and once to give the customary bucksees of one rupee to the coachman, when he was relieved. I woke up the next morning refreshed by a good ten hours' sleep. On waking I found the scenery quite different from that of the day before—in fact, during this day I passed through three entirely different kinds of scenery. In the first place, we were among the Rajmahal hills, the passes in which, and the views of which were exactly like hundreds of similar scenes in any hilly part of the Northern States of America. Leaving these towards the afternoon, we came upon a plain where the cocoa-palm, the orange and plantain trees, and other similar objects, told of the richness of the soil, and the vivifying power of the tropical sun. And again, on the same plain, and between these fertile and cultivated *oases* (which were always situated around villages), there were tracts of uncultivated land, stretching for mile after mile, with no grass, no trees, no house, or even hut—nothing to tell of life but a few low scrub bushes, or a lot of vultures, sharing with the foul pariah-dogs the rotting carcase of some camel or buffalo which had died upon the road. These pariah-dogs are miserable, unkempt, uncared-for brutes, devouring any filth that comes in their way, and making themselves useful in a humble walk as public scavengers; during the recent mutiny they have had dainty fare, having been fed by the Sepoys upon the flesh of their mangled victims.

The general neglect and want of cultivation, which meets the eye of the traveller everywhere in India, contrasts, as I have before said, most disadvantageously with the economy and thrift which are so remarkable in China. It is, however, necessary to bear in mind the very different incentives to labour in the two cases. The Chinese has a freehold property, and can always invest his savings profitably and safely (the principle of "limited liability" being, in China, carried to a greater extent than in any other country); or, if he has not a freehold, he has always the privilege of retaining his farm at the same rent as long as it is paid punctually. The poor Indian ryut (cultivator) on the other hand, at least in Bengal, farms the soil on shares for the *zĕmindar*, who hires many farms direct from government. The rent which the ryut pays, in Bengal, is always exorbitant, and would be increased if the production became greater under good management. The Chinese, too, always have some information, and can read and write to a certain extent, and the greatest exertions are made by a whole family to supply funds for the education of any one of the younger members, who may have shown good intellectual powers, in the hope that he may pass creditably at the Public Service Examinations, and obtain a government appointment. No such hopes, no such motives, present themselves to the Indian ryut—the bonds of caste, if nothing else, being sufficient to prevent any change of condition. In the last analysis, these results, so disadvantageous to the native of India as compared with the Chinese, are no doubt due to the difference of national character. The system of society, beyond a doubt, in one case fosters, in the other discourages, every effort. Still those systems are but the reflex of the national mind, and neither would long exist were the national character changed. The Chinese is active, industrious, enterprizing, and independent—the native of India, idle, living only for the day, never wishing or hoping to change his condition, always irretrievably in debt, and never able to work without a master. The remarks above, on the land tenure, apply only to Bengal, where the land was leased by government, in perpetuity, to a number of large proprietors, who do undoubtedly, to a certain extent, demand unreasonable rents from the cultivators of the soil. This system was preferred by the English government in their early days, when the extent of their possessions was still limited, as it was supposed that the existence of a large number of "landed gentry" would do much to consolidate their power, and would preserve at least one powerful class who had a great stake in the permanence of the English rule. As the dominions of the Company extended, and their sway became more unquestioned, such precautions became unnecessary, and in all the North-western Provinces, the Punjab, and both the lesser Presidencies, a tenure of land has been introduced, which amounts in fact to hiring directly from government. The rent, which includes all direct taxes, is fixed every few years, with reference to the average production of the land, the price of corn and other products, and various modifying circumstances, and varies, for the most productive lands from one eighth to one quarter of the proceeds. Now, if it be remembered that this tenure is in fact equivalent to "farming on shares," I think the proportion of the profits paid to the landlord will seem anything but exorbitant, especially as there are no direct taxes in addition. In the determination of the rent, the ryut is always heard and consulted, and the bargain between him and government is the same as between man and man in any country. Should he be dissatisfied with his assessment, he is at liberty to give up the land, and do what he pleases. This liberty, to be sure, is rather restricted, not only by the prohibitions of caste, but by the state of slavery to *buniahs*, or native bankers, under which most of the population labour and toil. The agents of the Company, however, never take advantage of the necessities of a native, but always endeavour to give the land on desirable terms—it being the policy of government to encourage in every way the cultivation of the soil, an occupation which is looked upon, by the natives, as about the lowest condition in life. It is, therefore, the aim of government to make farming a profitable, if not an honourable, career. Their efforts have been, however, quite unsuccessful. It might with reason have been expected that the condition of ryuts in the up-country would be superior to that of their fellows in Bengal, where the old zĕmindaree system obtained. No such difference, however is found to exist. The natives are so impacted in a mass of customs and prejudices, that the tilling of the land is all left to a class who have been so engaged from generation to generation, who are

6*

ignorant and lazy to a degree; who cannot appreciate any improvements in agriculture—and if they could, would not have the means to adopt them; who are so improvident as to be always completely in the power of their creditors; and so idle, so spiritless, and so bound about by an iron prison of prejudice and caste, that any amelioration of their condition seems hopeless. I really believe that the lower classes would be more comfortable and happier under a mild system of serfdom; while the soil would be cultivated as it has never been; millions of acres of prolific, but now unproductive, land would be made profitable; and, in the absence of native enterprise, encouragement would be given to the colonization of the country, and cultivation of the soil, by Europeans, who have hitherto been restrained and disheartened by the necessity for relying on the voluntary industry of the blacks.

But to return from moralizing to the description of the second day's ride. We had to cross many *nullahs*, as the beds of streams are called, and tiresome work enough it was, the bridges having been nearly all carried away during the rains. The streams had shrunk into small compass, and did not form much of an obstacle; but the gárrhee had to be dragged over hundreds of yards of soft sands, by the aid of *coolees*, (a term used by Europeans to designate the lower classes of labourers in many parts of India and China). I put on as many coolees as could get a hand anywhere on the gárrhee, but they are a wretchedly weak race, and hardly earn the paisa ($\frac{3}{4}$ ct.) with which they are well satisfied, after tugging, straining, and shouting for twenty minutes or more.

The groups that one passes on the road are motley and often very picturesque. Some tall, fine looking fellow with a fierce moustache, long lance and shield, will go by on horseback, and next will follow a train of bullocks of burden, with panniers, going to market. The next people may be a train of fifty or more women, going to, or returning from labour—all with some bright coloured paint on the forehead, most with silver bangles on the arms, some with gold rings through the nose, but almost all carrying a baby a-straddle on the hip.

The coloured paint-marks indicate the deity to whom the wearer has, that morning, performed *poojah* ; the bangles are of solid silver or gold, generally worn by even the poorest classes, and are commonly heirlooms which are not parted with except on the direst necessity; gold nose-rings, are not uncommon, nor do they look ill upon a pretty brown face. They are considered merely as ornaments, and are readily sold or changed by the wearers; the babies are often three years old, it not being the custom in India to wean children much before that age—they sit, as I said, a-straddle on the mother's hip, and are supported by her arm. This is not a bad way to carry a child, but far inferior to the Chinese plan, which consists in strapping baby like a knapsack on his mamma's back, thus leaving both her hands at liberty.

We may next see a long train of baggage camels, each one having his nose made fast to the tail of the one ahead; and an elephant may be the next object that meets the eye. Now we meet a *hackuree*, or bullock-cart covered with a gaudy red tent, and containing a whole family with all their goods and chattels—and the next vehicle is perhaps a *bailee*, a smaller, two-wheeled conveyance, covered with a rich crimson awning, and drawn by a fine pair of little bullocks who will trot bravely off their five or six miles an hour, and keep the pace up all day—the curtains are closed, and we guess that some rich lady is within, a supposition which is confirmed by the armed men who follow to guard the bailee. The mail-cart, shaped like a dog-cart, passes us in a trice, as their horse is going at ten miles an hour, and ours stops to look at a milestone or something else, just as we are getting him into a good pace. The mail-coachman blows a joyous blast on his bugle, and is lost in a cloud of dust. We in our turn, soon after pass in similar triumph an English travelling carriage, going at four miles an hour, drawn by coolees.

On the morning of the third day, I woke up in what struck me as the prettiest scene, that I had beheld in India. It was the environs of the town of Sahussuram, and the clear morning air and bright sun, made particularly charming, a picture that would at any time have been striking. As I caught sight of a fine mosque rising above the trees, I determined to stop for breakfast at the dâk-bungalow, and visit the mosque, which was the first native building of any pretensions that I had seen since landing in India. All the way from Calcutta I had not seen a single mosque or Hindoo temple—I suppose because the villages were too miserably poor to afford any edifices of religion. I had expected that there would be more outward respect for religion in India than in China, but was astonished to find the reverse the case. The Chinese are, however, doubtless, the most irreligious people in the world—all educated men being atheists of course, and on principle, while even the common people have only a very qualified respect for their idols. On the other hand I suppose, there is no nation in the world so utterly credulous, and so sunken in a debasing superstition, as are most of the inhabitants of India.

I stopped at Sahussuram three hours, and visited the mosques, which were primarily tombs, and never intended as places of public worship. Their shape was that of the Arabian mosques, of which we see pictures in the books of travellers in Egypt and Syria; the material, a light, red freestone, very fine grained and durable, the same as that of which all the fine buildings in Bĕnarĕs are constructed. Both of these mosques, like most other public monuments in India which are not actually in use, were falling into decay. A native scarcely ever repairs his own house, much less a public edifice in which he takes only an indirect interest. The smaller of the two mosques was first visited. I ascended to the roof by a staircase in the wall, which was elsewhere of solid masonry, and very thick. This mosque being in the town, was separated from the adjacent houses by a court yard, surrounded by cloisters, constituting a *surai.* It had formerly other buildings surrounding it, and particularly a large crypt under the court yard, but the crypt is now full of water, and of the other buildings, the *surai* (or free lodging house for pilgrims or travellers) alone remains in tolerable repair. The larger mosque is really a very striking building. Similar in design to the other, it is seen to great advantage, being situated on a stone platform in an artificial lake, perhaps 800 feet long by

500 broad. It is an octagon in form, each side being about 60 feet long, with four *minárs* (minarets) and a noble dome. The Chubootra, or platform, which supports it, is an artificial island, about 200 feet square, and faced with stone toward the water. It was formerly connected with the land by a stone bridge, but this has now nearly gone to ruin. The building is still very handsome, but when painted and gilded, as at first, must have been gorgeous in the glaring sun.

On the way back from the mosques to the dâk-bungalow, I saw a dancing cow, which I told them to make perform for me; but they said she was too young and not sufficiently trained to amuse so great a lord as I. We passed through the village bazár, and here I noticed for the first time, the women covering their faces as I passed, a custom introduced by the Moosulmans, which does not obtain in lower Bengal, and is not universal anywhere in India. In this place too, I noticed some signs of a greater variety in dress, the rich green, red and yellow muslins of Hindoostan being intermingled with the universal white of Bengal. I met also one or two tall, wild-looking fellows, wrapped in shaggy blankets, with a bright coloured turban and long spear—a species of animal which is not seen further down the country.

The village of Sahussuram, though the largest I had seen, is after all only a village, the houses being all of one story, and mere sheds, built of mud. At the doors of these dwellings the inhabitants were squatted industriously engaged in smoking the hookah. On the outskirts of the village were one or two larger houses, built of stone—the residence of the zĕmindar, and a few others who were comfortably off.

On my return to the dâk-bungalow, I was accosted by the zĕmindar of the village, a mild-looking young Moosulman, who asked permission to come in and see me. This being granted, he sat down while I breakfasted. It soon came out that his object was to practise his English upon me. He presented me with his card in Persian, and I gave him mine in English, and we kept up quite a conversation on the propriety of Moosulmans eating with Christians, which they refuse to do in India. He afterwards began begging for books, papers, &c.,

and offered to sell me his ring, when I became disgusted and dismissed him. His visit was rather longer than he intended it to be, from my ignorance of the Indian usage which forbids a visitor to depart until he has received permission from his host. I had been hoping he would go, and when he began begging, expressed my wishes to my servant, who advised me to say "Rookhsut hy," *i. e.*, "There is permission to depart," when he looked very grateful, put on his shoes, salámed, and left. This is a custom which it is somewhat hard for a stranger to learn, as it seems to us rude to turn away a guest. Some of our expressions, however, seem to point to its having once been usual in Europe, as, for instance, "to take leave" in English, and "prendre congé" or "donner congé" in French.

Soon after leaving Sahussuram we came up with an old fellow on a camel. As he did not get out of our way quickly enough, my coachman gave him a cut with his whip-lash, which so discomposed him that he tumbled off his beast, and must, I fancy, have had a pretty heavy fall. I spoke to my servant about it, and told him to reprimand the coachman, but he seemed to consider it a most excellent joke. There seems to be no sympathy with suffering in the East. A man may die by the roadside, with hundreds of people passing him, not one of whom will take the least trouble for his relief. The parable of the "Good Samaritan" must come with great force to men thus constituted. Among Christians, however inconsistent their general practice might be, no man could lie wounded and dying by a wayside, and not become the object of general attention and care. In India, on the other hand, were a Brahmun to touch such a person he would be defiled; were any of a higher caste to touch his blood pollution would ensue; so that both these classes would be forbidden to give relief by their religion itself; and no one of his own or of a lower caste, not even his acquaintances, would probably think it worth while to interfere unless they hoped for some advantage by so doing. When I was going from Agra to Bombay, with a retinue of twenty bearers, it happened several times that men were taken ill, and left by the others to die on the road without a rupee to relieve even their immediate necessities. I did not usually find such occurrences out till several days after, when a man would be missing when I counted the bearers; the miserable rogues always concealing the fact of one of their number having given out, in order to get the wages which are his due, and divide them among themselves.

After leaving Sahussuram the country is a flat, uninteresting plain, with hardly any trees, villages sparsely scattered, and cultivation in patches. We crossed the Ganges at midnight, in a large scow, and at two o'clock on the morning of the 5th of November, arrived at the hotel in Sĕroor.

Sĕroor is four miles from Bĕnarĕs, and is the military station of that city. It is just like Dum-Dum and all other cantonments in India—the same broad roads, the same ugly, low-walled, one-storied bungalows with steep, high, thatched roofs, in desolate compounds; the same hideous church, and the two stores. Sĕroor being a large station, and on the great route up-country, has two hotels, which are, like other Mofussĭl hotels, merely ordinary bungalows furnished by some native or half-caste on the chance of travellers requiring better ac commodations than they can get at the dâk-bungalow. They will not accommodate more than seven or eight lodgers.

CHAPTER XIII.

THE HOLY CITY OF INDIA.

The Sacred Apes—The City from the River—The Observatory—Oriental Science—The Golden Temple—Sacred Bulls—The Great Devil—Hindooism—The Goddess of the Skull-chaplet—Poojah—The Holy Well—Self-Torture—Caste—Brahmunical Regeneration—Supremacy of the Sacred Caste.

THE city of Bĕnarĕs is the Jerusalem or Mecca of the Hindoo; nay, it has in his eyes a far greater sanctity than have either of those two holy places in the estimation of Christians or Moosulmans, for he believes that Bĕnarĕs is not founded on the tortoise which is the common support of the earth, but rests on the point of Seewa's trident; that all who die in, or within nine miles of it, proceed directly to heaven; and that the material and visible Bĕnarĕs is not so much a city, *in se*, as a shadow or ektype of the celestial city, the heavenly Bĕnarĕs.

There are about 500,000 inhabitants in Bĕnarĕs, but the number cannot be exactly ascertained, as both Hindoos and Moosulmans regard it as impious to number the people—an opinion which seems to have prevailed among the Jews.

Colonel Mowatt, the commandant at Dum-Dum, had given me a letter to Captain Waddy of Bĕnarĕs, asking him to show me all the sights, and let me have an elephant on which to go through the market-place. Captain Waddy had, however, unfortunately, gone to Deenapoor, and a humble garrhee had to be substituted for the majestic elephant.

I engaged a young Armenian as guide, and we left the hotel at five in the morning, in order to be in time to see the bathers in the Ganges. A drive of three-quarters of an hour through a suburb of mud huts brought us to the river's edge, at the upper end of the city. On our way we passed what is called the "monkey-garden," an enclosure containing several temples and many hundred apes, sacred to Hooniman, the divine ape who conquered Ceylon for Rama. The apes are generally fine fat fellows, of a rich orange colour, and do not at all confine themselves to their enclosure, but range for a mile around, laying hands on all they can find. A Hindoo considers it a great honour and advantage if he can, by rich food and comfortable lodging, entice one of these animals to stay any length of time on his premises. The apes are very tame, as their sacred character protects them from all molestation. An Englishman was once drowned in the Ganges near Bĕnarĕs, for having ignorantly shot one of them.

We embarked in a dingee on the Ganges, and commenced pulling down the river. The sun was about an hour high, and shone full on the long line of palaces, temples, and mosques, built on the edge of the cliff on which the city is situated. The opposite bank of the river is perfectly flat and unoccupied. From the summit of the cliff, which is about eighty feet above the river, a long and continuous line of broad stone steps leads down to the water's edge. Near the bottom the *ghât* (steps) is broken by a broad platform, which serves as a thoroughfare, and gives accommodation to numerous small traders. From this platform jetties project into the river. At the further end of these jetties are graceful stone kiosks, sheltering some hideous idol before which a Brahmun may generally be seen performing poojah.

The buildings which crown the cliff, and form the water front of the city, are all striking in appearance. The dwelling houses are always large, being the residences of rajahs, and other rich men who come to Bĕnarĕs to end their days, on account of the sanctity of the place. Like the ghâts and temples, they are constructed of a fine light-coloured and durable freestone. The architecture varies somewhat, but the windows and doors are pointed—the former generally filled up with stone trellis-work, in lieu of glass. The mundrăs, or Hindoo temples form a striking feature in the *coup d'œil.* They are never of large size, and are surrounded by an enclosure, above which are seen the pyramidal spires which form the distinguishing feature in Hindoo sacred architecture throughout India. The larger mundrăs have three spires, the smaller, only one. Each spire is commonly decorated by a number of smaller spires surrounding it in diminishing rows up to its summit, where it ends in a gilt ornament. Rarely, the whole spire is gilt. The musjeeds, or mosques in India, two or three of which are visible from the river, have always either one or three bulging Saracenic domes, and at each extremity, a tall, slim minár, surmounted by a kiosk, and relieved from the effects of unsupported height by one or two narrow galleries.

As we rowed down the river the whole view was very striking, and came nearly up to what I had dreamed of Hindoo splendour—a dream, in the reality of which, like many others, I was most miserably disappointed, and which found a satisfactory realization only in this view of Bĕnarĕs, and one or two other cities, which it was my good fortune to visit.

The ghâts of Bĕnarĕs are covered in the morning by merchants, offering their wares for sale, in the shade of immense gaudy umbrellas; with men and women, dressing and undressing; with barbers, fukheers, brahmuns, and water-carriers. While on the lower steps of the ghât, which reach into the water, thousands of both sexes are occupied in bathing, and washing their garments in the river.

When it is recollected that the buildings above are a hundred feet or more long, and four or five stories high; that the ghâts are eighty feet in height, and are, in themselves, magnificent constructions of which any city might be proud; that this row of palaces, temples, and ghâts, extends for two miles along the river's bank, worthily terminated by the musjeed of Aurungzeeb, with its graceful minárs, and that the whole scene was lighted up by an eastern sun, bringing out the gaudy colours of the dress of the people, and the gilded ornaments of the mosques and temples, the reader may, perhaps, understand and pardon the enthusiasm excited in me by the splendid architectural effect of this river front, which cannot be parallelled or surpassed by any similar scene in India or in the world.

After descending the river about half a mile, we landed at the observatory ghat, and went to view the building. It is of stone, about 200 feet square, and 50 high. Within are many small courts and apartments, once appropriated to scientific purposes, but now in ruins. The chief interest is on the flat roof, where there still remain several charts of the heavens on stone, and some of the instruments which were formerly used in astronomical observations. There is an immense stone sun-dial in the form of an arc, perhaps twenty feet in diameter; a meridional wall of stone with two iron sights, besides several other arrangements which I did not understand, and piers and iron rings for the support of instruments which have been removed. This observatory is one of three, founded several hundred years ago, by Jai Singh, the Rajah of a Rajpootana State—the other two, were one at Delhi, and the other, at his own capital of Jaipoor. Hindoo astronomy is known to have made considerable progress long before the science was at all cultivated in Europe, but its study is now abandoned in favor of the more perfect systems of the West. It will scarcely be believed that so careful were the East India Company of all the religious feelings and prejudices of their subjects, that for years after they had established schools for the natives, the old Hindoo systems of geography and astronomy, which represent the earth as supported by a tortoise, the source of the Ganges as the centre of the world, and the sun as revolving daily around the earth, continued to be taught in colleges, to the support of which, the Company contributed.

This observatory, like the other two which I have mentioned, is now never used, and is fast falling into ruin, all except the solid walls. The revenues for its support are appropriated by the Brahmuns.

Leaving the observatory, we again took boat, and landing a little lower down, ascended the ghât, and visited the golden temple, the principal mundră in the city. The road from the bank to the temple lay through narrow streets, having on each side large, lofty, and solid stone houses, looking rather gloomy, as there were few windows, and those small. The streets were filled with worshippers going to the temple, each having a small basket containing offerings of flowers, rice, &c. The sacred bulls which once filled the streets of Bĕnarĕs, are still inconveniently numerous and tame, but they are not treated with as much respect as formerly, and many hundreds had recently been seized by government and put to work. The temple consisted of a small square court, having around it a verandah, filled with stone images of bulls, before which many worshippers were making poojah. The bull is the most sacred animal in the Hindoo mythology; he is called Nahadeo, or the little devil, and is the steed of Mahadeo (the great devil), which is one of the chief symbols under which the god Seewa is worshipped. A Hindoo considers the slaughter of a bull or cow, as a greater crime than parricide; and in old times this offence was punished with death—a penalty that was long permitted to remain in force in some parts of India, by the Honourable Company, so fearful were they of seeming to interfere with the religious customs of the natives. In the centre of the court was the temple itself, raised several feet from the ground, upon a stone platform. It consisted of three rooms opening into one another, each not more than twelve feet square—the roofs rising into those pyramidal spires of which I have spoken before. The interior of these rooms was perfectly plain, but in each there was a Mahadeo—a stone cylinder, three feet or so high, and rounded at the top, rising from a basin sunk in the stone floor. The Mahadeo is the deification of the *lĭngam*, or creative principle, and as it is an emblem of Seewa, the destructive element in the Brahmunical trĭmoortee, it must typify the eternal origin of life from death—that is, if it has any such deep meaning at all. It answers to the Phallos and Priapus, and is, perhaps, only an Indian phase of that Phallic worship, which seems to have been so general in various places, in the earlier stages of religious development. The Mahadeo, say the Brahmuns, is the only idol which has an intrinsic sanctity; the others must be consecrated, but any conical stone or rude mound of earth will be a worthy representation of the god, and can be rightly worshipped.

Speculators on Indian religion have made out the Brahmunical system to be one of the purest and most perfect that the world has ever seen, and we have derived from those theorists some very pretty and systematic notions about a Brahmunical Trĭmoortee, or Trinity, in which the Creative, Preserving and Destroying Powers were supposed exactly to counterbalance each other, and govern the universe in harmony. Such may have been the doctrines of the early vedas, but, at the present day, the fact is, that, in theory, the whole religious system is the most confused, contradictory, beastly tissue of incredible fables; in practice, it is even worse; the Trĭmoortee is altogether ignored, and it is only a very learned pundit who would know that his religion presupposed such a thing. Brahma is never worshipped; Vĭshnoo has some followers in the south; but Seewa and his wife Párbutee are the gods to whom most of the homage is paid. Seewa is always venerated in the Mahadeo; but his wife Párbutee has numerous forms, each more repulsive than the other. As Kalee, in Bengal, she presides over self-torture, swinging suspended by hooks in the back, burning villages, and murdering the inhabitants, and other amusements, of which her followers are so fond; as Bhowanee, in the centre of India, she is the mistress of the Thugs, in whose honour they drive their murderous trade, and whom the blood of a man slain for her sake is supposed to make smile for a thousand years; as Dévee, in the rest of India, she is the dread small-pox, which is so fearful a scourge among the natives. When one is taken ill of this disease, his friends say "*Dévee Nikala,*" "Dévee has manifested herself," and it is considered impious to attempt to dislodge the goddess, or to burn the body which she has honoured by taking up her abode in it. In all these forms, Párbutee presides over every form of torture and horror—infanticide being one of her favourite failings. It was formerly customary to offer to her sacrifices of men and horses, but these have been discontinued since the introduction of the Company's rule. It must be remembered that this most amiable and attractive goddess is worshipped by about half the population of India, while the greater part of the other half worship her husband, Seewa, who is a deity of equally bad character, only his qualities are not developed in the same obtrusive hideousness. He is supposed, however, to be an accessory before the act in all that his wife does.

The worship of the Mahadeo is very simple. It consists merely in putting upon the stone lĭngam, rice, flowers, bright-coloured powder, and some other things, which are then washed off by a stream of Ganges' water, poured by the attendant Brahmun, who keeps mumbling Sanscrit prayers. As each worshipper completes his offering, the Brahmun paints his forehead with certain stripes of bright-coloured paint, which show, during the whole day, to what deity the wearer has done poojah in the morning.

The Golden Temple was crowded with naked devotees, sacred cows, begging Brahmuns, &c., and was a nasty, wet place. We had to give the priests a fee of a rupee apiece, in return for which they put a garland of flowers about our necks. This Mundră is the property of an hereditary corporation, and its income is said to be a lakh of rupees, or £10,000, a year.

Leaving the court of the temple, we went into an adjacent enclosure, which contains the sacred well, into which flows the water that has been poured over the Mahadeo in the adjoining temple. The well being a mere sink, is of course putrid, but is, notwithstanding, worshipped with great reverence. There is a stone platform around it, about fifty feet by forty, covered by a solid stone roof, supported on rows of columns. The temple which I have described was formerly on the other side of the well, on what was the most sacred spot in the world. The old location was, however, unfortunately defiled by that violent Moosulman, the Emperor Alum Geer, and the gods and temple were transferred to their present position. One of the goddesses, however, who inhabited the old temple, is said to have been dissatisfied with the change, and to have plunged down this well, where it is thought she still is.

The platform around the well was filled with devotees and pilgrims—men of different races, dress, and appearance. There was one old *Yogee* (Hindoo religious mendicant), who, squatted on the ground, with his back to a column, and his hands on his knees, silent and motionless. He had made a vow never to move or speak, nor to eat, unless food was put in his mouth. By this process he had attained to great sanctity, but very poor condition. His head and body had been liberally anointed with cow-dung and Ganges-mud by some of his admirers, and I saw many persons saláming and making poojah to him, but no one seemed to feed the poor wretch. I gave a bystander a few anas, with which a most bountiful meal was purchased. The old fellow eat it with much appetite, but an expression of countenance which seemed to say, "I despise it while I enjoy it." In old times, this place was a great resort for these performers of self-imposed penances, of which we read so much in tracts; but the practice of self-torture is gradually, but steadily, dying out in Northern India. A great change having been effected by the abolition of the Churruk-poojah by government. This was a festival in which men were swung in the air, supported by iron hooks run under the muscles of the back. The performers used generally to intoxicate themselves by smoking *bhung* (the Cannabis Indica). We have all read in missionary tracts, of people throwing themselves under the Car of Juggurnath, of men with their limbs fixed in unnatural positions, the nails growing through their hands, &c., and suicide in the Ganges off Běnarěs used to be committed by hundreds every year, who wished to die within the sacred influence of that holy city, and thus secure an immediate transition to eternal felicity. All these barbarous practices, however, are now fast disappearing; and suttees, with the various other forms of self-immolation, have long been prohibited and abolished by the Honourable Company.

Both Hindooism and Mahommedanism would seem to be gradually breaking up in the Company's territories; not that there has yet been any great impression produced upon the mass of the population, or that any better creed is being substituted; only there are numerous signs to show that neither of the old religions is in as vigourous a state as it was some years ago, or as Hindooism, at least, is still, in the dominions of some native princes. The musjeeds are mostly out of repair, and in many instances fast going to ruin, except some of them which are kept up by government. The Moosulmans in India have long abandoned the purity of their old faith, and become more or less infected with Hindoo superstitions, and the great bulk of them rarely go to the mosques, or observe those daily prayers which are so striking to the traveller in other Moslem countries. Among the Hindoos the change is seen more in the gradually increasing disregard of caste. A few years ago a Brahmun would have been polluted for the day by the touch of a low-caste man, and would as soon have thought of wearing leather shoes, eating beef, or drinking spirits, as of killing his mother, eating her flesh, and drinking her blood. Now, however, patent leather pumps are very fashionable in the cities among them; the higher classes, whose wealth and position enable them to despise public opinion, eat and drink what they like—especially the latter; and the pollution by touch, if remarked at all, is too inconvenient to be long remembered. It must not be supposed, however, that this disregard of caste is yet at all general. Among the lower classes, that maxim, so general among oriental nations, that "that which goeth into the mouth defileth a man" is still universally and scrupulously observed, and any deviation from the rules of caste is severely punished. Even those *illuminati*, of whom I spoke above, are in many instances so hampered by the prejudices of their youth, that they would not eat at the same table with one of another caste or drink water from his cup.

I had a little illustration of the inconveniences of caste before reaching Bĕnarĕs, after crossing the river Sôn. The coachman had left the carriage to get a fresh horse, and as he was rather long gone, I took up the bugle, which is carried by all dâk-coachmen, to recall him. No sooner, however, had my lip touched it, than all the bystanders groaned in concert. I asked my servant what the matter was, and heard, in reply, that the coachman was a Brahmun, and would be unable henceforth to use the bugle without loss of caste, which, as he was a Brahmun, could not be regained. However it turned out that he was a very low-caste Brahmun (for they, like all other castes, are broken up into subordinate ranks, according to greater or less purity of blood) and could be reinstated by the payment of a fine, in the shape of a feast to his friends; so he finally made up his mind to blow the bugle, lose caste, and restore himself by standing treat, rather than have the greater expense of buying a new bugle. He would not touch his mouth to it, after all, without heating the mouth-piece in live coals, and scouring it with mud and cow-dung to purify it from the pollution of my lips. It may seem strange to some that a Brahmun should be coachman, but in fact they are found in all positions, and very commonly hire themselves out to natives as cooks, since the food which they prepare can be eaten by men of any caste. There are, however, a very large number, particularly among the higher castes of Brahmuns, who subsist wholly on their religious character—living on the charity and hospitality of one family after another. They are a very licentious race, and the customs of society give this tendency of theirs full swing, as, if a Brahmun leaves his shoes outside the door of a house into which he enters, it is unlawful for the owner of that house to enter until invited; and again there can never be any scandal with respect to them since a Hindoo would rather die than say anything to the disadvantage of a Brahmun. In old times, slandering a Brahmun was punished by cutting out the tongue; and death was the penalty for a blow given to one of the sacred caste. Of course these penalties have been inoperative since the government of the country by the Moosulmans, but the offences, which they were designed to prevent, are none the less rare. The dress of the Brahmuns does not differ from that of other natives, except that they all wear a piece of thread over the shoulder, falling to the hip, tied in a particular knot. This thread is put on the young Brahmun when he is about nine years old. Certain religious acts are performed on this occasion, and he is acquainted with a certain mystic sentence called the *gayootree*, which is in Sanscrit; and although now well known by foreigners, has at least half a dozen different translations. When all this is done, the novice is said to be twice born. Under the Hindoo system of government, the Brahmuns occupied a position of superiority which is almost incredible. All the other castes existed only for their use and advantage. If a Soodra (or member of the great caste which comprises the mass of the population, and of which the present castes are only subdivisions) presumed to learn by heart any portion of the Shastras, the penalty was death; if he only repeated a few of the sacred words without learning them, he was let off with a dose of boiling oil poured down his throat. The killing of a Soodra by a Brahmun was the pollution of a day; a blow inflicted on a Brahmun by a Soodra, was, as before stated, a capital offence. These and other exorbitant privileges have been lost, both by the rise in importance of the lower castes, by the degeneracy and impure blood of the present race of Brahmuns, and especially by the effects of the Mahommedan invasions which deposed them from their despotic pre-eminence. They are still, however, universally regarded by the Hindoos with a superstitious reverence, and are permitted to enjoy many privileges which they abuse. For instance, monogamy is the general rule among the Hindoos, except under peculiar circumstances, but the Brahmuns, and especially those of the high class called Kooleen, are allowed to marry several women. A Kooleen Brahmun can have as many wives as he pleases, and frequently weds as many as fifty or even a hundred girls, for the sake of the dowries which the parents are willing to give to secure the honour of so high-caste a husband for their daughter. As these Kooleens are frequently poor, they have no home of their own, but stop with such of their wives as they fancy—frequently never seeing the others after their nuptial day. This is, of itself, a fearful source of immorality, second only perhaps to the Hindoo custom of prohibiting the remarriage of widows. In some parts of India the Brahmuns have attained a social position even higher than that assigned to them by the laws of Mĕnoo, as they are looked upon as deities, and called by the same word which is used for a god.

CHAPTER XIV.

BĔNARĔS—CONCLUDED

Religious Ablutions—Aurungzeeb's Mosque—View from Minâr—Burning Ghat—Market Place—Hindoo College—"Native Gentlemen"—European Manners and Morals in India—Ruins of a Boodhist Monastery—Gold Brocade—Opium.

Leaving the Golden Temple, we returned to the ghat, re-embarked in our boat, and continued down the river. The ghats were still occupied by bathers, though the crowd was now not so great as earlier in the morning. Bathing in Ganges-water is a religious ceremony, which must be performed every morning, by all who live within any reasonable distance of that river. In case of persons who live more than twenty miles from the Ganges, the rule is so far relaxed as to allow them to bathe in any other river which may be more convenient. Next in sanctity to the Ganges, or Gunga as it is called by the natives, is the Nurbudda in Central India, which indeed is believed, by many of those who live on its banks, to be the Ganges itself, or to have a mysterious underground communication with it. Bathing being, as before remarked, a religious ceremony, is accompanied with prayers, joining of the hands, throwing up the water toward the sun, and numerous other rites. When the religious act is complete, the bather thoroughly washes every part of his person, scours his hair with mud, and cleanses his teeth with a piece of soft wood, which he has previously chewed into a brush, using the mud as tooth-powder. As this act is punctually performed every morning by every Hindoo, they are in person perhaps the cleanest people in the world. After bathing they take off their clothing and wash it, frequently putting it on again without waiting for it to dry. In Bengal, oil is rubbed into the skin after the bath, but in Hindoostan this is not customary. Men and women bathe together promiscuously, but although all the clothing has to be removed in the water, they contrive to do so without any immodest exposure.

We kept down the river, almost to the end of the town, and landed by the Musjeed of Aurungzeeb, where we landed and ascended the Ghat. The mosque itself is not a particularly handsome building, but the minárs are very fine, rising to perhaps 150 feet above the ground, which is about 100 feet above the river. All mosques in India have one shape, which is distinct from the form usual in other Moosulman countries. They consist of an open portico, forming the western side of a court. The portico is the place of prayer, and is supported by a row of columns on the side which is open toward the court. The other two sides are walled in. In the middle of the western wall is a niche, the *kibla*, which indicates the direction of Mecca. Close beside the kibla is a stone platform, raised a few feet from the pavement, on which the *moolah*, or preacher, sits. All this is on the western side of the court. On the eastern side is the main gateway. The court itself is frequently occupied by worshippers, when there is a crowd. In the centre is generally a pool of water, for the purification which the Korán enjoins previous to prayer. At each extremity of the colonnade dividing the open court from the portico, which has been described as the special place of prayer, is a minár. Every mosque has two. They are used as standing-places for the muezzins, who chaunt on their summits, certain Arabic verses which call the faithful to prayer.

We ascended to the top of one of the minárs of Aurungzeeb's musjeed, from which we had a view of all the city, the river, and the country for miles around. In the town itself, there were no buildings which stood out very prominently, except the Hindoo college. The houses generally had flat roofs, and were larger than in other towns which I saw in India. The Ganges had a very deserted look—there being only one or two boats upon it. In China, such a river would be crowded with vessels. Such parts of the country as we could see were all barren jungul.

Leaving the mosque, we again entered our boat, and returned a short distance up the river. We passed close to the "Burning Ghat," which I had not noticed as we went down, since we had kept in the centre of the stream. It was much like the corresponding establishment at Calcutta, and had quite as foul a smell, but there were not so many hurgilas to be seen. Two bodies were burning and two or three others, lying in the mud, wrapped in red muslin, awaiting incremation.

Landing again, we dismissed our boat and entered the garrhee. We passed through the chôk, or market-place, and the Burra Bazár, or great street of shops. They were, neither of them, very remarkable sights; but, in the afternoon, when I visited them again, were crammed full of people buying and selling—so much so that I had to leave my carriage and make my way through the crowd as best I could on foot. I had cause to regret not having the elephant, with which I should, no doubt, have been furnished, had Capt. Waddy been in Bĕnarĕs, as such an animated scene as the chôk of a large Indian city, at high market time, is much better seen from a howdah than in any other way.

We returned home by way of the Hindoo college, an extensive establishment, built and supported by Government. The material is the same light free-stone, which is so generally employed in Bĕnarĕs; the architecture, a sort of Indian Gothic, badly carried out. The tuition is free, and, as in all government schools, all mention of religion is carefully excluded. The school was not in session, the day being a Hindoo festival.

My companion of the morning offered to take me to see some Hindoos of eminence with whom he was acquainted—which I should have been glad to do—but he was afterwards prevented by business. Rich natives generally live in a very retired way, and foreigners do not get on intimate terms with them—they are, however, very glad to have acquaintances among the English, and receive visits from them, and are much disposed to adopt English customs in exteriors. There is, in fact, no such thing as intimacy among the natives. They have no confidence in each other, and so there cannot be any friendship among them. Again, a native's home is in his zĕnana, among his women—a place of retirement into which his most intimate friends are not admitted; so that any society, in our sense of the word, is, of course, impossible among them. The English, in India, have been censured for their haughty manner toward the higher class of natives, and the footing of inequality on which the latter mingled with the former. I do not think that they are open to this charge, to the extent which is supposed, as the Company always desired, and as far as possible enforced the utmost respect, in the manners of its servants towards all natives of respectability. For instance, there was an army regulation that the English officers should always invite into the house any native officer who might call, and give him a chair. These native officers were men who could neither read nor write, and had no further training than a perfect knowledge of drill, being therefore in education, as well as in character, infinitely inferior to the European sergeant who was required by the same regulations to stand up in the officer's presence. Besides even the best and highest classes of natives, were addicted to such low and foul vices, as our laws say cannot even be mentioned by any Christian man—how then were they fit companions to associate with honourable gentlemen? The manners of a native of standing, are as polished as those of the most refined nobleman in Paris, perhaps even more so—his mind and his character, as foul and depraved as those of the most degraded outcast of that capital.

I met at the hotel, in Sĕroor, a very intelligent and agreeable captain of infantry, from the North Western Provinces, going home on sick leave. He told me that he knew personally, Arnold, the author of "Oakfield," a work that produced much excitement in India, and made some stir in England, and even in America.

This officer told me that he could, as I can, understand how Arnold might have written the book in perfectly good faith, being a very quiet, religious, gentlemanly, highly-educated, but somewhat narrow-minded man; while he yet contended, as I fully believe, that "Oakfield" was a great misrepresentation of the Indian army as it now exists. The fact is, that like "Uncle Tom's Cabin," the work was intended to satirize certain *individuals*, and both books were supposed both by their friends and foes to be meant as representations of the entire class to which these individuals belonged. Moreover, I heard on all hands, in India, that within ten or twelve years a great change for the better had come over the Company's service; and if we go back to the times when the present generals were "griffins" or "griffs" (as they call cadets,) the alteration in manners is most essential. At that time India was so cut off from the rest of the world, and travelling from one part of the country to another so slow, that men were isolated, and became very like savages. Shut off from all communication with what was of general interest, and coming out too young to form literary tastes, (which even had they had, they could not have gratified,) they gave themselves up to playing, drinking, and other vices; generally kept native mistresses or wives, and for want of better society, associated familiarly with the sepoys, and their native officers; an association which shows the depth to which they must have sunk, and which must have tended to drag them lower still. In old times, some Englishmen became so lowered in character under the influence of the heathen wives and companions among whom they lived, that instances have been known where they actually painted their faces, and performed poojah at the Ganges. Nowadays, the number of Europeans is very much increased; their quality is improved, by which I mean, that they are men of higher cultivation before they leave England, and occupy a better standing in the society of that country than did their predecessors; communication with home and different parts of India is rapid, and manners have undergone a very great change for the better. Perhaps, what did more than anything else to effect this desirable result, was the increase in the number of English ladies, who give a higher tone to society than it ever had before, and exclude from their circle any man who has a native wife or mistress; in addition to which, Government took the matter up, and any officer who indulged himself in this respect, soon found that by so doing he lost the confidence of his superiors, and diminished his chance of promotion. The result of all these causes was to produce on the whole a most satisfactory state of morality among the Indian officers, who all feel that the eyes of society and Government are constantly upon them, since one is never unaccompanied by servants in India, and every act is by them made a subject of conversation in the bazár, whence any scandal soon makes its way throughout the whole station.

On the following day I went with the landlord of the hotel to see the remains of a large Boodhist establishment, about eight miles from Bĕnarĕs. This was formerly a great centre of Boodhism, and is described by contemporary Chinese travellers in works which still exist. It was, however, entirely destroyed during the contests between the Boodhists and Brahmuns. The remains consist of ten or twelve acres of brick mounds, which have been recently cleared away in some places, showing the foundations, which are very thick. The buildings must have been both strong and lofty, judging from the quantity of bricks that remain. The only building standing, is a sort of monument, being a round tower, perhaps, 60 or 70 feet in diameter, and about the same in height; it was once loftier, but the upper part has fallen to ruin. It is of stone, filled in solid with brick, the stone coating alone being twelve feet thick. Each stone is numbered. The exterior of this tower is decorated with most elaborate carvings of fruit, geometrical forms, and numerous other designs. The work is very deep and sharp, and in some places still remains incomplete.

As we drove to these ruins, our road lay through fields of indigo and sugar-cane; but the former had hardly sprung from the ground.

In the afternoon, I visited a manufactory of the kinkŏb, or gold brocade, for which Bĕnarĕs is famous. The establishment which I visited, although the largest in Bĕnarĕs, was all comprised in one small room, with an earthen floor. There were only four looms, which were placed close to the ground, the weaver sitting on the earth, in a little excavation. The material of the kinkob is silk, and threads of pure gold. Being exclusively used for pa*n*jama, the pieces are only 4½ yards long. It brings from 50 rupees to 150 rupees the piece.

Bĕnarĕs is one of the great opium depôts, the other being Patna. The Company's plantation is 87 miles from the city, but I did not care to visit it, as the poppy was not ripe. Opium is a Government monopoly in the east of India, and all private growers must sell their drug to the Company's agent at a fixed rate. In the west of India, however, that is to say, the Malwar country, private cultivators are allowed to sell to whom they will, only paying a duty to Government.

CHAPTER XV.

ALLAHABAD—"THE CITY OF GOD."

Arrival at Allahabad—Zubburdustee—Seekhs—Hindoostanees—Fort at Allahabad—An Invisible River—Sooltan Khooshroo's Surai—Hindoostanee Wells—Allahabad to Cawnpoor—Bullock Trains—Elephantiasis.

LEAVING Bĕnarĕs on the evening of the seventh of November, I found myself next morning on the north bank of the Ganges, opposite the city of Allahabad, which is situated on a narrow tongue of land between the Jumna and Ganges, at their point of junction. The position of Allahabad is not unlike that of New York, except that it is not an island. The fort, which is a large structure with high red stone walls, occupies a position corresponding to that of Castle Garden.

The Ganges was low, not more than a mile wide, and it took us a couple of hours to push the garrhee across the sandy bed of the river, from which the water had receded. Arrived at the river's bank, I found that the bridge of boats which connects the city with the northern bank of the Ganges, had been opened to allow of the passage of some boats loaded with troops.

Arrived at Allahabad, I put up at a tolerable hotel kept by a native, and drove in a buggy to the fort, to present a letter of introduction to Captain Russell, the Commandant. On the way I counted fifty-three native drays, employed compulsorily by Government to aid in the preparations for the expected visit of the Commander-in-chief, the late General Anson, who was then on a tour of inspection. The Government in India take by force anything that is required for the public service, whether belonging to natives or English, paying at a fixed rate, which is generally very fair. This system seems to us harsh and tyrannical, but has always been usual under previous Governments, who, however, seldom made any payment for what they took. The natives do not think this custom oppressive, as they consider it the height of folly for any one to pay, when he can avoid so doing; and have always a tendency to appropriate their neighbour's goods and services *zubburdustee* (by force) whenever they have the power so to do. When we were going from Agra to Bombay, our followers used constantly to steal vegetables growing in the fields; take, by force, food from the bazar, and press the services of villagers as guides. We found it almost impossible to restrain them, or to convince them that there was any wrong in what they did. The aggrieved villagers used also to take things very coolly, so that it was only rarely that their depredations became known to us.

Outside the fort a regiment of Seekhs were encamped. They are the best soldiers in India, and have proved themselves the most reliable in the recent revolt. In appearance they would be an honour to any army in the world. It is impossible to imagine a greater discrepancy than exists between the proud, martial, rough-spoken Seekh, and the mild-looking commercial and courtly Bengalee. The difference in appearance, of the races who inhabit India, is even greater than between the different nations of Europe. The national peculiarities have been, I suppose, perpetuated by the institution of castes. I was now regularly in Hindoostan, Bĕnarĕs being generally considered the boundary between that country and Bengal. The features of the people were more regular and finely cut than lower down the country, but the complexion of the lower classes was very dark—in many cases quite black. The costume worn here was entirely different from that of Bengal, which consists of voluminous folds of pure white muslin wound gracefully around the body. In Hindoostan the men dress in a long, tight-fitting cassock, (chupkun) and pa*n*jama or trowsers. I have before described this dress as worn by the Moosulman khitmutgrás at Calcutta; it was in fact introduced by the Mahommedan conquest, but has now become the general costume of Hindoostan. The

Hindoos, however, do not wear pa*n*jama, but keep the dhotee, and their chupkuns open on the right breast instead of the left. The Hindoostanee women generally wear very tight pa*n*jama, and a scarf (saree) wound around the upper part of the body and over the head. The material of the dress of both sexes is bright-coloured calico. In cold weather the women often wear a thick blue or green petticoat over the pa*n*jama. In Hindoostan men always wear turbans, which are small and generally bright-coloured, but in Bengal it is usual to go with the head quite uncovered. In cold weather the Hindoostanees wrap themselves in cotton quilts precisely resembling, in make and appearance, what we call "comfortables" in America.

The fort at Allahabad is, as I have said, situated at the extremity of the town, at the junction of the Jumna and Ganges. It was an old native stronghold, but has been so entirely remodelled that the armoury alone bears any traces of its former masters. Captain Russell, whom I found in his office, showed me all over the place, which covers many acres of ground. I saw, among other things, a siege-train which had been got ready before the annexation of Oude, in case that any of the strongholds of the country should hold out. Under the fort are extensive catacombs, into which we penetrated for some distance. They contain shrines of several gods, and two or three Mahadeos. There is also, in the court of the fort, a shaft of stone about fifty feet high, and covered with an inscription in one of the old languages of India. The kind of stone of which this pillar is made, shows that it must have been brought from an immense distance. Only two similar columns are known in India.

I afterwards drove through the city, which is as large a place as Bĕnarĕs, but not so handsome. There are none of those fine brown-stone residences which I admired so much in Bĕnarĕs. The houses are all low and small, and in the Moosulman style of architecture, which prevails throughout Hindoostan.

Allahabad is considered by the Hindoos as one of the most

sacred localities, being a place where three rivers join.* Only two of these rivers, however, are visible; the third is supposed to flow direct from heaven, and here, unseen by mortal eyes, to add its celestial waters to those of the sacred Gunga. There is a great religious festival held every year at this place, where the Brahmuns make an immense amount of money, since they have, as elsewhere, the entire control of the bathing ghat, and make all pay well for the privilege of washing away their sins in the purifying waters of the Ganges. They have also the monopoly of shaving, which is very profitable, as every one who is shaved at this fair gains a thousand years of Paradise for every hair removed.

The principal sight at Allahabad, beside the fort, is the Surai and Gardens of Sooltan Kooshroo. They may have been founded by that monarch, who died seven hundred years ago, but certainly the present buildings are much more modern. The surai is a quadrangle, about 500 feet square, surrounded by a high stone wall, against which are cloisters, affording shelter to travellers, while their camels occupy the centre of the court. Every town, and most large villages, in India, have at least one of these surais, built either by some rich individual, or by government. They are always free to all comers.

On one side of the surai is one of those noble gateways which form so striking a feature of Saracenic architecture. It is nearly sixty feet high, and about fifty feet deep, and leads to the gardens, which contain six or eight acres of land, and are well kept. At the further end of the garden are three tombs, raised over a princess and two princes. The tombs are of stone, about forty feet square, surmounted by marble domes, and raised on stone chubootras, fifteen feet from the ground, so that their fine proportions are seen to great advantage.

The public wells are among the prettiest objects in the towns

* Its former name was Deeg, which, I believe, means "the junction" in Sanscrit. It was called Allahabad, or "the city of Allah," by the Moosulman invaders, who were much struck with its situation, and were very fond of changing the names of towns which they conquered.

and villages of Hindoostan. They are generally octagonal stone platforms, raised four or five feet from the ground, and approached by four flights of steps. Four stone columns over the well's mouth, support cross pieces from which the pulley is suspended. In Bengal no pulley is used at the wells. In the north of India generally the women draw and carry the water. The only men seen at the wells are the bheestees, a peculiar caste whose occupation is to carry water in a goat's skin slung on their back. It is said that the constant pressure of the wet skin against the back, occasions the growth of a parasitic worm in the flesh, which occasionally causes death.

Toward evening I took a drive through the cantonments, which are considered the prettiest in India—there being many nice roads to drive on, shaded by avenues of trees. We drove around the parade-ground, the road about which is called in all stations "the Mall," and is the favourite drive of the officers in the evening. We passed a large number of carriages and buggies—the sáeeses were generally running beside the horses, instead of seating themselves comfortably on the foot-board, as they do in Calcutta. Every station of course has its parade ground, which is always admirably adapted for the purpose, on account of the perfect flatness and barrenness of most of the country in India. In fact almost any part of the country which is not cultivated, would do for a parade-ground. In this respect, India is, perhaps, the finest country in the world for military evolutions, and almost every part of it has been the scene of some bloody fight.

I left Allahabad the same evening, and breakfasting the next morning at Futtehpoor, arrived in Cawnpoor by seven, in time for dinner at the hotel. The country through which I passed between Allahabad and Cawnpoor, was, as before, a perfectly dead level, with hardly any trees or vegetation to be seen. There was, however, rather more cultivation about the villages, and I noticed several large fields of maize and other grains. I saw no palm trees between Bĕnarĕs and Cawnpoor.

During the day I passed an unusually large number of bullock trains. These are, as the name implies, trains of bullock-drays. They belong to the various dâk companies, and run the whole length of the Grand Trunk Road. The drays are built after European models, and are much superior to those of the native form. These bullock trains carry heavy goods, and also take native passengers, who are never very particular about speed on a journey, or, for that matter, in anything else.

After arriving at Bĕnarĕs I did not see any cases of elephantiasis—a disgusting disease which is very common in Bengal. It usually attacks one of the limbs, which swells enormously. I have often seen a very pretty girl ("mulier formosa superne") with a leg as thick as her body. I believe that death finally supervenes, perhaps from mortification of the affected limb.

CHAPTER XVI.

CAWNPOOR TO LUCKNOW.

The Station of Cawnpoor—Disorder in Oude—Cawnpoor to Lucknow—Elephants—Kaorees—Lucknow—Making Ice—The Weather—The Generosity of the Sovereign Company—My Man Brown—First View of Lucknow—A Moral—The Gate of Rome—The Taza—The Imambara—A fine Coup-d'œil—Situation of Oude—Splendour of the Court—Indian Misgovernment—Indian Gentlemen—Extortion and Tortures—Lord Canning's Confiscation—Brutal Degradation of the Court—Relations of the East India Company to the King of Oude—Violated Faith.

I REMAINED at Cawnpoor over night, and on the morning of the tenth, started for Lucknow by a branch of the Grand Trunk Road.

Cawnpoor was a large and important station, especially before the annexation of Oude, from which district it is separated by the river Ganges only. Oude was always a difficult kingdom to keep in order. Its population are mostly Rajpoot Hindoos—the governing class were Moosulmans of the sect called Sheeahs, who are considered by the orthodox Mahommedans as no better than infidels. The Rajpoots are a military caste, and when not in actual service, have generally employed themselves in robbing, Thuggee, or some similar occupation. The government of the King at Lucknow had no influence or authority in the rural districts, and was only heard of when there were taxes to be raised—the collection of which generally required the presence of the King's army, and a pitched battle between the tax-payers and tax-gatherers. The warlike Rajpoots held their land by a species of feudal tenure, and in cases of fighting, gathered round their zĕmindar, who commonly lived in a fortified village, and seldom yielded to the authority of law without showing good fight. Some of these zĕmindars had large possessions, many followers, and strongly fortified residences, and were almost independent of the King. When in want of money, they would organize predatory expeditions against their weaker neighbours, and slay, burn, torture and rob, until they had collected sufficient booty. When the exchequer of the King ran low, he used to send an army to one of these large villages, and demand of the zĕmindar either so many rupees or else so many bushels of ears. As the people did not like to part with their ears, and their leader was seldom inclined to shell out on a mere summons what he had gained with the red right hand, the result generally was a resort to arms, which in Oude was the *prima* as well as the *ultima ratio* of all disputants. In these conflicts, if the villagers were beaten, they were robbed, murdered, tortured, and frequently had their villages burnt down. If the king's troops had the worst of it, the villagers practised upon them the cruelties to which they themselves would have been subjected had the result been different. All the native states of India are a prey to the worst kind of tyranny, and in none of them is there much security for life or property; but in Oude, affairs were in a far worse state than under any other native government. There was absolutely no law outside of Lucknow; and the country swarmed with gangs of robbers, and professional murderers, who took refuge there from the police of the Company's territories, and emerged on predatory expeditions whenever they could do so safely and profitably. The result of this unsettled condition of the country, was that agriculture, trade, and all settled occupations were interfered with; large districts which were as fertile as any in India were allowed to become jungul, and there was a great and increasing emigration of the labouring and agricultural classes into the Company's territories. It may be imagined that the existence in the midst of their states of such a community, independent of their power, was a continual source of anxiety to the Company's government. The frontier stations were always on the alert, and of these Cawnpoor, as commanding the road to Lucknow, the only good road in the kingdom, was the strongest, and was always kept garrisoned by a large force. After the condition of Oude became such as was not only destructive of its own prosperity, but seriously threatened the peace and security of the adjacent possessions of the Company, the king was deposed and his territories annexed by the British government. Many of the troops, which had previously been stationed at Cawnpoor were then removed to Lucknow, so that the former station, had, at the period of my visit lost much of its old importance.

The ride from Cawnpoor to Lucknow occupied the whole day. The country was, as before, perfectly flat, and mostly jungul. Wherever it was cultivated, however, the crops indicated the fertile soil. The road led through two country bazárs, enclosures separate from any village, surrounded by a high mud wall and closed by gates—a peculiar arrangement which I never saw elsewhere. On the road we passed several elephants carrying passengers—the first time that I had seen them so employed, though I had often seen them used for other purposes. The natives sit on a broad pad upon the elephant's back—the howdah being a European invention. The Mahoot rides, a-straddle, upon the elephant's neck, and guides him with a sharp iron pike, about two feet long. In "old Indian" times, elephants were much used throughout the country, both by natives and foreigners, but the English carriage is now generally preferred as a conveyance, and elephants are not often seen far down the country. It is not, perhaps, generally known, that the elephant will not breed in captivity—they must always be caught wild, and tamed. Their numbers must, therefore, be always limited, and, when I was in India, Government had bought up all the good ones and sent them to the Punjab, where they were needed for military purposes.

In describing the country, above, I have several times used the word "jungul"—a Hindoostanee term, meaning "wild"—and when applied to land, meaning simply "uncultivated"—whether there is any vegetation or not. I think this explanation necessary, as I have noticed that both in England and this country, "a jungle" is supposed to be a cane-brake or forest. It may be so, undoubtedly, but much of all the jungul in India has hardly a single tree or bush upon it.

It was on the road between Cawnpoor and Lucknow that I

first saw *kaorees* used as money. Their use is general throughout India, but it so happened that I had not before seen them. They are small but solid shells, of a purple colour, which are only found in certain streams. Their value is about one eighty-fifth of a cent. Nothing can be bought with a single *kaoree*, but the existence of so small a medium of exchange, proves the cheapness of food.

We reached Lucknow about eight o'clock, and drove through the town, on the far side of which the dâk-bungalow is situated. I was surprised to find the whole city awake, the shops open and illuminated, and the streets crowded with people. It showed, at any rate, that I was no longer in Bengal, where the whole city would be asleep two hours after sunset. There was only light enough for me to see many large buildings, some tall minárs, and several fine gateways.

We drove more than two miles through the streets of the city, crossed the river Goomtee on an iron bridge, and keeping on for about a mile, arrived at the dâk-bungalow, which is on the outskirts of the cantonments. I found the dâk-bungalow rather uncomfortable, having only been built since the country came into the Company's hands, but there was no hotel, so I had to make up my mind to it. The room where I slept had no window-sash, an article of furniture of which I felt the want very much, as it was now freezing every night, and I was the more sensitive to cold from having been so long in hot weather. Throughout Hindoostan it generally freezes in the night time for two or three months in the year. This has been taken advantage of, for several years past, by the Europeans, to obtain a supply of ice for the hot weather. The plan is, to expose water to the cold air, in very shallow pans, having a net at the bottom. The water freezes during the night, to the depth of about a quarter of an inch, and the sheet of ice is lifted out in the morning, by help of the net, and carefully packed in an ice-house. Though the weather is so cool at night, and though even in the day-time one feels chilly within doors or in the shade, yet so hot is the sun, and so powerful are its rays, that it is quite unsafe to expose the head without the protection of a thick turban—or, as it is always called in

India, *pugree.* During the cold weather I generally found it necessary to wear flannel clothes, and even an overcoat indoors; but when I went out I put on a thin alpaca coat, taking care, however, not to expose my body to the sun's rays, and winding around my felt hat more yards of fine Dacca muslin, than a novice would believe it possible to arrange in a convenient and even graceful and picturesque pugree.

After I had eaten a curry and drank a bottle of beer, I dispatched my letter of introduction to the military Secretary of Government, Captain F. Hayes, and then heaping upon the *charpoy* (low native bedstead) all the shawls and coats I could find, got a better night's rest than could have been expected, considering the cold, and that as the Khansáhma*n* told me, much to my disgust, "Sircar, Koompanee, Bahadur kee Sukhawutne bichona koee nuhee*n* diya hy." (The generosity of the sovereign warrior company has not provided any bedclothes.) I had, by this time, picked up a good many words of the Hindoostanee, and was beginning to be able, by the help of a pocket dictionary, to dispense sometimes with the assistance of my servant, as interpreter, in which capacity he was not of so much use as I had expected, being often too stupid to understand my questions. He was a half-caste, and had a most peculiar character. He was awfully lazy, very extravagant, and generally stupid, but yet he was sometimes sharp enough, and once extricated me cleverly from a troublesome predicament in which I had put myself by beating a *moonshee* (native clerk and agent) of the dâk company, who filled some small office under the government.

Brown (my servant) used to take advantage of the delicate distinctions in the construction of the Hindoostanee sentence, to use forms in his conversation with natives which implied an equality in position between him and me. As soon as I began to understand the *lingo*, however, I put a stop to that. When I bought anything, he invariably exacted from the seller the dustooree of six per cent., which is always allowed in India, but he never kept the money for himself, giving it away to the servants at the dâk-bungalows, or wherever we were staying. He could never understand the difference between numbers. One day he told me that, during the Doorga Poojah at Calcutta, his uncle and he had driven out of town a hundred miles, and taken tiffin at some place of public resort. I asked him how long it had taken him to drive out. He said, "two hours," without seeming to remark any discrepancy between his two statements, and it was a long time before I could show him by the rate of our travelling that the distance could not have been as great as he supposed. At last he was convinced, and said, without the least confusion, "Ah! then, sir, it must have been ten miles." One day we were talking about castes, and he told me that all the Khitmutgrás in Calcutta were Christians. I was surprised to hear this, and asked him to what Church they belonged. "Oh, sir," he replied, "they do not belong to any Church, but they will all eat pork and drink brandy." Like all the natives, Brown seemed very insensible to the cold weather. He dressed in Alpaca clothes, and as he slept on the roof of the garrhee, without any covering, while we were travelling, I feared that he might suffer from the severity of the weather, and bought him a thick blanket. The next morning I asked him if he had found the blanket comfortable. "Very, sir," he replied; "I used it for a pillow." He used to lie, of course, as all natives do, but I expected that, and did not mind it. He remained with me until I arrived at Agra, when he left my service, returned to Delhi, and got employment in the office of the "Delhi Gazette," an English newspaper published in that city. At the massacre of the Christians, he was one of the few who escaped, and curiously enough, his safety was reported in the very mail which brought the first news of the mutiny, and his name was printed in all the newspapers in Europe, when the fate of so many more important people was a question of doubt and anxiety for weeks after.

Next morning I sent for a buggy to drive to the city. Just as I was starting, a chuprássee, or messenger, from Captain Hayes, arrived on a fast camel, with a letter from him inviting me to dinner, and promising me his advice and assistance in seeing the city on the following day—both of which offers I was happy to accept. After sending back the chuprássee,

I entered the buggy and drove to the town—about one mile off.

On crossing the iron bridge over the Goomtee, the view before me astonished even more than it delighted me. I knew, beforehand, that the city of Lucknow was a place of over two hundred and fifty thousand inhabitants, that it had been for years the capital of the most fertile portion of the Ganges valley, and that, until within some months of my visit, it had been the seat of the most considerable and splendid native court in India; still I had been so much disappointed by all the native towns which I hăd seen (except Bĕnarĕs, the architectural features of which are quite peculiar to itself and different from those of all other towns in India) that I was wholly unprepared for the magnificent *coup d'œil* which presented itself to me on the further bank of the river. The city, which extends for several miles along the bank, seemed one mass of majestic and beautiful buildings, of dazzling whiteness, crowned with domes of burnished gold, while scores of minárs, many of them very high, lent to the scene that airy grace for which they are so famous. The whole picture was like a dream of fairy land. I stopped the horse and gazed upon the view for a few minutes with unalloyed pleasure. Here, at last, I thought, I have come upon some real "Oriental magnificence"—this place will give me a vivid idea of the proud state of the Emperors of Delhi. True, the princes who built these mighty palaces no longer inhabit them; they no longer worship Allah in these glorious temples which they have reared as grand tributes to the supremacy of a pure monotheism; but still their buildings bear witness to their mightiness and wealth, and even if their strength was used in tyranny, and their riches gained by extortion, yet this employment of their power and money in promoting art and beauty, gives us a lurking feeling of regret that Justice should demand the utter abolition of the Moslem's rule.

A nearer view of these buildings, however, destroys all the illusion. The "lamp of Truth" burnt but dimly for the architects of Lucknow. You find, on examination, that the white colour of the buildings, which presented in the sunlight the effect of the purest marble, is simply white-wash. The material of the buildings themselves is stuccoed brick; and your taste is shocked by the discovery, that the gilded domes, of perfect shape, and apparently massive construction, which so much attracted your admiration, are merely thin shells of wood, in many places rotten. Everywhere you discover traces of disorder and want of repair. You come, at last, to the conclusion, that the whole thing is a gigantic sham, and, perhaps, think as I did, when recollecting my first impressions upon the further bank of the Goomtee, that the architecture of Lucknow is no bad type of the native rule, and the native character generally—very prepossessing *when seen and judged from beyond the water.*

I drove through the city to the Imambara, the principal mosque of the place. The streets were, as usual, narrow and crowded; the houses, as in all towns where the Moosulman influence prevails in the architecture, low and mean. This circumstance increases greatly the apparent height of the principal buildings, and to it they owe much of their effect.

After threading these narrow streets for half a mile or so, we passed through a great gateway, and entered an open paved square used as a market, and having on one side, a large but deserted and dingy-looking palace. At the further end of this square, was another gateway, the Room-ee-Durwázu*—the most magnificent structure of the kind I had seen. Passing through it we entered another square, similar to the first, but larger. It was also surrounded by several mosques, of which, by far the finest and most conspicuous, was the Imambara, on the left. These Imambaras are buildings peculiar to the Sheeah sect of Moosulmans, who differ from the orthodox Mahommedans, or Soonees, in permitting

* This means, literally, "The Gate of Rome." Rome being the name by which the natives of India know Constantinople, even at the present day, as it was the name applied to it as long as the "Eastern Empire" lasted. The gates of large native cities are usually called ostentatiously after the principal places in the direction of which they lie.

the use of images in worship. The original split between the rival sects, I believe was occasioned by disputes about the the succession to the office of Caliph. However that may be, they are now divided, also, on doctrinal points, and look upon one another as no better than unbelievers. Constantinople has always been the head quarters of the Soonees, Persia of the Sheeahs. In India, the Moosulmans of Delhi were Soonees, while those of Lucknow professed the Persian faith. The Sheèahs venerate the two brothers, Hússun and Hoosén, almost as much as they do Mahommed, and keep each year a season of fasting and mourning in memory of their death. The fast, the *mohurrum*, terminates by a grand procession, called the Taza, in which effigies of the prophet's winged horse, several angels, the two Imams, and other figures and representations of sacred objects are carried in procession amid the blaze of fireworks, and the lamentations of true believers over the untimely death of the two great brothers. The images and other objects carried in these processions are often made of precious metals, and being of great value, are, when not needed, deposited in a mosque, called the Imambara. The Lucknow Imambara consists of two courts, rising with a steep ascent, one above the other. Each of these courts is entered by a noble archway, and is, I should think, two hundred feet square. At the extremity of the furthest is a great gallery, perhaps sixty feet high, under which are kept the sacred images described above. Notwithstanding their value, they are very ugly. This portico is a curious combination of a sacristy, *garde-robe*, and cemetery. It contains the tombs of two or three members of the royal family, which are covered with showy and expensive tabernacles of silver and precious stones; and is, besides employed as a store-house of the more valuable curiosities collected by the various kings. There were a number of chandeliers, a blue glass tiger,, a great throne plated with silver, royal standards embroidered with gold and precious stones, and other heterogeneous objects —altogether, a collection of great value, but showing the most barbarous taste. The two courts of the Imambara are laid out as gardens, and on one side of the upper court is a large mosque, built at right angles with the portico described above.

On leaving the Imambàra, I visited several other mosques of great size. Their architecture left but little to desire, but the inferiority of the materials employed in their construction, and the general want of repair, were painfully evident. I also went to see the old Imambara, at no great distance from the new edifice of the same name. Its general arrangement is similar to that of the new one, but its size is greater, and it includes a college and other buildings. It is with reference to this building, that Bishop Heber says, "taken in conjunction with the Room-ee-Durwázu which adjoins it, I have never seen an architectural view which pleased me more from its richness and variety, as well as the proportions and good taste of its principal features. The details a good deal resemble those of Eaton, the Earl of Grosvenor's seat in Cheshire, but the extent is much greater, and the parts larger. On the whole, it is, perhaps, most like the Kremlin; but, both in splendour and taste, my old favourite falls far short of it." Since the construction of the new Imambara the old building is deserted, and its courts are used as a Surai. The walls are almost black with mould, and it sadly needs a coat of whitewash.

After viewing these mosques, I drove my buggy through the market-squares around which they are situated. The day was now so far advanced that the squares, which, in the morning were almost deserted, were thickly crowded with tradesmen and others. The spacious market-place, the gay dress of the inhabitants, the beautiful outline of the mosques, and the dark mass of the old Imambara and Palace, made a scene which I shall not soon forget, and not the least part of which was that noble structure, the Room-ee-Durwázu, separating the two squares. The material of which it is built, is, to be sure, defective, and the details are liable to criticism, but in size, grace, and the beauty of the general design, I do not believe that it is surpassed by any gateway in the world.

I returned to the dâk-bungalow, as it was becoming late,

and, after dressing, drove to the residence of Captain Hayes, for dinner. His bungalow was somewhat larger than these buildings generally are, and was built with a slight regard for taste, but in other respects was similar to all others I have seen, having no second story, the walls being low, and the thatched roof high and steep. Mrs. Hayes had also some flowers in the compound, and a little grass-plat, which were great curiosities; and they had even gone so far in innovation as to make a bold, although only partially successful attempt at a kitchen-garden behind the house.

Captain Hayes was the Military Secretary to the chief commissioner of Oude, and had, at the time, almost the whole administration in his hands, as his colleague, the Civil Secretary, was absent. The two together formed the ministry of the commissioner, who is charged with the supreme government of the province. It will be seen, therefore, that Captain Hayes' duties, in the absence of the other Secretary, were not light, as they amounted in fact to the Legislative, Executive, and Judicial oversight of a population of six millions. He and Mrs. Hayes were among the most agreeable people whom I met in India, and disposed to do everything in their power to make my stay pleasant. They pressed me to remain some time with them, but I was so hurried that I could only afford one more day at Lucknow, and was forced to refuse their hospitable invitation. Captain Hayes was one of the most thorough gentlemen I ever met, and, what is rare in India, a very accomplished scholar. He was a Master of Arts of Oxford; and, in addition to his heavy duties, made it a point to devote a portion of every day to study. In this way he had acquired about thirteen different languages—including Russian and the Oriental tongues. His knowledge of the latter was of the greatest advantage in his governmental capacity. Being thoroughly acquainted with the people and government, I found his conversation most instructive, and the information which he gave me was of the greatest advantage in enabling me to form correct opinions. He told me that I had lost a great deal by coming to Lucknow since the dethronement of the king—as the capital was formerly the residence of a host of nobles who lived in the most magnificent style, going about gorgeously dressed, seated in splendid *howdahs* on the backs of elephants, and accompanied by troops of followers—the whole presenting such a scene of real Oriental magnificence as is now to be found only in books—Oude being the last very large native Court that remained. The king of Oude, he told me, was nearly independent; at least, the amount of control exercised over him by the resident agent of the Company, was entirely dependent upon the personal character of the man.

Captain Hayes gave me a most lively picture of the tyranny and disorder which prevailed under the royal government. The king's power scarcely extended outside the city walls. Beyond that his orders met with obedience when the army was present to enforce them. Taxes were seldom collected without a fight, since the people knew that if they paid without opposition, the collectors would pocket the money, and then, reporting to head-quarters that they had been unable to collect the tax, would come again, reinforced by troops, and make the unfortunate villagers pay over again. The cultivators were completely at the mercy of their feudal landlords, who took from them all they could spare. What portions of their property they could not spare, they were relieved of by some adjacent landlord who had not been able to squeeze enough out of his own tenants, and resorted to predatory excursions upon the villages of his weaker neighbours. Should the wretched ryuts still save something from these harpies, the chances were that it would fall into the hands of the authorized agents of government, or be forcibly carried off by the bands of organized dukoits whom the lawless state of Oude attracted from the adjacent territories of the Company. The administration of justice was of course a mere farce—the man with the fullest purse being, as in most Eastern countries, nearly sure of his cause.

Misgovernment among an Eastern nation is quite a different thing from anything that has ever existed in the West, and the disorganization of society in Oude is almost incredible to a European. In Oude, rapine and murder, ferocious cruelty and abominable lust were common as the air. Assassination was not only raised to a doctrine but solidified into an institution. Female infanticide, in its most horrible form, was almost universal. In fact a large number of the inhabitants formed, what a European can hardly imagine, a nation of banditti. These men, whose hands were red with blood, and whose minds were blackened by the practice of the most loathsome vices, were at the same time persons of bland exterior and polished manners, and some of them associated freely with Europeans, by whom they were regarded as fine specimens of advanced native intelligence.

The awful cruelties and atrocious crimes committed by these men, especially in their predatory excursions into each other's territories, surpassed the most horrible outrages during the recent mutiny, and show that those acts of appalling horror which concentrated on this rebellion the execration of mankind, were far from being unparallelled, and were, in fact, the ordinary practices and every-day occurrences in the kingdom of Oude before its annexation.

One of these *gentlemen*, Dursun Singh, marched into the country of an adjacent Rajah who was temporarily absent. His fort surrendered, and his followers obtained leave to depart freely on giving up all their property. They crossed to a small island in the river, and there intended to await the departure of their invader; but no sooner had Dursun seen them collected into one spot than he opened his guns upon them and killed between one and two hundred—the rest fled. The son of Dursun, who was charged with collecting the revenue of a large district, so ruined the country under his care, that whereas it once supplied grain to all the adjacent country, after a few years of his management it had to import corn from Lucknow and even from Cawnpoor. In an incursion made by one of these individuals, as late as the year 1846, he drove off two thousand prisoners and eighty thousand animals. On the road pregnant women were beaten by the troops with bludgeons and muskets, and many of them gave premature birth to children. When the troops came to a halt the prisoners were paraded and tortured with all the hellish ingenuity of Orientals. Their sufferings, which included the public dishonour of women and such bestial cruelties as cannot be named, served as a mid-day recreation for their captors. The commander smiled, and the soldiers danced with delight as they elicited screams from their victims. Another of these model governors made war on his own brother, and when he had taken him prisoner, cut off his head with his own hands, and that, too, in violation of a solemn oath that his life should be spared. Buksh Ali, who passed sometime at Cawnpoor, associating on terms of intimacy with the European residents of the station, was considered a very fine specimen of a native gentleman. Yet his origin and his life were equally degraded. He was originally a drummer for a nach-girl. Having obtained admittance to court in this capacity, he became a favourite, and a large district was assigned to him. His territories soon became the most lawless in Oude. Not a day passed but some new act of cruelty and oppression occurred, and his seraglio was filled with girls kidnapped from the country around. Another famous character was Juggurnath Chuprassee. He and his five brothers were the terror of the country. They headed large bands of soldiers and joined harmoniously in the work of devastation. Juggurnath, however, wished to have all the pickings to himself, and with his own hands killed two of his brothers. A third was shot in a foray. The remaining two set up independently of each other and of their elder brother, and the miserable cultivators had thenceforth three bands of plunderers instead of one only.

The tortures and barbarities employed by these wretches for the purpose of extorting money are almost incredible in their atrocity. Women were stripped naked and had boiling oil poured over their skins. Men were plastered with moist gunpowder, which was fired when dry. Beating to death was the favourite form of execution. Mutilation was common, and was sometimes prolonged till the victim expired. Men and women were slain after bestial outrages that might make a devil blush.

Such was the condition of the country of Oude, and such the character of its barons. The above acts are not exceptional, but are only instances of what was done continually and in all parts of the country. These are the men who, this year, have offered a pertinacious resistance to the authority of the British, as well they might, knowing that under English rule such acts as the above could not be committed. The "confiscation" proclaimed by Lord Canning, after the capture of Lucknow, was aimed only at this class, that is, the landholders; as the *people proper*, the cultivators, held land merely as their tenants, and no greater mercy could be shown them than to rid the country of these locusts. Under the management of such landlords the country could not be expected to be very prosperous. Accordingly, we find that the revenue was always diminishing, while the value of a district of equal extent which was ceded to the British in 1801, has since that time increased nearly to double.

Such was the state of the country. As for the capital, Lucknow, it cannot be better described than in the words of Dr. Duff. He says, "Lucknow was a very Sodom and Gomorrha of iniquity, the hard-worn earnings of the ground-down and tortured ryuts and villagers, the spoils of cruelly ravaged districts and provinces, were there consumed in monstrosities of wickedness and vice which might put Pandemonium itself to the blush." It was to Lucknow that the barons and landlords above described resorted to spend in luxury and pleasure, the fortunes which they had collected as above described. Besides them and their troops of lawless retainers, the population of the city was principally composed of the trades people and others who lived by ministering to their pleasure. The only other inhabitants were the numberless dependents that are attached to every native court.'

The degradation and vice of the royal court can scarcely be imagined. The palace was a den of infamy, a sink of indescribable licentiousness and incredible degradation. Bad as were the native aristocracy still they were men, and the king shunned their society, and lived among his singers, and the creatures dedicated to his licentious gratification. The lowest and vilest minions were raised to the highest posts; old servants of government were degraded to gratify a whim, and aged members of the royal family were subjected to the lowest indignities to amuse a set of dancers, and were robbed of their property, and forced to flee to the Company's territories, to secure their lives.

This state of things may be thought to be unendurable, and in fact could never have lasted had it not been for the support which the Company afforded to the king. The throne of Oude was created by them. They had recognized the independence of a revolted vassal of the Emperor of Delhi, and had established him as the first King of Oude. The treaty by which this was effected, provided that that king should govern well and faithfully, and promised protection and support of the Company. From the time that the arrangement was entered into, it became a ceaseless source of anxiety and trouble. The Company's power had to be constantly exerted to support the authority of the king, and prevent usurpations. The court was utterly corrupt; the king was entirely without authority; the feudal lords were unrestrained in their lawless excesses; the country was becoming a nest of bandits and murderers from all parts of India; the soil, the most fertile in the valley of the Ganges, was relapsing into jungul; the wretched villagers were sinking into mere beasts of burden, and fled each year, in great numbers, into the Company's territories.

Again and again the English resident remonstrated with the king and called upon him to observe the stipulations of his treaties, which required him to govern with some show of justice, and maintain at least the appearance of order. The remonstrances met with no attention from the miserable imbecile, lost in the beastly pleasures of his zĕnana. The Company could no longer continue their protection without making themselves accomplices of all these wrongs. They could not withdraw their support and leave the king independent, for that would have thrown the kingdom into worse confusion than ever. The king had no authority or respect, and would not have remained upon the throne a day. The strongest of the zĕmindars would have usurped the royal power, and the whole country would have been plunged into a state of anarchy, the conclusion of which could not have been foreseen. In fact, such a usurpation was liable to occur at any moment, and might have given the Company the greatest trouble in the restoration of peace.

The disorganization of society had thus been complete. The government was a malignant and incurable cancer, eating out the very life of the body politic. Extirpation was the only remedy. The ravages of the disease threatened to extend to the English possessions. In their own interest, in the interest of their subjects, finally in the interest of humanity and civilization, only one course* was possible and that was bravely taken by Lord Dalhousie in the annexation of the kingdom. After the deposition of the king, he removed to Calcutta, where he was allowed a pension of £150,000 sterling a year, which was to be continued to his descendants.

The deposition of the king, as Captain Hayes' informed me, was not received with any great satisfaction by the inhabitants of the city, who had profited largely by the presence of the court, and into whose coffers had flowed much of the wealth extorted from the country-people. Even the ryuts did not find their position materially bettered at first, as the revenue-

* This course has been condemned as a violation of plighted faith. Without stopping to discuss the ethical question whether this was not one of the cases that constantly arise in politics, where a permanent engagement in writing may and ought to be set aside, from a total change in circumstances; it is here sufficient to state that by the treaty of 1837, the Company had a right to assume the *administration* of the country. This, it is plain, would amount practically to the course actually taken, and would be an equal infringement of the theoretical rights of the King.

The question whether the annexation of Oude was not a political blunder, is evidently quite distinct from the above. It may be contended that the great land-holders above described were too powerful a class for their resentment to be dared with impunity—that, however much they deserved punishment, it was unwise to attempt to inflict it. Such arguments may be used with great force, particularly since the rebellion in Oude. But whether the question be decided in one way or the other, the decision will not affect the justice or injustice of the act, and will not compromise the wisdom of the Company's policy, since, as is well known, the annexation of Oude was a measure entirely dictated by the English ministry, as almost all the aggressive acts of the Indian government have ever been.

administration had to be temporarily continued in the hands of the old native agents, who found their facilities for extortion increased by the restoration of the supremacy of law. The real benefits of the change would only be felt when the whole administration system had been altered and conformed to the admirable arrangements in force in the North-Western Provinces and the Punjab—measures which required time to introduce and perfect.

I noticed in Captain Hayes' house, that the ceilings were formed of canvass, painted in the Italian style. In Bengal the rooms are open to the roof. These canvass ceilings are common all over the North-Western Provinces, and were introduced by the Italian architects and artists, who were at one time attracted to these Indian courts, and whose influence is very often perceptible in the architecture of the buildings, and their decorations.

CHAPTER XVII.

LUCKNOW.—CONCLUDED.

A Morning Surprise—Salám—Native Polish—Hindoo Manners—Parade—Red Coat—Character of Sepoys—An Army of Priests and Kings—Caste misunderstood—Pariahs—India Conquered for the English, by Natives—Bullock Artillery—"Hathee pur Howdah" or Elephant Riding—Rich Dresses—Chokeedárs—Fukheers—A Coat of Paint—Royal Palace—Vanity—The Social Evil—A Modern Sodom—Defence of the Lucknow Residency—The Massacre of Cawnpoor.

After dinner I returned to the dâk-bungalow, and next morning again repaired by invitation to Captain Hayes', to accompany him to a review. As all parades take place before the heat of the sun becomes oppressive, I was obliged to get up very early, and after driving the two miles from the dâk-bungalow, arrived by five o'clock. I found the Captain not yet dressed. His house was shut up. On opening the door, I discovered ten or twelve servants asleep on the parlour floor, having chosen that resting place on account of the warmth of the house and the softness of the carpet. The noise I made in entering awoke them, and they all got up and salámed. The salám consists in opening the hands and placing them so that the little fingers touch, and both hands form one flat surface; then bowing and touching the hands to the earth and the forehead. This is the most respectful form and is employed by servants and inferiors. In it, the upper part of the body is bent as far as possible. There are less respectful varieties of the same salute, made by not bending the body so much, or lowering the joined hands so far. The lowest form of all is a simple inclination of the head, and touching the forehead three or four times with one hand. The salutation by salám was introduced by the Moosulmans, though it is now also practised by the Hindoos.

When used by one Mahommedan to another, the gesture described above is accompanied by the words "Salám Alékoom," to which the reply is, "Alékoom Salám." The Hindoo salutation, which is given only to a Hindoo, is Ram-Ram. Hindoos are, commonly, much less polite than Moosulmans. The former never salute any one whom they do not know—the latter salute all whom they have reason to believe superiors. The manly independence of Hindoo manners is, however, scarcely found in the north of India, where the Mahommedan influence has been very powerful. As a general rule, the manners of a native are cringing and slavish to his superiors—coarse and brutal to his inferiors. In addressing a superior, every deferential circumlocution is employed. The verb is never used in the second person, but always in the third, with the title "Sahib"—"lord;" "Gureeb Purwar"—"provider for the poor;" "Khodawund"—"representative of God;" "Huzoor"—"your worship;" "Sahib Bahadur"—"warrior Lord;" "Bahadur Shah"—"warrior king," or some such term used as the subject. On the other hand, the native speaks of himself as "bunda," "your slave," or by some title of humility. Mrs. Colin Mackenzie relates that one morning her husband was travelling by palkee, and saw some others behind on the road. He put his head out of the door and asked one of his bearers how many other palkees there were. The reply was, "There are two, three, or even four, if such be your Lordship's pleasure." Another story is told of one of the Lieutenant Governors of Agra, who took much interest in native schools. One day he was examining a remarkably clever protégé before some friends. After several other questions, he asked the boy, "what makes the earth go round the sun?" and was told, "the earth revolves by the favour of your Highness." The servants of Europeans, as is the universal custom of all natives, never wear their shoes in the house. When addressed by their master, they stand with the arms folded, and when speaking, join the hands in the attitude of prayer—a position well suited to the slavish style of their speech. When a native has a particular favour to ask, he kneels down on the ground, and puts his head under your feet. When they are flogged, they never think of resisting, but kneel down with their foreheads in the ground, and joining the hands above their heads shriek frightfully, crying to the Honourable Company to come to their aid, and now and then yelling out that they are dead.

The servility of the Moosulman manners, would be all very well if they implied any real respect—but when you know that they detest and despise you, that, if they dared, they would spit upon you for an infidel dog, and that they would feel themselves eternally disgraced by sitting down at your table—you cannot help feeling a hearty contempt for the miserable fawning, cringing, slavish cowards.

Soon after five o'clock Captain Hayes joined me, and we went together to the parade ground. We stood near the colours, and saw the troops march by. They were all Sepoys, but very fine-looking and tall men. Like all native regular regiments, they were officered by an equal number of Europeans and natives. The latter looked intensely proud of their red coats, showy accoutrements, and the strings of gold beads around their neck. The dress of the Sepoys, is nearly the same as that of English soldiers, and though not so pleasant or convenient as the native dress, is much preferred by them. The red coat takes the fancy of the natives, both on account of its colour and the *prestige* attached to it. It was adopted years ago in the armies of the independent native princes; and in the Punjab war the Seekhs were only distinguished from the Company's sepoys by wearing a turban instead of the military cap. Native soldiers march as well as possible, manœuvre admirably, and are better shots than Europeans. The only desiderata as regards drill, are a prominent chest, and physical strength. In all other respects they would be as fine soldiers as any in the world if they only had one thing—and that is manly courage.

Oude was the great recruiting ground of the Bengal army. Among its teeming population there is an unusually large proportion of Brahmuns, and Rajpoots, the latter the highest of the Soodra castes; and they had contrived almost to monopolize the army appointments. The pay of the army was so high, and the service so desirable in every way, that each soldier would induce his young relations to enlist, and at the same time would endeavour to prevent the enrolment of men of inferior caste. Though the Oude Brahmuns and Rajpoots, were the finest races in India, yet one quality alone of theirs would have totally unfitted them for a serviceable army. I mean their indomitable pride—which far exceeded that of the bluest-blooded Castilian noble. The hidalgo may trace back his descent for several hundred years of unspotted lineage, but the Rajpoot's genealogy ends only in the sun or the moon—the Spanish gentleman may fancy himself equal to any prince or nobleman, but the Rajpoot would not acknowledge his inferiority to a king, and would not even allow the equal rank of most monarchs. But if such is the Rajpoot's pride of birth, how much greater is that of the Brahmun. The former believes that he is the equal of any living man, the latter, that he is by far their superior. "You may say, if you please," they will observe, "that Brahmuns are men, like the rest of mankind—so it is true that cows and hogs are both animals, but you can never make a hog into a cow, nor pretend any equality between them. A wicked Brahmun is entitled to more reverence than the most virtuous Soodra—is not a vicious cow better than a well-behaved cat?" In speaking of this divine caste, the great law-giver Mĕnoo says, "Whatever exists in the universe is in effect, if not in form, the property of the Brahmuns—and so the Brahmun is entitled to everything by primogeniture and superiority of birth. The Brahmun who lives on another's charity is under no obligations; he eats but his own food, wears but his own apparel, and bestows but his own alms. It is, indeed, only by the benevolence of the Brahmuns that other mortals enjoy life." How could discipline be maintained in an army composed of men with such feelings; any one of whom would consider himself eternally disgraced by dining with you, my reader; and would almost prefer death to eating a meal prepared for him by the hands of his own general, whom he would consider as bearing the same relation of rank towards himself, that the unclean hog does to the pure and sacred cow.

This institution of caste is the most remarkable feature in

Hindoo society, and is, perhaps, scarcely at all understood by those who have not lived in India. Almost all the English books which I have read on the subject of India, seem to assume the actual existence of the original four castes, the Brahmun, Kshatrias, Vaishyas, and Soodras—whereas the two intermediate castes have wholly disappeared, and the Soodras, who comprise the mass of the population, have become broken up into innumerable subordinate castes, as entirely separate from one another as from the Brahmuns. Although the Brahmuns are properly priests, and the other castes are generally called by the name of some trade, so that they are, to some extent, guilds—yet a man of any caste is allowed to do anything which does not require him to touch substances or engage in occupations which are pollution, according to the rules of his particular caste. For instance, a Brahmun will be a coachman, a clerk, or an employé of government, and perhaps their most common occupations are cooking as domestic servants in the houses of natives, and begging. But no matter how menial is their occupation, howsoever poor and miserable they may be, whether squatted on the mud cooking, begging naked in the streets, or licking your feet for an extra bucksees, he always considers himself, and is looked upon by all Hindoos, as infinitely superior in rank to the mightiest monarch in Christendom. So also, any Hindoo will be a domestic servant—but he will not cook beef or take care of fowls; he will make his master's bed and mend his clothes, but he will not sweep the room or empty the dirty water, unless he be of a low caste. The higher the caste, generally, the fewer the occupations that the subject can engage in, and the more limited the number of articles he can eat. There are some castes so low that scarcely anything is a pollution to them, and they even eat the putrid meat of animals which have died a natural death. Still they are very punctilious on the few points which mark their caste.

Lowest and most degraded of all are the Out-castes, who, in Southern India, form a large part of the population. An English missionary describing the condition of this class, and comparing them with negro slaves, says: "The slave may tread the same floor with his master, without polluting the house, he may enter the room where he sits, touch the meat he uses, sleep under the same roof, and prepare the food he eats. He is not made to feel that his step defiles the room, that his touch infects the purest wares, and that he carries in his body, no matter how clean, a cursed incurable filthiness which fills with disgust all who have proper human sentiments. Above all he may possibly die free, or his children may become manumitted. But the Out-caste has no such hopes. He must bear his curse down to the grave, and bequeath it to his children, who like him will be compelled to live beyond the village walls, will be hunted from every door, scorned by the most base, loathed by the most vile, and know that the same malediction awaits his little ones." The condition of these Out-castes, who number some twenty millions, is only one of the curses of the caste system. No such insuperable barrier has ever been reared elsewhere between the members of the human race. It is an institution which destroys all brotherhood between man and man, and is therefore one of the deadliest opponents of the Christian religion—do not all Christians eat of one bread and drink of one cup? but the very essence and test of caste is eating and drinking. A man of one caste would not take a cup of water from one of another caste, though they had been life-long companions; nor would he touch to his lips the pipe used by the other. Caste, then, looses the bonds which binds society together, it prevents intimacy between man and man, destroys friendship, and supplants patriotism. The Hindoo has no attachment to his rulers, no care for a particular form of government, no sentiment of nationality, no love for freedom:—for these sentiments which exist in greater or less extent in every other nation of men, and have existed in all ages, are in the Hindoo centred and bounded by the limits of his caste.

It was by taking advantage of these differences in caste, and the indifference to nationality induced thereby, that the English obtained their power in India. A native will be a mercenary soldier to whoever pays best, and will fight his own neighbours as willingly as men of another nation. India was conquered for the English by the natives themselves, and it was only when the precaution of arraying caste against caste, and nation against nation was neglected, that the allegiance of the native soldiers was destroyed, and the magic chain was loosened by which India had been conquered and held.

The parade at Lucknow went off very well. After the troops had marched past the colours, the artillery were exercised. The guns were drawn by bullocks, and I was surprised to see how well these animals worked. The driver of each pair ran between his animals, and guided them with a short goad. On account of the great difficulty of obtaining good horses in India, elephants, camels, and bullocks, have all been employed with artillery. The experiments with the two former have now been abandoned, as they are not naturally adapted to draft labour; but the bullock batteries although they do not give entire satisfaction, are still in use.

The parade lasted for several hours, and I was glad when we returned to breakfast, as not having eaten anything, I found the sun's rays very oppressive. Breakfast was finished by eleven, and Captain Hayes informed me that his duties would prevent his going through the city with me, but that he had obtained an elephant from the Residence for my use, and would send with me one of his servants to show every thing.

The elephant was a very large beast, with tusks, and caparisoned with crimson. At the word *baith*, he knelt upon the ground and I mounted by a ladder into the howdah—a box with seats for two in front and one behind. When I was seated, my host warned me to hold on tight, and then told them to let the elephant rise, which he did at the word *ootha*. It was well I minded the warning to hold on tight, for I never experienced anything like the heaving of the ponderous carcase as it rose into the air—a small steamer at sea in a gale is nothing to it—I should think that people who ride elephants would not mind earthquakes.

The elephant walked at about three miles the hour. As he belonged to the Chief Commissioner, not only were his appointments splendid, but he was accompanied by half a dozen servants, beside the mahoot who sat a-straddle on his neck, and directed his movements, enforcing his commands by pricks with a sharp iron hook. One man walked beside the elephant's head and talked to him constantly, recommending him to take care of stones, holes in the road, &c. In the seat of the howdah behind me sat the servant whom Captain Hayes had sent in my company. He held over my head a gigantic scarlet *chattah* or umbrella. I did not particularly like elephant-riding, the paces are not comfortable until you are used to them. You are thrown first to the right and then to the left—occasionally the motion is backward and forward—but you cannot keep still for an instant, and I found my sides sore for several days afterwards, from violent contact with the howdah. Altogether it reminded me uncomfortably of riding on a slow trotting horse—you cannot help imagining that if he would go faster he would be easier, and yet if you succeed in increasing the pace, your sufferings are probably aggravated.

Wherever I went, the elephant and retinue attracted the greatest attention and respect. Horsemen faced round and saluted, some of them even dismounting and making saláms. The sentries all presented arms, and at one or two points they even turned out the guards. All that I could do was to make a military salute in acknowledgement, try to look as dignified as possible, and convey the impression that it was all my due, and something to which I was quite accustomed.

The streets were full of people, as it was a great Hindoo festival, and presented a most interesting sight- The dress in Lucknow is much more picturesque, and gave the impression of more wealth, or, at least, more luxury than the costumes which I had seen further down the country. Many of the men had shawls, some of them very beautiful and costly, worn as kummurbunds (sashes), or pugrees (turbans), or else thrown loosely over the shoulders. The great mass of the people, however, as elsewhere, wore little clothing, and that of the coarsest yellow cotton.

We met numbers of the chokeedárs, or native police, who

are so obnoxious to the people, and whose extortions, and abuse of power, are so difficult to control. They were dressed in the native fashion, wearing a blue cloth cassock with tight trowsers, and were armed with shields and spears. These weapons were necessary, as a very large proportion of the people in the streets carried swords, and sometimes shields also.

I noticed among the crowds a good many fukheers, or religious mendicants, who answer to the durweeshes of Persia. They generally wear little clothing, and are daubed over with white streaks or mud. One of them was entirely naked, his hair dressed with feathers, and covered from head to foot with a yellow powder. I thought he must be cool in this costume, but learned afterwards that it was a common dodge with the fukheers to rub this powder into the skin, as it occasions a slight cuticular irritation, and thus yields an artificial warmth.

Crossing the bridge again, and keeping down on the other side through a street parallel with the river, we arrived in a short time at a large gateway leading to the Furad Buksh, the palace occupied by the late king. It consists of a succession of courts, connected by gateways, and each surrounded by rows of two-storied buildings, in a plain, Saracenic style. The palace extends to the river, on the banks of which are three larger and more lofty buildings, surmounted by gilt domes. The courts behind these buildings were of considerable size, and laid out in the Italian style of gardening, with fish ponds, and marble copies of antique Grecian statues. The whole establishment covers many acres of ground. We passed through the stables, the courts for servants, those of the zĕnana, and many others, the former use of which I did not ascertain, and at length arrived in the garden court fronting that portion of the palace, used by the king for the reception of visitors. This building is four or five stories high. The lower story consists principally of a large room, open toward the court, and surrounded by several smaller apartments, used as breakfast-rooms, or for similar purposes—all furnished in English style. A billiard room, with an old table, occupied the side toward the Goomtee. I found three or four young officers quartered here and in the adjacent apartments. One of them had taken the billiard table for a bedstead, and a terrier dog was quietly sleeping on a tall gilt throne of Oriental shape.

We ascended to the roof, which, though not very high, commands a good view of the city. The houses are generally very low. I was surprised at the great space of ground covered by the Furad Buksh, and at the extraordinary number of palaces in sight. The king alone had five palaces at Lucknow, besides sumptuous country seats in the vicinity; and the great men of the court owned magnificent residences, many of which rival the Furad Buksh in size. Like the royal palaces, these edifices were closed and inaccessible to visitors, their owners having withdrawn to the country after the dethronement of the king, and dissolution of the court in the previous February.

None of the rooms which I saw in the palace were large, but they must have been handsome when the frescoes and gilding were fresh. At best, however, they never could have been so elegant as the rooms of very many private houses in New York—the decoration was often tawdry and in bad taste, and always perishable, as nothing but stone retains any freshness in the Indian climate. The weather, hot and rainy one-third of the year, and hot without rain for most of the remainder, makes all stuccoed buildings look shabby in a short time; and when it is remembered that such is the material of nearly all edifices in Lucknow, and that no repairs are made to them, it is easy to understand why it has been necessary for the kings to build one palace after another. Another reason for building so many palaces was the desire of each monarch to signalize his reign by constructing for himself a residence more splendid than those of his predecessors. This foolish wish each successive king carried out with that recklessness which is so characteristic of Oriental sovereigns in the gratification of every whim.

Mounting the elephant, and passing again through the deserted courts of the palace, I left the Furad Buksh, and passed through the bazár and chôk. The streets were again crowded with people, and were so narrow that the foot passengers often found it difficult to get out of the elephant's way. As I sat in the howdah, I was on a level with the upper story of the houses, and could look in upon the apartments. In the principal bazár these were mostly tenanted by young girls, dressed in fine sarees of green or red muslins, decorated with gold nose-rings and jewellery, their eyes darkened with kohl (antimony), and their hands tinged red with heena. These ladies are called in Hindoostanee *khusbees*, or more politely, *lallbeebees* (red-ladies). Not to be less polite than the natives themselves to those who are in India, as they were in Greece, the only well-educated class of women, we will call them bayadères, though it is a word which I never heard in India. The bayadères then sat at the windows, smoking their naichas, displaying their finest clothes and jewellery, and sometimes making remarks to me in Hindoostanee or English.

> "Ite quibus grata est picta lupa barbara mitra."

Sometimes might be seen beings still more repulsive—*men* with their pale faces, long, oily locks, decorated like their female correlatives, and gazing out of the windows with spiritless leering eyes:

> "Hispo subit juvenes et morbo pallet utroque.
> Talia secreta coluerunt orgia tæda
> Cecropiam soliti Baptæ lassare Cotytto.
> Ille supercilium madida fuligine tactum
> Obliqua producit acu pingitque trementes
> Attollens oculos; vitreo bibit ille Priapo
> Reticulumque comis auratum ingentibus implet,
> Cærulea indutus scutulata aut galbina rasa."

The city of Lucknow is spread over a large space of ground, but the best streets are all near the palace and Imambara, so that it did not take me long to see them all, particularly as I was on an elephant: in fact, there was such a crowd that, in any other conveyance, progress would have been almost impossible. Once or twice we met with other elephants, and then as the streets were too narrow for the elephants to pass or turn round, the other always had to retreat backward before ours, till he came to a cross-street.

After taking another view of the Imambara and Room-ee-Durwázu, we again passed the bridge to return to the bungalow. As we reached the opposite shore of the river, I turned round and took my last view of Lucknow. It seemed to me even more beautiful by the slanting rays of the evening sun than when I had seen it before, shining as if made of silver in the full blaze of an Indian noon. That evening I read Bayard Taylor's description of Lucknow, and the expressions of his feeling on seeing for the last time that magnificent home of vice and crime, represented my own feelings so well that I cannot forbear quoting the words: "The sun is setting, and the noises of the great city are subdued for a moment. The deep-green gardens lie in shadow, but all around us, far and near, the gilded domes are blazing in the yellow glow. The scene is lovely as the outer gate of Paradise, yet what deception, what crime, what unutterable moral degradation fester beneath its surface!"

In truth, every native capital in India is a nursery of the darkest crimes, a hot bed of the most disgusting forms of licentiousness ever invented by the depraved passions of man. Should the doom of Sodom descend upon these cities, no one who knows what they are would dispute the terrible justice of the punishment.

I again dined at Captain Hayes', who gave me much advice during the evening as to my further progress, and furnished me with letters to his friends in the stations whither I was going. Late in the evening I bade adieu, with regret, to my kind entertainer and his wife, for whom I had formed sentiments of sincere respect and esteem.

The subsequent fate of Captain Hayes was sad. He took command of a regiment of irregular cavalry, a service for which he was eminently adapted by his intimate acquaintance with the natives and their language; and fell, among the first victims of the mutiny, treacherously shot from behind, by one of his trusted followers.

The same evening I left the city of Lucknow, which was subsequently the scene of so much noble endurance, and such heroic gallantry. The siege of the Residency is, I believe, unparallelled in the world's history. The residency is a large, three storied house, of not more than average strength, and entirely unsuited for defence; and yet here a little band of noble hearts held out for month after month of sickening suspense, with unexampled courage, unflinching endurance of privation, and a never-failing trust in their countrymen, against countless hordes of well-armed, well-provisioned, and ferocious enemies. They were fighting to save their wives from barbarous indignities, worse than a thousand deaths; themselves and their children from the hellish tortures of the heathen, whose tender mercies are cruel; and the English name from disgrace and degradation. Their struggle was watched with breathless interest by the civilized world; their success and safety were hailed with universal applause—an applause shared by their heroic rescuers.

I arrived at Cawnpoor again on the morning of November 13, and, having breakfasted, left in gárrhee for Futtehghur. At breakfast I met some officers who offered to show me splendid sport if I could give a week to it. They were going with camels and tents to have some deer and antelope shooting; but I felt that I must push on as fast as was compatible with seeing the most remarkable objects, and was obliged to refuse myself the pleasure.

Six months after I left Cawnpoor, its troops revolted, and its European inhabitants fell a prey to the treachery and barbarous cruelty of Nana Sahib—a wretch, who, it is to be hoped, will soon meet with the just reward of his horrible crimes, and die amid the curses of the world; a monster whose name will always be mentioned with loathing, and heard with horror. To all his other vices he added cowardice. Miserably inefficient as were the hasty defences which the feeble band of Europeans had reared against the mutinous thousands, they were strong enough to hold those overpowering odds in check, and the leader of the rebels was obliged to resort to the basest perfidy, and perjure himself by the most sacred oath of his religion, to obtain that surrender, which he and his followers dared not force. Black treachery was followed by pitiless slaughter, and the blood of the innocent called on Heaven for vengeance. Nor was Heaven indifferent to the cry. Though every circumstance seemed to promise the mutineers immunity for their crimes, a stern and speedy avenger was found in the "Puritan" soldier, Havelock, and his army of "Saints." "Though only a few thousand in number, far away from all succour, and in the ends of the earth, they marched unfalteringly amid millions of disaffected people, and armies of trained mutineers, over thousands of miles, in the worst season of the year, besieging and overthrowing great cities, meeting intrepidly all sorts of surprises, against incredible odds of numbers, and defeating day after day, vast hordes of well-armed and desperate men. They did this while the air sighed with the dying sobs of English women and children perishing under horrors which *no pen has dared fully to tell.* Wrung to the heart with these sorrows, but cool and determined, they marched to avenge themselves and the human race against the demonism which had broken out around them."* Honour, then, to the brave soldier, whose life-blood was shed in doing his duty; pity and tears for the fearful fate of the helpless women and innocent children; but indignation and contempt for those who wrought this shame; the gallows and the cannon are a fit punishment for the coward and the traitor.

* New York *Christian Advocate and Journal.*

CHAPTER XVIII.

TO MEERUTH.

Appearance of Country—Bishop Heber—Christian Missions—Colonel Tucker—Country between Futtehghur and Meeruth—Ganges Canal—An Indian "Station"—Sirdhána Dyce Sombre's Tomb—Free Lances of India—An Ingenious Process for Collecting Money—A Female General—Success of the Bégoom—To Moozuffurnuggur—Dhoolee Travelling—Persian Inscription—Natural History.

After leaving Cawnpoor, the appearance of the country improved much. The population seemed thicker, the cultivation better, and the tôps more numerous. A tôp is a grove regularly planted, generally near a village, and used as a resting-place for caravans. The land on each side of the road was, in many places, overgrown with jungul-grass, a tall, thick sort of grass, which rises to the height of ten feet or more sometimes. Palm trees again became abundant, but I saw scarcely any banyan trees up-country.

I used to amuse myself in the gárrhee by studying Hindoostanee, and reading Bishop Heber's travels, which is the only guide-book for India, beside being extremely well written and interesting. His character must have been really lovely. He certainly made all with whom he was brought in contact, love him. It was related to me as a most remarkable proof of the great respect and affection entertained for him by all classes of both Europeans and natives, that at his death, commemorative religious services were held, not only in the churches of all the numerous Christian sects represented in Calcutta, but also in the mosques and temples of that city.

The Bishop's darling hope was the conversion of India, and he used to think that he saw hopeful signs. It would not appear, however, that the work is going on much more rapidly than in his time. The converts are few, and mostly of the most degraded classes. The pride of caste forms an almost insurmountable barrier to the reception of the Gospel; and ages of abject superstition seem to have eradicated all noble and manly qualities from the Hindoo character.

People in this country cannot appreciate the extreme improbability, I might almost say impossibility of the conversion of a high-caste Hindoo. Humanly speaking, it would be almost as reasonable to expect the archbishop of Canterbury to sacrifice a goat to Párbutee. As for arguing with a Hindoo of intelligence, it is like using cannon against Hindoo earth-works. He will grant every argument of the Christian, will admire his religion, admit his miracles, and acknowledge the truth of the Incarnation. At the same time he will contend that he has an older and a better system, miracles much more astounding, and numberless awatars, instead of one only. He is the most tolerant man in the world; will allow every religion to be true, and as his own system will not admit of converts, he recommends every man to adhere to his particular creed, and permit him to do the same.

I arrived at Futtehghur on the morning of November 14, and at once presented my letter from Captain Hayes to Colonel Tucker. He received me very kindly, and presented me to the ladies of his family, an honour for which I was not at all prepared, dressed as I was from head to foot in white flannel. I had come to Futtehghur with the intention of proceeding thence to Nynee Thal, one of the most beautiful stations on the Himalayas. I found, however, from the Colonel, that the journey would be exposing, and the trip would take considerable time. I therefore determined, by his advice, to alter my plans and proceed instead to Munsooree, also a hill-station, but much more accessible and affording an equally fine view of the snowy range. I dined in the afternoon with the Colonel, and started in the evening by gárrhee for Meeruth. Colonel Tucker was afterwards shot through the head, while defending, in company with a few other gentlemen, a place of refuge to which they had betaken themselves with the ladies. I believe they were all massacred.

The Lieutenant Governor of the North Western Provinces was encamped under a tôp near the dâk-bungalow at Futtehghur. His camp was quite picturesque, comprising numerous tents, regularly laid out, a dozen or two of camels, half a dozen elephants, several companies of sepoys, and camp followers enough for a European army.

The country between Futtehghur and Meeruth was the best cultivated that I had seen since leaving Raneegunj. I saw for the first time several plantations of castor-oil plant. Tôps were numerous, long strings of camels constantly went by, elephants were often seen, and we passed many drays conveying bales of cotton down-country. But notwithstanding these pleasant features in the day's ride, the greater part of the country through which the road lay, was the same flat barren waste which had been wearying my eyes ever since I began my trip—a very disappointing substitute for the luxuriant foliage and picturesque scenery which I had expected to meet in India. The villages through which I passed were just as miserable as those lower down the country. They consisted of the same collections of wretched, ill-built mud huts, and displayed the same want of order, energy, and economy. Though the weather was now cold, the inhabitants were very insufficiently clad. Many of them were nearly naked, and the children entirely so, if I except a bit of string round the waist, which, as some one told me, "illustrates the intention."

As the great plain of India has no decided natural features, the absence of cultivation near the road takes away its only claim to beauty. Still, it might be tolerable, if the long level prairies were only covered with vegetation; but I did not see a square foot of turf in India from the time I left Calcutta, except in gentlemen's compounds, and most of the uncultivated land is almost as unproductive as the Arabian desert. This defect is owing to the want of water, a difficulty under which most of this country used to labour greatly; widespread droughts, causing famine over large extents of country, and the death of many thousands, being of frequent occurrence. The Ganges canal, however, from near the source of that river to Cawnpoor, has done much to remedy the difficulty, and free the husbandman from all dread of losing his crop by drought. Its length is 450 miles, or, including its branches, 900 miles. Its breadth is eighty feet and its average depth eight feet. It is bordered by rows of trees and broad tow-paths, is everywhere finished with the greatest care, and has locks and bridges of massive masonry, beside ghâts at short distances for the convenience of bathers. It is probably the most extensive and perfect work of irrigation and transportation ever constructed, secures the fertility of nearly five millions of acres, and is one of the greatest benefits conferred upon India by the British rule.

I arrived at Meeruth on the morning of the sixteenth, and took up my quarters in a hotel, which, like those at Sĕroor and Cawnpoor, was merely a large bungalow, and had accommodations for only a very few guests.

I was busy all the morning writing and making arrangements for laying a dâk to Rajpoor, a place at the foot of the Himalayas. "Laying a dâk" is a technical term, and means simply bargaining with a chowdri (maître de poste) to have relays of bearers in readiness along the road for your conveyance to any point. In the afternoon I hired a buggy from the master of the hotel, and drove to a village called Sirdhana, above ten miles from Meeruth. I had to drive some distance before passing the limits of the station, which was one of the largest in the North-west, and consisted, like all others, of rows of low-walled, high-roofed bungalows in desolate compounds. Meeruth being a large station had two churches, each a tolerably exact copy of every other in India, and remarkably similar in form to a New England meeting-house. The only difference between stations is their size—in all other respects they are precisely similar. There are always the same broad, macadamized roads, crossing each other at right angles, and bordered by rows of puny trees; on each side of the road there are the same low stone walls, enclosing extensive compounds, which sometimes contain trees, sometimes are entirely uncared for; in the midst of each compound rises a bungalow, an exact model of any other within a thousand miles, looking like a hay-stack with its high, thatched roof.

In each compound is a row of low mud huts, built against the wall, where the servants live, and where all the cooking is done.

After passing the limits of the station, the road became very bad, and I was forced to walk the horse for fear of breaking the springs of the buggy. The last two miles of the way were along the tow-path of the Ganges canal. It is quite broad enough for two buggies to pass, and being perfectly level makes a very good road, so that I was enabled to increase the pace, and thus arrived at Sirdhána in time to see the monument in the church before sunset, which I should not have been able to do had all the road been as bad as the preceding five or six miles.

The church at Sirdhána is a large edifice of pukka, or stuccoed brickwork. It is in the Italian style, cruciform, and surmounted by a dome. It was built by the Bégoom Sombre, a native princess who became converted to the Romish faith. A large convent and school are connected with it.

The interior of the church is in no way remarkable, the only point of interest being the tomb of Dyce Sombre, the old Bégoom's great grandson and heir, who is buried in a chapel on the right of the altar. The tomb is of marble, and is decorated by an allegorical group of five life-sized figures, which is as incomprehensible as most allegories. There are also statues, as large as life, of the Bégoom and Dyce Sombre, which are said to be excellent likenesses. This tomb was executed in Italy, and cost altogether three lakhs of rupees ($150,000).

The Bégoom Sombre was a most remarkable woman. By birth a lineal descendant of the Prophet Mahommed, she married early in life a German adventurer named Reinhard, who had received the appellation "Sombre" from the melancholy cast of his countenance. Sombre commanded a regiment of free soldiery whom he hired out to whichever of the native princes would pay best. It is said that he always took care to be on the winning side, and if he found the battle going against his friends, he and his troops deserted *en masse* to the enemy.

In the stormy times which intervened between the decay

of the Mogul power, and the restoration of order by the English, such bands of adventurers, especially when commanded by Europeans, were eagerly hired by the petty native princes who sprang up on all sides, as they were of the greatest assistance in giving security to their power, and moreover could always be made useful in the constant wars which prevailed.

By hiring out his forces to one prince after another, and the *prudent* method of fighting described above, Sombre finally accumulated much property and attained considerable power. His troops, by an ingenious process, managed to obtain a share of the former. Whenever they entertained suspicion that he had accumulated considerable wealth, they put him in confinement until he confessed his hiding-place. When he was more than usually obdurate he was tied to a cannon, at the further end of which a fire was lit. In that position he was kept until the increasing heat compelled him to come to an arrangement.

Sombre died in 1778; seven years previously, his wife, the Bégoom, had been baptized by a Romish priest.

On her husband's death, the Bégoom took the command of his troops, which were now a very large, powerful, but disorganized and ill-disciplined body. She was formally commissioned by the puppet-Emperor Shah Alum, and intrusted the immediate command to a German called Pauly. He attempted to have a creature of his own appointed minister by the Emperor, when he would have obtained the exercise of whatever power now remained in the Grand Mogul's hands. The plot failed, and Pauly was assassinated. The troops now became very disorderly, and resorted to their old practices to obtain money. The Bégoom was a woman of great courage and energy, and determined to be obeyed. An opportunity occurred for asserting her power. Two of her slave girls set fire to some houses containing her valuables, which were then plundered by their soldier paramours. The offenders then eloped, but were captured and brought before the Bégoom. After a brief trial, she had them flogged nearly to death, and then buried alive within her tent. The severity of this punishment struck terror into the troops, and occasioned the greatest respect for the old lady.

After Pauly's death, the troops had various commanders. One of these was a man called George Thomas, who had been quarter-master of a ship, but, possessing great military talent, finally raised himself to a principality in Northern India. He was supplanted in the Bégoom's affections, and the command of her army, by a Frenchman named Le Vassoult. After losing his command he formed an army of his own, and made extensive conquests in the Seekh country. Indeed he would probably have deposed Runjeet Sing, and obtained his power, had it not been for the jealousy of certain French officers in the Maharatta service, whose troops, united to those of the Seekhs, were sufficiently strong to crush him.

The Bégoom now established her capital at Sirdhána, where she kept the larger part of her troops; the rest were at Delhi. The new commander, Le Vassoult, does not seem to have possessed the requisite qualities for his post. The troops broke out into open mutiny. He and the Bégoom took to flight; the soldiers pursued. When it became evident than they would be overtaken, they resolved to die. The Bégoom stabbed herself as she lay in her palkee. Le Vassoult seeing her clothing stained with blood, blew out his own brains with a pistol. The Bégoom's wound proved trivial, whether by intention or accident. Her soldiers kept her chained under a gun-carriage for a week, at the end of which time they released her, and acknowledged her authority. The troops now amounted to six battalions. They served under the Maharattas, and were present at the battle of Assai. After that event, the Bégoom, seeing which way fortune was turning, sought the alliance of the English. Beside the original six battalions, she had now a battery of European artillery, and a troop of cavalry. She built at Sirdhána, a gun-foundry, arsenal, and fort. The whole expenses of her establishment were six lakhs a-year, which the revenues of her territory barely sufficed to meet. The latter were, however, considerably increased under the protection of the Company's government. She built the church and convent at Meeruth, and had palaces in several cities of India. In her will she left a million of rupees for various charitable purposes—so that if her property was not very honestly obtained, at least part of it was well employed. She had only one son, who was a person of infirm intellect. His daughter married a Mr. Dyce, whose son became the heir to the Bégoom's fortune of sixty lakhs ($3,000,000), and took the name of Dyce Sombre. He was a miserable debauchee, went to England, married a nobleman's daughter, treated her shockingly, and finally died, a few years since, from burning his foot while sitting drunk in a chair before the fire in a London hotel. His constitution, shattered by a life of every excess, could not recover from the trivial injury. After his death his property became the subject of a long suit in Chancery. His tomb in the church at Sirdhána, I have described above.

After seeing Sirdhâna I returned to Meeruth. On the way I passed a camel harnessed to a dog-cart; it trotted along at a very good pace, although the camel is not well adapted to draught labour.

The native towns of Meeruth and Futtehghur are both considerable places, but I saw nothing of either. In fact a man might travel all over India by dâk, without seeing a single city, as the dâk-bungalows are always some distance from the city or village to which they belong, and when there are cantonments, they always contain all the hotels, bungalows, dâk-offices, &c., and are invariably several miles from the city, for obvious sanitary and other reasons.

I left Meeruth early in the morning of November 17th, by gárrhee for Moozuffurnuggur; arriving there at noon, and leaving again at four in the afternoon, by dhoolee.

On leaving Meeruth, I witnessed a parade of troops, and passed by their camp, which presented quite a picturesque scene, with the large numbers of camels and elephants, the bazár, &c.

The dhoolees, by which I continued my journey from Moozuffurnuggur to Rajpoor, are a rough sort of palkee. To make a dhoolee, take a bedstead, six feet by three; cut off the legs to six inches long, and the bed-posts to three feet or so, and cover the whole with *mamzama*, or waxed canvass.

Finally, pass a bamboo pole immediately under the roof, so that it shall project four feet fore and aft. A palkee is the same in principle, but made of wood and heavier. I had eight bearers, who relieved one another several times in a quarter of a mile—four carrying the dhoolee at once, the bamboo pole resting on their shoulders. One of the disengaged bearers carried a torch at night. Had I been in a palkee I should have had two torch-bearers to do nothing else. The stages were about ten miles long, and the work cannot be very fatiguing, as in one instance, when the fresh bearers had not arrived at the Chokee, the old bearers took me on with undiminished speed. The great annoyance in this kind of travelling is the moaning and grunting of the kuhars (bearers), sometimes dignified as their *song;* and a custom they have of waking you up at night for their bucksees, which is four anas, or twelve cents, for the ten men. This gives each man a little over a cent, which is considered a liberal gratuity. After all, this annoyance is not greater than that of being constantly waked up to pay tolls, when travelling by gárrhee. The worst trouble of all was the dust, which was almost insufferable. It lay five inches deep on the road, and the four extra bearers and banghee-burdar kept kicking it up. My sufferings were aggravated by being in a dhoolee, which hangs within eighteen inches of the ground. A palkee, being differently swung, is nearly a foot higher.

To give an idea of caste prejudice, I may mention here that in some parts of India, the same men that carry a palkee, will not carry a dhoolee; while in no part of the country will either of them carry a burden on the head or back. On the other hand, coolees can only, or will only, carry a burden on the head. The Puharrees, or inhabitants of the Himalayas, carry burdens on the back, shoulder, or head indifferently. My luggage was all contained in two small portmanteaus, which were slung one at each end of a bamboo pole and carried by a man called the banghee-burdar.

After leaving Meeruth, I noticed that the inscriptions on the milestones were in the Persian character. In Bengal they are in the Bengalee, and further up country in Hindee—both of which languages use the old Sanscrit character. In the North-west, however, where the Mahommedan population is very large, Persian is very commonly spoken, and its character is more generally understood than any other.

I was much struck with the beauty of the birds in India. There are many varieties, the more common kinds being the parrot and dove; but birds of the most remarkable shapes, with high crests, lyre-tails, and other peculiarities, that I have elsewhere met with only in ornithological collections, are constantly seen; others again have plumage the colour of every precious stone, and nearly as brilliant in the bright sunlight. The glare of the sun in India is something wonderful. It really seemed as if the ground and everything around me were a mirror. Although it was now winter, freezing every night, and quite cold enough during the day to make a flannel suit comfortable, yet a turban around the hat and an umbrella were indispensable accessories to a walking costume.

A remarkable characteristic of the birds in India is their tameness. The little birds fly into the house without the least suspicion of intruding, and the crows, of which there are immense numbers, will do the same thing, particularly during meal-time. They may often be seen riding about on the backs or horns of buffaloes, bullocks or goats. In fact, the utmost harmony seems to prevail between the different orders of the brute creation, and they have apparently no fear of man. Monkeys, foxes, jackals, deer and vultures will all watch with interest the traveller who passes within a few rods, but do not show any alarm. The reason, I suppose is, that so very few of the inhabitants ever hunt.

CHAPTER XIX.

THE HIMALAYAS.

A Night in a Dhoolee—The Turai Forest—First View of the Snowy Range—Siwalik Hills—Ram! Ram!—The Dhoon Valley—Rajpoor—Ascent of the Himalayas—Puharrees—Mu*n*sooree—Indian Hospitality—Landoor—View of Snow-clad Peaks—Hill-stations—An Accident—The Descent—Agriculture in India—Tea Plantation—Chinese Workmen—A Snake Fight.

MY first night in a dhoolee was rather uncomfortable. The road lay through the Turai forest, a belt of woodland running parallel to the Himalayas. This forest has a particularly bad reputation for jungul fever—an intermittent in its worst form, with a tendency to typhoid. In the hot season it is dangerous to pass through it even by day; the cold weather, while it diminishes the danger, does not make it entirely safe, especially for night travelling. Beside the fever, the Turai is full of elephants and tigers; and though I cannot say that I was at all afraid of them, as I knew wild animals to have more fear of man than he has of them, yet the fever and the tigers, added to the great and positive discomforts of my conveyance, made the night's sleep rather broken.

When I awoke the next morning, we had almost passed the limits of the forest. The trees do not grow very thickly, but are of large size—some of them entirely covered with creepers, and others bearing beautiful flowers. There were also several banyans, the first which I had seen since leaving Bengal. The ground between the trees was covered with tall jungul grass.

I did not have the good fortune to see any of the elephants, tigers or leopards, which are said to abound—but there were plenty of monkeys in the trees. The leopards (cheetas), are frequently tamed, or rather trained, and used instead of hounds in deer-hunting; which is said to make the sport more exciting.

After passing the forest, we arrived, about ten o'clock, in a valley from which I had my first view of the Himalayas—a range of mountain monarchs, sitting in state, looking over the broad plains of Hindoostan; covered, as to their heads, with turbans of clouds, as becomes sovereigns of the Orient. One snowy face alone, of a *Jungfrau* of the East, was visible, and she, as an Eastern maiden should, soon shrouded her countenance and was seen of me no more.

Crossing the valley, we had to pass the Siwalik hills, a low range, before entering the valley of the Dhoon, which divides them from the Himalayas. The pass through the hills was certainly not grand, but picturesque to one who had seen so little mountain scenery for a year; and had been travelling for a thousand miles over a succession of desert plains, as level as a bowling alley. The pass was about three hundred feet wide, its bottom was the rocky bed of a mountain torrent which had now almost disappeared; its sides were steep, from one to three hundred feet high, looking like the sections of hills in geological works.

All the natives whom we met on the road, gave the bearers the Hindoo salutation, Ram! Ram!—which I had not heard before, probably on account of having always travelled in a gárrhee. This Hindoo salutation is only used to a Hindoo. To a Moosulman, or a Christian, the Hindoo uses the Moosulman salám—an obeisance which is, I suspect, very much what the Greeks meant by προςκυνεῖν. All the polite forms of speech by which a superior is addressed, as "Ap"—"your Honour;" "Bundugee"—"releaser of slaves;" and "Gurreeb-Parwar"—"provider for the poor," were introduced by the servile Mahommedans, but are now universally employed in Northern India. The latter title is the usual one in the north-western provinces, and it is with respect to it that Bishop Heber made the mistake of supposing that he had earned it by his attention to the wants of his dependents.

After passing the Siwalik hills, we entered the valley of the Dhoon, about twenty miles broad, beyond which rose the

Himalayas. Being well watered, and protected by the two ranges of hills, it is very fertile, and I saw palm-trees and plantains in abundance. About half-way across the valley we changed bearers at the village of Dehra, which was the best looking place of its size that I had seen in India. The houses, though low and small, were constructed of pukka, instead of mud. They were generally whitewashed, and some of them decorated with gaudy pictures of nach-girls, or mythological designs. It was high market when we passed through the bazár, and as I noticed most of the people munching sugar-cane, I determined to do so likewise, having eaten nothing for over twenty hours, and found it very cool and refreshing.

About four in the afternoon I arrived at Rajpoor, a small village immediately at the foot of "the Hills," as the Himalayas are always called in Northern India. The hotel being very comfortable, I put up there for the night, as I was very tired, hungry and dusty.

Rajpoor is over three thousand feet above the level of the sea, and the summit of the first range about six thousand.

The next morning I ascended this on horseback. The mountains rise almost perpendicularly from the plain, and although the path is constructed with much engineering skill, I found the ascent so steep, from the very commencement, that I dismounted and walked most of the way, fearing that my weight was too great for the little pony I had hired.

The sides of the hill were covered with low trees. The road wound around the vast, narrow gullies which are the distinguishing feature of Himalayan scenery. They make a sharp, deep cut into the mountain range, and are apparently so narrow that you almost fancy you could throw a stone across. Should you be so deceived by the vastness of everything around as to make the attempt, your missile, if propelled by a vigourous arm, will lodge, a thousand feet below, on the precipitous side of the chasm.

On the way up we passed many Puharrees, or hill men, carrying burdens slung on the back. They are a small, light, but strong and agile race. Their dress is a shirt and trowsers of coarse brown woollen stuff, girt with a rope, and they wear woollen caps instead of pugrees. They are not so cleanly as the inhabitants of the plains—indeed, they are suspected of never taking off their clothes until no longer serviceable. Their religion is a very low form of idolatry, and they have no caste. They make excellent servants, as they will do any kind of work, and are considered thoroughly honest. I noticed by the side of the path several bushes decorated with rags, to show that they are esteemed sacred on account of some god's having, when wearied, sat down under a bush of the same kind. There was also a black stone which the hill-people stopped to worship, each "leaning on the top of his staff" like Jacob.

Mu*n*sooree is on the crest of a spur which puts out from the main ridge, and is a little lower and more sheltered than Landoor, which is on the very summit. They are both places of several miles in extent, and consist of one-storied bungalows scattered about on the steep side of the mountain.

On arriving at Mu*n*sooree I found, to my dismay, the only hotel closed. Not having any letters to a resident I began to fear that I should have to return the same evening to the plains. Fortunately, however, I went in my despair to the club-house, the khansáhma*n* of which, although he refused to do anything for me, recommended me to apply to Mr. Scott, a merchant. That gentleman received me with the greatest kindness and hospitality, offered me the use of an unoccupied bungalow, and invited me to take my meals with his family—and this without knowing anything about me except that I had no other quarters.

Indian hospitality is proverbial, and deservedly so. Any gentleman who finds himself without acquaintances in a place where no public accommodations are provided by government, need only apply at the magistrate's house, where he will meet with the readiest and most liberal welcome, and receive any assistance he may require.

Soon after arriving at Mu*n*sooree, I went with Mr. Scott up to Landoor. The ascent is about five hundred feet. We rode for several miles on an excellent road, around the summit of the ridge, which is in some places not a hundred yards broad The views, on the side toward the Dhoon valley and the plains, were magnificent, but when we crossed a low ridge, and came upon the northern side, the grandeur of the view was almost overpowering. At our feet was a dark and narrow valley, sinking almost perpendicularly for hundreds of feet; beyond were the parallel chains of the Himalayas, each more distant range a little higher than those which were nearer; beyond all, and towering high above all the others, were the magnificent peaks of the snowy range. At first I could not believe that the rounded, snow-white masses which I saw, far above the clouds, were really the summits of the mountains, but the cloud-bank soon passed away, and left the grand old hills unconcealed, in all the sublimity of realized vastness—a hundred miles distant, yet seeming scarcely as far off as the low range which I had crossed in the morning.

I have been asked to compare the scenery of the Himalayas with that of the Alps. The comparison is impossible. In the Alps you have the greatest variety; in the Himalayas the most unvarying monotony. The mountain views of the Alps have a beauty and picturesqueness which at once detracts from their grandeur, and is partially dependent upon the comparatively limited size of the features in the landscape. The Himalayas, on the contrary, are wholly deficient in the beautiful and the picturesque; their very vastness places them beyond the reach of the artist. They are simply immense and sublime.

Besides, how immeasurably do the traditions of the Indian mountains surpass those of the Alps. Their snows feed the Ganges and the Indus, rivers second only to the Nile in the venerable antiquity of their history; they are the scene of legends the origin of which is lost in the obscurity of bygone ages; they have been for countless generations looked upon by a large part of the human race as the actual residence of some of their most worshipped gods, and are still so regarded by one-sixth of the whole human family. They are the most formidable natural barrier ever interposed between a rich and fertile country, inhabited by a cowardly and effeminate race, and the warlike inhabitants of a more northern clime, and yet they have seen more numerous and more bloody invasions, more frequent and more sanguinary contests in the fair plains which they overlook, than have ever been the lot of any other portion of the world.

The height of the loftiest peak visible from Landoor, is twenty-three thousand feet; but the mountains become higher as you go eastward. The greatest height yet measured is thirty thousand feet; in future surveys, however, even this enormous measurement may be surpassed. In the west, the Himalayas are in several parallel ranges, nearly equally high; as you go eastward, the more northern range continually grows higher; the southern ranges, on the contrary, diminish, and one after another drops off, until, in the extreme east, where are the highest summits, the northern range stands alone.

I remained on top of the hill for an hour, and then descended with regret, but determined to have another view on the morrow.

On returning to Mr. Scott's I found that he had sent his servants to arrange for my reception the bungalow which he had offered me. Fires had been made, and everything was as comfortable as could be expected on so short a notice.

Before dinner we took a ride around the "Camel's Back," a steep and narrow ridge separating two gullies, each over a thousand feet deep. The road was a good and broad one, and there were people out taking their evening exercise. Some were riding, others carried in jan-pans, a kind of sedan chair, much used in the hills, and looking like the body of a small gig, with the top removed.

Mu*n*sooree is one of several hill stations. The others are Dárjeeling, Nainee Thal, and Simla. I do not know if there are any more. These are kept up principally as Sanitaria. Hither are sent the European soldiers, when their health becomes affected by long residence in the plains. Here, too, all the children of English parents must pass the greater part of each year that they remain in India. To these healthful heights resort all those English ladies whose fresh beauty has withered under the hot sun of India, and their society adds so much to the natural attractions of the hill stations, that every officer who can obtain leave of absence, and command the funds, passes the hot season, if possible, in the hills. There is the most excellent shooting, admirable tiger-hunting in the Turai, and all the gaieties of watering-place society, so that it is not surprising that "a summer in the hills" is looked upon as one of the few bright periods in the dreary monotony of an Indian existence. The good effects of the bracing climate were seen in such ruddy cheeks, such healthful complexions, and faces expressive of such exuberant vitality, as had not met my eyes since I was on ship-board.

During the evening, Mr. Scott pressed me to join him in a trip he was about making northward into the mountains. He said that we should have to walk most of the way, but could occasionally be carried in a hammock slung from a bamboo. I forget the name of this conveyance, which requires only two bearers, and is much used in the hills. Tempting as this proposal was, the limits of my time prevented my accepting the kind invitation.

The next morning I rose before day-break, and went up to Landoor to have an early view of the snowy range. I remained there an hour, and then descended to breakfast. On the way back, my horse slipped on some ice and rolled over, crushing and bruising my leg. I lay on the road for some time, waiting for my servant to bring me a jan-pan, but as none was procurable, I managed to limp to the house on one leg—two young Moosulmans, whom I caught, supplying the place of the other. On arriving at the bungalow, my leg had all sorts of doctoring, rubbing, &c., to undergo—Mr. Scott, coming down from his house every few minutes to see if I was comfortable, or suggest some improved treatment.

My accident made any further stay useless, as it was quite evident that I was to be lame for several days, at least, so I made up my mind to return to the plains, and set off the same afternoon in a jan-pan, bidding adieu, with many thanks to my hospitable entertainer.

The views in going down are much finer than in ascending.

The path is so steep that, when you go up, you always, as it were, have a blank wall before you. On the contrary, in descending, you realize at a single glance your immense height, as you look down upon the plain almost immediately under you. The reckless speed with which the jan-pan bearers run along the most frightful precipices, and around the sharpest turns, in a road which everywhere hangs suspended over giddy abysses, would, I should think, be trying to the delicate nerves of an invalid, seeking restoration of health in the mountain air, and creates in a stranger a certain feeling of apprehension that does not detract from the impression produced by the scenery; indeed, many critics hold Terror to be an essential quality of the Sublime.

I arrived at the Rajpoor hotel in about two hours after leaving Mu*n*sooree, and passed the night there.

The next morning I received a visit from the landlord of the hotel, Mr. Huzeltine, an old soldier of the Company, now pensioned. I found him very intelligent, and got a good deal of information in the course of conversation. We were talking about the tenure of land, and the great quantity of waste land. I suggested that, with so fertile a soil, labour so cheap, and the terms offered by government so favourable, it was strange that the waste land was not all taken up. He explained this by saying that the climate was such that no European could himself give that active supervision which would be necessary in an agricultural enterprise, and that reliable native superintendents could not be obtained. On the other hand, native capitalists will not embark in agriculture, so that the cultivation of the soil is left entirely in the hands of small holders, who are invariably deeply involved in debt to the native bankers. This state of things, by making the ryuts miserable, prevents the increase of population; and by rendering that misery hopeless (since they all owe more than they can ever hope to pay), checks the very feeble enterprise of the native character, and consequently prevents the thorough tillage of the soil, and puts restraint upon a more extended cultivation. As Mr. Huzeltine said that these debts were in the nature of inheritances, and had been accumulating for generations, I remarked that if they could once be wiped away, and the ryut could feel that his condition depended entirely upon his own exertions, a much greater scope would be given to whatever enterprise and industry he possessed, and, at any rate, such a change would give opportunity for forming a much fairer judgment of the capabilities of natives. The landlord replied that he had once undertaken to cultivate some land, and in order to start fair, had paid off the debts of all his ryuts, stipulating that they should repay him in instalments, as they should be able, with a moderate interest. All went on well for some time, only he was disappointed at not finding the good effects he had expected from the change. At length he was surprised by hearing that a few of his ryuts had contracted considerable debts with the buniahs, and, on making further enquiries, found that they had all returned to their old courses, like the sow that we read of in Scripture, that they were all again irretrievably in debt, and as much slaves as ever to the buniah, and that all his efforts for their good had been in vain. Since that time Mr. Huzeltine has despaired of any improvement in the condition of the ryuts.

Another interesting fact told me by Mr. Huzeltine is, that Polyandry, or the custom of one woman having several husbands, prevails among the Puharrees, as it does among several of the aboriginal races of India. Repulsive as this custom is to our notions, it is but the natural complement to the polygamy of the plains, and is not, *in se*, perhaps any worse.

I left Rajpoor about nine in the morning of November 21st. The landlord's son offered to accompany me to one of the Company's tea plantations, and as I found that I could sit in his buggy with the game leg outside, I accepted the invitation.

This plantation is one of several belonging to Government, and making altogether two thousand acres under cultivation. The Honourable Company has taken great trouble, and spent much money, in attempts to introduce the culture of tea into India.

They employed Mr. Fortune to travel in China, and collect plants and seeds of the best qualities; they have supported these plantations, and now offer land, plants and seeds almost gratuitously to any one willing to undertake tea-planting. Their hope is to make it a permanent branch of agricultural enterprize, and these hopes may be fulfilled, as the soil of India is considered by good judges better adapted to tea than that of China, and in fact, tea actually grows wild in Northern India. Another advantage of India is the great cheapness of labour; but it may be doubted whether this is not more than compensated by its inferiority. For instance, in this plantation all the picking of the leaves and manufacturing is done by Chinese, brought from their home at great expense, to whom very high wages were paid. They were originally brought out only to teach the processes to the natives, but it having been found utterly impossible to rely upon the faithfulness and care of natives, even in the picking of the leaves, it is probable that Chinese labour will have to be permanently employed.

Mr. Thompson, the superintendent, showed us over part of the plantation, which had at the time about 350 acres under cultivation. The tea-plant is a thick, round bush about three feet high. The leaf is similar to that of the box, but larger. Only some of the leaves are fit for manufacturing. The difference between the two kinds is very perceptible, and Mr. Thompson said was easily learned by the natives, who picked the good leaves only, with perfect discrimination, as long as they were carefully overlooked; but the moment supervision was removed they would pick leaves of inferior quality. Every plan of rewards and punishments had been tried to make them more careful, but all had been unsuccessful, and they were now reluctantly concluding that Chinese labour would be a permanent necessity.

We visited the manufactory, a pukka building where the tea is fired and prepared for the market. As it was not the proper season nothing was doing, and the empty rooms contained only some air-tight cases of tea-plants and seeds, which were to be sent gratuitously to any applicants.

We afterwards visited a neat row of cottages, the homes of the Chinese labourers, the comfort and order visible in which, contrasted strikingly with the wretched mud-huts that shelter the natives of India.

Mr. Thompson informed me that only the finer qualities of tea are manufactured or grown at the Company's establishment. The average price realized at the tea sales which had just taken place was one rupee and ten anas or seventy-eight cents a pound.

I was very glad to have seen this plantation, not only on account of the interest of the experiment, but because they were the first tea plantations I had seen, my China travels having stopped short of the tea districts; and they are besides the largest in the world, as in China the herb is generally cultivated by small planters who have each but very little land.

Besides the tea-plantations of the Honourable Company; there are in India others belonging to private individuals. Of these, the largest are those of the Assam Company, which I believe pay very well, their tea bringing a very high price in London, and being used exclusively to give a body and flavour to inferior Chinese teas.

After leaving Mr. Thompson's we were stopped in a narrow lane, by a crowd around a juggler, and, for a few anas we witnessed a fight between a mungoos and a snake. The mungoos is a small animal, like a weasel. It is particularly hostile to snakes, and remains uninjured by their venom. After witnessing the death of two snakes we kept on to Dehra, and young Mr. Huzeltine drove me to the house of Mr. Woodside, an American Missionary, where he bade me good-bye.

CHAPTER XX.

RETURN TO MEERUTH.

Rev. Mr. Woodside's—American Missionaries—Opening of the Ganges Canal—Excitement of Natives—Moral Effect—Missionaries' Opinion of the Company's Government—Its General Effects—Native States—A Seekh Temple—The Gooroo—Farewell to my Countrymen—Last view of Himalayas—Roorkhee—Workshops—Native Workmen—Repugnance between the English and Native Races—The Ganges Canal—Other Buildings—Meeruth Again—Mutiny at Meeruth—Conduct of Officers, and their Feelings toward the Sepoys.

I found Mr. Woodside's compound filled with tents, camels, horses, elephants, and servants, it being the convention of all the American Missionaries in that part of the country, and most of those who attended having to live, as they had come to Dehra, in tents. There were about twenty Missionaries present, some of whom had brought their wives and children. It was strange how my heart warmed at finding myself again in the company of so many of my own countrymen.

I was particularly pleased with the Rev. Mr. B———, who had served in the Mexican war, and had afterwards enlisted as a "soldier of the Cross." He was stationed in the Punjab, and recommended me very strongly to visit that country. Mr. B——— had come to Dehra by "marching," that is to say travelling with horses and camels and tents. The distance he had come was three hundred and twenty miles, the time occupied was thirty days, which will give a good idea of the slowness of the mode of locomotion, which was formerly universal in India, and is still the only practicable plan in many parts of the country.

Mr. B——— described to me very vividly some of the scenes at the opening of the Ganges Canal. It seems that the Brahmuns were very much opposed to its construction, as all the ghâts on the Ganges were in their hands, and they made their fortunes by contributions levied upon the bathers, whereas any one who pleased might bathe in the canal, and convenient ghâts had been constructed for the purpose by Government, at short distances. This opposition of the Brahmuns would have been enough at one time to have prevented the building of the canal; or at any rate they would have been reimbursed by government for their loss. I refer to the period when a Sepoy was turned out of the service for becoming a Christian, and when it was a standing regulation that "no natives but those of the Hindoo and Moosulman persuasions" should fill a post in the Honourable Company's service. On the day of the opening of the canal, Mr. B——— and a friend got into a boat and were carried on with the first of the water. The banks on both sides were crowded with thousands of natives from all the country round. It was night, and the ruddy glare of torches lit up the empty bed of the canal, and the close packed masses of black-skinned naked Hindoos, waiting with trembling anxiety to witness the result. They had been assured by the Brahmuns that the mighty goddess Gunga could not be diverted from her ancient and Heaven-appointed bed; that her pure waters would refuse to flow in any but the sacred channel. No doubt, in the minds of many of the spectators, the question to be decided was not whether the task of the engineers had been perfectly carried out; but whether the Brahmuns, the emanations from the godhead, nay, whether the very power of the gods themselves, would not be overcome by the irresistible might of that dread impersonality, "The Warrior Company."

As the water advanced wild shouts arose from the crowds, the mighty masses swayed to and fro with excitement, and finally they rushed headlong into the water. Many of them had never before bathed in the sin-absorbing waters—others had only done so in rare pilgrimages and at the expense of the greatest privations.

It is not too much to say that the opening of the Ganges Canal is the greatest blow that has ever been inflicted upon the infallible authority of the Brahmuns. The mighty goddess leaves her place at the bidding of an English engineer, and flows in a channel which he has constructed. The armies of Heaven do not interpose to prevent the sacrilege; on the contrary, blessings arise, both temporal and spiritual. Millions of acres are fertilized and yield abundant crops, the inhabitants have the highest privileges of their religion brought to their door, and the same stream which washes away the sins of the cultivator will bear his plenteous harvests, rapidly and cheaply to a market. The benevolent science of the foreigner, stands triumphant over the mercenary superstition and the money-getting lies of the Brahmun.

I dined at Mr. Woodside's. I was curious in questioning these missionaries with a view of obtaining the opinions of disinterested and well-informed men, on the actual working of the Company's government. All with whom I conversed spoke in the highest terms, both of the general policy of the Government, and the great improvements in the condition of its subjects. Especially, they said, that too much praise could not be given to the very high character of the civil service; and the integrity, equity, and benevolent spirit of its members, generally. At the same time they confessed that the greatest oppressions were continually committed in the name of Government; but assured me that they were, in every instance, traceable to the native subordinates, and could not properly be laid at the door of the European officials. The missionaries from the Punjab spoke with particular warmth of the great improvements in the administration of that country, during the few years that had elapsed since its annexation by the British. The revenue of the country had been considerably reduced; the quota of each tax-payer was equitably adjusted; and he no longer had to satisfy the extortion of the tax-gatherer, as well as the just demands of Government. Public improvements had been extensively planned, and their execution begun. Every man felt sure of his head, his wife, and his property—whereas, under the old rule, no man's life was safe, and if any one had collected wealth by industry, skill, or enterprize, he soon learned that his gains must be shared by his rulers small and great.

To show still further the effect of a transfer from native to

English rule, I quote the words of a missionary now in this city. "At one of the missionary stations of our church in Upper India, a native chief was in power when the missionary first visited the city, which then contained a population of sixteen thousand souls. Soon afterwards the old chief died and left no heirs. His principality, according to native usage, escheated to the British; if his town had been on the other side of the Sutlěj, it would have fallen, in like manner, to the miserable old king referred to above. British rule was set up, the reign of law commenced, people from neighbouring districts, still under native rulers, removed to this town, and in a few years its population was numbered at nearly eighty thousand souls. Facts like this confute whole pages of declamation."

No one who sympathizes with the restoration of order in France by the Great Napoleon, ought to object to the annexation of native territories by the Company. The two cases are almost exactly parallel. In both we have the forcible substitution of a good government for a bad one—of law for anarchy. In both certain rights were necessarily violated, and certain classes offended. Whatever differences there are in the two cases, are in favour of the English. The tyranny of a native government is worse than that of the Bourbons, or of the Revolutionary authorities. In France there was a large class who were much attached to the old Royal government; in an Indian State, such a class is small, and consists of the government officials who live by extortion, and the feudal princes who grow rich by violence and plunder. In France, too, if Napoleon had not arisen, the Bourbons would probably have been restored, and would have inaugurated a government purified of the abuses which had driven them from the throne. In India there was no such chance. Governments there never change or improve—they only become weak. The royal races degenerate, and, as vitality diminishes in the central organ of the body politic, the extremities become corrupt and disorganized. Then comes a bloody usurpation, and the same thing is repeated. Sometimes the catastrophe is a conquest; but, with that change, the above formula is an accurate description of the history of the native dynasties of India. Fortunate are those States which, at such a crisis in the affairs of their rulers, have been taken under British protection, and saved from the indefinite repetition of revolutions, tyrannies, anarchy, and conquest. The term "revolution," which I employ, may be misunderstood. I would not imply a popular movement. There never has been, and never can be anything of the kind in India, with reference to government. The great mass of the population have stood inactive for centuries, and seen their country invaded; their royal families in chains, or put to the sword; armies of invaders devastating their fields, and robbing their wealth. They have beheld, unmoved, every possible change in the supreme power; they have submitted without a murmur, to the most grinding cruelty and oppression; but they have never once struck a blow in their own defence—they only fled to the jungul and its tigers, when their country was overrun by robbers, like the Maharattas, of more than average cruelty; or took refuge in the British territories, when, as in the case of Oude, the tyranny of government was no longer endurable.

I was very glad to learn that during the Punjab war, the Punjabee proclamations of the English General were printed at the press of the American missionaries. This fact alone, shows the light in which our countrymen looked upon that movement. The English government has lately had the opportunity of repaying its obligations. During the recent disturbances a very large amount of American property was destroyed at Loodianah. As soon as order was restored, Sir John Lawrence assessed the sum upon the town, and thus promptly reimbursed the loss sustained by our missions.

After dinner, I drove out with Mr. Woodside, in his buggy. We visited a handsome new surai which has recently been built by public subscription; the school-house of the missionaries, a pukka building on the model of a Connecticut Seminary, and a Seekh temple—which last is a curious place. It consists of a court containing one large building on a raised platform, and four similar, but smaller edifices at each of the four corners. The Seekhs, it is well known, are a religious sect who arose at Lahor, about four hundred years ago. Their founder pretended to a new revelation, which is contained in a sacred volume called the Grunth. The new religion borrowed many dogmas from both the Hindoo and Mahommedan systems, and was embraced with equal readiness by the followers of either faith. This temple typified, to some extent, the two-fold origin of the Seekh creed. Its form, though similar to those of the mosques, also recalled the Hindoo temple. The shape of the arches and decorations may be described as impure Saracenic. The main building contains the tomb of the founder of an extensive sect of Fukheers, or Mendicant Friars, in whose hands the establishment is. The four smaller buildings at the angles shelter the remains of the saint's wives. He allowed himself four of these luxuries, but forbade marriage altogether to his disciples. All five of the tombs have domes. The larger one has a coating of polished white cement, but the four smaller buildings are beautifully decorated with colours, which have withstood, uninjured, the effects of the climate, for over a century and a half. As we were looking at the large temple, we were accosted by the chief Fukheer, a very tall, venerable-looking old man with a long white beard. His rich dress seemed somewhat incongruous with the poverty and mortification professed by the body to which he belonged; and contrasted forcibly with the naked sanctity of his followers. He made a profound salám and offered us some peculiar spices, after which, he made a long speech which I could not understand, but which Mr. Woodside said was a complimentary oration descriptive of the high respect entertained by him for missionaries generally, and Mr. Woodside in particular. The Gooroo afterwards accompanied us around the enclosure, and pointed out the beauties of the smaller tombs. One of them had met with a remarkable accident. During an earthquake, its wall had become cracked completely through, in a line parallel with the ground. The upper part remained stationary, while the lower and larger part had moved under it about three inches in a circular direction, in which position it now remains, and is apparently as strong as ever.

After making our salâms to the Gooroo, we returned to Mr. Woodside's, and had prayers and a very long sermon. The congregation was rather numerous, and contained several families of the station—the gentlemen of which had taken a great deal of interest in the Mission, and contributed a large part of the funds for the construction of the school, and the purchase, for the Mission, of the fine large house in which Mr. Woodside was residing.

Mr. Woodside informed me that he had just returned from a missionary tour in the Himalayas, during which he had ascended the snowy range to the height of twenty thousand feet, and he showed me a fragment of granite brought by him from that height.

The prayers being finished, we had supper; and after that meal, having bade farewell to my host and other countrymen, and having received from Mr. B——— two letters of introduction, which he kindly wrote for me to friends of his in the Punjab, I entered the dhoolee and started for Roorkee, at which place I hoped to arrive by seven next morning. We did not, however, arrive till ten o'clock, but I was consoled for the delay by the magnificent view of the hills and snowy range which was continually before my eyes for the last two hours of the road.

The situation of Roorkee is very pretty, as it is on a fertile and well cultivated plain, and is quite hid by groves of mango trees, from which emerge several minârs and domes. The dâk-bungalow is under the trees, just outside the town, which I did not have the curiosity to enter. After taking breakfast, I went to see the Honourable Company's Iron Foundry, and Machine Manufactory. It is a very extensive establishment. The iron used, comes altogether from England, and I could not at first understand the object of establishing a foundry at this place, nearly a thousand miles from the coast. The superintendent, however, who showed me over the works, explained that the real object was to test the ability of native workmen in the manufacture of iron; and to introduce to them a new branch of industry. The enterprize is prevented from being a great failure in a monetary point of view, by manufacturing mostly small articles, and parts of things, to supply defects and breaks-down in machinery—as men prefer to pay high prices for such articles, rather than have the delay of sending to England. I was informed that the natives learned the trade very much more quickly and easily than Europeans, but that they never could be depended on to perform their task with faithful care and accuracy, if their labour was not conducted under the vigilant supervision of Europeans. Here, as elsewhere, they find it impossible to entrust the supervising to natives, of whom an intensely narrow-minded selfishness, which cannot see the advantage of adopting another's interest as its own, seems to be an almost universal characteristic. I think this feature in their character, and the universal absence of truth and honesty, goes far to explain the want of sympathy between the English and native races—a want of sympathy, compared to which, our feeling towards negroes in America, is a warm affection. In fact, the two sentiments are quite different. The mass of the people in this country entertain a sort of contempt, nearly akin to physical disgust, towards the African race. We will not sit down with them, eat with them, or admit them to our society. There is no such feeling towards a native in India. The repulsion between the two races is almost entirely moral, and arises in great part from the scorn felt by the blunt, brave, open, and truth-loving Englishman, for the cringing servility, the abject cowardice, the unfathomable duplicity, lying, and hypocrisy of the native character.

After leaving the iron foundry, I went to see the aqueduct by which the Ganges canal is conducted over the river Sulanee. It is constructed entirely of brick-work, and is nearly two hundred feet broad. Its whole length is about a quarter of a mile, and it is supported by sixteen arches, the piers of which are sunk twenty feet below the bed of the river. The masonry of the arches is never less than four feet thick, to enable them to bear the weight of such a mass of water. The successful completion of this aqueduct is a great triumph of engineering skill, as from the peculiarly shifting character of the sand which forms the bed of Indian rivers, almost all bridges that have been built have given way when tried by the torrents of a single rainy season.

Roorkee also contains a Government college, a fine looking building, which, however, I did not visit. As soon as I had seen the aqueduct, I left for Moozuffurnuggur, where I exchanged the dhoolee for a gárrhee, and reached Meeruth at five o'clock on the morning of November 23.

I found the weather warmer than in the hills, but a fire was quite necessary at night. The natives of India, in the cold weather, wear wadded cotton clothes, wrapping themselves at night in thick ruzais, or what we should call "comforters." In this respect they form a contrast to the Chinese, who dress, during the winter, in velvet, silks, and furs; depositing them with the pawnbrokers for safe keeping in summer. I used to be surprised in India to see many of the natives without any provision at all against the cold, going about in dresses of the thinnest muslin, while almost all the children and babies were entirely naked, even in the severest weather. I used to find it necessary to sleep with my clothes on; in fact, for a month after I left Calcutta, I only undressed for the purpose of bathing and changing soiled clothes.

The 23d, being Sunday, I rested at Meeruth, and early next morning left this station, which became afterwards the scene of the first outbreak in the general revolt of the Bengal army. I say the first outbreak, although there can now be little doubt that the Barrackpoor mutiny was to have been the signal for the general insurrection, but the prompt extinction of that movement discouraged the other disaffected regiments, and deferred the catastrophe.

The mutineers at Meeruth shot their officers, set free thousands of criminals from the jails, and then having fired many of the bungalows and massacred the inmates, ladies and children, with that hellish refinement of barbarity, which is usual in Asiatic warfare, but which almost surpasses the belief of more civilized and Christian nations, they at once set out for Delhi, no doubt in virtue of a previous arrangement.

The conduct, on this occasion, of the commanding officers at Meeruth, has called down great censure; but only shows how entirely the whole revolt took India by surprise. The feeling of the older officers towards the sepoys was far different from that which exists between the officers of any European army and their soldiers. These men had grown up with the sepoys from their boyhood; they knew them, and loved them almost as their children,* and they would not believe that the troops, which had always displayed so much affection for them, and in whose fidelity they had such unbounded confidence, had really proved faithless. Even when men came in wounded and bloody to tell them the news, they were still unconvinced; they said it must be a slight matter, and that *they* could pacify the troops. Full of this confidence, they went to meet the mutineers, and fell, riddled with balls. Even after the revolters had left the station, after all the devastation and the fiendish outrages had been committed, men of this class still persisted in their error, and when the commander of a cavalry regiment offered to pursue the mutineers and cut them up, the permission was refused.

Everywhere was the same incredulity, the same blind confidence, incomprehensible to those who have not seen the light in which the sepoy was looked on by his officer. Officers felt that though all the other regiments were to revolt, yet theirs would prove faithful. They yielded to the prayers, the protestations, the tears, and the embraces of their men, and left them their arms, with which the treacherous scoundrels murdered them the same night.

Such things would be impossible in any other country.

* In fact, the sepoys were called by their officers "baba-lôg"—"the children," or "the dear children." The feelings entertained by the older officers toward their men, do not in the least contradict what has been said about the natural repugnance of the English and native character. They only show how entirely national prejudices may be obliterated by a residence in foreign countries, and by intercourse with their inhabitants. In this respect, there was a most marked difference between the feelings of the old officers, who had passed their life in the country, and those of the younger men, who did not intend to stay in India any longer than they could help, who had a thorough English education before they went out, and who never kept native women, or associated on terms of equality with the native officers of their regiments.

The deep dissimulation of the Indian character is fortunately the characteristic of no other race.

It is remarkable that the oldest officers, those who knew most of the people, and most of their men, were just those who, by a misplaced lenity, added fuel to the revolt. While the young men, who had just come out, with all their English prejudice fresh, were those who first appreciated the real importance of the movement, and who, had they been allowed to act, might, by vigour and well-timed severity, have moderated the terrific violence of the conflagration, or perhaps entirely extinguished it.

CHAPTER XXI.

THE IMPERIAL CITY OF DELHI.

First View of Delhi—Entrance to the City—The Palace—The Houses low—The Arsenal—Col. Skinner's—The Church—The Square of Death—The Signal Tower—Drive to Kootub—Ruins—Old Delhi—An Imperial Whim—Sufdur Jung's Tomb—The Kootub—Indian Sam Patches—The Observatory—Chandee Chok, the Broadway of Delhi—Dandy Moosulmans—The Mosque of Slaughter.

I LEFT Meeruth by gárrhee-dâḳ for Delhi, at two o'clock on the morning of November 24th.

I slept all the way, and was only awakened by the demand for toll at the bridge across the Jumna. On looking out of the gárrhee, I saw, on the opposite bank of the river, the bright red walls of the Imperial City, and above them, the white domes and beautiful minárs of the Júmma Musjeed.

Although Delhi possesses larger and finer edifices than Lucknow, and although the mass of tombs and ruins which cover the country around, give it the effect of immense extent, yet its appearance is not nearly so imposing as that of the capital of Oude.

There are not so many tall minárs, which always form a chief beauty of a Mohammedan city. The domes are fewer in number, and not gilt; while the material of the chief buildings is red sandstone, instead of the white pukka, which has so fine an effect at a distance. In Lucknow, too, all the principal objects are finely grouped, whereas at Delhi they are much scattered, and many of them are distant several miles from the city.

The walls of Delhi are over fifty feet in height, and broken by circular bastions. The battlements were not square, as in European architecture, but rounded with a Saracenic curve—a very effective decoration.

Crossing the river, we entered the city through two lofty gates, between which was a deep moat. We were now in a broad unpaved street—almost a square—which runs around the royal palace. All around this open space were low houses. The palace itself is not at all what we understand by that word. It is an immense collection of buildings, containing the king's residence, gardens, mosques, open squares, and buildings for servants, and the dependents of the court—in fact a small town. It extends for half a mile along the river's bank, and is surrounded by fortifications similar to those which defend the city, but loftier and broken by three gateways. These gateways, like all others of Saracenic style in India, are made a principal, instead of a subordinate, feature in the architecture. They are far higher and broader than the wall through which they give entrance, and their roofs are decorated with kiosks of white marble, and a low stone colonnade around the edge, supporting a row of little stone domes, looking like turbans—not a very pleasing ornament.

We drove around the Palace, which I shall call by this, its usual name, although a better title would be the Fortress "khila," as it is always denominated by the natives.

The dâk-bungalow is situated in a street not far from the Palace, and consequently inside the town—the only case of the kind I know of. As soon as I had got breakfast and dressed, I drove in a buggy to the bungalow of Captain Russell, of the 54th Native Infantry. I had to drive for about three quarters of a mile through the city, again passing through the open space in front of the Palace. After traversing several streets, the houses on which were small and low, I came in front of a large pukka building of English style, which I afterwards heard was the Arsenal. This was the most important establishment of the kind in this part of India, and the fact of its being entrusted wholly to the protection of native soldiers, shows what entire reliance was placed in their fidelity. At the time of the mutiny Lieutenant Willoughby was in charge of the Arsenal. As soon as he saw the danger, he came to the courageous resolution to blow it up with his own hands—although he must have fully expected to lose his life in so doing. The explosion was terrific, and killed many hundreds of the mutineers who were in the building at the time. By what seems a miracle, Lieutenant Willoughby escaped from the danger which he had so bravely faced in the discharge of duty.

Soon after passing the Arsenal, the road widened into an open space, having on the right, the Church of St. James; on the left, Colonel Skinner's house, and in front, the city wall and Cashmeeree Gate. Colonel Skinner was a half-caste, or descendant of a European and native. When the English arms were first carried as far as Delhi, he was in command of a very considerable body of irregular cavalry, known as "Skinner's Horse," which were of great service in the war. Having acquired a great deal of property, he built this splendid residence, where he lived in a style of mingled Eastern and Western luxury. I believe his wives were all natives, and in order to show the broad liberality of his views, he built not only the church of St. James, on the square opposite his house, but also constructed, at the same time, a Mohammedan mosque, and a Hindoo mundră. St. James' Church, which was used as the station chapel, was a considerable, cruciform, pukka building, in a sort of Doric style, surmounted by a dome.

It was in this square that the officers of the Fifty-fourth Regiment were murdered, and here, when Delhi was taken, the English troops were horrified by finding a Christian woman hanging in the agonies of crucifixion.

I passed through the Cashmeeree Gate, which being defended by outworks, was by far the strongest entrance to the city, and became subsequently the main point of attack for the English troops.

The cantonments were over a mile from the city walls. The road led past the Residency, an extensive pukka building of English castellated architecture, and then ascended a low hill, beyond which were the cantonments. On the summit of this hill was the Signal Tower, a round stone building, in which the ladies and some officers of the station took refuge on the outbreak of the mutiny. The Sepoys who accompanied them gave the strongest evidences of fidelity, and the most solemn promises of protection, but as soon as they were all within the tower, and apparently beyond the chance of escape or assistance, the cowardly wretches massacred all but one or two ladies and Lieutenant Vibart of the Fifty-fourth, with whom I was well acquainted. These jumped from the top of the building, a feat that I should consider very dangerous for a man, and almost impossible for a lady, and fortunately escaping with but few wounds from the volleys fired after them by the Sepoys, at last succeeded in reaching and fording the river. After wandering for many days in the jungul, weary, foot-sore, almost starving, exposed daily to insult and blows, and hourly in peril of death, they at length found safety in Meeruth.

Descending from the hill on which the Signal Tower was situated, and on which the batteries of the English besieging force were erected last autumn, I entered the station and drove to Captain Russell's bungalow. He received me very kindly and wished me to stay with him; but I had to decline, as I expected to leave in a day for the Punjab. After showing me a number of tiger's skins, elk, deer, and antelope horns, and other trophies of his skill with the rifle, Captain Russell took me to tiffin (luncheon) at the mess-house of the Fifty-fourth. I was introduced to the other officers, who showed me every kindness during my stay.

The next day I went in a buggy with Captain Russell to see the Kootub Minár, which is about thirteen miles south of the Delhi gate of the city.

The surface of the country is uneven, the soil barren and rocky, so that our drive would have been uninteresting had it not been for the ruins of palaces, mosques, temples, and tombs which were visible on all sides. The present city of Delhi is quite a modern place, having been built by Shah Jehan about the middle of the seventeenth century. It was called after him Shah Jehanabad, a name which literally translated means "The City of the King of the World." Although the English adopted the old Hindoo name of Delhi, or, as it should be written, Dihli, yet the Moosulmans retain that appellation which recalls the glory of their most splendid sovereign—just as they always delight in calling Agra by its later name of Akburabad.

Before the present city was built, Delhi had occupied various sites within a circuit of twenty miles to the south and west, most of which space is now covered with ruins. These changes of locality were owing sometimes to invasions destroying the old towns, and necessitating the construction of new; sometimes to the ambition of particular emperors who wished to found a more splendid residence than that of their predecessors; sometimes merely to the caprice of the sovereign. Wherever the king built his fortified palace, there the nobles clustered around him, and the other inhabitants of the old city soon followed the court, both on account of the trade which it controlled, and also because their old town being unprotected by the king's soldiery, became exposed to the assaults of the robber tribes.

The most remarkable removal to which the inhabitants of Delhi were ever subjected, was designed and carried out by Mohummud Toghluk, who occupied the imperial throne during the fourteenth century. He caused all the population to migrate to Dowlutabád in the Dĕkkun, where he established his capital and built what is to the present day the strongest fortress in India. Dowlutabád is eight hundred miles from Delhi, and the country between the two places is mostly jungul, so that a large portion of his unfortunate subjects died before reaching their new home. After the transfer was complete it was discovered that the new city had no natural advantages to enable it to support so numerous a population, so that it had finally to be abandoned, and the royal residence was again fixed at Delhi. A few years afterwards, however, the king again repeated his mad freak, and as the second march was made during a famine, the sufferings of the townspeople were much greater than on the first occasion. This was the same monarch who, driven to desperation by his inability to extort from his impoverished subjects the requisite funds to pay for his military expeditions, used to order out his whole army and form them into a circle enclosing a vast extent of country, after the manner of a *battue*. The army then closed in upon itself, murdering the inhabitants of all the villages so enclosed, without distinction of age or sex. Another feat of Mohummud was the flaying alive of his nephew who had ventured to oppose him in arms.

About half-way between the walls of Delhi and the Kootub is the magnificent mausoleum of Sufdur Jung, who was a wuzeer of the Mogul empire, and usurped the independent government of Oude, of which country he had been viceroy. This event occurred about a hundred years ago. The Honourable Company recognized his family in the government of Oude, and even conferred upon them the royal title, both of which they retained until within three years. The Delhi Moosulmans, however, never acknowledged the superior title conferred on the ruler of Oude by the Company, but always considered and spoke of him as a wuzeer, or minister of the Padshah.

The mausoleum is about a hundred feet square, having at each corner a round minár surmounted by a kiosk. It is elevated upon a marble terrace or chubootra, and is surmounted by a white marble dome of great beauty. The walls are constructed of red sandstone relieved by layers and arches of marble. The windows, of which there are two tiers, are not glazed, but closed by marble slabs most delicately cut into open fretwork. The interior contains one large apartment and four smaller ones. In the centre of the large apartment, under the dome, is the cenotaph, a plain white marble tomb; immediately under it, but beneath the terrace, is the real tomb, which protects the body.

The garden in which the mausoleum is situated is three hundred and fifty yards square. It has been at one time beautifully laid out, and is still filled with trees. The red stone wall which surrounds it is formed into a cloister on the inner side, and is used as a surai by native travellers. The gateways are very large and fine.

Outside the gateway we found several hundred natives encamped. They were the followers of a young relation of the Rajah of Jaipoor. He had come to Delhi to get married.

There were in the camp about thirty of his soldiers in a green uniform, on the English model, but very shabby. None of them wore shoes.

After driving about six miles from Sufdur Jung's tomb we came to the Kootub—the loftiest and most remarkable column in the world. Its form tapers from the base to the summit, and it is divided into seven stories by heavy balconies, the distance between which diminishes in proportion to the diameter of the shaft. The effect of this very peculiar and highly artistic arrangement is to add very much to the apparent height of the pillar by exaggerating the perspective. The lower story is polygonal, but above the first balcony the minár is round. Its surface is deeply fluted all the way up. The flutings on the first story are alternately semicircular and angular, on the second story they are all semicircular, on the third all angular. The first three stories are built wholly of fine red sandstone; the last two are principally white marble, and have a plain surface. The projecting galleries, which separate the stories, are massive, and richly decorated and supported by heavy stone brackets. Around the lower story are six horizontal bands of passages from the Koran, carved in the boldest relief. The second story contains two such bands, and the third one of them, but there are none above. The whole height is now two hundred and forty feet, but there can be but little doubt that it was once sixty feet higher. The base is fifty feet in diameter, and the summit only thirteen feet. It is now in perfect order, having been thoroughly repaired by the Company in 1826, at the cost of several thousand pounds sterling.

We ascended to the top of the minár, from which we obtained a most extensive view of the country, which was everywhere covered with ruins as far as the eye could reach.

After descending from the minár, we walked through the courts of a very old and now ruinous mosque, built by Kootub-ood-Deen, the deputy of Sooltan Mohummud, one of the early Pathán conquerors, in the year 592 of the Hijra, answering to 1195 of our era. The Moosulmans contend that the Kootub was intended as one of the minárs of this mosque, the Hindoos on the other hand assert that it existed before the advent of the Moosulmans. Each view has earnest supporters, who find very strong arguments for their respective opinions. Whichever party is right, the Kootub is certainly perfectly unique. If it was built by the Mahommedans, it is unlike every other minár in India or the world, both in form and decoration; if, on the contrary, it was constructed by the Hindoos, it is the only edifice of considerable dimensions erected by them which has come down to the present day. I suppose the question will never be decided, for no nation would willingly give up for its race the honour of having devised and completed a monument which so far surpasses in sublimity every other creation of oriental art, and which, whether we consider the grandeur and originality of the conception, or the workmanlike knowledge of art displayed in its construction, whether we look at the boldness, grace, and exquisite execution of the ornaments with which it is covered, or their perfect harmony and entire subordination to the grand features of the design, must, I think, be allowed a rank by the side of the most renowned triumphs of western architecture.

The mosque which I have mentioned as situated at the foot of the minár, was built as the Jumma Musjeed, or principal mosque, of old Delhi. It is doubtful whether it was ever completed; at any rate it would now be in ruins were it not for the care of the Company's government, which has caused the tottering walls to be strengthened, and restored the largest of the arches, which is of majestic proportions, and decorated with beautiful designs in scroll-work and Arabic inscriptions carved in the stone. In one of the court-yards of the mosque is the celebrated "Loha ka Lat," or "iron pillar." This column is really of bronze, about twenty feet high and two feet in diameter. It bears a short inscription, in a very ancient character, which was for a long time unintelligible. Its origin is unknown, but there is a legend that it cannot be moved from its present position, and the Hindoos point triumphantly to a dent in its surface, which they say was made by a cannon ball fired against it by the orders of Nadur Shah, who in vain tried to batter it down.

Leaving the pillar, we walked a quarter of a mile to the little village of Mehrowlee, to see the diving, for which the inhabitants are famous. The "locus in quo" is a *baolee*, a species of well which is not uncommon in the north and west of India. The excavation is perhaps sixty feet long by thirty broad, and the sides are supported by stone walls. The surface of the water, which is about forty feet below the level of the ground, is approached on one side by a flight of stone steps. The divers took their stand on top of one of the perpendicular sides and then *jumped* down, moving their hands and feet to and fro in their descent. On striking the water, they suddenly closed the legs together and drew the arms close to their sides. They made a tremendous splash on entering the water, and sunk so deep that before they rose again the surface was perfectly unruffled.

We afterwards took tiffin in the pavilion of an old surai, and returned to Delhi, by a different road, which led us by the observatory of Jai Singh, the scientific rajah of Jaipoor, who also built the similar establishments at Bĕnarĕs, Oojén, and his own capital, the former of which I have before described. The most remarkable object in this observatory is the great sun dial, the gnomon of which, built of stone, is one hundred and four feet in length, fifty-six in height, and about ten feet thick. The shadow thrown by this gnomon was received on two immense graduated quadrants, which, as well as the gnomon itself, were formerly cased with white marble. The observatory was founded one hundred and thirty years ago, and was formerly a great seat of astronomical science. It was, however, abandoned before the conquest by the English, and its numerous buildings have fallen into utter ruin, with the exceptions of the sun dial and two round stone towers pierced with numerous openings, the shadow of the sun's rays passing through which indicated his altitude.

We returned to the city, and after dinner I drove in a buggy through the Chandee chôk, or Silver market, which is altogether the handsomest street in India. It is about a mile in length, extending from the great western entrance of the palace, to the Lahóree gate of the city. Its breadth is one hundred and twenty feet, and an open aqueduct bordered by rows of trees runs through its centre. The houses on each side are mostly of pukka, and not over two stories high. Their roofs are tiled, and they have light wooden balconies in front which add much to the appearance of the street. The ground floor of these houses is commonly used for shops; the upper stories are often inhabited by what the natives call "scarlet ladies," and by other "great evils of great cities" in the East. When I was at Delhi, Chandee chôk was the gayest scene in India. Every native who could muster a conveyance of any description betook himself thither in the cool of the afternoon. Some came on elephants, which were magnificently caparisoned, and painted with bright colours around the eyes and on the trunk. Others rode milk-white horses, the tails of which were dyed scarlet, and which were decorated with housings of fine cloth and gold embroidery. Others rode in bailees, or two-wheeled carts covered with red canopies, and drawn by neat teams of bullocks. A few preferred palkees, or ton-jons, a vehicle very like the jan-pan of the hills. But at least half had abandoned oriental fashions, and adopting the manners and customs of their conquerors drove on the chôk in graceful English phætons or buggies, drawn by well-groomed and well-harnessed Arab steeds. All had as many followers as possible, who ran ahead armed with sword, spear and shield, shouting out their master's titles, and clearing the way, with words and blows, through the closely packed crowd. The dress of the inhabitants of Delhi is very gay. The tight fitting cassock (chupkun) is of some dark cloth or flowered cotton, and the turban and kummurbund are of scarlet or some rich colour, often fringed with gold. Sometimes Cashmeer shawls, or the imitation ones made at Delhi, are worn around the head, waist or shoulders. Some of the costumes are very rich and costly, but most of them are tawdry, and decorated with spangles and artificial jewellery. In Delhi there are a great number of "dandy Moosulmans." They are frequently sepoys, who pass their spare time as "coureurs d'aventures." Their dress is as showy as their limited means will allow, and they wear a natty little skull-cap, cocked on one side of the head, from which their long, straight, greasy hair hangs down upon their neck. Their appearance is altogether far from respectable, and they interchange salutations with the young ladies of the market, who sit at the windows of the upper stories, or parade their charms in open bailees. Now and then one may see an Afghan, a short, thick-set man, with loose grey woollen clothes, broad, heavy features, a dirty face, of the colour of leather, and brown tangled locks.. He evidently looks with the utmost contempt on the unmanly foppery of the effeminate race whom his ancestors have conquered and spoiled whenever they chose; and if asked his opinion, will express it in no measured terms, and in language far different from the courtly euphemisms of the Hindoostanee.

Half way down the Chandee chôk is a pretty little mosque, with three gilt domes, where, scarcely more than one hundred years ago, Nadur Shah, the Persian conqueror, sat with drawn sword, looking on while his troops sacked the city. The slaughter lasted from morning till night, and was accompanied by all the horrors of unrestrained lust, rapine and vengeance. Over a hundred thousand of the inhabitants perished, and the aqueduct in the Chandee chôk ran red with blood.

CHAPTER XXII.

DELHI.—CONTINUED.

A Juggler—Poses Plastiques—Entrance to Palace—Dewán Am—Emperor's Throne—Mosaics—Drawing first Blood—A Paradise on Earth—Peacock Throne—A Microcosmic View of the Mogul Empire—Shah Jehan in State—A Hundred Years Later—Native Tact—The Glory has Departed—Maharattas in the Palace—Gholam Kadur, the Rohilla, seated on the Royal Throne—Restoration of the Empire by the British—Their Majesties, and their "Particular Slaves"—The last Emperor—The last Tenants of the Dewán Khas—The Pearl Mosque—Palace Gardens—The Jumma Musjeed—View from Minár—Moosulman Worship—Feerooz's Walking Stick—Hoomaioon's Tomb—Chubootras—Peculiarities of Mahommedan Architecture—Capture of the King of Delhi.

THE next morning I had a juggler to perform for me, who did some most wonderful tricks with almost no preparation or means of deception. There came also to the bungalow some nach girls of a low class, who danced and sang—both indifferently; but afterwards they performed some feats, showing that wonderful suppleness which is so remarkable in all natives, but especially in this class. I put a four-ana bit (about as large as a dime) upon the ground. The girl then placed one foot on each side of it, and standing up, bent gradually backward until her head came between her legs; she then caught the silver piece in her eyelids and resumed the upright position. The performance was afterwards repeated, with variations, the paolee (four-ana bit) being taken up by the nostrils or ears.

Afterwards I visited the palace. I passed in my buggy through the lofty gateway and entered a small court, where I was requested to get out, as no vehicles were allowed to enter further. A number of shabby looking soldiers were lolling about. They wore a clumsily-made uniform, after the English pattern, and were Sepoys of the Emperor's army, commonly called the "Palace Guard." Captain Douglass, their commander, who was the first victim of the mutiny at Delhi, gave me two chobdars, or royal mace-bearers, to accompany me through the palace. They were an ill-dressed, slip-shod pair of Moosulmans, whose chief idea seemed to be "bucksees." The maces were heavy silver canes, about four feet long.

We passed through several very lofty vaulted galleries of stone, leading from one court to another, and at length emerged into a very large court, surrounded by stone buildings. Above the arched entrance is a gallery, called the Nowbut Khana, or music room, where the band used to play. On the opposite side of the court, and projecting into it from the wall of the zĕnana, is an extensive square stone terrace, approached by three stairways from the court. This terrace has a stone roof, supported by many stone columns. In the wall at the back, which separates the hall thus formed from the zĕnana, is a stairway that leads up to the throne, which is raised about ten feet from the ground, and covered by a canopy supported by four pillars. The canopy is all of marble, and the wall behind it is also of the same material. They are both covered with the most exquisite mosaics, representing the flowers, birds, and beasts of Hindoostan. These were executed by Austin de Bordeaux, a French jeweller of great skill, who, having committed some crimes in Europe, took refuge at the Mogul court. The throne has a doorway behind it, by which the Emperor entered from his zĕnana. On the stone floor of the hall is a raised slab, on which the wuzeer stood and handed up to his imperial master the petitions which he received from the suitors below.

This hall is called the Dewán Am, or Court of Public Justice. Here the Emperor in person administered justice every day. The parties concerned were examined by the monarch himself; judgment was summarily rendered, and the sentences executed without delay.

In the great court-yard which surrounds the Dewán Am, on three sides, the cavalry and retinues of the grandees used to pass in review before the Emperor, as he sat on his throne. Here also were paraded for inspection the royal horses and elephants, covered with splendid trappings. The latter carried howdahs of gold or silver, their foreheads were painted with gay colours, their ears bore choúrees formed from the white bushy tail of the Thibet ox, and around their necks were suspended massive silver chains, from which hung bells which tinkled as they marched in stately procession around the area. As each elephant came before the throne, he bent one knee, raised his proboscis into the air, and trumpeted. After these came antelopes, rhinoceroses, buffaloes, leopards, and other wild animals, trained to fight each other; then followed sporting dogs of all kinds, and the procession closed with falconers, bearing on their wrists every kind of bird used in falconry.

When I visited the Dewán Am, it had not been used for many years, and was in a wholly neglected and ruinous condition. The mosaics were in many places picked out, the terrace was dirty and uncared for, and the great quadrangle was filled with mud huts and stables. During the recent mutiny, it has again come into use; and here, it is said, the Shahzadehs, or princes, sitting on the marble terrace, "drew the first blood" from the trembling Christians in the court below, after which they were butchered by the Khasburdars. Of this story, it may be said, "Sinon vrai, du moins vraisemblable;" if it is not true, it is one of those illustrative stories, so many of which find a place in history, and which represent individuals performing acts which typify the feelings of whole classes. At any rate, it is quite certain that, if the royal family did not take an active part in the slaughter, they, at least, gave the orders, and that, too, after the most solemn promises and oaths that the lives of all who had fled to their protection should be spared. The Khasburdars, who officiated as executioners, were the highest servants of the palace, and were allowed to perform the task as a favour, since Indian Moosulmans believe that whoever kills a Kaffur, or infidel, wipes away by the act all his previous sins.

From the Dewán Am we went into a smaller court, on one side of which, upon a terrace of pure white marble, is the Dewán Khas, or private hall—where the Emperor held his levees, and received the higher nobles to audience. It is a square marble canopy, resting on massive square pillars and arches of the same material. The marble is very highly polished. There is but little decoration—a few exquisitely graceful flowers in mosaic work being the only ornaments. One side of the Dewán Khas opens on the court, a second side looks on the palace gardens, a third side commands a fine view of the broad Jumna, which runs below, and the fourth rests against the walls of the zĕnana. Between each pair of the outside rows of pillars is a very beautiful balustrade of marble, chastely carved in several designs of perforated work. The roof has at each corner a marble kiosk with a gilt dome. The shape of the building is oblong, and its greatest length not more than sixty feet. I cannot deny that my first feeling, after all the encomiums I had heard, was one of disappointment with the size.

The ceiling was once entirely composed of gold and silver filagree work, for which the goldsmiths of Delhi are still noted. In the centre stood the famous peacock throne, so called from its back being formed by jewelled representations of peacocks' tails. The throne was six feet long and four feet broad, composed of solid gold, inlaid with precious gems. It was surmounted by a gold canopy, supported on twelve pillars of the same material. Around the canopy hung a fringe of pearls, and on each side of the throne stood two *chattahs*, or umbrellas, the symbol of royalty; they were formed of crimson velvet, richly embroidered with gold thread and pearls, and had handles eight feet long, of solid gold, studded with diamonds. This unparalleled achievement of the jeweller's art was constructed by Austin de Bordeaux, by command of the Emperor, Shah Jehan, who founded the present city of Delhi, and built this palace. The value of the throne is estimated by Tavernier, a Frenchman who saw it, and who was himself a professional jeweller, at six millions of pounds sterling.

Here then, on this magnificent throne, in the most beautiful apartment of the grandest palace in the East, within the walls of his splendid and populous capital, sat the Emperor Shah Jehan, arrayed in the most sumptuous attire, sparkling in jewels of unparalleled beauty, and surrounded by the pomp and state of a court, in comparison with which even the costly splendour of Louis XIV., which ruined his kingdom and dynasty, grows pale. He was at the head of an almost countless army, the absolute sovereign of one-sixth of the human race; and as he sat in state and received the homage of his powerful vassals, he must have gazed with satisfaction on the proud legend which he had caused to be inscribed on the cornice of this his presence chamber, "If there be a paradise on earth, it is here, it is here." Little did he anticipate that all this should pass away from his grasp, and that he himself, after ten years of imprisonment, would die in the fortress of Agra.

A hundred years later, Mohummud Shah, a descendant of Shah Jehan, is sitting in this same apartment. He is still surrounded by all the insignia of royalty, but beside him sits a Persian soldier, in whose hands is all the power. Nadur Shah wills to be treated as the guest of his captive, and takes a pleasure in mocking humbled royalty by allowing the conquered Emperor to preserve the outward show of authority. Coffee is brought by the highest lord of the household, but he is uncertain to whom he should first offer the fragrant beverage—he knows that his head will be the penalty for the least apparent slight to either of the monarchs whom he is serving. But the native tact of the Indian Moosulman bears him safely through the trial, and with a graceful politeness that would have honoured a noble of the "old régime," he takes the salver to his old sovereign, saying as he presented it, "I know that your Majesty would not allow your distinguished guest to be served by any but your own royal hands." With a true Persian appreciation of courtly polish, Nadur Shah says to the Emperor, "If all your Majesty's servants had known their duty as well, and done it as thoroughly as this one, I should not now be sitting here."

So the coffee was served without bloodshed, and the two kings sat and sipped it, and talked together as if they were the best friends in the world. The next day Delhi was subjected to all the horrors of a general sack and massacre, and the old Emperor lay prostrate at the conqueror's feet interceding for the lives of his subjects. The month which followed was spent in plundering and torturing high and low to obtain their money, and in scarce six weeks from his first appearance in the capital, Nadur Shah led back his victorious army, bearing to his western home the golden peacock throne, the hoarded treasures of the Mogul Empire, all the money and jewels which could be collected, and leading with him into captivity many hundreds of those skilful artisans and workmen for which Delhi has always been famous.

Henceforth we read of one invasion after another. The power of the Mogul throne had passed away, the few treasures of the palace and the public buildings which escaped the rapacity of the Persians and Afghans were plundered by the Maharattas, who melted down the gold filagree ceiling of the Dewán Khas, and destroyed a magnificent crystal seat, which was one of its most remarkable ornaments, by lighting a fire round it. Two occupants of the imperial throne were successively assassinated. Their successor was forced to throw himself on the protection of the English, who gave him shelter and an ample income at Allahabad. Five years afterwards, in 1771, he again returned to Delhi, where he soon became a mere tool of the Maharattas. Six years later and the scene is again in the Dewán Khas. Delhi has been invested by a formidable body of rebels, to which the Maharatta garrison offered no resistance. The Emperor was dragged before the rebel chief Gholam Kadur, who is seated in the throne-room, and is commanded to show where his treasures are concealed. In vain he plead the utter poverty of himself and his family. The rebel general, incensed at his inability to extract the information, knocked down the aged monarch, and kneeling on his breast, put out his eyes with his dagger, while the poor old man could only murmur, "Why should I be deprived of those eyes which have been incessantly employed, for sixty years, in studying the sacred Korán ?"

The Maharattas, however, soon returned in great force. They deposed the rebel chief and caused him to be trodden to death by elephants. The Emperor was restored to a nominal sovereignty, but he was really only a little more comfortable than when a captive of Gholam Kadur. Sindiah, the rajah of the Maharattas, and his French officers, only allowed the imperial family a miserably insufficient annuity, retaining in their own hands nearly the whole revenue of the Crown property. Bishop Heber relates that during this period most of the marble and inlaid ornaments of the palace were mutilated; as they were actually sold by the Emperor to obtain bread for himself and his children. In 1803 the arms of the British triumphed over those of the Maharattas. The Emperor at once threw himself under the protection of Lord Lake, and begged to be delivered from his oppressors. Five years after he was deposed and blinded by Gholam Kadur, the poor old monarch again took a seat in the throne-room of his ancestors, the scene of his former humiliation. The splendour of the Mogul empire had long since departed, with its power, and the blind and feeble king had only a tattered canopy over his head to mark his royal rank. Lord Lake approached the Emperor with the utmost respect; he recognized him as the "fidoi," or feudal sovereign of the Company, and reinstated him in the enjoyment of his revenues. The deliverance of their Emperor from the combined tyranny of the Maharattas and their French officers, was a cause of the greatest rejoicing to the inhabitants of Delhi, and an immense concourse of people assembled to greet the solemn entrance of the English commander. For a long time the English continued to rule India in the name of the Emperor. Since 1830, however, the meaningless form has been abolished, but the Emperor was still recognized as a sovereign, although the imperial power was confined to the limits of his palace. The lowest member of the royal family, of whom there are hundreds living in the palace, always addressed the British Resident as "Our particular slave," and was answered, "Your Majesty's slave has heard your Majesty's commands, &c." The royal family received regularly an allowance of $750,000 per annum, on which the Emperor was enabled to keep up considerable state, and held regular courts in the long abandoned Dewán Khas, where Bishop Heber was presented. Of this ceremony he gives an interesting description in his "Travels."

For fifty years after this time Delhi enjoyed uninterrupted tranquillity, under the powerful protection of the British. The city was thoroughly fortified and drained; and its aqueduct, which had become useless under the Maharattas, was restored. The inhabitants were freed from the fear of invasion and pillage from without, or the oppressive rapacity of their native governors. The royal family were protected in the enjoyment of their throne, honours, and revenues.

The last Emperor, who was on the throne when I visited Delhi, appeared in public only once a year. The rest of his time he passed in the puerile amusements of his zĕnana. He is an old man, almost childish it was said, and might have died quietly if he had not been sufficiently foolish to join the recent revolt—a movement which, had it succeeded, would have thrown India back to the state in which it was after Nadur Shah's conquest—from which he could have expected no advantage (for no one who has studied the history of India will believe that he could have retained power for any time); and which, in its failure, involved the ruin of himself and his family, the devastation of his city, and the misery of what were the dominions of his ancestors.

The Dewán Khas is again occupied. The last monarch of Shah Jehan's line is again present in the throne-room of his empire. He is a mean-looking old man, plainly dressed, crouched upon a low native bedstead, and smoking a hookah. His hairs are white, and what little expression remains in his Jewish features, is not pleasant to look at. Before him, at a table, sit a row of officers in the English uniform. They are judging him for treason to the Power to whose protection and generosity alone he owed his position and ability to do mischief. After the most ample and pains-taking investigation, they convict him of treachery and murder.

Of all the remarkable events of which the Dewán Khas has been the theatre, certainly this was the grandest and most significant. If the trial of Charles the First was not merely his individual condemnation, but was also the practical denial and abolition of the Divine Right of English kings, and the adoption of the democratic idea in the government, then the judgment pronounced upon the king of Delhi was not only the decree of a British court upon a miserable old man, rendered almost imbecile by age and a long life of debauchery: it was the verdict of the civilised world on the whole line of which he was the last representative—it was the sentence pronounced by Christendom upon the utter incapacity, the childish folly, the hopeless corruption, the abandoned licentiousness, the fiendish cruelty, and the intolerable oppression of the effete dynasties of Asia—it was the decision of Humanity in the grand trial between Christianity and Paganism for supremacy in the East—a decision which, it is not presumptuous to say, has been ratified by the Eternal Justice of the King of kings.

The narrative of the various events that have taken place in the Dewán Khas, has led me away from the regular description of my visit to the Palace, and to that we will now return.

I had now seen the two reception courts of the Mógul emperors, the Dewán Am and the Dewán Khas. Leaving the latter, I wandered for a while among the extensive gardens which were once magnificent, but had long been sadly neglected, like the rest of the Palace.

I next visited the Motee Músjeed, or "Pearl Mosque," where the Emperor worshipped every day. It is a small building of the purest white marble, and without ornament. The domes were gilt, and the doors were of bronze, worked with much skill and taste.

I had now seen all that was exhibited to visitors, in the Palace. The zĕnana, or private apartments, were of course not visible, and the rest of the large space enclosed within the Palace walls was used for the residences of the many dependents of the court, and was not worth seeing.

From the Palace I went to the Jumma Músjeed, or principal mosque, which is about a quarter of a mile distant. It is situated on an elevation in the centre of the city, and is visible from every part of the town. Around the crest of the elevations runs a red stone wall, having three gates, each approached by a broad flight of fifty steps from the street below. The eastern gateway is the finest, and the steps leading up to it are the broadest; they are used as a sort of market, during the afternoon, by birdsellers, muraba (sweetmeat) dealers, and others. These three entrances lead into a quadrangle, about three hundred feet square, on the western side of which is the mosque proper. The court is paved with red sandstone, inlaid with white marble; and contains in its centre a large marble tank for ablutions.

The mosque proper, as I have said before, occupies the greater part of the western side, being the side toward Mecca. It is built of red sandstone, and is about two hundred feet in length by over one hundred deep. Toward the court it is open, the wall being supported by the arches, of nearly Gothic form. Within, it is paved with oblong slabs of marble, inlaid with borders of black stone, which define the space allowed to each worshipper. The western wall is also wainscotted with marble slabs. In its middle is the Kibla, a marble niche showing the direction of Mecca. Close to the Kibla is the pulpit, a solid marble platform, approached by a few steps from the ground. There are three domes, of great size and very graceful. They are formed of white marble, relieved by vertical layers of red stone; and terminate in delicate spires of gilt copper. The mosque is flanked by two minârs, one hundred and thirty feet high, composed of white marble and red stone, in alternate vertical layers. At about equal distances are three projecting galleries, and they are crowned with light pavilions of white marble.

The whole effect of the mosque is extremely imposing, and I suppose it is, as the natives claim, the finest building ever erected for Mahommedan worship.

I ascended one of the minârs, from which I obtained a magnificent view of the city and the surrounding country. The appearance of Delhi is quite different from that of Běnarěs. In the latter, the houses are high, and have flat paved roofs. In Delhi, on the contrary, although more than half of the population are Hindoos, the architecture is entirely Moosulman, as it is in almost all the other cities of Northern India. The houses are low, with tiled roofs, upon which the inhabitants amuse themselves with flying kites—a national amusement, which formed one of the most frequent and serious occupations of the royal family.

As I sat on the summit of the minár, looking east, the panorama was very striking. Before me rolled the Jumna, almost parallel with the front of the mosque. On the further bank of the river nothing was to be seen but the low shore, and the broad barren plain. Sometimes, they say, the Himalayas are visible, but that can only be in the fairest weather. Along the western bank, ran the Palace, which with its fortifications, its courts and streets, and the great variety of buildings which it encloses, presented just the appearance of a walled town. From the great gate of the Palace, the broad Chandee chôk ran west to the city walls, dividing the mass of tiled roofs into two nearly equal areas. Beyond this street was seen the house of the Bégoom Sombre, a splendid residence. This and the Palace are almost the only conspicuous objects in the city, except the mosques, which for size and splendour do not compare with those of Lucknow. Although so large a part of the inhabitants are Hindoos, I did not remark the pointed spire of a single Mundră.

Beyond the city walls all was desolation. On my left, that is on the northern side, rose the low hills which intervened between the city and the cantonments. On the south side of the city, were the ruins of old Delhi, conspicuous among which were the tombs of Hoomaioon and Sufdur Jung, the Observatory, and the old forts of former dynasties. Far in the distance I could see the Kootub Minár.

On descending from the minár, I made an unsuccessful attempt to enter a portion of the court which is partitioned off by a beautifully carved white marble screen. In it are kept certain relics of the Prophet, and of the two famous Imáms, Hússun and Hoosén. This enclosure, however, is so sacred that no Kaffurs are allowed to enter it; indeed, formerly, Europeans could not come within the great enclosure of the mosque without removing their shoes. This prohibition had, however, been removed by government, who obtained the right to interfere by the repairs which they have made to the building, and the sums of money which they allowed for its support.

It being Friday, the Mahommedan Sabbath, some hundreds of Moosulmans had assembled for worship. This may seem a small number for so large a city, especially as I did not see any worshippers at the other mosques; but I believe I have mentioned before that the Moosleem in India are far from displaying that regular attention to the forms of their religion which is so striking to the traveller in Arabian and Turkish countries. The devotions consisted in various genuflexions, and the rapid muttering of Arabic prayers, which are not "understanded of the people."

On the last day of the Ramuzán the Emperor always came in state to this mosque to break up the Fast. The vast enclosure of the building, which holds twelve thousand persons, was then filled with the faithful in their gayest attire, and marshalled in straight rows by the marble lines and spaces in the pavement. The spectacle is described as deeply impressive.

The Jumma Músjeed was built in 1630, by Shah Jehan, the same monarch who founded the present city and constructed the Palace. It is said that for many years prayers have been offered up in it for the restoration of the Moosulman Empire. This is very likely, as, although the government would certainly have known of it, they would not feel themselves called upon to interfere with the religious worship of the natives; and would look upon it as a matter of very small importance, whatever might be the tenour of the prayers. Since the taking of Delhi, certain persons have proposed that this building should be turned into a Christian Cathedral. As it consists mainly of a large court, it is plain that the plan is impracticable. It could only be carried out by walling up the eastern arches of the mosque proper, which would give a very awkward apartment entirely unadapted to Christian worship, and would utterly destroy the architectural effect.

From the Jumma Músjeed I returned to the dâk-bungalow and took tiffin, after which I drove to the tomb of the Emperor Hoomaioon, which is about three miles south of the Delhi gate of the city.

On the way I stopped to see a celebrated object called Feerooz Shah ka Lat, or the Emperor Feerooz's walking stick. It is situated among the ruins of the palace of that monarch, and is a round granite shaft, thirty or forty feet high. The material of the column is a sort of stone which is not found nearer than the Siwalik hills, a hundred miles from Delhi. It was originally set up in Meeruth, but was removed from that place by the Emperor Feerooz, a Moosulman prince of the Toghluk dynasty, who ruled in Delhi during the fourteenth century, and died ten years before Taimoor's invasion. The Lat is covered by an inscription, in a very ancient character, which was entirely unintelligible to the most learned Brahmuns, even in the time of Feerooz. European skill has, however, deciphered the writing, which proves to consist of certain edicts for the furtherance of religion and virtue enacted by a king called Dhumma Asoko Piyadasi, who reigned B.C. 320, and who must have changed his character after ascending the throne, as he only obtained that dignity by the murder of ninety of his relations who had prior claims. The column is therefore at least twenty-two hundred years old, and the inscription upon it is probably the oldest writing in India.

All around the Lat are the massive ruins of the palace and Jumma Musjeed, built by Feerooz at this place, which was then the centre of his capital city.

Hoomaioon's tomb is a square building of red stone and marble, built upon a terrace about three hundred feet square, and twenty high, formed of the same materials. The architecture is in the purest and simplest form of Indian Moosulman art. Each side of the mausoleum is over a hundred feet long, and contains three deep arched recesses, almost the whole height of the building, within which are the windows. The arches are almost pure Gothic, but a little flattened. The dome is of white marble, and is considerably lower than those of the later Moosulman buildings.

Within the building, under the dome, is a large circular room, containing in its centre the simple, unadorned tomb of the Emperor. Hoomaioon was the son of Babur, and father of Akbur. He did not long enjoy the empire conquered by his father, for, having been deposed by a successful rebellion, he became a fugitive from one Indian court to another, and finally had to take refuge with the King of Persia. At length he treacherously got possession of a city belonging to his protector, and with the money and forces obtained by this act, he succeeded in overthrowing one of his most formidable opponents, his younger brother Kamran. Having put out Kamran's eyes he continued the reconquest of his empire, and at last reëstablished his throne at Delhi, after sixteen years of exile. Six months afterwards he died, having fallen from the staircase of his library upon a marble floor. He was a great scholar, astrologer and patron of literature, and is considered one of the finest characters in Indian history.

The two wives of Hoomaioon are also buried in this building, which contains besides the tombs of other members of his house; among them that of Dara Shéko, the eldest son of Shah Jehan, who was murdered by the command of his brother, the Emperor Aurungzeeb.

The terrace, or chubootra, on which this mausoleum is built, is a distinctive feature of Moosulman art in India. It is always much broader than the building which it supports, and generally just so high that when the observer stands at the entrance of the court-yard, the lower line of the building is apparently on a level with his eye. The effect of these chubootras is really wonderful, and is like that of a good frame to a picture, or a pedestal to a statue. The arched recesses which are spoken of above, are also peculiar to this architecture. They begin at the ground, and commonly cover nearly half the surface of the building. The doors and windows, which are within them, may be of any size, but these recesses are always as large as circumstances will permit, and are the grand feature of every façade.

This magnificent mausoleum is enclosed in a quadrangle, nearly four hundred yards square, which was formerly laid out as a garden, with marble-fish ponds and other decorations, but is now neglected and uncared for. The quadrangle is enclosed by a lofty embattled wall of redstone, with towers and four fine gateways. Being a place of considerable strength, the enclosure of this tomb as well as that of Sufdur Jung's mausoleum, were formerly used as places of refuge by the inhabitants of the suburbs during the incursions of the Maharattas. It was here that the King of Delhi took refuge after the capture of the city last autumn; and here he was taken prisoner by Captain Hodgson. Nothing can give a better idea of the immense moral superiority of the European over the native, than this daring achievement. The enclosure, I have said, was strong, far stronger than the Residency at Lucknow. The king was within, surrounded by troops of armed followers. The Englishman was alone, far away from all help, and accompanied only by fifty black suwars (horsemen) who could not be relied on. He ordered the king to come out, promising him only his own life, and that of his favourite wife and her son. The disproportion of these commands with Captain Hodgson's power of enforcing them would be ludicrous were it not for the imminent danger to which he was exposed, and the confidence in himself and his race which he displayed. He knew the native character, and felt sure that under the circumstances no native would have the spirit to resist a command. The king yielded at once, and set forth with his followers towards the city. The procession moved at a foot pace, the road was bad, on every side were tombs and other ruins that would serve for ambush or refuge, but Hodgson coolly rode by the side of his prisoner, with drawn sword ready to kill him should a rescue be attempted. All around were thousands of armed men, any one of whom might have shot that lonely Englishman without dread of the consequence, but not a man dared to lift his hand; all were cowed by the calm courage and undaunted confidence of his expression. That was the grand triumph of the Anglo-Saxon blood. A native may fight as well as another when excited; he will even risk his life more readily than a European, but there is not a man in India who will not quail before an Englishman's eyes, and tremblingly obey his commands.

During the recent mutiny, English courage has nobly supported its ancient reputation. Feeble companies have borne the attack of countless adversaries, ladies have shot down the wretches who dared to assail their life and their honour, and have then killed themselves to avoid a worse fate. Everywhere the odds were a thousand to one. Everywhere the war was one of extermination, yet not one Englishman ever despaired, not one ever doubted the result of the struggle. But in the long list of acts of individual heroism which have distinguished this above all modern wars, and which, when we hear them told, carry us back to the days of chivalry, I think no single action is so thoroughly characteristic of British pluck, as the capture of the King of Delhi by Captain Hodgson.

CHAPTER XXIII.

DELHI AND UMBALA.

The Saint's Tomb—A Royal Cemetery—A Victim of the English—The Old Fort—A Nach at Mr. Skinner's—The Dinner—The Girls—Their Songs—Dancing Boys—Native Gentlemen—Snakes—The Bazárs of Delhi—The Streets—A Native Wedding—A "Public Night" at the Mess of the 54th—Dâk to Umbala—Sick—A Dandy Servant—"Vengeance is Sweet"—Sepoy Bands—The Native Army—Cashmeer Shawls.

From Hoomaioon's tomb I went to a village, half a mile north, where is buried a celebrated Moosulman saint, Nizam-ood-Deen, who died in the early part of the fourteenth century. The tomb is within a court paved with marble. It is a small but very beautiful white marble building, surrounded by a colonnade, and covered by a dome. Between the pillars of the colonnade are scarlet cloth purdahs, or curtains. In the centre of the building the body of the saint lies in a low sarcophagus of marble, which is covered with silk brocade, strewn with fresh flowers. The sanctity of this shrine is such that it still attracts pilgrims from all parts of India, whose contributions keep the tomb in order. Within this court-yard are buried several members of the imperial family, among others, the Emperor Mohummud Shah, during whose reign the invasion of Nadur Shah took place. Close by is the tomb of Prince Mirza Jehangeer, who was banished by the English government from Delhi, on account of frequent attempts to murder his elder brother, and excite insurrection. He killed himself by drinking cherry brandy, of which liquor he used to swallow a glass an hour, limiting himself to that amount, in order to protract the pleasure and delay intoxication. He was the favourite son of the old Emperor, who always believed that he died of "sighing." At his death, the limited resources of the imperial purse were drawn on to give him a handsome tomb in this place. Many other tombs lie around, among which the most remarkable is that of Jehanara Bégoom, the eldest daughter of Shah Jehan, and a very lovely character. All these tombs are of the same character. They are plain, square marble structures, about six feet long and two feet high, surrounded by screens of that exquisite marble trellis-work which is so beautiful a feature of Moosulman architecture. The tomb of Jehanara is shaped like the others, and, like them, is surrounded by a screen; but it is not covered with a slab. At its head is a stone, containing an inscription dictated by herself, and explaining this peculiarity. It runs as follows: "Let no rich canopy cover my grave. This grass is the best covering for the tomb of the poor in spirit. The humble, the transitory Jehanara, the disciple of the holy men of Christ, the daughter of the Emperor Shah Jehan." The allusion to Christ is thought by some to signify that she had become a convert of the Romish priests, others suppose that she belonged to some Moosulman sect who particularly revered the character of Jesus. When Shah Jehan was imprisoned by his son Aurunzeeb, Jehanara voluntarily resigned her liberty, and accompanied her father into confinement, where she continued with him till his death. She died soon afterwards—poisoned, it is said, by her sister.

Close to these tombs is a baolee, or deep tank, about sixty feet square, similar to that near the Kootub. Here the same feats of diving, which I had seen at the former place, were repeated; but the leap is far higher, being at least sixty feet.

On the way back to Delhi, I stopped to see the Poorana Khila, or old Fort, which was formerly the centre of the old Pathan city of Delhi. It is a very large building, with high and massive walls, of dark coloured stone. The top of the walls was plain, not decorated with those arched battlements which distinguish the later Moosulman fortresses. The interior of the "Old Fort" is now occupied by an extensive village of mud huts, but it still contains a very large and massive tomb of redstone, and another considerable building in good repair.

That evening I dined at Mr. Skinner's, or, as he is called

by the natives, Sĕkundur Sahib—Sĕkundur, being the Hindoostanee pronunciation of Alexander, which is his first name. The party was very large, as nearly all the officers in the garrison were invited. I suppose fifty sat down to table. All the guests sent their own servants, plates, and silver—which is always customary in India where many are invited. As I was not aware of this habit, I was rather at a loss, having come without servant or plates; but my friend, Captain Russell, was kind enough to provide me with all that was necessary, and lend me one of his two Khitmutgrás.

Mr. Skinner is a half caste, almost black in complexion. His father, the celebrated Colonel Skinner, whom I mentioned before, left his property to each of his sons in succession, on the condition that a certain large portion of it should be spent yearly in entertainments. Accordingly, the hospitality of the Skinners became famous in India, and the races, hunts, coursing-matches, dinners, and nach parties, which they gave, were considered one of the chief attractions of Delhi as a Station.

The house where this dinner was given was situated on the square near the Cashmeeree Gate, and opposite the church of St. James. It was built by Colonel Skinner, and was a spacious one-storied mansion, in a compound filled with shrubbery.

Mr. Skinner having a great deal more black blood than white in his veins, conformed in many respects to native usages, and kept a zĕnana, where he had several wives and concubines. One of the latter was said to be a sister of his eldest wife. These little peculiarities cut him off from the society of the ladies of the station, but he always found guests enough among the officers to enable him to comply with the hospitable provisions of his father's will.

The dinner was of the best that could be had, and on the most liberal scale, and the usual amount of "beershurab" and "simpkin," as the natives call ale and champagne, were consumed in honouring the old customs of drinking healths and toasting, which still reign in India.

After dinner we retired into a large drawing-room, where the remainder of the evening was spent in witnessing the performances of some nach girls.

I had always heard a great deal of these bayadères, so that I expected a treat; particularly, as Delhi is famous throughout India for its dancing girls, and Mr. Skinner would, of course, have the best that could be procured. The result, however, very much disappointed my expectations.

The girls were ten in number, of whom not more than two performed at the same time. They were dressed in pa*n*jama, or trowsers, of velvet, silk, or muslin, which reached to below the ankle, and trailed on the ground. These trowsers are so loose that they sometimes contain fifteen or twenty yards of stuff. The upper part of the body is entirely covered by a muslin saree, wrapped many times round the person, and brought over the head. The colours of the dress are generally green and red. The clothes of several of these girls were embroidered with gold thread, and they all wore gold armlets, anklets, nose-rings, ear-rings, and another ornament, which is a great favourite among Indian beauties, and consists of a precious stone, set in gold, which is glued to the forehead between the eyes, and really has a very pretty effect on the brown skin. Their hair was plainly dressed "à la Chinoise"—a mode which should be called "à l'Indienne," for it is universal in India, and by no means so in China. Of course, they wore no shoes, as natives never do in the house, but the soles of their feet and palms of their hands were stained red with "heena," and the languishing expression of their dark eyes was heightened by a border of kohl, or antimony, around the edge of the lids.

The songs they sang were in Persian, and were of two kinds.* The first was very simple, both in words and music, consisting merely of a repetition of such words as, "Oh, my mother-in-law, go to the river and fetch water," or, "My beloved prince, take me to Calcutta, with howdah on elephant, saddle on horse." The second variety they sung in the latter part of the evening. They were Amœbean strains, sustained by two voices, and representing a quarrel between women. The words were all curses, so foul that I do not believe they could have been invented out of India.

As the girls sang they swayed the body to and fro, bent

* See Appendix, at the end of the Book.

the hand upon the wrist, and assumed other positions, beating the feet upon the ground in time with the music, and jingling the circles of silver bells which they wore around the ankles.

The girls had each two or three musicians, jaunty-looking Moosulmans, who accompanied them upon the drum, sitar (native guitar), and other instruments. The drum was played with the fingers; and there were no wind instruments used. The music was in general slow and monotonous, as were also the postures of the girls—for their movements can scarcely be called dancing.

The nach girls are a peculiar class. Their lives are spent in debauchery, and they will drink more raw spirits than most men I have seen. Like women of the same character elsewhere, they do not bear children, but instead thereof they buy infants, sometimes from their parents, sometimes from kidnappers or slave dealers; for slavery, although abolished by law, still exists as a domestic institution in India. These children they train up to their trade, and it is said that their education must begin in early life, or they can never acquire the requisite grace and suppleness. The consequence of this strange custom is, that this class present the peculiar spectacle of women who never have had the slightest idea of virtue or modesty. Some of these dancing girls whom I saw at Colonel Skinner's brought two or three of these children with them. They were pretty little timid girls of five or six years old, with very graceful and winning manners; but when once encouraged to talk, they uttered sentiments and expressions which would bring a blush to the oldest habituée of the Haymarket.

The nach girls are rarely handsome—they say that all the good-looking ones are at once seized by the native princes for their zĕnanas. How this may be, I do not know, but some of them have certainly risen to positions of eminence and great power in Eastern courts. Their voices are very high, and frequently harsh and nasal—but that is not esteemed a defect. The ordinary pay is from five to ten rupees an evening, but some of them, who are very graceful, and have particularly high voices (for good looks and a sweet tone are not taken into consideration), occasionally get as high as five hundred rupees a night.

The entertainments at Colonel Skinner's were varied by the introduction of some nach boys. They were about seven years old, and although they did not possess the same undulating grace as the girls, their voices were sweeter, and they sang with more spirit, so that they were quite as interesting. They were dressed in clothes similar to those worn by the nach girls, and they danced in the same way. The characters of these boys were, if possible, more degraded than those of the women.

During the evening three Moosulmans, of high rank, joined the party. The eldest of the three was a thick-set man, of about forty, with a dark skin, and bushy black beard. He wore a very rich dress of blue cloth, embroidered with gold, and a large red turban, worked with gold thread. The other two were younger, and had much lighter complexions, and no beards. They were dressed simply in white, but wore kummurbunds and turbans of fine Cashmeer shawls. None of the three was armed, and they all took off their shoes before entering the room. Their manners had a high-bred polish, which would have done honour to a nobleman of the court of Versailles, and which is often found in natives of rank. I was particularly interested by the youngest two, who had very pleasing countenances, and regretted that I could not converse with them, since they did not speak English. I afterwards learned that they were near relatives of Shumsh-ood-Deen, who was hung at Delhi for the murder of his patron and friend, Mr. Frazer.

These native gentlemen, as well as my host, and a few of the officers, smoked their hookahs the whole evening. This is undoubtedly the most luxurious form of smoking. The hookah is similar in principle to a Turkish narghilé, but is much larger, and many persons keep servants whose only business is to attend to their hookahs. The smoke of these pipes has a very pleasant smell, the tobacco being perfumed, and the smoke being conducted through rose-water. They were formerly much used, and have this advantage, that it is allowable to smoke them at table in the presence of ladies, or in a drawing-room. Of late years, however, many new English ideas have been introduced, among which is the smoking of cigars and pipes, and I suppose hookahs will soon be entirely out of fashion among Europeans.

The people of India—men, women, and children—all smoke. Tobacco is so common and cheap as to be within the reach even of the poorest, and smoking is almost the only consolation of the poor ryut, whose idea of enjoyment is limited to perching like a monkey on the top of some wall, with his beloved hookah at his lips.

The next morning, as soon as I awoke, my servant told me that there was a snake-man, (samp-wala,) as the natives call snake charmers, outside the bungalow, who longed to have the honour of amusing me. Accordingly, I opened the venetians, and found two or three black fellows squatted on the verandah, with some earthen chattees, or pots, which contained the snakes. The natives made their salám, and the performance commenced. One of the men played on two pipes, the ends of which were fitted into a hollow gourd, into which he blew. As soon as the music began, his companion removed the cover of a chattee from which a large cobra soon reared his head. The snake seemed to be so pleased at getting his liberty, as to be quite peaceably inclined, and had to be poked with a stick before he became angry. When his temper was excited, he dilated the skin of his neck, which stood out several inches from his head, in shape like a monk's hood. It is from this remarkable property of this animal, that it derives its name of "cobra di capello," or "snake of the hood." The name was first applied by the Portuguese, and was afterwards adopted by the English. After the snake had come out of his pot, he looked around for a moment, and then stiffening his body, he raised his head a foot from the ground; and gazed at the musician, at the same time swinging himself slightly from side to side, which I was informed was dancing. It was certainly quite as much like that exercise, as the performances of the nach girls, the night before. I was afterwards shown other snakes of various kinds, and a mungoos was finally produced, who concluded the entertainment by killing several of them.

After breakfast, I walked out through the different bazârs, and made several purchases. Delhi is famous for its shawls, made in imitation of those of Cashmeer; I saw a number of very fine ones. Another manufacture in which the artificers of Delhi excel, is the gold and silver jewellery, and especially filagree work, which is even finer than that made by the Chinese. The artists of Delhi are very celebrated for their exquisite miniatures upon ivory, the execution of which is as good as anything of the sort I ever saw in America. They represent public buildings, and celebrated personages; the pictures of buildings being much the best, as the anatomy of the figures is defective. I used to think that some one of these fellows must have taken lessons of a European, and that the rest of them only copied his pictures, because Delhi is the only town in India where you see any even tolerable pictures by natives, and at Delhi all the likenesses of the same individual which you may see, no matter by whom taken, resemble one another in every minute detail of dress, posture, and expression.

The streets of Delhi are very gay, much gayer than those of any other native town which I saw, and I found much interest and amusement in observing the people. The Moosulmans in Delhi seemed to me to have nothing to do but to strut about, and show their fine clothes. But I do them injustice—they have one serious occupation, and that is, flying kites, which they construct with so much skill, that they do not require tails, as in other countries. The expression on the faces of these dandy Moosulmans was one of the most insufferable arrogance and insolence; equally removed from the timid manner and cunning smile of the Bengalee, and from the really martial, though somewhat gasconading bearing of the Rajpoot. To afford food for the bodies of this noble race, shops of confections and sweetmeats occupied every corner, while the constant *tomashas*, or shows, which were to be seen in the streets, nourished and strengthened their minds. Of these shows, there were two kinds: the standard, and the occasional. Among the standard shows were jugglers and snake-charmers; but by far the most popular of all was a rude sort of puppet-show, infinitely inferior to Punch. This amusement was not, like the performance of that hero, intended for the diversion of children, but was witnessed by crowds of men with shouts of admiration and enthusiasm.

Among the occasional shows, weddings were the most common and most popular. In India, this ceremony generally takes place when the parties to the marriage are not more than seven or eight years old. The wedding lasts eight or nine days, and is celebrated with as much pomp as the circumstances of the families will allow. Once performed, the marriage is indissoluble, although the bride does not reside with her husband until she is sixteen years old. Should the husband die in the meantime, his bride is considered a widow, and by the Hindoo law a widow can never marry again, a custom which is productive of great immorality, and a thousand evil consequences. I saw several marriage processions, but none so imposing as one of a Rajah's son, which is described by Mrs. Mackenzie. I extract the description, both because she tells the story better than I could hope to do, and because the thing described was grander than any similar scene which I witnessed. Occasionally I have taken the liberty of altering a phrase, to make the meaning clearer. Mrs. Mackenzie occupied a window in the Chandee chôk. She says: "The procession was passing down the street, on the side furthest from us, and turning at the end of the street, it paraded before the bride's house, which was a little way above us, and then came close under our windows. It was more than a mile long! The balconies and flat roofs of the houses, which were generally low, were covered with people; here was a variegated group of men and children, there a bevy of shrouded Mahommedan women. The gay dresses of the crowd gave it the appearance of a bed of tulips.

"Just as we had seated ourselves, numbers of empty palkees were passing; then a crowd of tonjons, some empty, some with one or two children in them. Many of these were gorgeously dressed in brocade or velvet, with Greek caps of gold or silver; and some of them were borne by four men in scarlet, and attended by a man on each side with a chouree, or brush formed of the tail of the yak, or Thibet ox, to keep the flies away. All the friends of the bridegroom's family do him as much honour as they can, by sending their led horses, elephants, and vehicles of every description to swell the procession. The ladies of the Emperor's family were also there in bullock-carts, with scarlet hangings. His Majesty had also sent his guards, and his camels carried small swivel cannon, which were fired at intervals. The led horses formed a very picturesque feature in the procession; some of them were painted; a white one had his legs and tail dyed red with heena, and splashes of the same on his body, as if a bloody hand had been repeatedly laid on his side. Then came a body of men, dressed as English soldiers, at the Rajah's expense, and a band in the same costume played a Scotch melody. Next appeared a number of magnificent elephants, their faces elaborately painted in curious patterns, and their bodies gaily caparisoned in scarlet, green, and other bright colours.

"On a small baby-elephant, most richly adorned, sat a little boy, with an aigrette of jewels in front of his turban. His dress was a robe of lilac gauze, edged with gold, reaching to his feet, and carefully spread out, fan-wise, on each side, as he sat astride on the elephant. Then came the little bridegroom, who was a mass of gold. He sat alone in his howdah, with a careful servant behind him; his turban was covered with a veil of gold tissue, which he held up with both hands, that he might see all that was going on. Bearers of peacock fans, and others with gold pillars walked by him, while his elephant was as splendid as could be. A few other elephants closed the procession, the head of which now passed under our windows on its return. It consisted of huge trays filled with artificial flowers, the effect of which, as we looked down the street, was exceedingly pretty, like a parterre of the gayest colours. Then there were moving pavilions, with beds of flowers in front of them, peacocks on the top, and bands of musicians inside. Such music! fancy flutes in hysterics, drums in a rage, violins screaming with passion, and penny trumpets distracted with pain, and you will have a good idea of native harmony. A crowd of women and boys, of the humblest class, then appeared, carrying little flags.

"Eastern processions are like Eastern life—comprising the greatest contrasts of poverty and magnificence. They seem to think that everything, no matter what, helps to make a show. After, and among, the moving flower-beds came trays of huge dolls, and others of little puppets, one set of which represented a party of European officers at dinner, with their khitmutgrás waiting on them." These dolls were stuffed with sweetmeats, and were finally given up to be scrambled for by the crowd. They were followed by "several nach girls, splendidly dressed in red and gold, their muslin trowsers full of gathers, and very wide, and their long hair hanging down their backs. They were each carried by men on a canopied platform." The manners of these nach girls, and their postures, were bold to a degree which struck Mrs. Mackenzie as "most unpleasing in a woman;" but it is not very clear what else she could expect. This closed the procession, but Mrs. Mackenzie drove to a point opposite the bridegroom's house, which was illuminated by torches. As soon as he entered, the gate was closed after him, a custom which reminded her of the expression in the Gospel, "the bridegroom came, and they that were ready went in with him to the marriage; and the door was shut." This description is written by a lady, and for that very reason is much more accurate and particular than if the scene had been observed and described by a man. I hope that its interest will be a sufficient excuse for its insertion.

I dined that evening at the mess of the fifty-fourth regiment. It was a "public night," that is, an evening on which it is permitted to any member of the mess to invite as many of his own acquaintances as he may choose. The officers of the other regiment then stationed at Delhi were present, so that with the exception of a few black-coated civilians, who came by invitation, the company was the same that I had met at Colonel Skinner's. The evening was long and pleasant, and I did not return to the dâk-bungalow till midnight.

I left Delhi in gárrhee for Umbala, on the morning of November 29th. My intention was to make a rapid tour through the Punjab, which I supposed could be accomplished in a little over two weeks. In order to accomplish the trip in this time, I meant to travel beyond Umbala by the mail-cart, which goes ten miles an hour, only stopping to change horses. Although this conveyance is fatiguing and exposing, I felt quite in a condition to endure it, and accordingly left my servant, and all my luggage except a small carpet-bag, at Delhi.

The bridges not being completed beyond Peeplee, ninety miles from Delhi, the gárrhees do not run beyond that place. The remaining thirty miles I went by dhoolee, and arrived at Umbala on the morning of the thirtieth. I had been in robust health up to the time of leaving Delhi, and started from that place with every prospect of a pleasant and rapid trip. But after entering the dhoolee at Peeplee I began to be troubled with the premonitory symptoms of dysentery, and was much relieved when deposited at Umbala dâk-bungalow. Once there, I soon found that it would be impossible to think of continuing my trip on that day; so I determined to go to bed and endeavour to cure myself as soon as possible. Unfortunately, however, I mistook the nature of my complaint, and commenced doctoring myself with mutton broth, beef-steak, and hot brandy punch—a course of treatment which, by the following day, threw me into a high fever. The next morning I felt very ill, and began to think how I could get medical advice—not a very easy question to answer, for the only physicians on an Indian station are the surgeons attached to the various regiments. I was engaged in puzzling my brains on this question, and had almost made up my mind to do without a doctor, when the postmaster came in to give me notice that I must leave the dâk-bungalow, as several parties required the apartment which I occupied, and no traveller can claim accommodation in one of these establishments for more than twenty-four hours. I was in a complete dilemma—so ill that I could hardly move, without medical attendance and shelter, or any claim on any one for either. I now regretted that I had not taken the letters which my friends in Delhi offered me to their friends in Umbala. My perplexity was fortunately relieved by the arrival of Mr. Vauquelin, the assistant agent of the dâk company, in the carriages of which I had come from Calcutta. As soon as he saw my condition, he at once offered me the use of the bungalow belonging to Mr. Powell, the dâk agent, who had gone to Rawul Pindee—Mr. Vauquelin, who invited me, having charge of the business.

I had very comfortable quarters at Mr. Powell's, whither I was carried in a dhoolee. The bed had sheets, between a pair of which I had not slept since leaving Calcutta; a mattrass, even, being a stray luxury in dâk-bungalows and Mofussil hotels, the beds of which generally have bottoms of cane, or of plaited cotton listing, like those used by the natives. Such a couch, with a sheet spread over it, makes much the best bed in hot weather. In cold weather of course a mattrass is used; and travellers generally carry one with them, and find it useful in the dâk-gárrhee, and almost necessary in the dhoolee. Indian travelling has this peculiarity: the more baggage you have the more comfortable you are. Your baggage is no trouble to you, being all taken care of by your servants, and if you do not carry your own comforts with you, you will not find them on the way. Many men take even their wash-basins with them. I shall know better if I ever go to India again, but on this occasion, being inexperienced, I took with me neither sheets nor mattrass. On this part of my trip I was even worse provided than during the rest of my journey, for, having left my servant and luggage in Delhi, in expectation of travelling by dâk-cart, and having with me only the few indispensable articles that could be contained in a very small carpet-bag, I was of course quite unprepared for a month's sickness and detention, which was my lot at Umbala.

Mr. Vauquelin provided me with a physician, a young assistant-surgeon, who, on first seeing me was forcibly struck, as he afterwards confessed, with the impression that he would have the pleasure of attending my funeral. The disease with which I was affected is very dangerous in India, and I had it in an aggravated form, so that the doctor's apprehensions were not without foundation, particularly as several soldiers, who were taken down at the same time, and whose symptoms were not so bad as mine, died within a week.

I was waited on, or rather ought to have been waited on, by a young and dandified Moosulman servant, to whom I promised abundant bucksees if he would take good care of me. But seeing that I could not get out of bed to chastise him and enforce obedience, he used to absent himself nearly all day, so that I was quite alone except two visits a day from the doctor, and one from Mr. Vauquelin. For this treatment on the part of my servant I kept nursing up feelings of revenge, and at length I had an opportunity of paying him off. For the first few days the doctor would not let me eat anything, but on the third day he told me that I might have a little arrow-root in the evening. The method of preparing this article of food was fully explained to the "bearer," and he faithfully promised to have it ready at eight o'clock. Accordingly I kept awake past my usual hour of going to sleep, but eight o'clock came, and no bearer; another hour passed—it was nine, and still no signs of the servant. Yet another hour I lay there, almost frantic with the mingled emotions of hunger, sleepiness, hope deferred, and impotent rage. At length at ten o'clock my dandy made his appearance. He brought me my supper. At the sight of it all my anger vanished. I seized the bowl with eagerness, and beheld—not the rich gelatinous mass, upon the expectation of which my fancy had been gloating for twelve hours, but a pint of tepid water upon which floated some lumps of undissolved arrow-root. This was too much for a sick man's endurance. I knew the fellow would not have dared to treat me so if he had supposed that I was well enough to get out of bed and chastise him for his carelessness and inattention. I felt as if my life depended on that bowl of arrow-root, and having tasted one spoonful of the nauseous mixture, and spit it all back again into the bowl, my long pent up exasperation found vent, and I threw the whole thing at the fellow's head. It did not hurt him much, but it deprived him of caste. The food which I had tasted had touched his lips. "Oh! Representative of God, oh! Releaser of Slaves, oh! Provider for the Poor," he cried, "I am dead! my caste is gone!" I told him that he ought to take more care of a sick man, and the lesson had a good effect, as he was pretty attentive after this occurrence. The next day the other Moosulman servants held a Panchayut, or Council of Five, over him, and read him out of caste—a thing they do on the least pretext, as the person so ejected has to give them a feast to procure his readmission. All the rest of the time that I remained at Umbala this servant kept wearying me with entreaties for three rupees to give the above-mentioned feast. Sometimes he would put his head under my feet, and after my recovery, whenever I went out, I was sure to find him on my way ready to prefer his prayers. But, although wearied with his importunities, I never gave him anything for the purpose, as I considered it a very just punishment, and besides, the wages which I paid him, and which were far more than he had earned, were amply sufficient to defray these expenses, and leave something over for his trouble.

My days passed rather wearily. I was awakened before dawn by the morning gun, and bugles sounding the reveillé. From that time sleep was impossible. The thunder of artillery and the rattle of small arms lasted until eight. From that time there were no events, except the visit of the Doctor and Mr. Vauquelin. I used to lie in bed and calculate the probability of dying from the length of the Doctor's face. I even began writing a letter, to be sent home in case of my demise.

After a week's starvation, we got rid of the fever, and I began rapidly to mend. As soon as I could get out of bed, I went in a dhoolee to the station hotel, as Mr. Powell, whose room and bed I had been occupying, was expected back soon.

The hotel was very pleasant and comfortable. I remained there over ten days, and gained rapidly in strength and weight, both of which had been much reduced during my short illness. In one week I had lost twenty pounds of flesh.

Umbala was a very large station, and a band from some one of the native regiments used to play every evening on the parade-ground, where all the fashion of the station congregated. I frequently went there to hear the music, which was quite good. There is never any difficulty in forming a band of natives. Almost every man has the requisite ear and skill, and they learn the European notation with wonderful facility; but they never could be made to play with any spirit. It seemed as if they never entered into the meaning of occidental music. However, it is much the most fashionable among the natives. At their great weddings and feasts they always engage, if possible, the services of musicians who play English tunes; and it is said that a few days before Lucknow was captured this spring, the bands of fifty-three regiments had united in a monster concert, while the leaders of the mutineers were celebrating a great banquet.

During my stay at Umbala, and after my return to Delhi, I saw a good deal of the sepoys, in their every day life. Their dwellings, like those of other natives, are mere mud huts, which the soldiers of each regiment generally build for themselves. When off duty, the sepoys wore a dhotee of coarse cotton wound around the loins, and forming below a loose trowser, which reached as far as the knee, and was open at the back of the leg. They were usually beautifully formed men, very tall, and rather thin. The upper part of the body was commonly clothed in a short white jacket, with tight sleeves; and on the head they wore a white cotton skull-cap, jauntily set on one side. Being of high-caste, warriors by birth and profession, and also, as they expressed it, "servants of the warrior company," they felt a pride in themselves and contempt for the ordinary natives, which they showed very clearly in every motion, as well as in their intercourse with the common people. Whenever they met a European they always gave the military salute, by stopping, facing about, drawing up the body to its full height, and then extending the arm and bringing it round with a sweep, on a level with the shoulder, until the thumb of the right hand rested on the forehead. I have read recently an article in an English periodical, blaming the English residents for not having foreseen the late mutiny. Among other things, the author says that the "officers received daily, the respectful salutes of the men; they replied to them as a matter of course, and drove on regardless of the flashing eye, which gave the lie to the outward respect of the act,"—these are not the exact words, but they convey the meaning, and I only quote them because I wish distinctly to assert that I do not believe the writer, or any one else, ever saw any flashing eyes, unless he returned the sepoy's salute with his left hand, which is, with them, a great insult.

The native commissioned officers, although they took rank with the English captains and lieutenants, and were paid many times as much as the common sepoys, did not seem to be at all above them, in social position. They lived in the same mud huts, and might be seen squatted naked on the ground, cooking their food in a mud furnace. After the late rebellion, they rejected their native titles, and became colonels, captains, and lieutenants of the revolted regiments. In fact, one of the most remarkable features of the rebellion is the way in which all the revolted troops preserved the organization given them by the English. They always made a point of carrying off the regimental colours. This is perhaps not so wonderful, as they were in the habit of worshipping them as gods; but it is strange, that they should continue as they did to wear the uncomfortable English uniform, and that they should even impose this dress upon the new levies which they raised during the revolt.

There are a number of shawl dealers in Umbala, who used to bring their wares to the hotel for me to see. The shawls nearly all come from the Punjab, only a few from Cashmeer. All shawls that come to this country from India are called "Cashmere," or "Camel's Hair," but really, there are scarcely any true Cashmeeree shawls in America—and none anywhere of "Camel's Hair." The Cashmeeree shawl is made of the inner wool of the Thibet goat, which is brought from Ladak in Thibet, and woven into a fabric called pushmeena, which forms the basis and centre of the Cashmeeree shawl. The embroidery of the shawls is sometimes *woven*, sometimes *worked with the needle*, in either case the work is done by men, and requires an incredible amount of time. The Maharajah of Cashmeer does not allow any of the workmen to leave his dominions. If caught attempting to escape they are hung; but, notwithstanding this risk, many of them have made their escape to the Punjab, where, at the towns of Lahor, Loodiana, and Umritsur, they have long established manufactories of shawls, from which the markets of the West are supplied. Every shawl manufactured in Cashmeer, has a few square inches of work left incomplete. After the shawl is bought, it is finished in the private manufactory of the Maharajah, where it pays him about one hundred per cent. of its value, as duty. This regulation also gives the Maharajah the opportunity of ascertaining the party to whom the shawl is sold—which he always wishes to know, as he will not allow the shawls to be sold to traders.

CHAPTER XXIV.

RETURN TO DELHI.

Desertion—Life of an Indian Officer—Christmas Evening at Mr. Beresford's—The Mutiny at Delhi—Murder of my Friends—Fate of the Beresfords—The Revolted Emperor's Government—The City while held by the Mutineers—Uniform Defeats of the Mutineers—The Siege and Assault—Taking of the City and Flight of the Mutineers—News of the Taking of Delhi—The City after its Occupation by the English—Wholesale Punishment.

It was nearly too weeks after I moved to the hotel, before the doctor considered me strong enough to continue my journey. I had to give up my intended trip through the Punjab, having spent at Umbala all the time and money which I had appropriated to it. After I became strong enough to sit up, the time passed very pleasantly. The hotel was remarkably well kept, the weather was just cool enough for a fire, there were two officers lodging at the hotel *en permanence*, whose company I found very agreeable, and we had a constant succession of pleasant guests.

At length, on the 22d of December, the doctor told me I might leave; and on the evening of that day, having bid good-bye to my acquaintances, and thanked Messrs. Vauquelin and Powell very warmly for all their kindness to me, I started in a dhoolee toward Delhi. About the middle of the night I was waked up by my palkee stopping, and on looking out was informed that four of my bearers had run away, and taken the back track in company with two other dhoolees, which we had met going toward Umbala. I at once jumped out, sick as I was, and clothed only in my night-dress, and ran barefoot for a quarter of a mile, followed by the mussalchee or torch-bearer. I came up with the other palkees and my truants, just as they were crossing a river. I began to think it was all up now, as it was impossible for me to go in the water;

but, much to my surprise, I enticed them out by threatening to jump in and kill them if they did not return. As soon as I got them on *terra firma*, I asked them why they had deserted. As they could give no explanation, I tied them together with the turban of one of their number, and flogged them back to the dhoolee, where the head-man of the party also bestowed some blows on account of himself and the other bearers. Had I not caught these fellows, I might have been obliged to pass all night on the road, as the four bearers who remained could not have carried me to Peeplee, five miles or more from the place where the difficulty occurred.

In reading over my notes to my friends since my return, some of them have considered this occurrence a little extraordinary. But in truth those parts of the incident which excited their wonder were only those which were characteristic of the native character. In any other country it would seem strange that a sick man, entirely unarmed, could bind and beat four men, any one of whom was quite a match for him, even if he had been well. But in India it is the most natural thing in the world, and similar occurrences are constantly happening to every one. I felt quite sure there would be no resistance, and I am certain they never thought of offering any. The only difficulty I found was, that whenever I gave them a blow they would all fall down on the ground, yelling and joining their hands over the head, so that we did not get back to the palkee as soon as was desirable, considering that it was a cold night and I was scarcely clothed at all.

On arriving at Delhi I put up at the bungalow of Lieutenants Anderson and Butler, as my friend Captain Russell, who had asked me to stay with him when I should return, was absent at a coursing meeting.

I remained four days at Delhi, partly because the doctor had advised me not to travel fast, and partly because it was difficult to lay a dâk, the horses being all taken up for several days by parties going up country. Although on some accounts this delay was annoying, yet on the whole I liked it, as I had very pleasant quarters, and could thus pass Christmas in civilized society.

During my stay I saw something of "the life of an Indian officer;" which struck me as far from luxurious. Two men generally occupy a bungalow together. Each of the "chums" has one or two rooms to himself, and there is a large centre apartment which they have in common. The furniture consists of a bed, a table and a few chairs, generally of different patterns. The walls are bare or only decorated with an elk's head and horns, or some such trophy of the occupant's prowess. In one corner are a pair of foils and a gun. Against the wall are two large trunks, made to strap on a camel, which contain the officer's wardrobe. A few books in Persian and Hindoostanee, and the last magazine (six months old) lying on the table, complete the description of the "Oriental luxury" in which the young unmarried officers of the Company's service live.

As they advance in rank and pay, and particularly when they get married, they of course manage to collect around them some of the comforts of an English home—but still the above is a fair description of the interior of most of the bungalows.

The officer's life is as follows: He is wakened by his servant long before sunrise, dresses in uniform, and attends morning parade. This is over by seven or nine o'clock, according to the season. He then returns to his house, takes a bath, and dresses in civil costume. About ten, comes breakfast, known as *burra hazree*, or "great breakfast" to distinguish it from *chota hazree*, or "little breakfast" which consists of a cup of tea or coffee and a bit of toast taken before the parade. Some officers prefer to take this first meal at the mess-house, and it is then called "coffee shop." The burra hazree usually includes meat or fish or fruit, and is often followed by a hookah. Then comes business, either regimental, or the officer's study with a moonshee, or native interpreter—an occupation to which of late years they have been nearly all addicted. At two o'clock there is tiffin at the mess-house—cold meats, mulligatawney soup, and ale. After tiffin there is generally a game of billiards—nearly every regiment having a billiard table in its mess-house. After tiffin there are calls to be made on the ladies of the station, or else there is more regimental duty and study. At about five the officer dresses again in uniform and goes to the course (or drive around the parade-ground) either in buggy or on horseback. Here all the residents and ladies of the station are to be found on the afternoons when the band plays. If there is no band, the "afternoon parade" occupies the time that would otherwise be spent on the course. Dinner comes as soon as it is dark, and concludes the day. As there are no other amusements for the evening, it is made as long as possible, and very pleasant indeed the dinners were of which I partook at the mess of the Fifty-fourth. After the table was cleared we would draw around the wood fire, some of the men smoking their hookahs, others cheroots. An hour or so would be passed in conversation, or a quiet game of cards, and by half-past nine or ten every man had returned home and gone to bed, in readiness for the early call next morning.

On Christmas day I went with several officers to a large dinner at the house of Mr. Beresford, the manager of the Delhi bank. His house was a large and handsome mansion in the city, near the Chandee chôk. It was built and at one time occupied by the Bégoom Sombre or Sumroo of Sirdhána. Mr. Beresford came out to India as a common soldier in the Company's European army, and had raised himself by his talents to the opulent position which he then enjoyed. The Misses Beresford, two very charming young ladies, who had just returned from England, where they had been educated, and other ladies of the station were present.

After dinner we had music, and dancing; and the evening concluded with the old fashioned games of snap-dragon, blindman's buff, and hunt-the-ring. At the latter, Colonel Riddle, who was on his way to Agra, to take charge of the newly-raised Third European regiment, distinguished himself greatly. Among the decorations of the room were several misletoe boughs, which had been brought with much trouble from the Himalayas, but there were so few young ladies that kissing would have been personal, so the old custom went unhonoured.

Altogether the evening at Mr. Beresford's was one of the most delightful and homelike that I spent during my travels; and the whole time that I spent at Delhi, became by the kindness and attention of the officers, one of the most agreeable periods of my journey.

Four months after I left Delhi, one hot morning in May, the Christian inhabitants were startled by hearing that the mutinous Mahommedan cavalry of Meeruth were crossing the bridge and entering the city, massacring all the "infidels" on whom they could lay hands.

The news was probably no less unexpected and unwelcome to the Hindoos, who, after the fashion of their people, at once shut up their shops and secreted their property.

The officer in command of the Cashmeeree gate at once sent to cantonments for reënforcements. The sepoys of the Fifty-fourth, on learning the news, demanded to be led against the mutineers. Their request was complied with. As they marched to the city they vied with one another in professions of fidelity, and threats against the insurgents, but no sooner had they entered the gate and met the mutineers in the square before St. James' Church, than they separated on each side of the road, leaving their officers unprotected. My unfortunate friends had felt so confident of the result that they had come out without even their side-arms. A suwar galloped up to each and pistolled him like a dog.

The Christian inhabitants of Delhi, including the English, the half-castes and the native converts, concealed themselves as best they might, or sought safety in flight. All who were taken were mercilessly put to death. A few fled to the royal palace, and were promised protection by the Emperor, but they too were afterwards slain by his orders.

The cantonments were plundered by the mutineers and rabble of the city. A very few of the officers and ladies escaped, some to Umbala, some to Meeruth. One party, comprising several ladies, entrusted themselves to a sepoy guard, who swore to protect them, but when they had conducted them to a secure place, turned round and butchered them. All who were found in the cantonments were slain, and among the horrible sights that met the English troops when they arrived, was the body of a little boy, who had been nailed, head downwards, to the wall of one of the bungalows, and so left to die.

As I was travelling in Germany last summer, I met a German who had escaped from Agra during the mutiny. He told me of the fate of the Beresfords, which he had learned from a native who was in Delhi at the time. The details were sickening. The whole family, parents, and five children were "done to death" in the presence of each other, with such refinements of mental and bodily torture as Hell itself might learn a lesson from.

When the city was fairly in the hands of the revolted soldiery, they proclaimed the supremacy of the Emperor, and established a sort of government, the forms of which seem to have been largely derived from those of their English masters. The Emperor was to be supreme, but had a "council," at the head of which was a "Sĕkĕtur" (secretary). This council was composed of the "Kurnuls" of all the revolted regiments. A document emanating from it has been discovered, by which it appears that but few of these high officials could even sign their names.

As the revolt spread through the Presidency, the mutinous troops all poured into Delhi. Their support must have been a tremendous burden on the Hindoo inhabitants. On the first day they shut up their shops, but afterwards they were ordered by the Emperor's government to open them and sell their property to the soldiers considerably below cost. These orders being enforced by flogging and the fear of death, were complied with. By the same means large subsidies were forced from the reluctant bankers and other rich men—a class wholly composed of Hindoos, and the only class in the country who possess wealth, and have any very great stake in the preservation of order. They must often have cursed a state of affairs, which compelled them to support, by their hard-earned wealth, the mad movement which was ruining them, and which forced them to contribute to the establishment of a government under which they well knew how insecure would be the tenure of any property which they might preserve or acquire thereafter.

While all this was going on, Delhi was besieged on the north side by a feeble force of English under General Anson, the commander-in-chief. They established themselves upon the range of low hills between the cantonments and city, the distance from the walls averaging three-quarters of a mile. Here they remained through the burning heat of an Indian summer. The want of guns and the paucity of their numbers prevented any offensive movements. One commander-in-chief after another sickened and died—of cholera, it was said, but some persons think that native servants can produce cholera.

Meanwhile the numbers of the mutineers received daily accessions; they had two hundred heavy guns which they used with that skill for which the native artillerymen are famous; the arsenal, in their hands, contained countless stores of warlike *matériel*. Every advantage of position, numbers, climate, and arms were theirs, and yet, all summer long, they never got the advantage in a single sortie.

When it is recollected that these were men of that same sepoy army, which, fighting side by side with English troops, had gained by their bravery the admiration and applause of every General who commanded them, some may be inclined to wonder at their total want of success when fighting for themselves, and they may even be condemned as cowardly. This would be a hasty and not a just decision. They might be cowards in our estimation, and yet their courage might not be less than that of a European, but only of a different kind. Asiatic courage is of one kind, European of another, and the former bows before the latter, just as the nations of Asia kneel before the supremacy of the European. The sepoys could fight as well as any, on the same side with Englishmen, but they were powerless against them.

If any one thing has been demonstrated by the recent mutiny, it is the indescribable *moral inferiority* of Asiatic races. Great as has been the ukbal* of the English, henceforth it is greater and more awful than ever in the eyes of the native.

* *Ukbal*, a native term signifying "good fortune"—or the "prestige which arises from success."

So passed the summer of 1857, at Delhi.

Early in September the besieging force was strengthened by a siege train and additional forces from the Punjab. Their whole strength now amounted to 6,000 infantry, 1,000 cavalry, and 600 artillery, including Ghoorkas and other native regiments. None of the reïnforcements sent from England arrived in time.

On the eleventh of September, the batteries, which contained only eight 8-inch howitzers, ten heavy mortars, and forty-two other guns, the heaviest of which were twenty-four pounders, opened fire.

On the fourteenth the assault was made, principally on the Cashmeeree gate, which had to be blown in by gunpowder. The "forlorn hope" which undertook this arduous service had to advance in broad daylight to the gateway, in the teeth of a hot fire of musketry from above and through the gateway, and on both flanks. The powder bags were coolly laid and adjusted, but Lieutenant Salkeld, who commanded the party, was by this time disabled, with two bullets in him. Sergeant Carmichael then attempted to fire the fuse, but was shot dead. Sergeant Burgess then tried and succeeded, but paid for the daring act with his life. Sergeant Smith, thinking that Burgess too had failed, ran forward, but seeing the train alight, had just time to throw himself into a ditch and escape the effects of the explosion. With a loud crash the gate was blown in, and through it the column entered the city, just as the other columns had carried the breaches in the walls.

The English were now firmly established, but it was six days before the city was completely in their power. The loss of the English during the siege was three thousand, or between one-quarter and one-third of all the troops that were at any time engaged. The assault cost eight hundred men—over eleven hundred, one-third of the force engaged, being put *hors de combat* by death or wounds on the first day.

The six days which intervened between the assault and the complete occupation of the city, were occupied by the mutineers in decamping. The larger part of them went to Lucknow, but others escaped in different directions. The Emperor seems to have been abandoned by the sepoys. He also left the city, with a part of his family and a large number of followers. The other inhabitants of Delhi did likewise, concealing or carrying away with them the most valuable part of their property, so that on the twentieth of September there was not a living soul within the city except the English forces. The Palace and Jumma Músjeed were occupied as quarters by the Punjab and Ghoorka regiments with a few English troops; the rest were quartered in various parts of the city. The houses of Mr. Skinner and Mr. Beresford, which I have mentioned, were taken by the principal officers as quarters.

Soon after the capture of the city, the Emperor and his favourite wife were taken by Captain Hodgson, as I have mentioned before, and brought as prisoners into the city. Three of the Shahzadehs, or Princes, who were with the old king, were shot by Captain Hodgson, who thus, (in order to prevent the chance of their escaping on the way to the city,) forestalled what would have been their certain fate at the hands of the court-martial. All three of them had been in command of bodies of the mutineers, who seem to have deserted them when the city was taken. The youngest of the three, Aboo Bukhur, rivalled the worst of the mutineers in the atrocities which he committed, and is said to have hacked several poor creatures to pieces with his own hands. The bodies of these scions of royalty were brought to the city in a common bullock-cart, and thrown into the open sewer near the Kotwalee, or native mayor's office. An English officer writing home, says of this arrangement: "They lay open and exposed for any one that liked to see and take a lesson—a very ghastly and suggestive spectacle, I can assure you. How long they remained there I neither know nor care, but I suppose until, as in life so in death, they had become a foul and disgusting nuisance—rotten and intolerable."

The Reverend William Butler, an American Methodist missionary, gives an interesting account of the appearance of Delhi after its capture. He had been driven from his station by the mutiny, and had taken refuge at Almora, on the Himalayas. His description of the way in which he first learned the fall of Delhi, is too affecting not to be quoted. As he was sitting in his cottage, he heard a gun from the fort near by. "A brilliant hope flashed across my heart; I snatched my hat, and ran up the hill, while peal after peal thundered out, making even the Grand Himalayas reverberate. At last I gained the summit, and stood while I counted the 'Royal Twenty-one.' It needed no one to tell me what that meant, our commanding officer had received an express announcing that Delhi had fallen! that Britain was triumphant!

"I stood there wrapped in thoughts that can never be forgotten, and a luxury of feeling flowed through my very heart, that will make that moment a bright spot in my life and recollection forever.

"How often before has the thunder of these British cannon proved the inlet of salvation to the oppressed and persecuted! I am not the first American missionary to whom they have announced 'glad tidings of great joy.' I thought of Judson and his heroic wife, to whose ears, in his melancholy dungeon, these cheerful peals proclaimed approaching liberty.

"None but those who, like ourselves, have been practically captive for months, not knowing but any day our doom might be sealed by the hand of violence, can imagine how every gun, as it rung the knell of the Moslem city and power, while it 'proclaimed liberty' to the Christian and missionary of the cross—none but those so situated can appreciate the luxury of such an hour as that. May Heaven bless the British Nation! May God save the British Queen! Ah, yes! and let every lover of liberty, of civilization, and of Evangelical Christianity in our own happy America, say, from the depths of his heart, Amen! to that prayer!"

Mr. Butler afterwards came to Delhi. He walked through the Chandee chôk which was wont to be thronged by gaily dressed crowds. Not a soul was to be seen, all was silence and utter desolation. The shops where the gold and jewels and precious shawls of India were sold, had all been plundered and gutted. The houses were open and tenantless. "The wretched cats were silently moping about, and the dogs howled mournfully in the desolate houses. Far rather would

I see a city knocked down and covered in its ruins than behold a scene like this. A tomb, or Herculaneum, can be contemplated with interest; but Delhi is now like an open grave, rifled of its contents, and its dishonoured condition lying bare to the gaze of day.

"As I stood that night in the midst of this stern desolation I was forcibly reminded of the regular lesson in the calendar, for the 14th of September, the day in which the assault was given. The lesson was the third chapter of Nahum. It begins: 'Wo to the bloody city; it is all full of lies and robbery;' and the whole chapter is as applicable to Delhi, as it ever was to Nineveh; and here was her 'woe,' and she is 'naked,' a 'gazing stock,' and 'laid waste,' her 'nobles in the dust,' her people 'scattered;' so that with truth it may be said of her 'There is no healing of thy bruise, thy wound is grievous; all that hear the bruit of thee shall clap their hands over thee, for upon whom hath not thy wickedness passed continually?'"

As soon as the English were fairly established, a court-martial began to sit permanently for the trial of the rebels. The great body of the mutineers had escaped, so that there could be no "wholesale punishment," but fortunately a number of the leaders and prominent men were captured, tried, and executed. A gallows was erected by the Kotwalee, where deeds were done in May and June that fiends might blush to own, where Englishwomen

"Perished
In unutterable shame."

The scene of their sufferings witnessed their wrongs revenged.

As soon as order was restored a proclamation was published inviting all peaceably disposed inhabitants to return to their homes. This, however, was complied with but slowly. All suspected persons, and particularly Moosulmans, were either excluded, or had to produce a written pass before they could enter. The effect of these measures, and of the trials in the Dewán Khas, is thus described by Mr. Butler: "This rigid exclusion of the suspected Moosulman population; this calm, quiet and continued investigation by the authorities; this searching out and bringing to justice the perpetrators of the outrages of May and June; this discrimination; this justice even to the most suspected wretches, to whom every opportunity is given of proving their innocence (one trial alone lasted ten days*); the prompt execution of those who are proved guilty; this manifest anxiety to separate friends from enemies, and to take care that only the guilty suffer; all this with the disposition of government to acknowledge and reward fidelity, is producing an immense impression. It is all so contrary to the rash and indiscriminate mode of Oriental despotism, and argues in their estimation such resources, and justice, and calm resolve as are invincible; and which it is therefore folly and madness to resist. We have seen, I believe, the last rising against British authority that India will ever witness."

* This was written before the trial of the Emperor, which occupied much more time.

CHAPTER XXV.

AGRA.

Arrival at Agra—The Taj—Its Proportions—Mosaics—The "Tribe of the Infidels"—"The Ornament of the Palace"—Cost of the Taj—The Fort—The Pearl Mosque—The Dewán Am—Dewán Khas—A Seat for a Sovereign—A Court of the Zĕnana—The Palace of Mirrors—The Terrace—Sleeping Rooms—Town of Alexander—The Printing Establishment—Akbur's Tomb—Akbur's Character—His Legislative and Administrative Acts—His Religion—An Unexpected Meeting—Dine with my American Friends—"Young Bengal"—Illumination of the Taj—Revisit the Palace—An Indian Oubliette—The Old Hindoo Palace—Hindoo Art—A Great Well—A Pleasant Summer Residence—Presentation of Colours—Commander-in-Chief's Camp—Manly Sports—The Cathedral—Ram-bagh—Tomb of Aktmud-ood-Dowlah—"The Light of the Harem"—Her Ambition and its Success.

I LEFT Delhi, by gárrhee-dâk, on the evening of December 28th, and arrived in Agra the next day about noon. On the outskirts of the city there were ruins of many gardens, tombs, and other buildings, but neither in number or beauty did they compare to those which cover the country outside the walls of Delhi.

The city of Agra is situated on the south side of the Jumna, a hundred and fifty miles below Delhi. Its buildings and public edifices are quite equal to those of Delhi, as it was the capital of the great Emperor Akbur, and was a favourite residence of several other sovereigns.

The cantonments were situated about two miles from the town. I put up at one of the hotels, which compared very unfavourably with that at Umbala.

On the day after my arrival I drove to the Taj,* the mag-

* This word is a corruption of the last syllable of Moomtaz, the name of the Queen whose tomb it is. The "j" should be pronounced *soft*, as in French, or as if the word were written "tarshj"—remembering to give the "a" a broad sound, as in the word "father."

nificent tomb erected by Shah Jehan, the most splendid of the Mogul Emperors, over the remains of his favourite wife Moomtaz-ee-Mahul.

The Taj is built apart from all other buildings, on the banks of the Jumna, two miles east of the city. It is in a beautiful garden, surrounded on three sides by a lofty wall of redstone. The garden is entered by a magnificent gateway, which is approached through several large paved courts, used as surais.

The northern side of the garden is occupied by a chubootra, or platform of redstone, over nine hundred and fifty feet in length. It is open toward the river, and the side of it which is washed by the waters of the Jumna is protected by a water wall of squared redstone.

At each corner of this vast chubootra is a tower, with a white marble kiosk. Two mosques occupy the east and west sides. Like the towers, they are of red sandstone, inlaid with white marble. Their domes are of the latter material. The western mosque only was used for prayer, which must always be made in the direction of Mecca. That to the east was built as a jowáb, or *answer* to the other, in order to preserve the symmetry of the group.

Upon this redstone chubootra is reared another of white marble, which supports the Taj. The marble chubootra is over three hundred feet square, and has at each angle a round minár, one hundred and fifty feet high, with two projecting galleries, and a light kiosk, or dome, supported by columns. In the centre of the chubootra, between the minárs, is the Taj itself. Its form is octagonal, but the sides which face the four cardinal points, and contain the entrances, are by far the largest. Each is about one hundred and thirty feet long, but if produced, so that the building should be a square, would be nearly a hundred and seventy feet in length. The roof is seventy feet from the surface of the chubootra; above rises for fifty feet the circular neck of the dome. The height of the dome from where it begins to swell is seventy feet. It is surmounted by a gilt copper ornament, the top of which is two hundred and twenty feet from the marble chubootra, and nearly two hundred and sixty feet from the ground level.*

The proportions of the Taj are then as follows: The chubootra, on which it is situated, is one-third as long as the one of redstone which supports it, and forms the north end of the garden. The four minárs are twice as high as the walls of the Taj, and the highest point of the ornament on the dome is three times as high.

The entrances to the building are through doorways, in the back of large arched recesses, which also contain the windows, and which occupy nearly one-third of each principal side. These *niches* are as high as the roof, and the wall around them is continued up, as a screen, above the general level of the eaves.

The shape of the dome, which is high in proportion to its diameter, and the great length of the circular neck on which it rests, are evidences of the late period at which the building was erected. They have been objected to by some as defects, but are really like the great size of the entrance-niches, only the carrying out of the idea and genius of Moosulman architecture, which is to give prominence to the principal features at the expense of the general mass of the building.

The Taj, its dome, the minárs, and the chubootra, are all of the purest white marble, highly polished. Every part of the whole external surface is inlaid with the most beautiful designs in various coloured stones, and yet with such surpassing skill has this been done that the general effect of the pure white surface is not interfered with, and it is only on close examination that the elaborate ornamentation is detected.

The interior of the building is a circular hall, with a dome-shaped roof. The walls are all of polished marble, ornamented with designs in sculpture and mosaic. The pavement is alternate blocks of white marble and jasper. An octagonal screen

* I think it right to state that these numbers are not the result of actual measurement by me. I computed them by comparing various authorities, so that I cannot vouch for their entire accuracy. The proportions I believe to nearly correct.

of the most delicate marble filagree work surrounds the ceno taph of the Queen, which is immediately under the centre of the dome. The tomb of the Emperor, her husband, is by her side. These are both covered with elaborate mosaics, delicate as the work of Florentine jewellers. One single flower contains a hundred precious stones, each cut to the exact shape required. The Queen's tomb has upon it certain passages from the Koran, inlaid in black stone. One of these extracts, facing the entrance, terminates with the words, "And defend us from the tribe of the Infidels"—the same *tribe* which now governs the country of Shah Jehan, and keeps his tomb in repair. On the Emperor's tomb, which was erected by his *pious* son Aurungzeeb, there are no passages of the Koran. They were omitted for fear the foot of man might perchance some day tread upon the "holy words"—a very possible contingency, as things turned out.

I have now described, as well as I can, this flower and ideal of Saracenic art. I must leave it to other and more eloquent writers to dwell upon its perfect harmony, its purity, its almost heavenly beauty. It has been often said that one sight of the Taj was worth a journey from England. I will not dispute it, and I feel sure that one might make the pilgrimage, visiting on the way all the great triumphs of European art, and not find among them all anything that would compare with the Taj at Agra, in chaste beauty, perfect simplicity, and exquisite grace.

The Taj was built in the latter part of the seventeenth century by Shah Jehan, the same Emperor who founded the present city of Delhi, and built the Palace there. He had intended to build a precisely similar structure on the opposite bank, as a mausoleum for himself, connecting the two edifices by a bridge over the river. This ambitious design was begun, but never carried out, and his remains now repose in a sarcophagus beside that of his Queen.

Moomtaz-ee-Mahul, "the ornament of the Palace," for whom Shah Jehan erected this magnificent mausoleum, was the niece of the famous Noor Jehan, the wife of Jehangeer, who is the heroine of Moore's poem, "The Light of the Harem."

He calls her "Noor Mahul," the "Light of the Palace," a title which she afterwards altered to "Noor Jehan," or "Light of the World."

The gardens of the Taj are filled with beautiful trees, forming avenues, which shade raised walks of marble slabs. In the central avenue is a row of fountains, extending from the great gateway to the foot of the chubootra. The water of these fountains is conducted in open canals down the centre of the other avenues, and serves to irrigate the plants and trees. The garden and all the buildings are kept in perfect order by the Company.

The accounts of all the expenses of building the Taj are still preserved. From them we learn that the whole cost was three crors, seventeen lakhs and a half, of rupees, or three million, one hundred and seventy-five thousand pounds sterling—a sum which, allowing for the diminished value of money, and the difference in the price of labour, would be equal to over twelve millions of pounds sterling, at the present day in England.

The next day I drove to the town. The interior contains little that is worth seeing, except the fort. The general appearance of the buildings is far inferior to those of Delhi, and the only large mosque, the Jumma Musjeed, is sadly in want of care and repairs. The town and fort were both built by the great Emperor Akbur, who reigned in the latter half of the sixteenth century. Agra is still always called by Moosulmans Akburabad, or the city of Akbur.

The fort is within the walls, along the river's bank. It is defended by high fortifications of redstone, with strong buttresses, and lofty gateways. The top of the wall is ornamented with arched battlements, like those upon the palace-walls of Delhi.

Driving through one of the gates, and up a steep inclined plane, I found myself in a large open court-yard, having on my right the palace, and in front the Motee Musjeed, or "Pearl Mosque," which I first visited. It consists of a court, about one hundred feet square, paved with polished marble, surrounded by marble walls, and having at its further end a marble colonnade, all of the purest white, exquisitely polished, and without a speck or flaw in any part. It well deserves its name.

From this Musjeed I was conducted to the palace, which was built by Shah Jehan, who also constructed the Taj, and the city and palace of Delhi.

The first room which we entered was a large hall, having its stone roof supported by rows of pillars. This was the Dewán Am, or public reception hall of the Emperor, and was formerly open to the court. Now, however, it is walled in. and when I visited it, was used as an armoury. The walls were covered with panoplies, and rows of various arms; and from the pillars hung little blue flags, on which were inscribed in English, Persian, and Hindee, the names of the various victories of the English in India. At one end of this hall, surrounded by drapery, are two elaborately carved doors of sandal-wood, bearing evident marks of age and hard usage in their injured and worm-eaten appearance. These gates belonged to a celebrated idol-temple called Somnath, in Goozerat, on the west coast of India. In the year of the Hijra 415, or A.D. 1024, the temple was taken and sacked by Sooltan Mahood, an Afghan prince, who carried the gates back with him to his home, the city of Ghuznee, in Afghanistán. There they remained until the late Afghan war, when Lord Ellenborough had them removed, with a view of taking them to Calcutta, but the expense of transport amounted to so large a sum by the time they arrived at Agra, that he made up his mind to deposit them in this arsenal.

Opposite the door of the armoury is the Emperor's throne, a recess in the wall, like the box of a theatre. It is decorated with marble, inlaid with mosaics, and now contains a sofa and two chairs of marble open-work, which were presented to Lord Ellenborough by a Caboolee chief.

The royal throne was approached by a door from behind. Passing through this, we came upon a stone terrace, enclosing a court-yard about fifty yards square. Three sides of this terrace were protected by a roof, and surrounded by buildings. The fourth was open, and overlooked the river. This part of the terrace was very broad, and paved with white marble. At one end was a marble colonnade, with a roof of the same material. Here the Emperor used to sit during his státe receptions, and this court was the Dewán Khas of the Agra Palace.

The whole effect of the court was fine; and the view across the water to the Taj, which is situated around the bend of the river, is very striking. The Jumna is here so wide, that it is very shallow, not being navigable for vessels of any size. Two elephants were standing nearly in the middle of the stream, yet their legs were only just covered by its waters. They were washing themselves, an operation which they accomplished by drawing up the water into their trunks, and then squirting it out upon their bodies.

On this terrace are two large and thick slabs, one of black marble, the other of white. They were both used as thrones, the latter by the great Akbur Shah. Each of them has a corner broken off. When and how this damage occurred, is not known. The black marble slab is regarded with great reverence by the Moosulmans, who always salám to it, and say that no one but an emperor or king can sit on it. I answered the question practically by taking a seat upon it, and requested the guide, a Moosulman, to do the same. But he said the stone would not bear him, and that on the occasion of one of the Maharatta conquerors impiously sitting upon the stone, it bled in two places, pointing to some red spots. He accounted for my impunity by the supposition that all Europeans are sovereigns, (sircar-lôg,) which, with a little change in locality, is, I believe, a part of every true American's creed.

Leaving the Dewán Khas, I went into one of the courts of the Zĕnana. Part of it was laid out as a garden, at one end of which was a broad marble terrace, sheltered by a canopy of the same material, supported on colonnades. Between the garden and this "loggia" was a marble tank, perhaps forty feet long by twenty broad. In its centre was a fountain which filled it with water, and all around the edges were marble stalls, where, the guide said, the ladies of the Zĕnana used to sit up to their necks in water.

We next went to the Sheesh Mahul, or Hall of Mirrors, the walls of which are completely covered by little mirrors, embedded in a kind of stucco, which gleams like frosted silver. On one side is a recess, where a stream of water entered, and running down an inclined plane, tumbled into a marble basin in the centre of the room. The whole was so arranged, that the hall was entirely lighted by powerful lamps, placed behind the waterfall, and beneath the marble tank. When I saw the place, the water had long ceased to flow, and the ceiling and walls were blackened by the smoke of the guide's torches.

From the Sheesh Mahul we ascended to the story above the Dewán Khas. Here there was a magnificent terrace running along the battlements of the fort. Seventy feet below was the moat, and beyond it the Jumna. Along the edge of the parapet are several pavilions of white marble, which partially overhang the water. Their floors are of marble, and have a fountain in the centre, and from within the Jumna and Taj are seen through panels of that wonderful marble open-work which can only be compared to the lace of Europe or the most delicate ivory carvings of the patient Chinese. The walls of these pavilions, as well as those of some other parts of the Palace, are inlaid with mosaic designs, to which the highest praise that can be given is, that if possible they surpass those of the Taj. The exquisite taste of the whole and of every detail, and the perfection of the mosaic ornaments and the most fragile open-work, after the lapse of two hundred years, surpassed anything that I had expected.

We now went through the numerous sleeping apartments of the zĕnana. They were small and mean, all the taste and splendour being reserved for the courts and terraces where the day was passed. After visiting two small mosques where the ladies of the harem attended religious services, which were held by a little boy (for no *man* would of course be allowed within the zĕnana), my guide informed me that I had seen all that there was of interest. So I dismissed him with a bucksees, reëntered my buggy, and returned to the hotel.

The next day I drove out to Sĕkundra, a place about six miles from Agra, called after Alexander the Great, whose name, pronounced by the natives Sĕkundur, is still held in great respect in India. There are many towns of the same name, just as there are many "Washingtons" and "Jacksonvilles" in America, but the invasion of the Macedonian conqueror did not extend beyond the river Hydaspes, now called the Jhelum.

The drive to Sĕkundra is very pleasant, the road being bordered with fine trees, an unusual thing in India. On the road there are two coss-minárs, or pillars, to mark the distance. They are found on all the roads leading from Delhi and Agra. Their form is a cone rising from a cylinder, about fifteen feet high; the material of which they are constructed, is rubble work covered with stucco. They were erected by the Mogul Emperors, and do not seem ever to have borne inscriptions. The coss, the usual measure of distance in India, varies in length in different parts of the country; but in Hindoostan it is one mile and a half English.

On the road to Sĕkundra I passed the ruins of many large buildings, and the place itself contains many such remains of antiquity. It is now inhabited principally by people employed in a large missionary publishing establishment, the presses and workshops of which are established in one of the largest tombs.

The principal object of interest is the tomb of the Emperor Akbur, erected by his son Jehangeer. It is situated in a large quadrangle surrounded by redstone walls, the inner side of which, as is usual in these buildings, is formed into a roofed verandah and used as a surai or resting place for travellers. In the middle of each side is a lofty and massive gateway, from each of which a broad stone causeway leads to the chubootra in the centre of the quadrangle. The space between the causeways is laid out as a garden, and filled with mango, lemon, orange, and other trees. The tomb rises in the centre of the quadrangle. It consists of five terraces, rising pyramidally one above the other. The material of which it is constructed is redstone, like the chubootra, on which it rests.

The lowest and largest terrace of the building is three hundred feet square. The highest story, which alone is built of white marble, is not more than two thirds of that size. The pavement of the highest story, which is at the same time, the roof of the building, is formed of white marble blocks. In its centre is the cenotaph, a plain marble tomb on which are carved the "ninety-nine names" of God. The Emperor's body lies directly under this cenotaph, on the ground floor of the building, as is the case in all the Mausoleums.

The monotony and heavy appearance of the redstone, which forms the material of the tomb and gateways, was once relieved by bold and free decorations in the gaudiest style of "polychrome," but of this, nearly all traces have been removed by time and the weather.

The Emperor Akbur, whose last resting-place this is, was the best and greatest of the descendants of Tamerlane. He carried his arms to every part of India, and for the first time thoroughly subjected the whole peninsula to the supreme power at Delhi. He not only gained the power, but by his wise administrative measures, so strengthened and bound together the whole empire, as to lay the foundation of the greater splendour of his successors, Shah Jehan and Aurungzeeb.

He introduced reforms into the whole civil and military service, and subjected all his territories to a uniform system of government. But the greatest and most important of his enactments concerned the revenue, which was then, as now, principally derived from the tax or rent of land. For this purpose he caused exact surveys to be made, and divided all the cultivated soil into three classes according to its yield. The demand of government was one third of the produce.* Although this may seem to our ideas excessive, yet it was considered at that time a great reduction from the previous assessments; and this enactment has always been looked on as the most important and beneficial act of his reign.

* The land-tax of the East India Company, now amounts to from one sixth to one eighth of the produce.

Besides being a general and legislator, Akbur was a man of letters, a theologian, and a philosopher. He caused Persian translations of several of the old Sanscrit writings to be made for his perusal, and was the first and only Moosulman Prince who took an interest in Hindoo literature.

As a theologian, he caused the professors and teachers of Hindoo and Mahommedan religions to argue before him in defence of their respective faiths; and he even brought some Christian priests from the South of India to be present and join in their disputations. An account of one of these debates is preserved in the Akburnameh, a Persian work of the time. The Christians seem to have had the advantage, both in temper and argument, and the dispute is ended by Akbur's reproving the Moolahs for their violence, and declaring that in his belief, God could only be rightly worshipped by following reason, and not relying on any system of revelation.

In accordance with these views, the Emperor invented a religion of his own, which was a system of pure Deism. He abolished all ceremonies as unessential observances; but allowed his disciples to pray if they found it necessary for their weakness. If any external symbols of worship were to be chosen, he recommended the sun, or fire. Although his reason led him to frame a system so averse to external observances, yet he seems naturally to have had deep religious feelings which found vent in superstitious practices, and even magic arts. It was this feature in his character which led him to kiss and place upon his head, the images of our Lord, and the Blessed Virgin, presented for his adoration by the Christian priests.

On the whole, Akbur was by far the greatest, wisest, and best of the Mogul Emperors, although he was neither the most powerful, or the most splendid. Of all the rulers of India, he is the only one on whose character and acts, the Christian student of history can look back with admiration and respect.

My original plan had been to go from Agra to Bombay by the mail-cart, which does the eight hundred miles in about five days—sometimes a little less. This mode of travelling is, I have said before, very exhausting, and my sickness at Umbala, from the effects of which I was still suffering, made it impossible for me to undergo the exposure and fatigue.

I then thought of going by dhoolee. But finding that there were no chokees, or places where relays of bearers could be obtained, that the dâk-bungalows were few and far apart, and that I should be quite alone for over a month, I gave it up, and reluctantly determined to return to Calcutta, and proceed thence homeward by the Peninsular and Oriental Company's steamers.

With this intention I went to the dâk agent and engaged a dâk down country. After transacting this business I wished to go to the other hotel, about a mile off. A young English Engineer, Mr. Gibson, who happened to be in the office at the time, offered to take me in his buggy. On the way he informed me that he also, was bound homewards, and intended to go by way of Bombay, if he could get any one to join him. This entirely changed the aspect of affairs, and as soon as I arrived at the hotel, I sent off a messenger to countermand my dâk.

At the hotel, the landlord happened to mention that two American gentlemen were staying in his house. I was delighted at the prospect of seeing some of my countrymen and at once sent in my name. I found them to be two young men travelling like myself for pleasure and information. One was from Boston, and knew several of my friends there; the other was a Virginian. To my surprise and delight I found that they also wished to go to Bombay, and had even bought palkees and engaged bearers for the purpose. They were to start in two days for Delhi, but would return in a week and leave at once for Bombay.

Their plans so nearly coincided with those of Gibson and myself, that we soon came to a compromise and agreed to unite our forces.

Gibson had been in favour of "marching" with camels, horses and tents, which would have been the pleasantest and cheapest plan—but as time was a matter of importance to the rest of us, he gave up his preference. The other two had proposed to go by way of Gwalior, which is the regular mail-road; but as I had been reading a description of the country, and knew that by making a detour of two hundred miles we could see the most interesting sights of Western India, the others yielded in this respect, and we determined to go by way of Jaipoor.

The chance which brought us together, and enabled me to go across the country to Bombay, was very remarkable. In the first place, travellers of any kind are very rare in India, but American travellers are still rarer; and that three of these *raræ aves* should meet by chance, was still more remarkable. Then it was extraordinary that our plans should coïncide as they did, and that we should all be going by a route which, being through a wild country, where there is almost no road, is scarcely ever travelled over. Lastly, our meeting with Gibson was most fortunate, as his acquaintance with the country and language enabled us to see much more than we otherwise could, and saved us a great deal of trouble.

I dined the next day with my two countrymen. At their hotel I saw a Calcutta Baboo, who was on his way to Delhi. He belonged to "Young Bengal"—a class of natives in Calcutta, who have cast aside more or less the prejudices of their nation and religion, and adopted the habits, manners, and dress of Englishmen to some extent. This specimen was enormously fat and sleek, and very dark skinned. He was almost a Christian, being in the habit of drinking brandy profusely, wearing his shoes in the house, and eating without scruple in the company of Europeans. He still, however, retained a heathen prejudice against beef.

After dinner we went in carriages to the Taj, which we caused to be illuminated by coloured lights. The effect was beautiful beyond description. The view by moonlight is said to be better, but I can hardly think so. One of the party had brought with him a flute, and played some slow and plaintive airs. The rich tones rose to the dome and floated around its sides, each successive note mingling with those that had gone before, till they were all blended in one rich harmony, which hung throbbing in the air, like the music of the spheres, for long minutes after the flute had ceased to play.

The next day my two American friends went to Delhi. I occupied the time during their absence by seeing the remaining sights of Agra, and making preparations for the journey to Bombay.

During this time I went again over the palace, in Gibson's company. I again saw and admired all that I had seen when last there, but on this occasion we succeeded in seeing much more, through the influence of Gibson, who understood managing the natives. The guide took us through several courts, with flower-gardens, tanks and white marble pavilions; through endless galleries; and one suite of rooms after another. At the end of a long, low passage, far removed from all the other apartments, we found a small arched vault, in which the faithless wives of the Padshah* were hung. The beam with the hole for the fatal rope yet remained in its place. After the culprit's death, her body was thrown down a dark and deep oubliette, opening immediately under the gallows, and leading to the river.

This was how the Padshah got rid of his women. The capital punishments reserved for men were to be trodden, or gored to death by elephants; or else cut to pieces by sharp knives attached to the feet of these animals.

We also visited the remains of a very ancient Hindoo palace, which are contained within the fort. They are almost the only specimens of an ancient Hindoo dwelling which I saw in India. These remains consisted of two small grass-grown courts, surrounded by many-storied buildings of dark brown stone. The court-yards were dark, gloomy and mysterious. Within the buildings all was the same dingy stone, looking as if it would fall and crush him who ventured inside. Even the floors and low ceilings were of great blocks of stone, supported by columns carved into serpents, dragons, devils, and all foul and hideous forms. The *arch* was no where to be seen.

There is nothing grand about Hindoo art. All of their buildings which remain (if we except the Kootub at Delhi.

* Padshah, *i. e.*, Emperor.

the authorship of which is not known) are small, heavy and gloomy. Their temples have exactly the same form all over India. The tall and heavy pyramid, the low entrance, and the small dark chamber in the centre are the same in all. Bishop Heber says that there is something impressive and awful in these temples. I think this is the case ; the cruelty and immorality of the religion, reacts upon the architecture of its temples, and you feel within them that you are in a shrine dedicated to the worship of devils.

In the great court-yard of the fort is a noble well, about fifty feet deep, and thirty in diameter. A flight of broad stone steps, the entrance of which is about a hundred feet from the mouth of the well, leads down through the ground to the surface of the water. The ground over the stairway is supported by an arched roof of stone.

The fort of Agra proved of the greatest service during the mutiny. As long as the troubles lasted all the Christian residents of the station, city, and from the country around, remained in safety within its walls.

Recent disclosures have made it probable that the mutiny was to have come off on New Year's day. If it had taken place at that time, and I had escaped with my life, I might have been compelled to pass last summer within the Fort of Agra, which would have been a much warmer and less agreeable residence than the mountains of Switzerland, which I was enabled to reach by the miscarriage of the original plan for insurrection.

After leaving the fort we drove to the parade-ground, and witnessed the presentation of colours to the "Third Europeans"—a new regiment which had just been embodied, in accordance with a resolution of the Indian Government, allowing three regiments of English soldiers, instead of two, to each Presidency. The colours were presented by Mrs. Anson, wife of the commander-in-chief, who was then at Agra on his tour of inspection. The regiment was commanded by Colonel Riddle, whose acquaintance I had made at Delhi. His speech and that of Mrs. Anson were both very good, and the affair was quite brilliant, as all the ladies and gentlemen of the station had come in carriages or on horseback to witness the ceremony.

Afterwards we walked over to the commander-in-chief's camp, which, with its various tents, elephants, camels, and other accessories, occupied a space three times as large as Washington parade-ground in New York.

The next day was devoted to the "old sports" of leaping, running, throwing cannon balls, running in a sack, and others. They were joined in by the men of the Third Europeans, and attracted a large number of spectators from the station.

Wherever the English are they must have their manly exercises. Climate is not the slightest obstacle. The soldiers in India play cricket bareheaded in the sun's rays, when the thermometer stands at 100° in the shade; their officers dare both the deadly sun of summer and the pestiferous miasms of the jungul, in hunting the tiger. Every English colony or settlement has its races, every station in India has its racket court, every Englishman in India will ride a hundred miles without rest for a single day's snipe-shooting, and even when the forces were collecting at Cawnpoor for the relief of Lucknow, when more sentimental soldiers would have been thinking of what they had passed through and of what was still before them, the English army engaged in the sports of the olden time, with as much zest as if they were on the peaceful shores of "merrie England."

On the following Sunday I went to mass at the Romish cathedral, which is a large pukka building in the Doric style, but cruciform, and covered with a dome. The music of the service, which was sung by the nuns, was exceedingly good. After church I called on the Bishop, whose palace is in the same compound with the cathedral. I had received a letter of introduction to him, from Fra Raffaello, the Romish priest of Umbala. I found "his Lordship," as he is called, a very pleasant, gentlemanly man. He was a capuchin from Naples. We had quite a long conversation, during which he informed me that there are about five hundred thousand native Christians, of the Romish persuasion, in India; but confessed that now-a-days but few converts were made; all the efforts of the priests being required to retain Christian families in the faith. Agra once contained twenty-five thousand Christian families, according to M. de Thevenot, who visited the city in 1666. This number may be a little exaggerated, but there must have been a very large number of Christians. They were mostly French, or Dutch, or their half-caste descendants, who were employed in the artillery, arsenals, and gun-foundries of the Emperor. These duties were, in all parts of India, entrusted exclusively, by the native rulers, to Europeans, who were all Christians, and formed in the aggregate quite a large Christian population. When M. de Thevenot visited Agra it had half a million of inhabitants—while now it has not over seventy-five thousand.

I was anxious to see whether the opinion of the native character formed by the Bishop, as an Italian, a Romanist, and one who had been for years in daily intercourse with natives, would differ at all from the impressions which I had myself derived from observation, history, the conversation of Englishmen and such intercourse as I had been able to hold with the natives themselves. I found that he entertained exactly the same opinions which I had formed, and have expressed, and he said that in all parts of India the missionary priests, who live almost as natives, have come to the same judgment.

The following day I crossed over the river to the "Ram Bagh" or "Garden of Ram"—a beautiful and extensive garden on the bank of the Jumna. It was founded in the time of the Mogul Emperors, but is now kept in order by the Company. The stone pavilions and marble villas which it contains, are always occupied in the summer season by pic-nic and other parties, who often remain several days.

On the way back I stopped at the mausoleum of Kwaja Aeeas, commonly called "the tomb of Aktmud ood Dowlah." It stands within a quadrangular enclosure, upon a marble chubootra. The mausoleum is of white marble, about fifty feet square, and twelve feet high. At each corner is a round marble tower, about forty feet in height, surmounted by a marble kiosk. In the middle of the roof, is a square, dome-shaped canopy of marble, resting on supports of marble openwork.

The whole tomb was once covered with decorations in mosaic and painting, but both are now in bad repair.

In the interior is a circular apartment, with marble walls, and an arched marble roof, both richly decorated with graceful designs in various colours and gilding. In the centre of this room lie the remains of Kwaja Aeeas, one of the most remarkable characters of Jehangeer's reign.

He came originally from Western Tartary, being attracted to India by the hopes of procuring employment in the court of the Emperor Akbur. So poor was he that he started on this long journey, with only one bullock, which carried his wife and their little baggage. On the way his wife was delivered of a daughter. Once arrived at Akbur's court, he rapidly rose to a high position, both by his intrinsic merits, and the favour of some relations who had long been in the Emperor's service. His daughter, Noor Mahul, had now grown up to be a prodigy of beauty. Being freely admitted to the royal zĕnana she was accidently seen by the Prince Mirza Suleem, afterward the Emperor Jehangeer, who at once conceived for her that violent passion, which forms the subject of Moore's poem, "The Light of the Harem."

Sheer Afgun, a Toorkman noble, had long been espoused to Noor Mahul, and, notwithstanding the opposition of the heir-apparent, he married her. As soon, however, as Jehangeer was seated on the musnud, as Akbur's successor, he caused his successful rival to be murdered, and took possession of his wife, whom he married. From this time Noor Mahul, or as she now styled herself Noor Jehan, exercised an absolute sway over the Emperor, and became a paramount authority in the government. Her father, over whom this tomb was erected, was raised to the rank of Aktmud ood Dowlah or high treasurer; and afterwards promoted to be the prime minister of the empire. Her relations from Tartary flocked to the court, and were well provided for.

She never had any children by Shah Jehan, but her one daughter by her first husband, she married to a younger son of the Emperor. In order to secure the crown to her son-in-law, she induced the Emperor to put out the eyes of his eldest son Khosroo. His mother was then invited by Noor Jehan to visit her apartments. She led her out to a well in the court, which she asked her to look down. Her victim complied, and Noor Jehan at once threw her in. Khosroo was afterwards taken to the South of India by Shah Jehan, the Emperor's second son, who said "he could not bear to be separated from his poor blind brother" and was there murdered by his orders.

Notwithstanding the efforts of Noor Jehan, the Emperor's second son, Shah Jehan, succeeded to his father's throne on his death. He put the Empress in confinement, and blinded his brother Shah Reear, her protegé. His other relations were all strangled by his orders. With the accession of Shah Jehan the influence of this remarkable woman ceases. For ten years she had in fact governed the empire, had even led the imperial troops in battle, and had caused her name to be struck on the coin of the royal mint—a solitary instance of that honour being awarded to a woman in India.

The new Emperor Shah Jehan, had married her niece, Moomtaz-ee-Mahul, over whose remains the Taj was afterwards erected. She seems to have inspired her husband with an affection as deep and powerful as that of which Jehangeer felt for her aunt; but Shah Jehan being a man of greater ability than his father did not leave the reins of his government in the hands of a woman.

CHAPTER XXVI.

AGRA TO JAIPOOR.

Chowdris—Combination *versus* Competition—Our Retinue—Price of Labour—Commercial Integrity—Leaving Agra—The Departure of "a Warrior Lord"—A Loan to the Sovereign Company—The Royal Pilgrimage—"Seekree, the City of Victory—Tomb of a Wealthy Saint— A Magnificent Gateway—Bishop Heber's Guide—Throne-room —Human Chessmen—Blind-man's Buff—The Old Lake—A Triumph for Religion—Irreverence—Dining in a Palace—"Pointing a Moral"—Four Rupees' worth of Picturesque Piety—Fording a Jheel—Bhurtpoor—English Protection and its Fruits—The Fort—Its Sieges—An Indian Sebastopol—Rajah's Palace—Battle of Deeg—Quail Fighting—A Boxing Match—Deer—Bosawur—Breakfast at 3 P. M.—The Village—A Native Distillery—People on Road—Antelopes—Manpoor—Walled Villages —Naked Sanctity—Pilgrim to the Shrine of Juggurnath—Buranah—Pigeons—Dress of the Rajpoots—Hills of Jaipoor—Palace of the Rajah—Jaipoor.

On the 12th of January, my American friends had returned from Delhi, and we were all ready to start for Bombay. The previous week had been occupied in making arrangements, and bargaining for the bearers. We at first made application to a Chowdri* who lived near the hotel, but not liking his terms we had recourse to all the others in the place. These fellows were ostensibly in opposition to each other; but as we discovered that they were really in league, we gave our custom to the first man with whom we had spoken. This is a curious feature in the habits of all native tradesmen. As some one has remarked "they do not understand competition, but are masters of combination." All trades and occupations are in the hands of certain castes or guilds, who unite their forces against the customer. By an apparent competition they will induce purchasers to buy at a price far exceeding the real value of the article; and the surplus profit is then divided among all those who have joined in the plot. This

* Chowdri, a native *maître de poste* from whom kuhars or palkee-bearers are hired.

custom makes it impossible for a stranger or European to buy anything at a reasonable price in the bazárs. It is much better and cheaper for him to make such purchases through a native, and submit to the cheating of one rather than be defrauded by a combination of a dozen.

Gibson and I went in dhoolees, which are more commodious than palkees, and which being lighter required only twelve bearers each. The two other Americans had palkees, and sixteen kuhars each. Our baggage was carried upon bamboo poles by eight banghee-burdars. We also took a servant who was in the pay of the Americans, but cooked for the whole party. He went in a dhoolee with twelve bearers. Besides these there were six extra banghee-burdars to carry cooking utensils and provisions; and four mussalchees, or torch-bearers, for the palkees, so that our retinue amounted to eighty-six men exclusive of the servant.

In the northern part of India, as I have before stated there are lines of chowkees along all the principal roads. At each chowkee a fresh relay of bearers is obtained, so that the same set only carry the palkee for a stage of ten miles, but in Central India there are no such arrragements, and we had to hire in Agra, a sufficient number of men to carry us all the way to Bombay. The road is regularly divided off, before starting, into day's marches—the estimated number, by the route which we took, being thirty-nine. If we remained a day at any place we agreed to pay a fixed sum to the men as demurrage.

To give an idea of the cheapness of labour and living in India, it is only necessary to state the terms on which we hired the kuhars for this trip.

The distance was nearly a thousand miles; they were to feed and clothe themselves; and would have to return all the way on foot, without the chance of carrying another palkee back, that being forbidden by the rules of their guild. For this service, the hire of each man was seventeen rupees, of which pittance an ana per rupee goes as commission to the chowdri, and ten per cent. is retained by the hotel-keeper at whose house you are staying, so that the poor kuhar only gets about fourteen rupees, four anas ($6 84), for his two months' labour, and even that is considered high pay, and exceeds the wages paid to other labourers.

Gibson and I paid a little more than these rates. We gave each bearer eighteen rupees ($8 64), and paid the commission out of our own pockets. We did this to make our men contented, and were in hopes that they would work better than the others. In this expectation we were disappointed, and for a long time could not understand the cause. At length, when we were almost at the end of our journey, the men confessed that they had actually been fools enough to pay all the commissions over again, for fear of offending the chowdri, on whose good will they were dependent for work. So that our liberality had only gone to enrich the chowdri who lived on the life-sweat of these poor wretches.

We made the best bargain we could with the chowdris but yet they contrived to cheat us considerably in this and other respects. As all the money passed through their hands, they made arrangements with some of the bearers to desert during the early part of the journey—the chowdri, of course, retaining the larger part of the wages which we had paid supposing that the stipulated number of men would continue with us all the way down. We did not discover this little game for some time, and afterwards prevented its repetition by counting our men every few days. Another dodge which we discovered, was this: whenever a man became foot-sore, or too sick to go on, they would say nothing to us of what had occurred, and not supply the man's place as they were bound to do by agreement. The profits of this arrangement inured to the kuhars in this way. We had paid half their wages through the chowdri before starting. The other half was paid by us in instalments on the road. Now whenever pay-day came round, they would get a man from the next village to personate the missing bearer, and would then divide among themselves the wages of the poor man whom they had left sick or dying upon the road. This cheat was also stopped by the plan of frequently mustering the bearers.

We left Agra on the 15th of January, 1857. The day was cold and drizzly, but by two o'clock it cleared off, and we had magnificent weather during nearly all the rest of our trip—a matter of great importance in travelling by dhoolee, which affords but a slight protection against rain.

The scene presented as our long procession set out on the road, was very lively; and the shouts of the bearers added much to the effect. At starting, and at every village which we passed, they would sing out in chorus: "Sahib Bahádur, kee jaee!" "Kalee, kee jaee!"* words which mean nearly, "Help us, oh Kalee! A warrior lord is pleased to travel!" The people of the villages all replied by calling down blessings on our heads. Crowds of beggars ran alongside our dhoolees while we were in the villages, supplicating alms in the name of all sorts of gods, and calling us Shah Bahádur, warrior king, and Búndugee, or releaser of slaves.

We soon determined to walk and did so for eight miles, as far as Futtehpoor Seekree.

On the way we were passed by several very fierce looking suwars (native cavalry), wearing a dirty native uniform, and armed with spears and shields. One of these fellows stopped his horse, made a salám, and asked us, "Sahibo*n*, upne tush-reef kidhur lejate?" "Whither are my lords carrying their honour's effulgence?" On learning that we were going to Bhurtpoor, he informed us that he belonged to an escort of cavalry, which had come from that place to Agra, with eight lakhs of rupees ($400,000) as a loan from his master, the Rajah of Bhurtpoor, to the "Sircar Koompanee," or Sovereign Company, as the Honorable Company is called in that part of India.

The Indian government was then in considerable financial trouble, as Lord Dalhousie's great stroke of calling in the five per cent. loan, and re-issuing it at four and a half per cent., had proved a failure, as might have been expected in a country where twelve and fourteen per cent. is the usual interest paid for large sums. The difficulties of the government were, on this account, so great, that when I left Agra, it was currently

* This is the same in form as the old war-cry of the Sepoys: "Gunga jee, kee jaee!" "Oh, Lady Ganges, give thy aid!"

believed that Lord Canning had resigned the post of Governor-General.

About two o'clock we arrived at Futtehpoor Seekree, which is twenty-four miles from Agra. It consists of a mass of fortifications, palaces, gateways, and other splendid buildings, situated on the summit and sides of a range of sandstone hills, three miles long, which rises abruptly a hundred and fifty feet above the alluvial plain.

The story of the foundation of this city is as follows. The Emperor Akbur lost all his children in their infancy. Filled with despair at this misfortune, and dreading the extinction of his line, he undertook a pilgrimage to the shrine of a celebrated Moosulman saint in Ajmeer. The distance was three hundred and fifty miles. The court and all the royal family marched on foot with the Emperor. Kannats, or cloth walls, were raised on each side of the road; and a brick tower was erected at the end of each day's journey, which was only four miles. At Ajmeer the saint appeared to Akbur, and bade him seek the prayers of a holy hermit, Suleem Cheestee, who lived at Seekree. The Emperor did so, and to his great joy, a child was soon afterwards born to him, who showed every sign of a strong and long-lived constitution. This son was named Suleem in honour of the holy man, and received the additional title of Jehangeer, "Conqueror of the World," by which he became known on ascending the throne.

To testify his gratitude Akbur built this magnificent city on the hill where the saint resided. He said he wished to live always near one whose prayers were so availing with heaven. The new town was called Futtehpoor Seekree, or "Seekree, the City of Victory."

We passed through an arched gateway and ascended the hill by a paved street, on each side of which were rows of redstone houses, once the residence of Akbur's lords. At length we found ourselves on a plateau, which had been formed into a great square. On one side was the massive palace of Akbur's prime minister—on the other, that of the Emperor himself. Both were of redstone, in the simple Saracenic architecture of the period. Time seemed to have left them uninjured—every angle was sharp, the most delicate sculpture was perfect, and one could almost imagine the king and his court had gone forth to hunt, and would return by evening to their homes.

We left our dhoolees in the courtyard, and having given orders for dinner, at once set out to explore the place.

The first object was the tomb of San* Suleem.

It stands within a marble-paved quadrangle, four hundred feet square, upon the very summit of the hill. A redstone wall forty feet high, with arched battlements surrounds the court, on the west side of which is a great mosque, with domes of white marble. The principal entrance is on the south side. It is a magnificent gateway of redstone, inlaid with marble. Its height is one hundred and twenty feet, and its breadth nearly the same. From it a noble flight of redstone steps descends pyramidally to the ground. On the right side of the entrance are the following words in Arabic, inlaid in the stone wall:—" Jesus, on whom be peace, has said: this world is merely a bridge; you are to pass over it, not build your dwellings upon it."

The quadrangle is surrounded by a pillared cloister leaning against the wall. On the east side, opposite the musjeed, is a smaller entrance leading to the palace square. In the centre is a large tank and fountain.

The tomb is just north of the fountain. It is a small square building, approached by steps on each side, surmounted by a dome and surrounded by a closed verandah—the whole of the purest white marble, polished. The interior is elaborately decorated with carving, gilding, painting, mosaic, and inlaid work of mother-of-pearl. The ornamentation has been managed with so much skill, that notwithstanding its richness and profusion, it does not interfere with the exquisite taste of the architecture, or the simple purity of the white marble.

The body of the saint lies within this building, surrounded by a screen of that delicate marble openwork, which looks as Bayard Taylor says, " as if it had been woven in a loom."

* Mahommedan saints have the word "San" prefixed to their names in India.

The quadrangle in which this tomb is contained, was considered by Bishop Heber so magnificent that "no quadrangle either in Oxford or Cambridge, is fit to be compared with it, in size or majestic proportions, or for beauty of architecture."

The whole is said to have cost thirty-seven lakhs, ($1,850,000),* which, it is said, was all defrayed from the property left by the saint, so that, although a hermit, he seems to have been a considerable capitalist.

As we were leaving the quadrangle, we were met by the old guide, who forthwith took us in hand to show us the other sights. The old fellow was quite a character. Although then over sixty-nine years old, and very infirm, he persisted in acting as guide, which he had done for all strangers ever since the place was first visited by Europeans. Among his written recommendations was one from Bishop Heber, and numerous others from men whose names have become famous in India. He suffered dreadfully from asthma, and it would have been ludicrous, had it not been a serious matter, to see him dragging his fat body up the steep staircases, at every few steps stopping to get his wind, blowing and grunting out sentences of the Korán in a deep and dissatisfied voice.

He is one of a number of the saint's descendants who live at Futtehpoor, and who are supported by the rent of lands left by the Emperor Akbur. The proceeds of the legacy are punctually paid by the government, who also keep the tomb of the saint in perfect repair.

We went with the old guide through the various courts, rooms, and passages of the vast palace. Two pavilions were pointed out to us as the separate residences of the Emperor's chief wives—Mariam, who is supposed to have been a Portuguese Christian; and another, who was the daughter of the Room-ee-Padshah, or Emperor of Rome, as the natives of India call the Sultan of Turkey. The apartments of the latter and, indeed, all the others in the palace, have stone walls

* In naming the cost of these buildings, the amount should be multiplied by four to obtain the corresponding sum, at the present day, in England.

arched above, and covered with deep and elaborate carvings of foliage and animals.

What is called the "throne-room," is one of the strangest things in the palace. It is a circular apartment with a dome-shaped roof. From the centre of the floor rises a stone shaft sixteen feet high, which supports a small platform from which six stone radii diverge to the walls of the building. The tradition is, that Akbur used to hold his council sitting upon the capital of this column, while his ministers sat around him, one on each of the radii. A very original idea, and not altogether an improbable whim in a man so eccentric as Akbur.

In the court-yard before this throne-room, there was a low stone canopy, on a chubootra. Here, it is said, Akbur used to practice magic rites—but it is probable that the charge arose only from his rejection of the Mahommedan faith, and the general liberality of his religious views.

One court contained a large stone building known as the "Panch Mahul," or "Five Palaces." It consists of five stories rising pyramidally one above the other. Each story is surrounded by a row of columns, and the whole reminded me much of the style of Akbur's tomb. Its special use is not known.

Another court-yard in the portion of the palace appropriated to the Zĕnana, was paved with stone of various colours so as to form a gigantic "tric-trac" board. Here the Emperor used to play at pacheesee, a native game resembling "tric-trac," or "backgammon"—the girls of the Zĕnana acting as "pieces," and going from one square to another as the "moves" were made. Off this court there was a small stone apartment divided into various recesses and alcoves. Here it is said the ladies of the Zĕnana used to play "blind man's buff," and the building would be certainly admirably adapted for the purpose, although rather too small. But our guide described to us the real nature of the game, the principal features of which are altogether too disgusting even to be told, in this day and country.

This great palace contains numerous other courts, vestibules, and corridors, as well as a mint, Dewán Am, and all the other accessories of an Indian Emperor's residence, including long ranges of stables, and apartments for servants; but we went through the rest of the building so hurriedly, that I feel myself incompetent to describe it. A whole day, at least, is necessary to see it thoroughly, and more than a day's study would be required for a perfect description.

As evening was now falling we ascended a lofty point from which we had an extensive view of the surrounding country. The mist, which always rises at sunset in India, now covered the level plains and gave them the appearance of a lake. Indeed, in old times there used to be a lake at the foot of this hill, and the dam can still be traced. The lake furnished water for the use of the palace and town, and also for the terraced gardens, with which the hill sides were covered. After Futtehpoor was abandoned by the court, the lake dried up, and the surrounding country became quite barren, from the want of the irrigation which its waters afforded. Of late years this has been remedied by government. The whole country is every year overflowed by cutting through the banks of a small river near Bhurtpoor, and the water is drawn off below into the Jumna in time for the springing of the crops. The ground is now, therefore, more fertile than ever.

Although Akbur went to the enormous expense of building this splendid residence and capital, he did not long occupy it. The saint found his devotions interfered with by the bustle of the busy city, and the gaieties of the court. At last, when the Emperor wished to surround the hill with a chain of massive fortifications, the holy man could no longer restrain himself. He told his royal master that he had gone twenty times on pilgrimages to Mecca, and never before had had his comfort and quiet so much disturbed; accordingly he said that either the Emperor or he must depart. "If it be your Majesty's will," replied the Emperor, "that one should go, let it be your slave, I pray."

Akbur therefore built the city of Agra, upon what was then an unpeopled waste. The court and the townspeople removed thither, and Futtehpoor Seekree, with its massive palace, its noble residences, and its deserted streets, remains to the present day, a monument of the splendour and wealth of its founder, and a testimony to the despotic power which a reputation for sanctity has in all ages conferred.

When we returned to where we had left our palkees, the sun was setting, and our old guide, who was a Moosulman of the "straitest sect"—a class of which there are now but few in India—spread his praying-carpet upon the ground, and sat down on it, with his face to the west, for his devotions.

He began chaunting the Arabic prayers in a loud voice, and apparently with entire abstraction. Soon, however, he was interrupted. Our Hindoo bearers, who were standing around, began to make jokes at him. Upon this he stopped and cursed them roundly, and then turned again to his prayers. Delighted that they had succeeded in annoying him, the Hindoos renewed the attack with twofold vigour. The old fellow stood it for a long time, but at length his patience was exhausted, and he scared them with such strength of imprecations and lungs that they walked away.

It was dark before we got dinner, which was served in one of the rooms of the Prime Minister's palace, an apartment arranged by Government for the reception of visiters. The rooms were not large, but very lofty; the walls were of red stone, decorated with sculptures and arched niches. The ceiling was a solid dome of stone. The place and occasion were rather romantic. That we, from the opposite side of the world, members of the latest branch of that Christian race which are hated and despised, and at one time were nearly enslaved by the followers of Mahommed, should be dining in a palace chamber of what was once the capital of one of the mightiest Moosulman monarchs—and that, not by the invitation of his descendants, but by the permission and favour of a company of merchants, belonging to that same hated race, who had appropriated all that monarch's power and glory, and whose sway now extended over all that was once his dominions, and over countries whither he and his descendants in vain attempted to carry their arms and extend their power—here was certainly food for reflection, and a text, the comments upon which might, with good management, be made to fill a book.

Before sitting down to dinner, we dismissed our old guide with a handsome bucksees. He recompensed us by imploring the blessings of Heaven on our journey, praying that "we might arrive, whither we would go, in safety, peace, and coolness." The latter part of the prayer struck me as unseasonable, as we were all sitting with our over-coats on, and it was almost freezing out of doors; but as the old man stood with upturned eyes and hands raised in supplication, his fine figure and long grey beard, with the really earnest expression of his countenance, formed a noble and impressive picture. However, I believe that the same scene, with variations in the words to suit occasions, is got up for any party who will give him four rupees for an afternoon's work, as we did. We bade him good-bye, and shook his hand; he retreated backward, with saláms, from our presence. As he walked away across the court, we could hear him puffing and blowing for a long way, and every now and then grunting out a verse of the Korán, or the words "Allah! Allah Akbur!" in those same indescribably wretched and guttural tones which we had heard in the morning. At length the sturdy blows of his iron-shod stick against the pavement became fainter and fainter, and died away, and that was the last we saw or heard of Bishop Heber's guide, the most original native I met in India.

At midnight we started for Bhurtpoor, and had a disagreeable march, as the bearers lost their way and got into a jheel (shallow lake), where they floundered about for half an hour, to my great discomfort, as I was afraid the water would get into my dhoolee. I did not find travelling by night in the low plains at all pleasant, as there was always a mist, which made the air very chilly, and frequently caused the kuhars to lose their way.

We awoke next morning at Bhurtpoor, where we occupied an empty bungalow belonging to the Rajah, and appropriated by him to the accommodation of Europeans.

Bhurtpoor was the first place that I had visited in India beyond the limits of the Company's "raj," or sway. We were now passing beyond the Mahommedan part of India, and coming to the Rajpootana states and other Hindoo territories, which have always preserved a sort of independence, both of the Mogul power and the Company's Government.

The territory of Bhurtpoor is inhabited by Jats—a Hindoo tribe from the banks of the Indus, near Mooltan. They come of the same stock as the Seekhs, and will still intermarry with them. In settling in this part of the country, the Jats began as cultivators and robbers on a small scale. Becoming enriched by this trade, they ventured to plunder the tributes as they were being conveyed to the imperial capital. At length they rose to making war on the neighbouring states, and before the death of Aurungzeeb, in the beginning of the last century, they declared and maintained their independence, which they retain to this day. The independence of these native states is, in general, merely nominal, as they are entirely at the mercy of the Honourable Company, and the advice of the resident ambassador becomes, in fact, a *command.* Such a government is, of course, not so good as that in the English territories, but is infinitely preferable to the unlimited despotism of native rulers. The independent chieftains, who are almost numberless, are now compelled to live in peace with each other, whereas formerly they were engaged in endless wars, rebellions, and free-booting expeditions. Taking the dominions of this one rajah alone as a specimen, we find that "the thick belt of jungul, three miles wide, with which the chiefs of Bhurtpoor used to surround their fortress while they were free-booters, has been fast diminishing since the capture of the place by the English troops in 1826, and will very soon disappear altogether, and give place to rich sheets of cultivation and happy little village communities."* In fact, the change spoken of in the above sentence, which was written fourteen years ago, has already taken place. The people, no longer dreading the warlike incursions of neighbouring rajahs, and secured against flagrant oppression by the watchful super-

* Colonel Sleeman's "Rambles and Recollections of an Indian Official."

vision of the English Residents,* are every year extending the cultivation of the soil, reclaiming waste land, and more and more turning their attention to agriculture and useful industry, instead of war and robbery—two pursuits which formerly gave constant occupation to a large number of the population. The first effect has always been to occasion great discontent among a large and powerful class, namely, the predatory chieftains and their feudal followers; but in a few years these murmurs cease, and general peace, plenty, and prosperity, with a rise in the value of property, resulting from the security of its tenure, testify to the good effects of the change.

In the afternoon we walked into the town, which, although very populous, is a mere collection of mud-hovels, traversed by narrow and dirty streets. The fort, containing the palace, is situated on one side of the town, upon an elevation of ground. It is a very extensive and exceedingly strong fortification. The moat is broad and deep, the walls thick and lofty. There are two lines of defence, formed of stone and earth respectively.

This place sustained two sieges from the English—the first in 1804, under Lord Lake, the second in 1826, under Lord Cambermere. The attack by Lord Lake was occasioned by the Rajah having taken side with the Maharattas, who took refuge in this place. Lord Cambermere's attack was in behalf of the Rajah, who had become an ally of the British, and whose throne had been usurped by one of his relations.

In both sieges, the defences of earth proved a most formidable obstacle. Cannon were found wholly ineffective against them, as the balls buried themselves without doing injury; and tedious mining operations had to be resorted to before the place was taken. The garrison resisted vigourously, especially during the first siege, when the loss of life was so great, in storming the walls, that the British army was almost repulsed. The earthworks are now in great want of repair, but enough remains perfect to show how formidable they must once have been.

* "Residents"—the title of the English Agents of the Honourable Company at the courts of native princes.

The Rajah's palace, situated within the fort, is of redstone, whitewashed. It possesses no architectural merit, being merely a great square building, four or five stories high, with marble pavilions on the roof. We were not allowed to enter, but did not much regret our exclusion. There are in the city one or two other palaces of similar construction, inhabited by the Rajah's relatives.

We walked around the walls of the fort, admiring the beauty of the country, which is principally owing to the fine groves of old trees; and the very great fertility of the soil, which is all alluvial, and overflowed every year, as I have described when speaking of Futtehpoor Seekree.

The fortifications were dismantled, but there were still a few cannon remaining. They were of immense size, but of ridiculously small bore.

When we had made the circuit of the fort, we descended, and passed out of one of the gateways, which had bronze doors of great size, and very finely decorated with carved work.

Crossing the bridge over the moat, we returned to the bungalow, first going over several large mud fortifications, now deserted, but showing, like the large fort, that there were Todlebens in Central India, before Sebastopol was thought of.

We had intended to make an excursion to Deeg, a place twenty miles distant, which is the summer residence of the Bhurtpoor Rajahs. It contains several fine buildings; and gardens, which; with the pavilions they contain are, I should fancy, the finest in India. However, finding that we could get no conveyances but camels, and that it would delay us at least a day, we gave it up.

Deeg was the scene of a great battle, in 1804, between the English and Maharattas. The loss of the English was two-ninths* of their whole force—a very large proportion, but not greater than that sustained by them in many other engagements in India. These great losses are not to be attributed to what is called "a hard-fought field," but to the habit of the

* Even in the battle of Waterloo, the English loss was only one in six; and that is a very large proportion for a European battle.

English soldiers of dashing up to the enemies' batteries, in the face of a deadly and rapid fire, (for natives are among the best artillerymen in the world,) and carrying the guns at the point of the bayonet, thus finishing the battle at a single stroke; for the natives do not long resist after their guns are taken, and generally disperse as soon as they are brought to close quarters.

Not being able to go to Deeg, we spent an hour or so of the morning at the Rajah's menagerie, where there were a number of animals, among others, two giraffes, in large bamboo cages. We could not learn were these came from. A number of game-cocks and fighting quails were kept in the menagerie, the combats of these birds being a favourite amusement of native princes. The keepers set some of the quails at each other, without spurs, but it seemed poor sport, as one of the combatants was sure to run away after the first encounter.

We also got up wrestling and boxing-matches among the boys, by offering rewards for the best performers. The wrestling was exceedingly good, as it is everywhere a favourite exercise among the supple Hindoos; but the boxing did not succeed. The first blow in the face made the receiver whimper, and the "set-to" was so evidently a sham, that we withheld the promised reward.

We dined at eight in the evening, and started at midnight for Bosawur, thirty-seven miles to the westward.

On awaking, the next morning, we got out of our dhoolees, and walked eight or nine miles. The country generally appeared fertile and well cultivated, and the path by which we were travelling (for we had left the road, in order to make a short cut,) was bordered by well-tilled fields, and orchards of trees, bearing a fruit like the plum. Although this was the general character of the country, yet we passed through several miles of jungul, upon which we saw a very large herd of deer. They were, like all wild animals in India, not at all shy, and let us approach quite near, but not near enough to be within range of our smooth-bore guns.

During this journey we often regretted not having a rifle

in the party, as we might without any trouble have shot a deer almost every day, which would have been no bad thing in a country where chicken and goat's flesh is the only meat procurable; and even that not always to be had.

Before reaching Bosawur, we came in sight of some hills, the view of which, although they were distant, was a great relief after the monotonous dead-level of Northern India. In fact, we were now entering a hilly region, in which we may be said to have continued all the way down to Bombay, for although we frequently marched for days together over broad and perfectly level plains, yet, even there, there was almost always a mountain or range of hills visible upon the horizon to remind us of what we had come through, and of what we had still to pass.

We arrived at Bosawur dâk-bungalow at two in the afternoon, and ordered *breakfast*, to the great astonishment of Khansahma*n*, who had never heard of taking that meal in the afternoon.

After breakfast, we took a walk in the town of Bosawur, which is small and dirty. The houses are almost all mere mud-huts, and the streets narrow, unpaved, and filthy. However, having nothing better to do, we wandered all over the place, and finally came upon a native distillery, a very rude establishment under a thatched shed. A crowd of natives accompanied us in our walk, and we treated them to as much liquor as they could drink. The liquor is a kind of whiskey made of wheat, and is only used by the poorer classes. They drink it unmixed with water, and in incredible quantities. The price is fabulously low.

We got dinner about half-past nine, and left at midnight for Manpoor, distant four-and-twenty miles.

Our walk on the morning of the 18th was again interesting. The country was hilly, and perfectly barren. Numerous travellers passed us on foot, on camels, on horseback, or in bullock-carts. They all treated us with the greatest respect, and saluted us with courteous salâms.

Just before arriving at Manpoor, we crossed a broad sandy *nullah*, or river's bed. A little way off we saw a herd of several hundred antelopes. They let us approach until we got within a hundred and twenty yards, and then trotted slowly off. I fired, notwithstanding, but with no other effect than causing them all to leap up eight or ten feet into the air, and then make off at full gallop.

We reached the bungalow at noon, and after breakfast walked into Manpoor, which is a walled village, though very small.

This was the first walled village we had met, but from this point, almost every place which we saw, however insignificant, was defended by mud walls and ditches. Until within a few years, such defences were absolutely necessary. They were used to protect the inhabitants, sometimes against invading armies, sometimes against organized bands of robbers, but oftener against the freebooting incursions of neighbouring rajahs, and not unfrequently against the agents of their own ruler. The existence of these fortifications, so entirely disproportionate to the size of the places which they protect, is a striking proof of the perfect lawlessness which must have prevailed in these countries until quite recent times. At the present day, they are mostly falling gradually to ruin. In fact, they are no longer needed. The omnipresent arm of the East India Company protects the inhabitants in the enjoyment of their lives and property, far better than any defences which they can erect; and peace and prosperity now reign where marauding incursions, bloodshed, robbery, and devastation were formerly matters of constant occurrence.

Within the walls, Manpoor was a wretched collection of mud huts. We entered several Hindoo temples, the courts of which were decorated on the inner side with fresco representations of mythological scenes, painted in very bright colours. We were obliged to take off our shoes before entering these temples.

Another object of interest was a *yogee*, or Hindoo religious mendicant. He was a youth of about twenty years, entirely naked, smeared with mud and cow-dung, and altogether one of the most disgusting beings I ever set my eyes on; still, the inhabitants seemed to treat him with great veneration.

We were followed in our walk by sixty or eighty boys and young men, and when we left the village, the people crowded along the ramparts to see us off; the great interest and curiosity which our appearance excited showing evidently that we had come to a country where Europeans are seldom seen.

We left Manpoor about midnight for Buranah, twenty-eight miles off, and next morning, January 19th, after an early breakfast on the road, of ham and eggs, biscuits and coffee, we made our way through a barren and rocky tract of country to Buranah dâk-bungalow—which we reached at half-past two in the afternoon.

Just before arriving, we passed a zĕmindar, making a pilgrimage to the shrine of Juggurnath, on the eastern coast of India, south of Calcutta. He was travelling in a bailee, or bullock-cart, shaded with a canopy of scarlet cloth. His train was very numerous, and comprised several well-armed men, a large number of servants and camels, horses and bullocks. The zĕmindar was a fine-looking, fat old fellow, but being a Hindoo, did not think it worth while to salám to us.

Arrived at the dâk-bungalow, we did not get anything to eat till four in the afternoon, and by the time we had finished breakfast it was so late that we gave up our usual walk through the village, and went out with a gun instead, to get some breakfast for the next day. We succeeded in bagging some ducks, pigeons, and a peacock. At ten in the evening, we dined, and about midnight left for a thirty miles' march to Jaipoor.

At eight on the following morning, we took breakfast outside a village, the whole *public* of which came out to look at us, and squatted around our palkees in admiring circles. While the bacon and eggs were being cooked by our servant over a fire of sticks built on the road, we took our guns and shot a great many pigeons, which afterwards did us good service at Jaipoor, where we could get scarcely anything to eat.

After breakfast we walked for about ten miles. The country was again jungul, but we occasionally passed villages, around which the ground was cultivated, and seemed productive. The road was covered with people. We passed many travellers with escorts, and bullock-carts conveying merchandize eastward. We now began to notice, what is a striking feature in Rajpootana, namely, almost every man is armed with a sword, and many with a shield and spear in addition. This custom, which is common to all states under native rule, and is particularly noticeable in Oude, arises from the insufficient protection to life afforded by native governments. In the Company's dominions it has almost disappeared.

About ten o'clock we came in sight of a high range of hills, beyond which the town of Jaipoor is situated. By one o'clock we entered the pass, where the road is very good, and the scenery exceedingly picturesque, as the sides of the pass are steep and the hills well wooded and green.

We stopped the palkees near the entrance of the defile, and visited a large Hindoo temple and gardens belonging to a thakoor,* who has a country seat here. The buildings are all of white marble and well worth a visit.

After walking for a quarter of a mile further, we came to a country palace of the Rajah, which we entered, and saw the gardens, and two large and handsome temples of Párbutee, who is represented by a hideous black doll, with a necklace of bleeding heads. The whole establishment is very extensive, reaching, with the gardens, more than half a mile on each side of the road. Free use had been made of the beautiful white marble for which Jaipoor is so famous, and which was conveyed on carts from this place to Agra and Delhi, for the construction of the Taj, and other architectural monuments of those cities.

The road led for about half a mile further through the pass, and soon after emerging upon the plain we came in sight of Jaipoor, the extent and beauty of which much surprised us.

The city of Jaipoor, which was built by Rajah Jai Singh, less than one hundred and fifty years ago, is situated in the midst of a beautiful plain, eight or ten miles broad, and completely enclosed by lofty hills, the crests of which are crowned

* *Thakoor*, a name given in Rajpootana to the great vassals; elsewhere called jagheerdars, or zĕmindars.

by a long fortified wall, with towers at intervals. The town is more than a mile square, and surrounded by lofty walls of red sandstone, above which appear the marble walls of the palace, several domes, and a tall, square minár. Outside the walls are fine groves which give shelter to caravans of travellers, and on two sides the suburbs extend for some distance beyond the limits of the city proper. The situation of Jaipoor far surpassed in picturesqueness and beauty that of any other city which I saw in India.

About five o'clock we arrived at the dâk-bungalow, which is about a mile from the town. In the evening we had a call from a young lieutenant in the Bombay army, stationed at Jaipoor in command of a company of Bombay sepoys, who formed the Resident's guard. The Resident himself was absent, but this gentleman promised to get us elephants for the next day.

CHAPTER XXVII.

JAIPOOR.

Elephants—Beauty of the City—A Beautiful Temple—The Zĕnana and Palace—Its Rooms—Novel Stairways—View from Roof—A Court—Revenue Department—The English Resident sitting Cross-legged on the Floor—Dewán Khas—Sitringees—Native Furniture—Curtain-ladies—A Lovely Character—Palace Gardens—His Highness' Toys—"Composite Architecture"—Native College—Marriage Nach—Observatory—Palace in Lake—Palaces of Ummeer—Splendid View—Tiffin in the Reception Court—Bishop Heber's Praises of the Palace—Bazár of Jaipoor—History of Jaipoor.

THE following morning two fine elephants with howdahs, scarlet jhools, or trappings, and several attendants and spearmen, took us to view the sights of the place. On entering the gate we were surprised by the breadth and splendour of the principal street, used as a bazár, and extending in a straight line through the town from gate to gate. It is crossed in the centre by another similar street, dividing the city in the opposite direction. At the point of junction is a broad square, having in the centre a marble tank. One side of this square is occupied by the Rajah's palace, which, with its gardens and courts, occupies one-sixth of the town.

Jaipoor, having been all built by one man, presents a regularity and uniformity of design unusual in Indian cities. The houses are generally two stories high, but those on the two great streets have three and even four stories. The material is commonly white-washed pukka, the style of architecture quite Moosulman, and the houses are decorated in front with ornamental windows and stone balconies, which are often finely carved. The whole population of Jaipoor must be nearly a hundred thousand, almost exclusively Hindoos.

The first object visited by us was a small but very rich temple in a side street. It was entirely built of white and beautifully polished marble, the interior being richly decorated with bright colours and gilding. Under a graceful and elaborately carved marble canopy was the idol, a diminutive black doll, in a long dress of rich brocade. This was Párbutee, the incarnation of all the most inhuman and barbarous qualities of the Hindoo gods. Throughout the Rajpoot states, her worship seems largely to have supplanted the Phallic worship of her consort Seewa, who is the most popular deity in the rest of India.

Leaving the temple, we went through one of the principal streets before described, along the wall of the zĕnana, which extends for half a mile from the palace. In one of the courts of the zĕnana rises a lofty square minár of stone, used, I believe, as a watch-tower, and being one of the most conspicuous objects in the city, as it is visible from every part of the plain around the town.

At the end of the zĕnana we came to the palace, which presents to the square a lofty front, seven or eight stories high, flanked by two towers which rise above the roof, and are topped by marble kiosks. The architecture, like that of the city, is impure Moosulman, the arches being flattened and cusped.

Within the palace we were led through numerous apartments, which, like those of all other Indian palaces, were very small, though much decorated. The walls of one of the rooms were entirely covered with little looking-glasses, embedded in a sort of cement, which at a distance looked like frosted silver. The whole reminded me of the "Sheesh Mahul" in the fort of Agra. Our guide, one of the Rajah's servants, evidently considered this room the gem of the palace, and asked us if there were such another in Europe; to which question we answered, much to his satisfaction, that there was not.

The different stories of this palace were approached, not by stairs, but by inclined planes, similar to those by which the visitor ascends to the roof of St. Peter's church at Rome.

From the top of the palace, or rather from one of the marble pavilions upon the roof, we had a magnificent view of the city, with its numerous palaces, temples and domes, the slender minárs of a mosque, and the rows of fine buildings on the great streets, all of the purest white. The square and bazárs were filled with busy and picturesquely-dressed crowds; beyond the walls we could see the suburbs, and the broad groves which surround the city; further off were lakes, with palaces upon islands in their midst, and the scene was bounded by the circle of hills, and the long lines of defensible walls. The whole view was so striking that we remained gazing for half an hour, and only descended because we were pressed for time.

Having descended from the roof, we were led through several low and dark passages, and finally reached an open court, one half of which was occupied by a marble portico, raised upon a chubootra of the same material. This was used as a cutchurree,* or court. The judge sat upon a carpet close to the wall, and was undistinguished from the crowds of natives squatted around him, except that he was smoking a hookah, which is, in Indian courts of justice, a privilege conceded only to the sitting magistrate. The open space below the chubootra was crowded with a motley throng of suitors and spectators.

The next court which we saw was larger, but similarly arranged. The portico was appropriated to the revenue department, and the floor was occupied by over fifty clerks, writing upon narrow slips of paper† which they rested on one knee. Several of the older officials in these courts wore the old Rajpoot pugree (turban), which is narrow, high, and bent back from the head. It is now but little used, most of the inhabitants wearing the small low jaunty turban of Hindoostan.

From this court we proceeded to the Dewán Khas, or hall of private audience, where the Maharajah is accustomed to hold Durbar, and receive his high functionaries and vassals. On these occasions the Resident is accommodated with a seat on

* This designation is also applied to the courts of the European magistrates in the Company's dominions, and is generally spelt cutcherry.

† Native paper (kaghuz) is very thick and brittle, made, I believe, of some woody fibre. It is very expensive. The ink is merely soot and water thickened with gum. It can be easily washed off—a circumstance often taken advantage of in inconvenient treaties or contracts. The pen (kullum cf. calamus) is made of a sort of reed, and writes very well, being stronger and more durable than a quill, though not so fine.

the floor, since the Rajah has not, like many of the other native princes, become so Anglicized as to use chairs.*

The Dewán Khas consists of a marble platform raised five steps from the pavement of the court. It is covered with a roof of polished white marble, supported by columns and arches of the same material. It is about eighty feet square and open on all sides to the court, which is of considerable size, paved, and surrounded by the buildings of the palace, which are five stories high and of red sandstone. On two sides of the court the palace front has on every story broad verandahs, arched in front, and lined with white marble.

We went through one of these buildings, the rooms of which, like those of the other palace, were all small but richly decorated. The windows were formed by small panes of stained glass, said to be Venetian, inserted in slabs of marble openwork. As in all native apartments, there was no furniture, but several of the rooms contained sitringees, or quilts of scarlet cotton cloth wadded, which are spread over the floor for the guests to sit on when the rooms are used. These form the whole furniture of a native sitting-room, there being no tables or chairs. The bed-rooms contain only a low pullun, or bedstead, which is taken out during the day into a court. These peculiarities of native habits make the rooms in all the palaces look as desolate and deserted as the abandoned palaces of Agra and Futtehpoor Seekree.

* Chinese sit on chairs, but natives of India never do, except when they have acquired the habit from Europeans. When they sit on the ground, they squat in such a way that the legs are doubled, the soles of the feet are flat on the ground, and the knees touch the chin. In fact they sit upon their heels. This position is quite impossible to a white man, but is very favourite with the supple Hindoos. The lower classes are particularly fond of perching in this way upon a wall, when they look exactly like monkeys. The upper classes, or those who sit on carpets, often cross their legs like Turks, but more generally kneel down, and sit upon the ground with the legs slightly spread and bent backwards. This position, also, is impossible for a white man. But perhaps the most common position is to kneel down, and sit upon the lower part of the legs, the insteps touching the ground. The only substitutes for chairs ever used by the natives are very low stools, which they sit upon in the mode above described. A few Mahommedan princes had thrones, which were always very high, and intended to be used in the same way.

Each suite of apartments is entered by a strong and heavy wooden door, with a massive lock of the rudest construction, looking as if it had been copied from a prison-door of the Middle ages. The arched passages between the separate apartments of the suite are, however, closed only by a purdah, or wadded curtain, or sometimes by a *chik*, a sort of blind of bamboo shreds, so arranged that those *within* can see out, whereas those on the outside cannot see in. From this custom comes the expression applied to the ladies of the zĕnana, "purdah ke undur," within the purdah, i. e. on the inside of the curtain which separates the zĕnana from the public apartments; and hence, also, women of rank are called purdah-beebia*n*, or curtain-ladies.

We were particularly struck with one room in this part of the palace. Its walls were of white marble, decorated with carving, gilding and painting, in a style elaborate beyond belief. Some of the panels contained paintings of various deities, and among them one of Bhowánee, the patroness of the Thugs. She is the same as Párbutee, two of whose temples I have described. Bhowánee was represented as a naked black female figure, wearing around her neck a necklace of human heads, bleeding. She had ten arms, with two of which she was tearing a baby in pieces. In another hand she held half of a man's body. The other half she had eaten, and her jaws dripped with the blood. A fourth hand was bearing an elephant and its rider to her huge red mouth, glittering with a row of sharp, projecting tusks. This amiable character is supposed to smile a thousand years at the death of a single man slain in her honor. She is the patroness, and receives the homage of the Thugs and Dukoits, classes of professional robbers and murderers, who look upon the crimes which they commit as a religious duty, and who were fearfully numerous throughout India, until the great and successful efforts made during the present century by the Honourable Company for their suppression.

This room overlooked the Gardens, to which we next descended, after swinging for a few minutes in a swing with a cushioned seat suspended by silken cords from the roof of one of the verandahs.

The gardens were extensive, laid out in Italian style, and well cared for. The alleys were paved with marble, and bordered by rows of trees. In the middle of the pavement was a marble canal, down which a stream of water, recruited at intervals by fountains, ran, to irrigate the various beds and grass-plots. There were several marble fish-ponds, and *jets d'eau*, and graceful pavilions, terraces, and kiosks of white marble were distributed through the grounds.

Having now seen all that we were allowed to, and a great deal more than we could have seen had not the Rajah been absent at one of his country residences, we prepared to leave the palace. Before doing so, however, we stopped in a sort of lumber room on the ground floor. Here we found a collection of the most curious and dissimilar things that can be imagined. A model steam engine, an electric machine, a go-cart, saddles, old guns—in short, all the broken and used up toys of the Rajah. A native, seated by a table was repairing a French musical box, and upon the same table lay half a dozen valuable watches of English and Genevan construction, some of them enamelled, and all of them, as the workman said, the property of the Sircar,* who had been pleased to break them.

We next went to see a new palace which is building for the Rajah, next door to the old one. The new building is of red-stone, and will be of great size, but was only completed as far as the first story. It was designed by a pundit high in the Rajah's service, who undertook to gratify a desire of his master for a residence "in the English style." Accordingly he read up some English works on architecture, and selected whatever he considered desirable. The full effect of the result of his studies could not be seen in the building itself on account of its incomplete state, but we were shown a plaster model, presenting the most extraordinary combination of the Grecian, Roman, and Gothic styles. When finished it will look as Mr. Russell, the "*Times*'" correspondent says of the Martinière

* Sircar—*i. e.* Sovereign. In Calcutta, the upper servant, who makes the purchases, is so called.

at Lucknow, "as if it were the result of a competitive examination of mad architects."

We now again mounted the elephant and went through the streets of the town, passing many fine houses belonging to thakoors and other great men.

Returning to the principal square, we visited the college, a large building opposite the palace. We were too late to see the students, but went through the lecture-rooms, the walls of which were hung with good maps and mathematical diagrams, published in England, but having the names of the countries and other words and letters in Sanscrit characters. The back part of the college is devoted to a temple, which is a feature in all palaces and large edifices of Hindoo construction.

After visiting the college, we went home on the elephants, passing a large menagerie of tigers and leopards belonging to the Rajah, to whom also belonged a number of animals of the deer kind, that we saw in enclosures around the city. On the way home we stopped for a few minutes to see a marriage-nach in the open air. The young couple were laden with finery, and sat upon a carpet. The relatives and friends of the family in their best dresses squatted around, forming a circle about the nach girls. Outside stood the general public. As soon as the nach girls saw that we stopped, they turned round and began singing a song in our honour—a proceeding that very much disgusted the bridal party. Making the girls a present of two rupees, and receiving their low salâms, we took our departure and returned to the dâk-bungalow, where we dined and passed the night.

The next day, we again mounted the elephants and went to a place called Ummeer, three miles from Jaipoor, at one end of the valley in which the latter city is situated. Ummeer was formerly the capital of this raj, until Jai Sing built the present city called after his name, and transferred to it his capital, about 130 years ago.

In order to take the Ummeer road we had to pass through the town, and, in so doing, stopped at the palace to see the observatory connected with it, which we had omitted to visit on the previous day. The observatory is a large establishment, contained in a vast unpaved court, but does not merit a description here, being very similar to those at Bĕnarĕs and Delhi—all these having been founded by Jai Singh.

The road to Ummeer was very interesting, being bordered on each side by a succession of groves, country-houses, and beautiful gardens containing pavilions of redstone and white marble.

About a mile from Jaipoor we passed a large lake, upon an artificial island in the midst of which, was built a white marble palace, surrounded by gardens and terraces—the whole much larger and more beautiful than the famous "Isola Bella" in the Lago Maggiore.

Ummeer is situated in a narrow gorge, at the head of the valley. A lake occupies the lowest ground, and around it are the ruins of the city, which must have been once a large place. The only perfect buildings which remain, are several temples of a hard grey stone, very elaborately sculptured. But the principal objects are the palaces and fort, three immense lines of buildings on the steep side of the hill. The lowest of the three was four hundred feet above the lake. The fort, which is the oldest and strongest, was perched on the very crest of the hill, and the third palace was half way between the other two.

We were not allowed to visit the two higher forts, on the usual plea of there being a zĕnana there, but the lower palace, over which we were conducted, surprised us greatly by its extent and beauty. The architecture and general arrangement were similar to those of most of the palaces which I saw. There were the same broad courts of reception, the same long ranges of small, but elaborately decorated rooms, the same beautiful little garden courts with marble fountains and arched marble porticoes, the same delicately carved balconies; but from these latter we got such a view as I did not see elsewhere in India. The valley is here narrow and dark, the hills are steep, rugged, and thickly wooded; at the bottom lies the lake surrounded by gardens and temples. Where the valley closes on the left, are the solemn grey ruins of the old city; its opening on the right shows you the green valley of

Jaipoor, the lake and palaces; and far in the distance the city itself, with its minár and domes, shines white over the dark-green groves which surround it.

The view was intrinsically striking and picturesque; the romance of the locality and its architectural features gave it an additional charm; but no one who has not travelled as we had for months, over the bare dead level of northern India, can appreciate the unalloyed enjoyment with which we gazed upon the scene.

The Dewán Am is one of the most striking features of the building. It is a very large square platform of white marble, open on one side to a great court, and on the other looking out upon the valley. It is covered by a heavy white marble roof, supported on low square pillars, without arches; the absence of which, and the massiveness of the roof, gave the architecture a very Hindoo air. We found a sitringee in the building, and sitting down upon it, took lunch and a bottle of beer, after which one of the party read aloud Bishop Heber's description of the building, in the laudations of which we all concurred. It concludes thus:—"The carving in stone and marble, and the inlaid flowers and ornaments in some of these apartments, are equal to those at Delhi and Agra, and only surpassed by the beauties of the Taj Mahul. My companions, none of whom had visited Ummeer before, all declared that, as a whole, it was superior to the Castle at Delhi. For myself, I have seen many royal palaces containing larger and more stately rooms, many, the architecture of which is in finer taste, and some which cover a greater extent of ground, (though in *this*, if the fortress on the hill be included, Ummeer will rank, I think, above Windsor,) but for varied and picturesque effect, for richness of carving, for wild beauty of situation, for the number and romantic singularity of its apartments, and the strangeness of finding such a building in such a place and country, I am able to compare nothing with Ummeer."

After our tiffin we visited a small and dirty temple, the floor of which was stained with the blood of sacrificed goats. Three or four dirty Brahmuns, who were squatted on the ground, humming their poorans* in a monotonous voice, scowled at us as we entered. We found there was nothing to see, and as this was the last sight of the palace, we went out of the gate and descended the hill by a steep carriage road paved with blocks of redstone. The road passes under two large archways belonging to two separate lines of fortification for the protection of the palace.

At the bottom of the hill we found our elephants, and returned upon them to Jaipoor. The road varied slightly from the one by which we had come, and passed through a grove, the trees of which were perfectly full of monkeys. There are plenty of these animals and peacocks in all the country about Jaipoor, but in this place it really seemed as if there were not room for one more.

On our return to Jaipoor we walked through the bazár to make a few purchases, preceded by the spearmen and other servants, and followed by our elephants and a large miscellaneous and admiring public. We noticed in the streets several tame leopards tied to bed-posts, to accustom them to the sight of men. They were not chained or muzzled, and played like cats with their keepers.

We returned to the dâk-bungalow late in the evening, and getting through dinner about midnight, started at one o'clock in the morning for Bugroo.

A few particulars with regard to the history of Jaipoor may not be out of place here. The Rajahs of Jaipoor were once the wealthiest and most powerful of all the rulers of Rajasthan, or Rajpootana. Their revenue was a cror of rupees, or a million of pounds sterling annually. Although nominally subjects of the court of Delhi, their position and power always enabled them to maintain a virtual independence. Their prosperity

* *Poorans.*—A word derived from the Hindee *poorana*, signifying old. It is applied to all the sacred writings of the Hindoos; but in a narrower sense is sometimes confined to the later writings. Although these last were written between the eighth and sixteenth centuries of our era, and are a mass of as absurd, incredible and contradictory fables as were ever got together, yet they are now regarded by the Brahmuns as of equal age and authenticity with the Vedas, and are almost exclusively studied.

may be judged of from the great works executed by Jai Singh: the four observatories, the palaces, and the city. This prosperity was blighted by the conquests of the Maharattas. The thakoors took advantage of the disturbances to revolt, and were continually engaged in feuds and in predatory excursions which stripped the unfortunate inhabitants of the little left them by the bands of Pindarrees, a nation of robbers who devastated the country as each year came round. The power of the Rajah was almost extinct, and his revenue was reduced to almost nothing. In his despair he applied to the British, who reinstated him in his dominions and restored order. After his death, one of his wives assumed the government, and administered it so badly, rejecting the authority and counsel of the English Resident, that when Bishop Heber visited the place, she had nearly lost all authority over the thakoors, who were resuming their old practices, and the country was fast relapsing into a state of anarchy which would encourage a renewed invasion of Maharattas. Subsequently, however, British influence again became predominant, public confidence and prosperity were restored, peace at home and security against foreign invasion were guaranteed by their power, and when I visited Jaipoor the authority of the Rajah's government was recognized throughout his territories and his revenue was steadily growing to something like its old proportions.

CHAPTER XXVIII.

RAJPOOTANA—"THE COUNTRY OF PRINCES."

Bugroo—Peacock Shooting—Thakoor's House—Dhoodoo—Superstition about Wells—Jain Temple—Kishinghur—Visit from Baboo—Rajah's Palace—Excitement of the Public—A Dancing Elephant—Road to Ajmeer—Scenery—Dress and Manners of Rajpoots—A Providential Rencontre—Fort of Ajmeer—Shrine of the Saint—Ruins of a Hindoo Palace—Nusseerabad—Bombay Sepoys—The Shop of a Fire-worshipper—Bunai—Hindoo Cooking—The Fortress—A Native Huntsman—Dáblah—Filial Grief—Bunaira—Remarkable Castle—Road to Ummeerghur—Cheap Meat—The Day of Rest.

On the morning of January 23d we arrived at Bugroo dâk-bungalow. It is situated on a vast and barren plain with nothing in sight but a garden of large trees a quarter of a mile behind the bungalow. After breakfast we went out and shot a good many pigeons, as well as some peacocks which we found in the trees of the garden. The latter are easy to kill, and looked like meteors as they came tumbling down to earth through the leaves and branches of the trees.

In the afternoon we took a walk through the village, which is about half a mile behind the garden. We found it a mere collection of mud huts, the inhabitants of which looked sufficiently dirty and wretched. In the centre is the residence of the thakoor, surrounded by a moat and fortifications. The town also is surrounded by a high and broad wall of earth. We learned that this thakoor has to pay a tribute of three lakhs ($150,000), in return for which he has the absolute government of a large tract, and rents to probably double that amount.

The following day we stopped at Dhoodoo, twenty-three miles from Bugroo. This place was also on a plain, with hills visible on the horizon. The village was about a quarter of a mile off, surrounded by mud walls, above which was seen the thakoor's residence, a large white building. After breakfast we walked into the village, which was, like the others, a collection of miserable hovels. In the centre was an unpaved square containing the thakoor's house, which was defended by stone walls and bastions. On the walk back to the bungalow we passed a fine well going to ruin, and which will never again be used, as the water was defiled by a man falling into it and being drowned.* The country around the village was all cultivated in cotton and tobacco. We saw some deer, and heard of plenty more, but there was no getting a shot at them as our guns were all smooth-bored. In the afternoon we went out to shoot some wild ducks in a pond near by, but the ducks were *too* wild, and we had to be contented with getting some pigeons.

Towards evening I walked again into the village with Gibson and visited a temple of the Jains, a sect which sprang from among the Indian Boodhists when they were persecuted by the Brahmuns. They practised their religion secretly for a long time. Now they are quite numerous in some parts of India, and count among their ranks many wealthy men.

This temple was built of white marble, and consisted of a small court, at one end of which was an arched portico, where were the idols, three in number, under a finely carved canopy. I could see no resemblance in the figures to the statues of Boodh in China.

At ten in the evening we dined, and at one o'clock the next morning we left Dhoodoo.

Daylight found us on a desert and rocky plain, with hills not far off, and plenty of deer in sight. We breakfasted beside a well, and walked to Kishinghur, which was about two

* A remarkable illustration of this Hindoo prejudice was afforded during the siege of the English and faithful native regiments in the Lucknow Residency. One of the garrison was killed while drawing water, and his body tumbled into the well. From that time the Sepoys of the garrison refused to drink the water, although what could be procured from other sources was inferior in quality and uncertain in supply.

miles off. The town of Kishinghur is the capital of an independent native state. It is situated on the banks of a small lake, surrounded by rugged hills, and is fortified by high and strong stone walls.

In the centre of the town there is a hill about two hundred feet high, on which the Rajah's castle is built. It is surrounded by fortifications, and the space between the foot of the hill and the shore of the lake is laid out as a garden.

We entered Kishinghur through a very large gate, and walking through the long bazár, passed out on the other side of the town, and found a garden of pomegranate trees beyond the wall, where it is customary for European travellers to put up. In the garden was a stone pavilion where we took up our quarters. A baboo in the Rajah's service soon paid us a visit. He said that his Highness sent his salám and wished to know if he could serve us. We expressed a desire for some provisions, and wood for cooking, and also a wish to see the Rajah. They afterward sent us what we had asked for, except meat, which was not procurable; at the same time we were informed that his Highness lamented that he would be unable to receive us on account of an indisposition (attributable no doubt to our not being in the Honourable Company's service). The rajah, however, sent us two of his elephants, upon which we visited the town and castle. The latter is quite extensive, and the defences are strong. We were not allowed to enter the palace, which is situated within, so after a walk around the ramparts, from which the view is very picturesque, we descended to the gardens near the lake. These were not well cared for, and after a short walk we got tired of them and crossed in a boat to an island in the lake, on which there were two small summer-houses or pavilions of white marble, very pretty and graceful.

We afterwards went through the principal streets of the town, which seemed well built, and contained several very fine stone houses. A crowd of at least a hundred idlers and boys followed us all through the town, yelling and shouting, as the street boys of New York would do if a Hindoo Rajah were to drive up Broadway in a sulky.

On our return to our quarters in the garden, we were informed that one of the elephants danced and walked on his hind legs. Accordingly, we gave orders to have him perform, which he did to our entire satisfaction. The sight of the huge beast walking toward us, with his forelegs in the air, and his trunk raised perpendicularly, was one of those things that are exactly on the boundary line between the sublime and the ridiculous.

Soon after sunset it began raining very hard, so that it was impossible to think of continuing our journey. We had our palkees and dhoolees set under the roof of the pavilion, and slept in them that night.

Next morning, January 26, the storm was over, and we started at noon for Ajmeer—seventeen miles distant. We walked three-quarters of the way, and found it very pleasant, as there was a delightful breeze blowing.

The road, which was a mere wagon-track, led among wild and rocky hills, many of which were crowned with forts and castles, now deserted. We saw many sheep, and some deer.

The travellers whom we passed were few in number. They wore their beards shaven under the chin, and brushed back towards the ears in the Rajpoot fashion. Their dress was the dhotee, or cotton cloth wrapped around the waist and descending in loose folds to the knees. The upper part of the body was covered with a short and tight-fitting jacket. All of them were armed, and had quite a martial look. As they passed us, they did not deign to salute, but looked us full in the face with an insolent stare, which would have been alone sufficient to show us we were no longer in Hindoostan.

The women wore the old Hindoo dress, the dhotee below the waist, and the sáree, or vail, covering the upper part of the body, and falling over the head.*

* In Hindoostan many of the women wear thick petticoats. The Moosulmanee women wear tight trowsers, with or without a petticoat. As regards man's dress, the pa*n*jama, or trowsers, introduced by the Moosulmans, is worn by all of that religion, and sometimes also by Hindoos. All over India

We arrived at Ajmeer about eight o'clock in the evening, and were at a loss where to put up, as there was no dâk-bungalow. Fortunately, we met the magistrate in a shigram,* drawn by a pair of bullocks. He was kind enough to conduct us to an empty bungalow, in the use of which, he said, we should not be disturbed. Had we not met the magistrate, I do not know how we could have managed, except by sleeping in our palkees on the road, and giving up dinner.

The town of Ajmeer, as well as Nusseerabad, fourteen miles off, where there is a station of troops, belong to the English, and are the first places in the Company's Raj† that we had been in since leaving Futtehpoor Seekree.

The bungalow that we occupied had no furniture, so we had our palkees and dhoolees brought into the large central apartment, to be used as beds. Fortunately, we found a table and some chairs in the dining-room, and late at night our servant managed to get us some dinner.

Next morning we walked into town, a mile and a half. It is situated on the gentle slope of a hill which rises behind the town, steeply, to a great height, and is crowned by a large and very strong fort, now deserted, as are all the hill-forts in the British territories.

The native princes always fortified their towns and palaces, and many of them, for greater security, built their castles on almost inaccessible crags. This was necessary, not only for protection against external enemies, but also against their own vassals and subjects. This policy, however, was never pursued by the English. Even in places where there were forts of great strength, the English troops were stationed outside the towns in cantonments, which were not defended by

Hindoos and Moosulmans are distinguished by the way in which the double-breasted jacket, or chupkun, is fastened. The Moosulmans invariably tie it on the left side, the Hindoos, and all other sects, on the right.

* *Shigram.* A two-wheeled, covered cart, much used by European travellers in the Bombay Presidency.

† Raj, *i. e.*, jurisdiction. It is the word from which Rajah, Rajpoot, &c., are formed.

even a wall of earth. The old native strongholds were suffered to go to ruin, with the exception of the fort of Delhi, which was kept up by the titular Emperor from his allowance; and that at Agra, which was preserved and kept in repair, principally as an arsenal, and also as an interesting architectural monument. The forts of Calcutta, Bombay, and Madras, which were constructed by the English, stand on a different footing, as they were intended principally for defence against foreign nations.

The calm confidence of the English, in thus neglecting all means of defence, produced a most powerful impression on the natives, contrasting, as it did, with the conscious insecurity of former rulers, who immured themselves in their castles, surrounded themselves with foreign troops, when they could be obtained, and lived, as it were, with the sword always drawn.*

Ajmeer is a considerable and well-built town, but possesses few objects of interest. We went into a large and fine house, belonging to a banker, in the court-yard of which we found a number of Brahmun cooks preparing the dinner. There were many other large residences, all, like the first, built of stone, several stories high, and with flat roofs, like the houses of Bĕnarĕs. We admired much the oriel windows, which we here saw for the first time. They were made of elaborately-carved brown stone, and, in place of sashes, had slabs of fine marble open-work.

Feeling tired and hot, we now hired a bailee, or bullock-carriage, and went to see the tomb of a Moosulman saint, which is an object of great veneration, and the resort of pilgrims from all parts of India. It was to the tomb of this saint that the Emperor Akbur made a pilgrimage, when in despair on account of the premature death of all his children, and here the saint appeared to him in a dream, and directed him to

* Some of the native princes used to have looking-glasses set in the front of the howdah, when they went out on an elephant, for fear the chattah-burdar, or umbrella-bearer, who rode behind them, should stab them in the back.

San Suleem, at Seekree, by whose intercessions he obtained an heir to his crown.

They would not let us go within the enclosure without removing our shoes, so we gave up the attempt, as what we could see through the gate did not look very interesting.

On leaving the shrine of the saint we visited the remains of an old Hindoo palace, a little way up the hill. The ruins were extensive, but the only part that remained at all perfect was a lofty hall with a brown stone roof, supported on numerous columns of the same material. The columns were slim in proportion to their height, and each differed from every other in shape; one would be square, one round, another hexagonal, another fluted, and so on for all the others, but all were most elaborately carved, as were also the deep panels of the ceiling, each of which had a different design. This hall was used as a mosque by the Moosulmans, who built a marble kibla in the west wall, and a series of lofty brown stone arches in front of the building. The arches are as large as those near the Kootub at Delhi, and at least as remarkable, there being the same beautifully sharp-cut inscriptions from the Korán in front. The mosque, however, like the more ancient building upon which it was constructed, has long since fallen into disuse and ruin.

On the whole, our expectations of Ajmeer were disappointed; since we expected to find it a very interesting place, as it was once the capital of all the Rajpoot states.

Nusseerabad is only fourteen miles from Ajmeer, and we arrived there at sun-rise on the 28th of January. The native town is not large, and the place derives its whole importance from its being a large station of the Company's troops, whose presence preserves order in all Rajpootana. When we were in Nusseerabad the soldiers all belonged to the Bombay army —"Ducks," as they used to be called in Bengal. The Bombay sepoys are not nearly so soldierly in appearance as were the soldiers of the Bengal army. The latter were the pick of the Rajpoot race, the former were of all nations and castes. They were much inferior in size to the Bengal troops, and had a way of wearing their uniform when off duty, which a Bengal sepoy never did, and which had two disadvantages. In the first place, it spoiled the uniform for parade, and then it made the men appear to disadvantage, for a native never looks so badly as in European clothes. Notwithstanding this deficiency in their appearance, the experience of last year has shown them to be much the most faithful, and has stamped with approval the system of indiscriminate enlistment which was about being abandoned in Bombay in favour of the Bengal system of receiving into the army only the members of one or two favoured castes.

At Nusseerabad we made a few purchases at the shop of a Parsee. In the Bengal Presidency the stores of the stations are all kept by Europeans, and contain large assortments in which everything is of the best quality. The style of living in the smaller Presidencies is, however, much less expensive, and the shops are all kept by natives, generally Parsees, and are much inferior in the variety and quality of what is sold in them.

We left Nusseerabad at midnight, and at six o'clock on the morning of the 29th arrived at Bunai dâk-bungalow, which is situated half a mile from a semicircle of high and bald hills, at the foot of one of which the village is built, and on top of another is the Castle. A short distance in front of the bungalow is a row of noble trees. As soon as we arrived, our bearers as was always their custom, went into the village bazár to buy food, which they afterwards cooked under the shade of these trees. Cooking is, among the Hindoos, a long and laborious operation, and each man has to cook his own food, unless he be rich enough to hire a Brahmun to do so for him. In the first place, a little mud-furnace, which can never be used a second time, has to be built. Then water must be drawn, by each man for himself, and in his own lota, a brass vessel of which every Hindoo possesses one, and which he always takes with him when travelling. When the furnace is built, the water drawn, and the fire, which is generally of dried cow-dung, lighted, the man squats on the ground and draws a circle which encloses himself and all these things. Cooking then begins in the ordinary way, but each step of the process is accompanied by religious ceremonies, and the meal must all be prepared and eaten within the magic circle. If anything unclean, such as a man of another caste or an ordinary fowl, comes within the circle, the food has to be thrown away and the operation begun anew. On this account whenever we came near our bearers at their meals, they would at once cry out, "Rotee kháta, Sahib, rotee kháta," "We are eating bread, Sir," to drive us away.

If anything remains unconsumed from one meal, it cannot be eaten the next day; and if the laborious cooking operation cannot be gone through, the Hindoo can eat nothing but parched gram, a sort of pulse which tastes not unlike roasted peanuts. I have seen sepoys, at sea, living for a week together on this alone, and some of the higher castes will not eat even the gram, instances having been known where they have starved on shipboard rather than break the rules of caste.

The absurdly stringent ceremonies of cooking, with the ablutions which precede, occupy a great length of time, and Hindoos, therefore, eat only one meal a-day—still this custom occasions an immense waste of time, and is one of the most oppressive and injurious restrictions of that heavy chain of caste-rules and prejudices which cramps every action of the Hindoo.

In the afternoon we walked through the village, which has heavy mud walls; and climbed up the hill to the castle, which is a massive structure on the very summit. From the foot of its walls the rocky hill-sides descend almost perpendicularly for a hundred feet, and the only approach is by a narrow stairway cut in the stone. After toiling up the ascent we were disappointed by finding the door closed, so we descended and returned to the bungalow, where we found a shikarree, or huntsman, who informed us that having heard of our illustrious names, he had come to offer us his salám, and to lay at our feet an antelope which he had shot. We accepted both, and gave him a rupee, with which he was well satisfied.

The natives of India are remarkably good shots, but their guns are of the rudest description. The barrel is very long, and the stock straight. The charge is ignited by a match, which is held over the pan of priming by a sort of "hammer." When the aim is taken, the shooter presses upon a button, below the stock of the gun. The button communicates with the hammer, and brings it and the match down upon the priming.

At half past eleven we left Bunai, and arrived at Dáblah on the morning of January 30th. The country around the bungalow is most uninteresting and level. The village is half a mile on the left, and contains nothing of interest but a Thakoor's Castle in ruins.

We were startled during the morning by hearing some loud shrieks, and much weeping. We all sprang up at once, and running out, found that all the noise was made by two young women, who were walking slowly at a short distance from the bungalow. As they went along they continued to cry, and throw their arms about, with much apparent grief. Whenever they met any other women, they embraced, throwing their arms around each, one by one, and leaning their heads over the shoulders of the woman whom they were embracing—first to the right and then to the left. We were informed that they were two young wives who were returning to their husbands after a visit to their parents, and that it was considered only proper that they should thus testify their sorrow.

Our next stopping-place was Bunaira, where we arrived very early, as it is only fourteen miles from Dáblah. The town of Bunaira was a mile from the dâk-bungalow, so that we did not visit it; but we had a fine view of the castle, which is a very large building situated on the crest of a hill overhanging the town, and having all the appearance of a large European fortification—even to the white palace, seen above the battlements, which with the turret on its roof looked from the distance very like a whitewashed chapel.

Having only done such a short distance the previous night, we determined to push on, after getting breakfast. The distance to the next bungalow was twenty-four miles, and a hard enough march it proved. We walked most of the way, to relieve the bearers, who had been awake since midnight. The country was mostly hilly and wooded jungul, in which the road was so badly marked, that we several times lost our way. We, however, found some cultivation around the one or two villages which we passed, and saw a field of poppies, which showed that we were approaching Malwa, the great opium country of Western India. The poppies were in flower, and looked very beautiful, especially to me, who had not seen any other flowers in India, except those used in the worship of idols.

We did not arrive at Ummeerghur till after eight o'clock, and got dinner at midnight. The next day we had to rest, as our bearers were quite used up by the twenty hours' march of the day before. We therefore spent the 1st of February at Ummeerghur, and treated our men to some goats, which cost us eight anas, (24 cents,) apiece, and were, I suppose, bought by the men for one-half or two-thirds of that money.

During the day, we walked out to the borders of a lake, just outside the town. Its banks were shaded by parallel lines of beautiful trees, in the shade of which we took our seat, and watched the women washing clothes, and the Brahmuns worshipping a shapeless stone, which they painted red, and decorated with silver ornaments. They could not venture to do the latter further north, as some sacrilegious Moosulman would be sure to walk off with the idol's jewelry.

Towards evening, we walked into the town. It is of moderate size, walled, and built at the foot of a hill, on the summit of which is a ruined stone castle. The only objects of interest in the town were three very regular and handsome Hindoo temples, built in a row.

CHAPTER XXIX.

COUNTRY OF THE MAHARATTAS.

Arrival at Chittôr—The Town—Remarkable Situation of the Fortress—Seven Miles of Ruins—Tank—The Moon Lady—The Great Temple—Hindoo Religious Architecture—The Great Tower—Antiquity of Hindoo Ruins—Religious Pic-nic—Enter the Maharatta Territories—"Zubburdustee"—"The Good Old Rule"—Poppy-fields—Neemuch—Noble Banyan Tree—Irrigation—Mundissoor—A Pleasant Resting-place—Jowra—Nawáb's English Palace—Khachród—New Style of Architecture—Wrestling—The Soobah's Politeness—Oojén—The City—Temple of Kunaia—The God's Carriage—Indian "Punch"—The Maharattas—A Native Government—Professional Robbing—Spread of the Maharatta Power—Nature of their Government—Their Subjugation by the English—Gwalior States—The Police—Indirect Utility of Native Misrule.

We left Ummeerghur on the evening of February 1st, and next morning I awoke on a jungul, separated from the other palkees, my bearers having taken a short cut which compelled us to go a mile down the river for a ford, so that I arrived at the dâk-bungalow of Chittôr at eight o'clock, half an hour after the others. The march was twenty-two miles.

After breakfast, we went out to see the place, which had much excited our curiosity, as well from Bishop Heber's glowing description, as from the view of the minárs and other prominent buildings which were visible from the dâk-bungalow.

We had a very hot walk of a mile, over a bare and sandy plain, and then, crossing by a fine stone bridge over a river which is a tributary of the Jumna, we entered the town through a gateway in the stone wall which surrounds it.

It is a place of about five thousand inhabitants, and was once the capital of an independent raj. We stopped in the bazár to eat some cocoa-nuts, and while we were so engaged, two chowkeedars, or native policemen, armed with sword and shield, came up with the kamdar's salám,* and said that they had directions to accompany us to see all the objects of interest, and that the kamdar regretted having no elephants to offer us.

The fortress is situated on the level summit of a hill, rising behind the town, and extending for some distance on each side of it. The line of fortifications extends for ten or twelve miles around the edge of the hill, the sides of which are naturally precipitous, or have been artificially scarped, so that it presents on all sides a perpendicular wall of rock, from eighty to a hundred and fifty feet in height. Lower down, the hill-side slopes more gradually to the plain on which the town is built.

The only approach is by a road, beginning in the town, and winding along the side of the hill. It is broad enough for a wagon, well paved, with a stone wall on the outside, and five fine gateways, now in ruins, but anciently capable of defence.

The summit of the hill is nearly level, and comprises within the fortifications a space of six or seven square miles, full of palaces, temples, tanks, minárs, and the remains of many dwelling-houses. The latter were quite ruinous, but many of the other buildings were in good preservation, and some of the temples still in use.

We first went down into a deep tank, cut in the solid rock. The tank is supplied by a fine spring, which gushes out of a marble temple richly carved. On the other side is a large pavilion of brown stone, with steps descending into the water. The place was delightfully cool and shady, the trees which grew on the bank above, leaned over the pool, and kept away the scorching beams of the sun; and their boughs hung down almost to the water's surface. We found it so pleasant a resting-place, after our hot and tiresome walk, that we could not persuade ourselves to quit it, and sat for a good hour on the steps of the pavilion, with our feet in the cool water of the tank. Our guide occupied the time by telling us of a great and powerful princess, the Chand Beebee, or Moon

* The kamdar's salám, *i. e.*, the compliments of the mayor.

Lady, who once held her court here. The Emperor Akbur, he said, asked her in marriage, and when she refused, he besieged the fortress for seven years. At the end of that time, the place yielded to the assault, and Pudda Mahoot, (for that was the real name of the princess, and Chand Beebee was only a title,) collected all her women and treasure in a little house built upon a lake above, and there, rather than fall into her captor's hands, set fire to her place of refuge, and was burned up, with all her treasures, women, and children—a voluntary Joár, or human sacrifice to Bhowánee. This was the substance of what he said, freed from the decorations and inconsistencies, which were many, as he told it. How much truth there is in the story, I do not know. Something like it happened, as Bishop Heber says, at Oudipoor, and I heard nearly the same legend at several other places. The name of the Chand Beebee certainly appears in history as one of the most powerful and obstinate opponents who resisted the conquest of the Dĕkkun by the Emperor Akbur. She sustained a long siege from his forces, in the fort of Ahmudnuggur, and was finally slain by a revolt of her own soldiery, during a second siege of the same place, conducted by Akbur in person.

When we were sufficiently rested, we visited a deserted temple, immediately above the tank. It was very remarkable, not only for the elaborate carvings of dancing women, and other figures upon the outside, but for the curious idol in the interior. This was a colossal bas-relief of a head, eight feet high, quite unlike anything else which I saw in India, and looking as if it had come from Egypt.

We had next a walk of half a mile in the sun, through the ruins of palaces and other buildings, which would no doubt have repaid examination, if we had had the time. We also passed several large tanks, hollowed out of the rock, and having stone pavilions on their banks, or sometimes upon artificial islands in the water.

At length we arrived at the largest temple, which is built entirely of white marble, very elaborately and deeply carved. Its form is the same as that of all Hindoo temples—the essential part of which, the shrine, is everywhere a little dark apartment, over which rises the pyramidal spire which is a universal characteristic. This is the type of all mundrăs in India, the only variations being in the details and decorations. The approach to the shrine is by open porticoes, the roofs of which are supported by columns, and each of which rises a few steps higher than the last. The whole is situated within a court.

The colonnades, or porticoes, and the court, are both non-essential features, and not often seen. In a few instances the roofs of the porticoes are supported by double or even triple rows of columns, and in one or two cases the courts which enclose the temple are very large, in one instance as much as four miles square; but however extensive such accessory features may be, the shrine is always very small, massively built, and lighted only by a low door.

This temple had two open porticoes, and was built in the midst of a court, perhaps a hundred and fifty feet square. The material of every part was pure white marble, elaborately sculptured. The goddess worshipped was Bhowánee, represented by a hideous black figure, with her hands full of weapons and instruments of torture, her mouth smeared with blood, and her neck circled by a chaplet of skulls. There were three or four Brahmuns in the temple, who clamoured for bucksees, and when we refused it became very insolent. After we left the temple they brought water and washed the whole place, to free it from the defilement which it had contracted from our presence. The trouble which we had caused them did not cause us the slightest compunction; on the contrary, we were pleased by finding that we had been the means of interrupting their habitual laziness. One of our native guides considered it a most excellent joke; but the other looked upon it in a serious light, and seemed to be afraid of the revenge of the Brahmuns, though whether their anger would affect his spiritual or temporal prosperity we could not quite understand.

A little beyond this temple was the largest tank, upon the banks of which was a considerable palace of brown stone, and in the centre another similar building upon an artificial island. The latter is assigned by tradition as the spot where the Chand Beebee and her ladies burned themselves to death.

The ruins extended for some distance further, but we had no time to make more extensive explorations.

On the way back we visited the minár, which is almost a unique object, there being but one similar building in India, and that is in this same place, about a mile off. The minár is a rectangular tower, 120 feet high, and about 25 feet square at the base. It is built with two walls, one inside the other; the inner wall enclosing the stairway, and the outer wall forming an open verandah at each of the nine stories. The two upper stories project considerably beyond the line of the building, and the whole is surmounted by a cupola, which looks like a late addition. The whole is built of the finest white marble, and almost every part of its surface, inside and out, is decorated with the most elaborate and intricate designs, representing either the exploits of Seewa, or naked men and women celebrating the phallic orgies of his worship. The building itself typifies the Lĭngam*—the form under which Seewa is always adored. From the top of the minár we got a fine view of the table land on which all these ruins are situated, the town at the foot of the hill, the river flowing eastward to unite its waters with the Jumna, and the broad level plain, stretching with almost unbroken uniformity to the foot of the distant hills.

The minár is in the most excellent preservation, even the most delicate sculptures being almost perfect throughout. It is said by the natives to be five hundred years old, but that is probably an exaggeration. In fact, nothing in India disappoints the traveller so much as the age of the monuments. Almost all the buildings of great architectural pretensions were erected by the Mahommedans, and very few are more than 300 years old. The most ancient of these buildings is the Kootub at Delhi, which was completed about the year

* *Lĭngam*—a wide-spread religious emblem, called by the Greeks Φαλλός, and by the Latins, Priapus.

1200, although it probably was begun earlier. The Hindoo remains are very few, and a very small proportion of them are at all remarkable for size or grandeur. The most ancient of them are undoubtedly the cave temples, but even these are now proved to be not more than a thousand years old, and many persons attribute to them a much later date. Of the other remains, but two or three temples are as old as the thirteenth century, and most of them would be modern when compared with the age of European cathedrals.

As we were leaving the top of the hill we went into a court-yard containing two small temples. Here we found about two hundred people from a neighbouring village, who had come to celebrate poojah for three days at this shrine—a sort of religious pic-nic. The people in this part of the country are a much more open, manly race, than those in Northern India. They at once asked us to have something to eat, and seemed much pleased when we consented. They brought us some bread, muraba, or sweetmeats, and dhal, which is a kind of pulse, eaten as a stew. The latter they served to us on broad green leaves, plaited into a kind of bowl. The bread was coarse, but well baked, and the dhal we found quite savory, especially as we were very hungry. It was a great satifaction to know that the food was certainly clean, as the religion of the Hindoos obliges them to observe the most scrupulous cleanliness in cooking.

The sweetmeats which I have described above are an article of food of which the natives are immoderately fond ; and many of those who can afford it, eat scarcely anything else. They are made of the ordinary soft brown sugar,* and have its characteristic taste.

After thanking our entertainers, and rewarding them with a present, we returned to the dâk-bungalow, took dinner, and at ten in the evening started for Neemuch, thirty-eight miles off.

* Sugar is commonly used by the natives in its raw state. They call it *sukkur*, a Sanscrit word from which all European names of sugar are evidently derived. The only process of refining practised is by crystallization; the result of which is called *khand*—the same word as *candy*. When prepared for use by pulverization the khand is called *misree*.

This was the last day's march in the Rajpoot states, Neemuch being in a tract which belongs to the Rajah of Gwalior, or Sindia,* as he is more generally called. In fact, for the next three hundred miles the road led through a great many different independent states, many of them so small that they are quite surrounded by the dominions of other princes; and we were scarcely ever for twenty miles together in the territories of the same Rajah.

On the morning of February 3d we awoke in a desert looking country, and soon stopped at a village for breakfast. Our kuhárs commenced stealing the wood of the villagers to make their fires, a proceeding which we at once stopped—but we never could cure them of stealing and taking by force anything that they fancied from the villagers, and they used even to compel the peasants to accompany them by night, without reward, as guides. Such acts are called in India "zubburdustee," a term which means "by force," and is a short condensation of that great law which is the only rule universally recognized and acted upon by natives:

> "The good old rule, the simple plan
> That they should take who have the power
> And they should keep who can."

We applied to the kotwal, or head-man of the village, for provisions, but could only get some maida, a coarse kind of flour, and a little ghee, or boiled butter. We asked for fowls; but the kotwal said that the villagers were all Rajpoots, and could not eat them, so that there were only three or four fowls in the place, which were kept in case the Maharatta governor should come that way, for the Maharattas, being low caste men, can eat fowls.

After breakfast we kept on our way through a country the greater part of which was barren, but around the villages

* The three great Maharatta princes are each known by an hereditary title. The Rajah of Gwalior is called Sindia; the Rajah of Indor, Holkar; and the Rajah of Baroda has the title of the Gaikwar. These appellations are sometimes spelt Scindeah or Sindheeah, Holcar, and Guicowar or Gykwar, and in other ways also.

were patches of maize and poppies. About half a mile from Neemuch we were overtaken by a very violent rain storm, which obliged us to take shelter under a banyan tree. The delay which this caused, and the length of the march prevented us from getting to Neemuch before evening. On arriving, we found that there was no dâk-bungalow, so we hired a bungalow from a Parsee merchant, and rested there the next day.

Neemuch is a station of the Company's troops, and looks exactly like all the stations that we had seen in the north of India.

The native town is a small place, and belongs to Sindia, the Honourable Company owning only the ground actually within the limits of the cantonments.

The bungalow which we occupied was in the next compound to the mess-house of one of the regiments. We took advantage of this to procure a good dinner from the mess-khansáhma*n*, a Bombay Parsee. He got us up a splendid meal, the best part of which was the English bread, which was the first (except what we had at Nusseerabad) that we had tasted since leaving Agra. We had been compelled to subsist on chupattees, a sort of pan-cake, made of flour (atta) and water, much used by natives as a substitute for bread. During the day one of the officers of the place called, and was kind enough to enquire whether he could be of use, and to offer his services and those of the rest of the mess.

We left Neemuch on the evening of February 4th, and found ourselves the next morning in a beautiful and highly cultivated country. After a short walk, we came to a magnificent banyan tree, which covered nearly two acres of ground. This was the finest tree I saw, though there are many of them in that part of the country, and the baolees are often placed under their shade. These are very large and deep wells, the water in which is approached by a flight of steps. The water is used both for drinking, cooking, and irrigation. When needed for the former purposes, each person must descend the steps and draw it in his own lota. The water for irrigation, however, is drawn up in a very large leather bucket. The power used is supplied by a pair of bullocks and a single pulley. The rope which draws up the bucket (or as it might be better called, bag,) is so arranged as to empty the water when it arrives at the top of the well into the main channel, from which it is conveyed by a thousand ever-subdividing arteries to every part of the field. The whole method is as rude as possible, and much inferior to the "Persian wheel" used in Egypt, and the chain pumps which I saw in China; though I am doubtful whether the latter could be used where the water has to be raised to so great a height, as from these baolees.

At about ten o'clock we arrived at Mundissoor, a large town on the banks of the Chumbul, which flows into the Jumna a hundred miles below Agra. Just outside the town we met the jumatdar, the highest police officer of the place. He was a very fine-looking and light-complexioned old man, handsomely dressed, and riding on a white horse, surrounded by eighteen or twenty chowkeedars. After an interchange of salutations, and a short conversation, he conducted us to a garden on the further bank of the river. We found there a stone pavilion, in which we took up our quarters, and the jumatdar soon sent us some provisions from the bazár. During the day the old man paid us another visit, bringing with him a very pretty boy, his grandson, who wished to pay his respects to the foreign gentlemen (Bulattee Sahib-lôg).

The garden contained many large and fine trees, under the shade of which we passed the day, even more comfortably than in a dâk-bungalow. The ford across the river presented a most lively scene. Men, women, and teams were constantly crossing in both directions, and throughout the day the water was filled with people, bathing and washing their clothes.

On the further bank rose the city, upon a slight inclination, but although it contained several buildings that looked as if they might be worth seeing, the weather was so warm that we could not muster courage to leave the shade of the friendly trees.

At seven o'clock in the evening, after an early dinner, we left for Jowra, distant twenty-eight miles, and arrived there at eight o'clock on the morning of February 6th. We put up in an empty bungalow, in a garden outside of the town. It belonged to the Nawáb, and was a rickety affair, appropriated to the temporary accommodation of Europeans. The day was too hot to allow us to think of walking to the town, which was distant more than a mile, but one of our number sent for bearers, and went thither in his palkee. On his return he reported it as not worth seeing.

About eight in the evening we left Jowra, stopping, as we passed through the town, to have a moonlight view of the Nawáb's Palace, or rather of his "English Palace," for the natives told us that he had eight in all, and kept one of his eight wives in each. The "English Palace," which we saw, is an exact copy of an English country residence of the last century.

The night's march was to Khachrôd, twenty-three miles. We awoke on Saturday morning just outside the town, and having passed through it, took up our quarters in a large tôp of fine mango trees, where we were much amused during the day by the boys from the town, who got up wrestling matches for our entertainment.

Towards evening we walked into town, which had quite a different appearance from any that we had seen before, the architecture being that which distinguishes the south-western part of India. The houses were generally three stories high, and built with wooden frames, painted black, and filled in between the frame-work with white-washed pukka. The houses in the bazár were built over the side-walk, and supported upon arches, forming arcades, similar to those in London and Paris. As we were walking through the streets about dusk, we met the Soobah, or Governor of this district, which forms part of Sindia's dominions. The Soobah was mounted on a splendidly caparisoned horse, and surrounded by a large retinue of cav-

* Mahommedan princes are called Nawábs, the feminine of which is Bégoom. Rajah is a Hindoo title, the feminine being Ranee. The title Nawáb was corrupted by the English into *Nabob*, which is really the French spelling of the Oordoo word.

alry, armed footmen and torch-bearers. We took off our hats as he passed, and, in return for this civility, he sent six of his attendants after us, to deliver his salám, and see that we wanted nothing. On returning to our camp, we found six chokeedars, or armed policemen, keeping watch with spear and shield. They also had been sent by the Soobah.

The next morning we breakfasted in a tôp of banyan-trees, on the banks of a little stream, just outside a small village. Leaving our palkees under the tôp, we crossed the stream on our bearer's shoulders, and went into the village to buy the materials for our breakfast. The place was a miserable collection of mud hovels, but fortified by high and thick walls of earth. We could buy nothing but some coarse flour, ghee, and a little milk. However, with these materials our servant made some chupattees, and with a cup of coffee, and some fried slices of bacon, (which we had brought in tins from Agra), we made a hearty meal.

After breakfast we marched on again through a country made beautiful by banyan-tôps and fields of poppies in bloom, and, having fine báolees near the road side at short distances from each other.

The whole march was forty-three miles. By dark we arrived at the branch of the Chumbul on which the city of Oojén is situated. This branch of the river is much larger than that which we saw at Mundissoor, and our dhoolees almost touched the water as they were carried over the ford. After crossing, we found a fine ghât, and, passing up a street bordered by large and substantial stone buildings, we entered the town, and traversing its streets for over a mile, passed out through a gate on the further side. The dâk-bungalow is a mile from the town. We arrived there at eight in the evening, having been over twenty hours on the march. We found the bungalow a large and fine one, with a Delhi Moosulman for khansáhman, who got us up an excellent dinner.

The next morning, on application to the Nana Sahib,* an

* *Nana Sahib.* This is not a name, but a title, or agnomen, meaning "the Lord Grandfather." Such titles are often assumed by natives of high

elderly relation of Sindia, who governed this part of his dominions, we obtained an elephant to view the city. Only one elephant was furnished us, the excuse being that all the others were at Gwalior, Sindia's capital. We afterwards found this to be a lie. The elephants were a great acquisition, as a walk of a mile to the town in the sun would have been rather a severe task.

On the way to the town we passed a considerable sheet of water, upon the banks of which were several stone pavilions. The walls of the Oojén are of redstone—about forty feet high. The principal streets are broad, but rather winding. The houses upon them are large, several stories high, and built with frames of black wood like those of Khachrôd. We were shown the outside of two palaces, belonging to a female relative of Sindia, who was allowed by him to appropriate the revenues of this part of his territory. They were both large pukka buildings stuccoed on the exterior. The only *sight* which we visited was a large and fine white marble temple, dedicated to Kunaia. The door of the shrine was decorated with richly-worked silver plates, worth, we were told, some thousands of pounds. Within the portico of the temple was a car, all overlaid with silver plates. This, we were informed, was the carriage of the "Moort Bahádur," (his Highness, the Idol,) in which he took the air, on great festivals.

We afterward rode on the elephant through the principal streets and bazárs, and then returned to the dâk-bungalow. This was all I saw of the city, but one of our party, who became disgusted with riding four on an elephant, got a horse from the Nana Sahib, and visited a fine palace and gardens upon the banks of a lake some miles from the town.

During the afternoon we were much amused by a native puppet-show, representing a Durbar, or state-reception at the

position, to prevent their real names becoming known to sorcerers, or evil disposed persons, who might use them in charms. "Chand Beebee," already spoken of, is an instance of this kind. These titles are not confined to the natives, but are often given to Europeans—for instance, Mr. Skinner at Delhi, was always called by the natives, "Sĕkundur Sahib," or, "the Lord Alexander"—Alexander being his first name.

Court of the Rajah of Jaipoor. The whole exhibition was exceedingly well managed, and included a fight of wild animals and some judicial proceedings. The latter were quite characteristic. An itenerant trader complains to an inferior officer of his goods having been stolen just outside the palace. This official promises him redress on condition that the recovered property shall be equally divided between them "ada mera, ada tera"—half mine, half thine—as he says. The unfortunate man accepts these terms, but finds that he has to make a similar compromise with so many other officials, that when the money is actually recovered from the thief, the rightful owner gets little or nothing of it. The puppets were all well dressed, and had moveable arms and legs, which gave them a very natural appearance. They spoke in exactly the tone of "Punch," and their conversation had all his wit.

The city Oojén is, as I have said, one of the chief towns in Sindia's dominions. This Rajah is the most powerful of the Maharatta princes. The dominions of his ancestors extended over all Western and Northern India, including the greater part of what was once the empire of the Moguls. It was from them, and not from the Mahommedan emperor that the East India Company conquered the Empire of Hindoostan. The description, therefore, of the territory still subject to their rule, may not be uninteresting, as it will show not only what is the practical working of a native government, but also what would have been the condition of the most fertile provinces of India, if they were not protected by the power of the English. In the description, I have borrowed largely the language of Colonel Sleeman, not only because he was one of the best-informed men in India, but also because, from the nature of his family relations, and from the intimacy in which he lived with natives of all ranks, he will be allowed not only to have been an unbiassed observer, but even to have been in some respects prejudiced in favour of native rulers and native society.

The Maharatta princes were robbers by profession and by caste. They conquered the countries which they governed, and ruled them as robbers might be expected to do. They never made a pretence of protecting the lives and property of their subjects—the whole administration consisting of revenue-officers, whose duty was to squeeze out of the inhabitants every farthing that could be obtained.

Robbing, is, in India, a regular profession. It is also hereditary. A man is born a robber, just as he is born a Brahmun. It is a caste recognised by the constitution of Indian society, and having its place in the religious system and its tutelary deities in the Hindoo Pantheon. All robbers take the field in the month of November, whether they are sovereigns of great states, or leaders of little bands from an obscure village. They all invoke the protection of Heaven, and take the auspices in the same way—asking and expecting the protection of the Deity, with as much confidence as those who are engaged in any other occupation. Nor is the robber regarded as less respectable than the soldier by the circle in which he lives, provided he spends his income as liberally, and discharges his social duties as well, and this he generally does to secure the good-will of his neighbours, whatever may be his depredations upon other and distant communities. In any other part of the world such a state of things would be impossible; but in India, under the weak and disorganized native governments, the system had spread to an incredible extent. There was scarcely a village that was not yearly subject to an incursion of one of the bands of plunderers. If they were weak, they prevented the interference of the authorities by dividing with them the spoils; if they were strong they overrode the governments and became territorial conquerors.

Of the latter class were the Maharatta princes. Every year they set out with their armies to rob and plunder the territories of their neighbours. Every year saw their territories broader than the last, until, in 1760, their frontier on the north extended to the Indus and Himalayas, and on the south nearly to the extremity of the Indian Peninsula. They had a large and well-trained army, officered to a great extent by Europeans. When the English conquest began, this vast extent of country was groaning beneath their intolerable yoke. The Emperor of Delhi was a prisoner in their hands, with an allowance so penurious that he and his family were in want of the absolute necessaries of life. The wretched inhabitants of these countries were subjected to organized and unsparing extortion, compared with which the exactions of their Moosulman rulers were just and liberal. The government cannot be said to have been oppressive, for there was really no government at all except the revenue administration. No pretence of administering justice was made. The country was left in a state of the most complete anarchy, and, beside all the disorders that naturally attend such a condition, the feuds of small princes, and the unrestrained excesses of lawless classes, they were subjected to periodical invasions of another robber nation, the Pindarrees, who only differed from the Maharattas in being even more ruthless and unsparing; since, as they did not aim at territorial acquisition, it was not worth their while to leave a "nest egg," and, accordingly, they carried off whatever they could, and destroyed and burnt up what was not portable.

These hordes of robbers were overcome by the English, and confined within the limits of their early possessions in Central India. Here for many years they chafed in impatient restriction, losing no opportunity for a quarrel which promised to unite them all in an effort to shake off the paramount influence of the English. They felt and still feel that they could easily extend their depredations if that power was withdrawn; and they know no other road to wealth and glory but such successful depredations. Their ancestors rose by them, their states were formed by them, and their armies were maintained by them. They look back upon them for all that seems honourable in the history of their families. Their bards sing of them in all their marriage and funeral processions; and, as their imaginations kindle at the recollection, they detest the arm that is extended to defend the wealth and industry of surrounding territories from their grasp. As the industrious classes acquire and display their wealth in the territories around, during a long peace, and under the protection of a strong and settled government, these native chiefs, with their little disorderly armies, feel precisely as an English country gentleman would feel with a pack of fox hounds in a country swarming with foxes, if he were denied the privilege of hunting them.

In 1835, Colonel Sleeman paid a visit to Gwalior. He found the road a mere footpath, unimproved and unadorned; and, except the path, and a small police station, there was absolutely no sign to indicate the dominion or even the presence of man. And yet it was the highroad between two capitals, scarcely a hundred miles apart, one occupied by one of the most ancient, and the other by one of the most powerful native sovereigns of India. The cultivation was every where wretched. Scarcely a tree was to be seen, as all were swept away to be made into gun-carriages—a proceeding which showed a most philosophical disregard of the comforts of the living, the repose of the dead (who planted them with a view to a comfortable berth in the next world), and the will of the gods to whom they were dedicated. There was nothing left upon the land of animal or vegetable life to animate or enrich it. The cultivation was of the sort that looks to one crop for its entire return. There were no manufactures, no trade or commerce, save the transport of the rude produce of the land upon the backs of bullocks, for want of even a cart-road. No one lived in the villages but those whose labour was absolutely necessary to the rudest tillage.

The colonel met twelve men wounded and bleeding. They told him that they had just been robbed outside the town near which they were. They had at once applied to the native governor. His answer was characteristic. "Look after your own affairs," said he. "Am I here to take care of merchants and travellers, or to collect the revenues of the Prince?" Upon this the colonel remarks, "Neither he, nor the prince himself, nor any other public officer, ever dreamed that it was their duty to protect the life, property, or character of travellers, or indeed of any other human beings, save the members of their own families. In this pithy answer was described the nature and character of the government. All the revenues of Sindia's immense dominions are spent entirely in the maintenance of the court and camp of the prince; and every officer considers his duties to be limited to the collection of the revenue. Protected from all external enemies by our forces, which surround him on every side, his whole army is left to him for purposes of parade and display; and having, according to his notions, no use for them elsewhere, he concentrates them around his capital, where he lives among them in the perpetual dread of mutiny and assassination.* He has nowhere any police, or any establishment for the protection of the life and property of his subjects. As a citizen of the world I could not help thinking that it would be an immense blessing to a large portion of our species if an earthquake were to swallow up this court of Gwalior and the army that surrounds it. Nothing worse could possibly succeed; and something better might.

"The misrule of such states, situated in the midst of our dominions, is not without its use. There is, as Gibbon observes, 'a strong propensity in human nature to deprecate the advantages, and magnify the evil of present times;' and if the people had not before their eyes such specimens of native rule to contrast with ours, they would think more highly than they do of their past Mahommedan and Hindoo sovereigns, and be much less disposed than they are fairly to estimate the advantages of being under our government. The native governments of the present day are fair specimens of what they have always been—grinding military despotisms; and their whole history is that of 'Saul who killed his thousands, and David his tens of thousands,' as if rulers were made only to slay, and the ruled to be slain. In politics, as in landscape, ''Tis distance lends enchantment to the view,' and the past might be all *couleur de rose* in the imagination of the people, were it not reproduced in these ill-governed states, where the 'lucky accident' of a good governor is not to be expected in a century, and where the secret of the responsibility of ministers to the people has not yet been discovered."

Since this description was written the administration of government has somewhat improved under the influence of

* Another traveller, who saw the Rajah of Gwalior at a nach, describes him as sitting with a drawn sword in one hand and a naked dagger in the other.

the English Residents; but in many of its features the picture is true even to the present day. Wherever there has been improvement it has been wholly through British influence, and this vivid sketch of a native government, without that influence, enables us to realize the condition in which India would be at the present day if it had never been conquered by the English; and the state into which it would at once relapse were their supremacy withdrawn.

CHAPTER XXX.

TO ELLORA.

March of Sir R. Hamilton—Indor—The Rajah's Palace—Strike into the Mail-road—Revolt of Kuhárs—Cavalcade—Origin of the present Rajah—Mhow—Goojree—Kurrumpoora—A Stray White Man—Manners of Natives—Sindwar—Fortress in Ruins—Sirpoorah—Peculiar Police Regulation—Old Venetian Coins—Enter the British Dominions—Dhoolia—Native Town—Evidences of having entered British Territory—Malligaum—Cantonments—Native Town—The Fort—Parallel Defences—Nandgao*n*—Camp in a Grove—Sakigao*n*—Put up in a Temple—Enter the Dĕkkun—Physical Geography—The Nizam—"Might makes Right."

We left Oojén on the evening of February 9th, for Indor, distant thirty-eight miles. The next morning we breakfasted by the roadside, just outside a village, where were pitched the tents of Sir R. Hamilton, the Resident at Indor, who was marching from that place to Mehidpoor. During the breakfast, parties of soldiers; ladies and gentlemen on horseback, in carriages, or in shigrams; elephants, camels, and hăckurees belonging to his train, were constantly coming in; and all day long we were passing people belonging to the camp, on foot, or variously mounted.

Marching is a most delightful mode of travelling. You go into tents, taking with you all your furniture and attendants, and in this way may travel any distance with all the comforts of home. The march, which is generally from twelve to eighteen miles, is made in the early morning, on horseback, or in a carriage. On arriving at the camping-ground, you find a breakfast-tent already pitched, and breakfast ready. During the discussion of the meal, the large tents and attendants come up, and a most comfortable home for the day is arranged in an inconceivably short time.

Indor is a large town strongly walled, and the residence of Holkar, one of the great Maharatta princes. The Rajah's palace fronts on an open square, in which we found a great mela, or fair, going on. The palace is over three hundred feet square, and six stories high. Its style of architecture is impure Saracenic. Within, there is a court surrounded by tall pillars of black wood. We were not admitted into the interior of the palace.

The town seemed thriving, and the streets were filled with people. The houses were generally high, and built with frames of dark wood.

At Indor, we struck the mail-road between Agra and Bombay, and consequently got along much more easily, as our bearers could do the same distance in shorter time, and the bungalows were at regular intervals on the road. All the way from Agra we had hardly seen anything better than a mere wagon track, and for part of the way there was not even that. Most of the merchandize we saw on the road was being conveyed on the backs of bullocks, of which we sometimes met droves of five or six hundred. After leaving Indor, we used to see the mail-cart every day, which reminded us that we were not entirely out of the reach of civilization; but in the country in which we had been, the only mails were those for the few places in which English officers were stationed, and they were easily carried by a running hurkáru, or postman.

We were detained a day at Indor, by a revolt of our kuhárs, who refused to go on, unless they were paid some demands for demurrage. We were finally obliged to call in the aid of the law, in the shape of a police jumatdar, who read them the ĕkranama, or Persian agreement which they had signed before leaving Agra; and soon brought them to reason by threatening them with imprisonment in case of noncompliance with our requisitions. These men had been dissatisfied for a long time, but were too wise to make a complaint in the native territories through which we had been passing, knowing, as they did, that however right they might be, they would stand no chance of justice from a native judge. They chose Indor as the scene of the revolt, because they expected that the case would come before Sir R. Hamilton, or an English magistrate. Luckily, however, they were all absent, and the jumatdar arranged matters, without giving us any trouble, for the small reward of two rupees. He even promised to have some of the mutineers flogged, if we liked.

On one of our walks to the town, we met a long cavalcade of chobdars, (men with silver maces,) couriers, native cavalry, and sepoys; the latter of whom wore the Rajah's uniform of dark green, made in the English fashion. They were escorting one of the Rajah's young relations, (I believe a brother,) who had been visiting a garden near the city. He was a little boy, not over eight years of age, very splendidly dressed, and riding a large white horse, richly caparisoned. The Rajah himself was quite young, and was originally a poor shepherd boy. On the death of the last Rajah, without descendants, the Company might easily have annexed his territories, but instead of doing so, they at last discovered this distant relative, and raised him from his humble position to a seat on the Musnud.

We left Indor on the 12th of February for Mhow, distant thirteen miles, which is a station of the Honourable Company's troops. From Mhow we marched the next day to Goojree—twenty-seven miles—arriving there on the 14th. The following day's march was to Kurrumpoora, twenty-five miles. On the way, we crossed the famous and sacred river Nurbudda; but we did not see much of it, as it was three o'clock in the morning when we reached it, and the night was very dark. We had now left the great plain of Northern India, the waters of which flow into the Ganges. Even at Indor there is a branch of the Chumbul which eventually flows into that great stream. But after leaving Mhow, the slope of the country was to the westward, and the road descended to the coast over successive plateaux, separated by ridges of hills, high to the westward, but low to the eastward.

Kurrumpoora is situated in a barren and hilly country; the village is small, and composed of mud huts, but contains a fine large surai, or open court for the accommodation of travellers. It is built at the foot of a low, but steep hill, on the top of which is the dâk-bungalow. During the day, as we were sitting talking within the bungalow, one of our servants announced that the jumatdar of the village craved an audience. He was accordingly admitted, and after profuse saláms, and a great deal of circumlocution, informed us that he had caught a stray "gora," and had come to ask what he should do with him. We supposed he meant "ghora"—a horse; and were surprised that he should find any difficulty in disposing of the animal, if it had come into his possession. He said his men had caught it wandering about the country, a week before; that since that time he had kept it in a cage, and was now desirous of getting rid of it, as he found its feeding expensive. Finally, we told him to bring it up for our inspection. In a few minutes he returned, followed by a crowd of nearly naked blacks, with swords and spears, surrounding a white man. The mystery was now all explained, and we recollected that "gora" is the native word for a white man, a term, however, scarcely ever heard, as it is not applied to any person of respectability, who is always called sahib—a lord. The "gora" proved to be a poor German sailor, who had a relation at Agra, and had started to walk from Bombay to that place. He was very pale and thin, and said that he had been treated hardly by the natives, all the way up. He could not speak a word of English, or any native language, and might have remained a month in the cage if the jumatdar had not luckily thought of applying to us. His feeding, he said, could not have cost much, as they gave him only coarse bread, and short rations of that. We recommended him to turn back, as he was likely to receive even worse treatment further up the country; but as he persisted in his original design, we supplied him with some funds, and dismissed him and his late jailors. This little anecdote, although uninteresting in itself, shows the light in which a poor white man is looked upon by natives, and the amount of consideration and kindness which he may expect. They regard such persons, in fact, very much as the blacks of the Southern States do the "poor whitefolk." We had frequently experienced the same thing ourselves, when we had walked far ahead of our bearers. The natives know that the consideration which they will receive depends entirely on their rank, and therefore surround themselves on all occasions with all the evidences of their position. All who can afford it go on horseback, and if possible, have with them at least one follower, and as many more as they can command. We, of course, did not mind such fictitious honours, and therefore used often to walk some distance ahead of our train, clad, frequently, in merely a shirt and trowsers. The puzzled or insolent demeanour of those whom we met only amused us, but, at the same time, we saw enough to show that a pedestrian tour through India would not be the most agreeable way of seeing the country, although it might give an accurate knowledge of the real character of the inhabitants.

The next day's march was thirty miles to Sindwar. The bungalow was unfit for a stable, and showed clearly that we had left the limits of Bengal influence. The village was a miserable huddle of mud huts, but near it was a large stone fortress on the plain. It is now in ruins, but contains the remains of a fine palace and tank, and must once have been a place of considerable strength and importance.

From Sindwar we marched thirty miles to Sirporah, where we arrived on the morning of February 17th. In Sirporah bungalow we fell in with the first traveller that we had seen since leaving Agra. He proved to be Lieutenant Black of the Bombay service, who was going by mail-cart to Bombay from Agra. He had held a civil appointment in Oude, and was well acquainted with Captain Hayes of Lucknow, and some others whom I had known there. We invited him to join our breakfast, and found his company and conversation very pleasant, as he was almost the first Englishman that we had spoken to since leaving Agra. After breakfast, we saw Lieutenant Black off; and in the afternoon we walked into the village, which is of large size, but exclusively composed of mud huts, and surrounded by a mud wall.

Outside the town were a number of baskets, about six feet long and three feet high. Each stood on a little raised platform of earth, and was sheltered by a thatched roof. One end was open and used as an entrance, but could be closed by a frame of basket-work which fitted into the aperture. We, at first, could not understand the use of these remarkable structures, but discovered that they were the residences of certain women, who, in this part of India, are not allowed to enter the villages. The specimens which we saw were dressed in gaudy cotton, and were by no means seductive in appearance. One part of their ornamentation, however, was curious, and, indeed, inexplicable to us. They were strings of old European gold and silver coins, which they wore suspended from their ears and noses. The women said the coins were not really gold, but were copied from real coins by the soonar (goldsmith). How he got hold of the originals I cannot imagine, unless they were relics of the Indian trade carried on in ancient times by the Venetians.

Sirporah is in the Bombay Presidency, and we were now again fairly in the British possessions, within which we continued for the next 130 miles.

From Sirporah we went to Dhoolia, thirty-two miles. The next morning we awoke on a great barren plain; and, after walking a few miles, descended a *ghât* (step), as these hills are called, and found the town of Dhoolia in the valley below.

In the afternoon we walked through the station, where there were then no troops, but the bungalows of a few European officials. The native town is of some size, and apparently a place of considerable activity. There were no walls or other defences: a peculiarity which was alone sufficient to show that we had now left the territories of native princes.

Dhoolia contains a large jail,* the convicts in which are employed in the manufacture of cotton goods. The bridge, over a tributary of the Taptee, is a very fine structure, high, long, and substantially built. It was another evidence that we had passed the limits of native rule.

As we walked into the town we met troops of boys, returning from one of the Company's schools. Like the other inhabitants of the place they wore the extraordinary headdresses peculiar to the Bombay Presidency. They are im-

* Jails are institutions unknown to the native governments of India. The punishments prescribed by the Korân and Hindoo codes are fines, flogging, the bastinado, mutilation, or death in various forms.

mense turbans, of various rich colours and grotesque shapes—the particular form being determined by the nationality or caste of the wearer. As much as fifteen yards of heavy muslin are often employed in their formation—rather a formidable burden for the head of a boy of eight or ten. In the north of India the turbans are small, and consist of about ten or twelve yards of fine and narrow muslin, which the wearer winds round his head each morning afresh, and will often re-arrange during the day. But the turban of Bombay is so complicated a structure that it has to be made up by a professor of the art, and when once formed is not unwound for a month or more.

We left Dhoolia on the evening of the 18th, and the next morning arrived at Malligaum, thirty-two miles distant. Like Dhoolia it is situated in a plain at the foot of a hill. The country around is quite barren and jungly, as was all that we saw after leaving Indor. However, we really did not see much of it, as the road was so excellent after entering the Bombay Presidency that our bearers completed each night's march, before we awoke.

Before arriving at the dâk-bungalow we had to cross a long and fine stone bridge, even larger than that at Sirporah, and, like it, of English shape and construction. From the bridge the native town and its castle were visible, a short distance down the river.

Malligaum is a considerable station. We walked through the cantonments, and listened to the band, which, like all the other bands of the Bombay army that I heard, was far inferior to those in the Bengal service, where they were carefully trained under European band-masters. The cantonments' church was very pretty, being a neat edifice of rough hewn grey stone, in the early pointed style—showing far more taste and knowlege of ecclesiastical architecture than most of the chapels in India, in which, indeed, those qualities could hardly have been expected, as they were mostly designed and built by the Company's engineer officers.

We also visited the native town, which, although a considerable place, had no walls. The only object of interest was the fort, built at a bend of the river. It was once a place of some strength, but is now in ruins. The defences consist of three parallel walls, one within the other, an arrangement rarely seen in India. The walls are of grey stone, at least fifteen feet thick. We found the fort entirely deserted, except that in one of the courts there was an encampment of Bheel troops.

Since entering the Bombay Presidency we had had an excellent road and good bungalows, but we were now again to leave these comforts and strike off from the direct Bombay road, in order to visit the caves of Ellora which are in the Nizam's dominions, about sixty miles from Malligaum.

Leaving Malligaum on the 20th of February, we found ourselves next morning on a villainous cross-country road. The country was hilly and very rugged, in some places covered with bushes or trees. Before arriving at Nandgao*n** we saw several wild hogs in the jungul.

The village of Nandgao*n* is built upon the banks of a little stream, and the country for some distance around it was well cultivated. Crossing the stream, we found what they called a "bagheechi"—a fine grove of tall trees, under the shade of which we passed the day very comfortably.

The next morning we awoke near a small village, in a very barren country. As there was not a tree or any other shelter to be seen, we had to push on to a somewhat larger and mud-walled village called Sakigao*n*, twenty-four miles from Nandgao*n*. At this place, also, there were but few trees, but outside the gate we found a mud temple, dedicated to Gunesi and Hooniman—the Elephant and Ape gods. In this we took up our quarters for the day. The idols were rude and hideous representations of these two animals. During the day we were several times disturbed by the priests' coming in to paint them, and to make poojah, which consisted in walking many times round the idol, and pouring over it the sacred water of the Nurbudda; at the same time bowing and touch-

* Nandgao*n*.—The final syllable in this word, gao*n*, means a village, and is the same as the last syllable of Malligaum, the spelling of which is corrupt. It should be Maligao*n*, meaning "The gardener's village."

ing their foreheads with their hands joined in the attitude of prayer.

Between Nandgao*n* and Sakigao*n* we had crossed the range of hills which divides the valleys of the Taptee and Godaveri. North of the hills all the waters flow westwardly, but the country in which we now were is drained by the Godaveri and Kistna, rivers that empty into the Bay of Bengal. We were now, therefore, fairly in the Dĕkkun, a term that is by some confined to those parts of the Indian Peninsula which are south of the Nurbudda valley and drained by eastward-flowing rivers, but which, as generally used, includes all the country south of the Vindya chain.

We had also entered the territories of another native prince, the Nizam, as he is styled. His capital is Hydurabad, and his dominions are almost four times as large as was the kingdom of Oude, or three times as large as Ireland, with twice its population. The founder of this dynasty was a Soobahdar, or governor, under the Mogul Emperor. During the disturbances that accompanied the decay of the Delhi empire, he asserted his independence, which was afterwards recognised and confirmed by the English. Unfortunately, there is no treaty which gives the English the power of interfering in the internal management of the Nizam's territories, and although a Resident is stationed at the capital he can do little but remonstrate whenever an act of more than usual folly or oppression occurs. The country is therefore misgoverned, Right and Justice are set at naught, the power of the Nizam is in many places defied, the whole country is a nest of robbers and a secure resort for Thugs, and the Company's officials can do nothing to remedy this state of things; what is worse, they are compelled by their treaty obligations to sustain the corrupt and powerless government, the inefficiency of which occasions all this disorder, and which, without their support, would soon be supplanted.

During the day that we remained at Sakigao*n* our kuhárs went into the village to buy materials for their food. When they came out again they were followed by the village buniahs, who with many tears and groans declared that the bearers had not half paid for the food which they had taken. This accusation was rendered only too probable by their whole conduct since leaving Agra, and on investigation we discovered it to be true, and compelled them to pay the whole value of the flour. In this case, therefore, the unfortunate villagers were righted, but we had good reason to believe that such occurrences often took place without our knowledge, and that those who were imposed on hesitated to complain for fear that we should side with our followers, in which case the latter would be sure to take revenge.

This was another instance of that "Zubburdustee"—the law of "Might makes Right"—which is so universally recognised in India. He who has the power takes, and he who is wronged gives up without question. Rarely is complaint made to the officers of justice, who, even in the Company's territories,* are looked upon with fear and distrust. In fact a native regards a resort to the courts and police very much as we do the conduct of the doves in the old fable, who called upon the hawk to defend them from the kite, and were subsequently eaten up by their champion.

* It will be remembered that the officials of the Honourable Company's police, and their judges in the courts of first resort, are all natives, who, from the very slight supervision that can be exercised over them by their European superiors, are scarcely less venal and tyrannous than in native states.

CHAPTER XXXI.

THE CAVE TEMPLES OF ELLORA.

General Description of the Temples—Khailas—Fine Sculptures—"The Work of Gods or Devils?"—Other Caves—A Heavenly Carpenter—A Disorderly Household—View from Hill—Saint's Tomb—Roza—Aurungzeeb's Tomb—His Character—Splendour and Power—Decay of the Mogul Empire—A Night in Paradise—Indra Sabha—Sonorous Obelisks—The Doorma Lena—Architectural Ornaments of the Caves—Hindoo Religious Mendicants—Peasantry—Their Complexions.

On the morning of February 23, we arrived at the caves of Ellora, which are fourteen miles from Sakigao*n*. They are the most perfect, and best known of the rock temples which abound in this part of India, and it was therefore with no little interest that we got out of our palkees and began to explore them. The caves are hollowed out of the rock, at the foot of a ghât, or range of hills, which rise steeply from the plain to the height of six hundred feet. Their name, Ellora, is a corruption of Weroola, the name of a small village about a mile distant. The caves extend for three miles along the foot of the hill. They are of various ages, the most northern, and the southern caves being of Boodhist origin, while those in the middle are Brahmunical, and about nine hundred years old, or even less.

We first visited the cave called Khailas, or Paradise, which, although one of the most modern, is at once the largest and most elaborate of the series. It is a quarry-like excavation—of which the depth is 250 feet, and the breadth 133 feet. There is a wall of solid rock, separating the enclosure from the plain. The interior of the quarry is occupied in the centre by the temple. This is of the usual form, consisting of the shrine with its pyramidal dome, and several pillared porticoes and halls. The sides of the quarry are steep, and hollowed out into successive stories of halls and galleries, into which light is admitted by open colonnades. All these buildings, the great temple, its porticoes and galleries, as well as the other apartments and the massive wall which divides the whole from the valley, are carved and quarried out of the solid rock.

The temple is about eighty-five feet high to the top of the pyramidal spire over the shrine. Its length, including the porticoes which are connected with it by hanging galleries of stone, is not less than 150 feet, and the greatest breadth is about ninety feet. The largest apartment is sixty-six feet by fifty-five. Its ceiling, which is supported by heavy square columns, is not more than twelve feet high, and carved to represent rafters. At the end of this apartment is a low door, opening into the shrine, which is a small and dark room, containing only a gigantic Mahadeo, four feet high. The columns and walls of the apartment were most elaborately carved, as was also the whole exterior of the building, the designs of which represent the exploits of Ram in Lunka or Ceylon, where, with the assistance of the monkey-god Hoonimán, and his army of apes, he delivered his wife Seeta from the captivity of a demon. The chambers and galleries in the sides of the quarry were similarly decorated. Sometimes the devices are uncouth, as is the case in one of the apartments, the roof of which is supported by huge stone lions and elephants fighting with each other. In the enclosure between the temple and the gateway are two obelisks, seventy-five or eighty feet high, supported on the backs of elephants. Like all the other buildings and accessories, they are carved from the solid rock. On coming out we met two Hindoo devotees, or Sooniasees, and asked them who had built the temple. "How do I know," one of them replied, "whether it was a god or a devil?"—implying that it was beyond the power of men.

After seeing the Khailas, we paid a hurried visit to the caves which lie to the south of it. They are mostly square apartments, about a hundred feet deep, cut into the steep face of the cliff, and approached by a terrace running along the hillside. The roofs were generally twelve or fifteen feet high, and supported by many solid columns. Some were approached from court-yards, excavated in the hill-sides, and others consisted of several separate apartments, joined by corridors. There was, however, a great uniformity of design, the most remarkable exception being a cave known as the "Carpenter's Cabin," which is not open in front like the others, but has only a small door for entrance. The interior is oblong in form, about fifty feet long and twenty-five broad. The end opposite the door is apsidal, and the roof is ribbed, and pointed with a perfect Gothic arch. Altogether, it would do remarkably well for a Christian church. This cave is singularly plain, the only figure of any kind being the colossal statue of the "Carpenter," or architect, as the word *maistree* would be better translated. This statue is situated in the apse, and represents the maistree as sitting cross-legged, with one hand on each knee. The natives told us that he was a son of Seewa—that he excavated all these caves, and finally died from a cut in the finger, wounded by an ill-directed blow of the chisel. In fact, one of his hands was represented in the statue as bleeding. This must have been a late legend, as this cave, and the others near it, are of Boodhist construction.

We now ascended the ghât, which proved a hot and fatiguing business, as it was nearly eleven o'clock and we had had no breakfast. On the top of the hill we came upon a broad plain, upon which there were several large stone tombs of Moosulman architecture. One of these, we found, was used as a bungalow by the officers of the Aurungabad mess, and was completely fitted up with a table, chairs, and cotton carpet. Here we ventured to take up our quarters, and wrote off to the commandant of Aurungabad for permission to remain all night. Opposite the tomb was a bungalow belonging to a retired English officer, who was a hundred years old, the natives said. He sent us over some mutton and vegetables, and offered to assist us in any way in his power. We thanked him for his kindness, in a note, and asked leave to call upon him; from this, however, he excused himself on the ground of illness and the fatigue of dressing. However, we found out afterwards that the real reason for objecting to our visit, was that the old gentleman's house was all zĕnana, and over-run with old and new favourites, whose number, as we were told by the bungalow-khansáhman, was "beyond account."

The heat was so great that we remained indoors nearly all day. Towards evening we ascended the hill behind the tomb, from the top of which we got an extensive view. In the valley below us was the town of Roza, almost buried in trees. In the distance rose a steep mountain, crowned with the fortress of Dowlutabad. On the right, in the valley, was the pretty village of Weroola, and behind us was the table-land upon which was situated the tomb where we had passed the day, and several others which we visited on descending from the hill.

One of these was quite an elaborate structure, in a fine court, surrounded by splendid trees. It is the burial place of a disciple of Nizam ood Deen, a saint whose tomb I saw at Delhi. The mausoleum of the disciple was larger than that of his master, if not so handsome, and the number of pilgrims encamped under the shade of the trees seemed quite considerable.

After seeing these mausoleums we walked on to the city of Roza, a walled town built by Aurungzeeb during his residence in the Dĕkkun. The architecture of the buildings, therefore, and general appearance of the town, precisely resemble those of the cities built by the Mahommedans in Northern India. Here, for the first time since leaving Jaipoor, we saw the minárs of a musjeed.

Roza, though well fortified and when first built doubtless a pretty city, has now a most decayed look. Many of the buildings are quite unoccupied, and the stuccoed exteriors of all were black with dirt and mould. The population are nearly all Moosulmans, and have a most shabby appearance. The fact is that this city, like many other towns in India, was built to satisfy the whim of a tyrant, who ordered the building of a city without regard to anything but his own pleasure, and when it was built transplanted inhabitants into it by force.

The principal sight of Roza, the name of which signifies a tomb, is the grave of the Emperor Aurungzeeb. It is covered only with a white marble slab, which is protected by a canopy of wood. A cloth of white silk, strewn with fresh flowers, was spread over the grave—a usual mark of respect shown to the graves of all Mahommedans who have left a fund to pay for it. The plainness and simplicity of the Emperor's grave contrasted very much with the elaborate splendour of several marble mausoleums which were contained within the same court. The moollahs in charge told us that the tomb had been prepared, in accordance with his own directions, before he died, which is quite possible, as he was rather given to asceticism.

Here, then, lie the remains of Aurungzeeb, the third in descent from Akbur, and the last, as Akbur was the first of the great Emperors of Hindoostan. He ruled an empire of immense extent, which had never been well consolidated, and which, during his reign, was distracted by formidable rebellions in various directions, some of them even led by his own sons; and yet he not only preserved in great measure the integrity of his dominions, but he even ventured to enforce upon the Hindoos odious taxes, prescribed by the Koran indeed, but which none of his ancestors had dared to maintain. He set at naught the religious prejudices of the great body of his subjects; forbade the public celebration of Hindoo festivals; demolished temples and built mosques where they had stood, and refused to admit Hindoos to any government situation of honour and responsibility. His zeal for religion was shown not only by these acts, but by the simplicity of his dress, the abstemiousness of his diet, and his habit of constantly perusing and expounding the Koran. At the same time his religion never interfered with measures of state. He made his way to the throne by deposing and imprisoning his father, and putting to death his three brothers and all their sons, and during his whole reign no scruples prevented the perpetration of any crime that was requisite for the gratification of his ambition.

Although abstemious in his private life, the splendours of his court and camp almost exceed belief. His army was composed of thousands of cavalry, infantry and artillery, the soldiers of which were drawn not only from all the provinces of his vast empire, but from other Asiatic countries, and even to some extent from Europe. A long train of war elephants, and a numerous stud of magnificently-caparisoned horses, for the Emperor's use, always accompanied his camp. A menagerie, also, was taken wherever he went, from which the rarest animals in the world were frequently brought forth and exhibited by their keepers before the Emperor and his court; while hawks, hounds, hunting-tigers, trained elephants, and every accompaniment used for field sports, swelled the pomp of the prodigious retinue.

The walls of cloth which encompassed the royal tents formed a circumference of twelve hundred yards, and contained every species of apartment found in the most spacious palace. There were halls of audience for public assemblies and private councils, with all the courts and cabinets attached to them, each hall magnificently adorned, and having in it a raised seat or throne for the Emperor, surrounded with gilded pillars, with canopies of velvet richly fringed and superbly embroidered; separate tents for mosques and oratories; baths and galleries for archery and gymnastic exercises; and a zĕnana as remarkable for luxury and privacy as that of Delhi. Persian carpets, damasks and tapestries; European velvets, satins and broadcloths; Chinese silks of every description, muslins, and cloths of gold were used in the utmost profusion and arranged for the greatest effect. Gilded balls and cupolas surmounted the tops of the royal tents. Besides all these there were separate tents for the household and servants, for the stable, the armoury and the kitchen; and every tent of the whole camp had its exact duplicate, which was sent on in advance to be prepared for the Emperor's arrival. His march was a grand procession, and when he entered his pavilion a salvo from fifty pieces of ordnance announced the event. In all places and circumstances he assumed and maintained every form and ceremony observed at the established residences of the imperial court.

The last twenty-two years of Aurungzeeb's life were spent in the Dĕkkun, in vain endeavours to overcome the rising power of the Maharattas. Yet, notwithstanding his absence from the seat of government; his being engaged in a vast and costly war, never successful, and at last purely defensive; the continued rebellions of different nations under his rule, and the treachery of his own family, he maintained his supremacy to the last; enforced the taxes necessary for his vast projects and expenses, and even, as before mentioned, carried into operation a series of acts calculated to offend the dearest rights of the great mass of his subjects. He did all this by his great natural abilities, never-sleeping vigilance, and minute personal supervision of every department of his government. In person "he planned campaigns, and issued instructions during their progress; drawings of forts were sent to him to fix on the points of attack. His letters embrace measures for keeping open the roads in the Afghan country, for quelling disturbances at Mooltan and Agra, and even for recovering Candahar; and at the same time there is scarcely a detachment marching, or a convoy moving in the Dĕkkun without some orders from his own hand. The appointment of the lowest revenue officer of a district, or the selection of a clerk in an office, is not beneath his attention, and the conduct of all these functionaries is watched by means of spies and of prying enquiries from all comers; and they are constantly kept on the alert by admonitions founded on such information."*

Aurungzeeb died in 1707, at the city of Ahmudnuggur, after a disastrous retreat from the Maharattas. On account of his splendour, power, and abilities, and the zeal which he showed for the Mahommedan religion, he is looked upon by the Indian Moosulmans as the greatest of all their monarchs. After his death, the Empire, which had no homogeneity, and no real elements of strength or unity, and which had been only held together during his reign by his extraordinary and commanding talents, underwent a speedy decay and gradual dismemberment. The governors of provinces revolted and founded new dynasties; the Maharattas, whom it had been the task of his life to hold in check, spread, and conquered, until nearly all his dominions fell into their hands, and the

* Elphinstone's History of India.

occupant of his throne was their prisoner and puppet; lastly, a power, feebler in its beginnings than either of these, which, during his reign, had secured a precarious footing on both sides of India, accomplished that which Aurungzeeb, with all his wealth and power, had never been able to effect. They subdued the Maharattas, who had grown to be a great and powerful nation; reduced the revolted governors to order and dependence on the central power; reinstated the Emperor in his position and rank; and having spread their conquests beyond what were the farthest limits of India, established a government the most liberal, and at the same time the most united and powerful that India has ever known, and the first which ever secured the unquestioned respect and obedience of *all* its different nations and rulers.

We took dinner in the "bungalow-tomb," and were afterwards preparing to go to bed, when our messenger returned from Aurungabad, announcing that we could not occupy the tomb, as it had been previously engaged by an officer who would arrive late that night. This was rather annoying intelligence, as it was past ten o'clock. However, we called up our kuhárs, and marched down the hill to the Khailas cave, where we slept in our palkees.

The next morning, as soon as we awoke, we went to visit the caves which we had not seen on the previous day. The first which we saw was the most northern of the series, about a mile from the Khailas, and known as Indra Sabha, since it contains a colossal statue of the god Indra, and his wife Indranee. This cave, which is one of the finest, consists of a series of chambers, each about fifty feet square, hollowed out of the sides of a quarried court. On each side of the court is a tall stone pillar, one of which has the remarkable property of ringing when struck, and is, in consequence, worshipped by the natives. The rooms have the same general appearance as those of the other caves, and are decorated with the same taste. The court is entered through a wall and gateway of solid stone, on one side of which is a monolithic column, and on the other a colossal elephant of stone.

Leaving the cave of Indra, we passed through numerous

others of minor note, and finally visited the Doorma Lena, which contains the largest single room of any one of the caves. This is one hundred and thirty feet in width, and of nearly the same depth. Besides the large apartment, there were numerous smaller rooms arranged in suites. One of these had a colonnade opening upon the precipitous side of a deep and wild ravine, at the upper end of which was a pretty water-fall. Besides the usual sculptured ornaments, the Doorma Lena contained many images of Seewa and his wife Párbutee, the latter of whom was represented in the congenial occupation of impaling a baby.

Whatever may be the size of the chambers in these apartments, the roofs are always very low, and the columns which support them broad and heavy. The latter are usually divided into about equal heights of capital, shaft, and base, the decorations of each being remarkably similar to the acanthus-leaf designs of Grecian architecture, and quite different from anything that I had seen elsewhere in India. In fact, these might be supposed to be the first rude attempts of art seeking for the perfect grace of the Corinthian capital, did we not know that the choragic monument of Lysicrates at Athens was completed twelve hundred years before these caves were excavated.

These caves are supposed to have been originally dug by the Boodhists, and subsequently altered by the Brahmuns to suit their worship. In some of them the alterations have been much more important than in others, but in almost all there are greater or less traces of a Boodhist origin. The figures of the gods, and the carvings which represent the obscene rites of Seewa's worship, are evidently late additions. The interiors were once decorated with paintings in very bright and durable colours, as the similar caves at Ajunteh are to the present day, but those in the caves of Ellora were all defaced and removed by that great iconoclast, Aurungzeeb.

After breakfast, we all went into the Khailas again, and occupied ourselves until two o'clock in sketching some of the ornaments and capitals of the columns. While thus engaged, we were accosted by two yogees,* who had come from

* Yogee, a Hindoo fukheer, or religious mendicant.

Hurdwar, the origin of the Ganges Canal. One of these fukheers had made his hair of a dirty tow colour by keeping ashes and lime on it. He asked whether one of our party, whose locks were somewhat of the same hue, had made them so by the same means. In another of the caves we saw one of these same gentry, who was sitting gathered up in a heap, and had occupied the same position for a year without speaking, having taken a vow to do so for the remainder of his life, as his servant told us.

While going through the temples in the morning, we saw a great many peasants, who had come from Weroola, where a fair was going on. They were going through the sights under the guidance of a Brahmun, who narrated the various legends connected with the gods represented, and demanded a contribution of money after each story. The peasants were mostly Maharatta girls, and very fine-looking. They were generally tall, stout, and well-made. They were clad in a saree, or veil, and a dhotee, tightly girt up around the loins, as is the custom near Bombay. These clothes were made of blue cotton, and their arrangement was well adapted to show the graceful forms of the wearers. The complexions of these girls were light, and their foreheads were marked with a cherry red spot of paint. All the natives in this part of the country had very light complexions, some scarcely darker than a Spaniard, and none so dark as the Bengalees, who are sometimes as black as any African. Even in Northern India I seldom saw the skin so light as the usual colour in the Bombay Presidency. What is a strange thing, the *Portuguese*,* as they are called, or the half-caste descendants of Portuguese, as they are really, who form a large class in Bombay, are often much darker than natives of unmixed blood, and are even occasionally as black as a Bengalee.

* The population of India, of Portuguese descent, is reckoned at one million, while the number of the English in India, until the recent revolt, did not exceed fifty thousand, including the soldiers.

CHAPTER XXXII.

TO BOMBAY.

Road to Dowlutabad—"The City of Riches"—A Stronghold—The "Master of the Plain" —Meet "the Moon-Lady" again—Aurungabad—A Magician—Tomb of Aurungzeeb's Daughter—Another Revolt—Separation of our Forces—Toka—The Godaveri—Brahmuns—A hungry God—Rope-and-boat Bridge—Imampoor—Ahmudnuggur—Meet our Friends—The Fort—The Kingdom of Ahmudnuggur—The Largest Brass Cannon in the World—Duelling among Natives of India—Chand Beebee again—Death of Aurungzeeb—Bombay Kuhárs—Sĕroor—Kondapoora—The River Kistna—Poonah—Dismiss our Kuhárs—Good-bye to Dhoolee-travelling—Irregular Cavalry.

About two o'clock we left the caves, in order to arrive at Dowlutabad, six miles off, in time to see its castle by daylight. We again ascended the Ghât, and passed through Roza. The road was very bad, in fact merely a path leading through a wild, hilly, and deserted country, so we did not reach our destination until five o'clock, and consequently were obliged to see the celebrated fortress rather hurriedly. Dowlutabad, the "City of Riches," is a walled town built on a level plain which is surrounded by hills. The town is a considerable one, and entirely in the Moosulman style of architecture, having been rebuilt by Aurungzeeb. It contains several gardens of trees, and a tall, but now rather ruinous, minár erected by the Moosulmans to commemorate the taking of the place. In the centre of the city rises a very steep and rocky hill, about 700 feet high, upon the summit of which is the castle, considered by natives the strongest fortress in the world. It was built by the Emperor Mohummud Toghluk, who had a fancy for making this place his capital, and twice compelled all the inhabitants of Delhi to remove hither. Both migrations were attended with great suffering, but in the last a large proportion of the people died of starvation, as a famine prevailed at the time.

The ascent to the fortress is alternately by a steep road and flights of stone steps. At intervals there are lines of strong defences surrounding the hill. The rocky summit of the hill, for a height of one hundred to one hundred and fifty feet, is scarped perpendicularly, and is further defended by a deep ditch filled with water. From this point the only approach to the castle is by a subterranean passage, with steps hollowed out of the rock. The top of the hill is entirely occupied by the castle, which has very strong walls, and contains various tiers of fortified ramparts. We were led through the apartments of the zĕnana, and one or two small garden-courts. The whole pile is quite extensive. On top of the highest tower we found a great cannon, twenty feet long, called "Maidan ka Malik" or "Master of the Plain." Close beside it, the standard of the Nizam, a triangular flag of tattered blue cotton, floated from a flag-staff. This fortress is said by the natives to have been besieged twelve years, by Aurungzeeb, to obtain the hand of a princess, the "Chand Beebee" —a not very probable story, as the Chand Beebee died fifty years before his reign began.

The fortress of Dowlutabad must have been quite impregnable before bombs were used in warfare; and even they would not do the garrison much injury so extensive are the subterranean passages and apartments. Still, like most of the other fortresses of India, it is valueless to the English, as it commands nothing, and is only adapted for the stronghold of a robber-prince. It is, therefore, left in the hands of the Nizam, and garrisoned by a few of his sepoys, who are as miserable excuses for soldiers as I ever saw.

Dowlutabad is famous for its grapes, which are very large, and resemble those produced in our hot-houses. Before leaving, we laid in a good supply of them to eat in our palkees. About eleven in the evening we arrived at the dâk-bungalow of Aurungabad, seven miles from Dowlutabad. We found that it would be impossible to get dinner, and were obliged to go to bed fasting, although we had had nothing but a cup of coffee and a biscuit during the day. However, we had been getting gradually used to irregularity of meals, and bore it like men.

It was on the evening of February 24th that we arrived at Aurungabad. The next day was very warm, so we remained indoors eating the excellent grapes, oranges, and figs of this region, and witnessing the performances of some jugglers, which were by far the most wonderful feats of the kind I have ever seen, particularly as they were performed upon the gravel road, and without the least preparations. One of the tricks consisted in wrapping a boy in a net so tightly that he could neither move his feet nor his arms, which were folded across his chest. The net was then tied by a firm knot behind. The boy thus bound was placed in a basket only just large enough to hold him, and the basket, which lay on the ground, was covered with a cloth. After some ceremonies, the magician assured us that the boy had gone to the bazár, to prove which he called him, and was answered by a childish voice far in the distance. Whether this was effected by ventriloquism or a confederate, I do not know. He then approached the basket, and, to further prove that it was empty, thrust a spear through it in all directions. This part of the performance was quite incomprehensible, as the basket was so small that the boy could hardly be crammed in, in the first place; and it, as well as the spear, were submitted for our inspection, to show that there were no false bottoms, or other similar devices employed by European stage-jugglers. A few more ceremonies recalled the boy, who jumped out of the basket, unembarrassed by the net, which was rolled up and held in his hand.

Toward evening we walked into the city, which is two miles from the cantonments where the bungalow is situated. Outside the walls is a tomb of one of Aurungzeeb's daughters, which is said to be a model of the Taj at Agra. It is, indeed, a good deal like it, but not nearly so large, and, moreover, built of pukka instead of marble. From the top of one of the minârs we had a view of the whole city, which is a place of much greater extent than I had supposed. It was built by Aurungzeeb, as its name implies, and is, like Roza and Dowlutabad, purely in the Moosulman style.

On returning to the dâk-bungalow we informed our kuhárs,

as usual, that we should start after dinner, and were surprised by their refusing to go on until some demands for an advance of wages were satisfied. This we had previously refused, as well from principle as from necessity—the ready money of the party being almost exhausted. We could, of course, do nothing that night, but determined to apply to the authorities next day. In this, however, we were forestalled by the bearers.

Although Aurungabad is in the Nizam's territories, and the cantonments are occupied by his troops, yet the magistrate is English, as are many of the other officers in the Nizam's service. This accounts for the revolt being made at Aurungabad, as the previous one had been at Indor.

As we were breakfasting next morning we were surprised by the arrival of a peon,* with a summons to appear before the commandant and answer to a complaint of our kuhárs. When breakfast was finished, two of our party accordingly proceeded to that officer's house. He caused our Persian and English agreements to be translated, and as it appeared from them that we were entirely in the right, he ordered our men to go on quietly under pain of losing all the wages due to them, and of being imprisoned if disorderly.

We supposed that this would prevent further difficulty, and after dinner were prepared to start, when the bearers of one of the party refused to move. As this was becoming intolerable, he gave the mate and several others a beating, upon which all his men took to their heels and ran away. The other bearers, however, professed their readiness to go on, so my two American friends left us for Ahmudnuggur. I remained, although my men were quite ready to proceed, as I was afraid that the kuhárs who were beaten might cause trouble. We, however, heard nothing more of the mate and six of the number, but toward evening five of those who had deserted returned and proffered their services, with whom, and eleven new bearers obtained at Aurungabad, we started on the evening of February 27th.

* *Peon*—A native attendant on a court of justice. The word is Spanish, and is also used in India to designate a class of servants employed for errands and to oversee work.

On awaking next morning we found ourselves at Toka dâk-bungalow, twenty-nine miles from Aurungabad. The bungalow is situated on the right bank of the Godaveri, which here forms the boundary between the Nizam's territories and the Bombay Presidency. On the opposite bank is the town of Toka, at the junction of another river with the Godaveri, and there are two other towns in sight, one on each of the points of land formed by the junction of the two rivers. During the afternoon we walked through two of these towns, which, though not large, we found well built of stone, with large high houses and a beautiful stone ghât along one part of the river's bank. One of the towns seemed a place of some sanctity, and contained four very handsome temples, around which there were a large number of Brahmuns idling, who at once assailed us with demands for eenám, as they call in the Děkkun what is known as bucksees in Northern India. We amused ourselves by pretending that we had no money, and asked alms of them, pretending that we were poor travellers—an assertion well borne out by our scanty and tattered attire. They would not at first believe us, but when they had once swallowed the story they became so insolent that it required all our self-command to restrain the avenging hand. Luckily, we remembered the danger that there is in striking a god, and prudently retired. The Brahmuns are, I think, the most disgusting and presuming wretches I ever met. One day while we were resting under a grove, a great dirty fellow, smeared with cow-dung and wearing the sacred thread over his shoulder, with no clothing but a rag six inches wide, marched boldly up to us and asked for paisa (farthings). I, being paymaster, wanted to know "what for?" when he answered as coolly as possible, "because I am a god and am hungry." If I could have mustered Hindoostanee enough, I would have told him that if his divine character could not protect him from hunger it certainly should not secure him unmerited charity. As it was, I could only recommend him, in terse and vigourous language, to remove himself, as speedily as possible, beyond the reach of personal chastisement.

There is a rope-and-boat bridge across the river at Toka, on a principle which I have seen applied in France and Minnesota. The waters of the river were considerably shrunken from the long drought, and a regular bazár had been established on the sandy bed which was left dry. Here we laid in a fresh supply of the fine grapes of the country. Outside of the bazár were a number of those little basket houses, some of which we had seen at Sirporah.

The next morning we arrived at Imampoor bungalow, which consists of an old Moosulman tomb, repaired and fitted up for the reception of travellers. It is built at the top of a steep hill, and the country around is utterly barren, although the enclosure of the bungalow contains some fine trees.

From Toka to Imampoor is twenty-six miles, but after breakfast we determined to proceed to Ahmudnuggur, twelve miles further, where we hoped to overtake the two members of our party who had separated from us at Aurungabad. We accordingly started at three in the afternoon, and walked into Nuggur* by seven, where we found our friends at dinner. We were all very glad to meet again, and passed the evening in recounting our adventures since separating.

The next day was so warm that it was afternoon before we ventured out of doors. We found Ahmudnuggur to be a considerable station, but the native town, although of some importance, has nothing worth seeing but its fort. This is of large size, but has been entirely modernized and the interior cleared of the mass of buildings which always encumber a native stronghold. The fort is now garrisoned and used as an arsenal.

Ahmudnuggur was once the capital of a large and powerful kingdom, under a Moosulman dynasty, which arose on the dissolution of the Bahmunee empire in the Dĕkkun. The founder of this dynasty was Ahmud, after whom the city was called, its name signifying "The City of Ahmud." He was originally a slave, but having attained a position of influence under the Bahmunee Emperor, succeeded in founding

* Although the real name of the city is Ahmudnuggur, it is usually called simply Nuggur, both by the inhabitants and by others.

an independent kingdom for himself and his descendants. The throne was occupied by members of his family from 1490 to 1637. These sovereigns ruled over a great extent of country, and it would appear that they possessed powerful armaments, not only from the long resistance which they offered to the Mogul Emperors, but also from the fact narrated in the history of Furishta, that in one campaign they lost six hundred cannon. Many of these were doubtless mere swivels, to be fired from the backs of camels, but one at least was of immense size. It is still in existence, and is four feet eight inches in diameter at the muzzle and fifteen feet long. Its calibre is two feet four inches, and its weight forty tons, being probably the largest piece of brass ordnance known.

Furishta mentions the prevalence under this dynasty of duelling, a custom almost unknown in Asia. Duels were occasioned by the most trifling disputes, and it was considered dishonourable to decline a challenge. No blame was attached to the death of one of the parties, provided the combat was fair. These duels were always fought with sabres.

It was during the wars carried on against this kingdom by Akbur, that the Chand Beebee or Chand Sooltana, as she is often called, displayed that heroic character which has made her name famous throughout Western India. Her most celebrated exploit was the defence of the Ahmudnuggur fort, during which she fought with her own hands in the breach, and finally compelled the Hindoostanee forces to come to terms. The common tradition among the natives is, that during the siege, after the supply of cannon balls was exhausted, she loaded her guns successively with copper, with silver, and gold coins, and did not consent to make terms until the only missiles remaining were her jewels. She died about the year 1600, murdered during a mutiny of her soldiers. Her infant nephew, for whom she had been acting as regent, was confined in the fort at Gwalior by the Mogul Emperor, and soon died. In 1637, under Shah Jehan, the dynasty was finally extinguished, and its territories were added to the agglomeration of conquered countries which formed the empire of the Mogul sovereigns.

It was in Ahmudnuggur that the Emperor Aurungzeeb, exhausted with twenty years of ceaseless and disastrous warfare, at length found in death that repose which the activity and energy of his character, and the continual fear and suspicion in which he lived, never allowed him to enjoy during life. Even on his death-bed he would not permit the presence of his sons, for fear that some treachery on their part should curtail the few hours of existence which he knew were all that remained to him. He had waded to the throne through the blood of his relations, and during his whole life he was tormented by a not ill-grounded apprehension that the same fate, by which almost all his ancestors and family had perished, would in the end overtake himself.

About five in the evening we walked to the parade-ground to hear the music, which was tolerably good for a Bombay band. Only a few of the officers and ladies of the station were present. Afterwards we returned to the bungalow and dined. In the evening we started for Sĕroor, forty miles distant. Gibson here dismissed the bearers whom he had hired at Aurungabad, and proceeded in a "nuggur-cart"—a conveyance resembling the gárrhees on the Grand Trunk road, except that it is mounted on two wheels only, and drawn by a pair of bullocks. The five or six of his original set of bearers who had remained faithful, accompanied us as supplementaries as far as Poonah, where we received a supply of money and paid them all off. Gibson's men were apparently glad to get rid of the Aurungabad kuhárs, who did not seem to *fraternize* at all. They had a different step, a different grunt (three notes instead of two*), and would neither eat nor smoke with the Agra bearers.

We arrived at Sĕroor bungalow on the morning of March 3d. It is situated in the midst of an utterly barren and desolate country. As far as the eye can see around there is no evidence of vegetable or animal life, except the pariah dogs, looking like mangy wolves, and the flocks of kites and solitary vultures which form a feature in every Indian landscape.

* A better distinction would be to say "three neighs instead of two grunts."

Dreary as this picture is, it is not an exaggerated description of much of the country in India.

The next day we passed at the dâk-bungalow of Kondapoora, forty-six miles from Sĕroor. Between the two places we crossed several rivers, branches of the Kistna which empties into the Bay of Bengal. Indeed all the rivers of this part of India, even those which rise within thirty miles of the western coast, flow eastwardly and pour their waters into the sea which washes the Coromandel Coast.

Kondapoora is in the midst of that desolate and jungly scenery which wearied our eyes from the time that we left Indor.

The following day, March 5th, we arrived at the dâk-bungalow of Poonah, one of the largest stations in the Bombay Presidency, and within 120 miles of that city. At this point we paid off our bearers, and bade adieu to dhoolee travelling. Since leaving Agra we had come nine hundred and sixty-six miles on men's shoulders, and were getting heartily tired of that mode of locomotion. At the same time, on looking back, I must say that there is not a more agreeable conveyance than the dhoolee in use anywhere (except it be the gárrhee of Bengal), especially where, as in India, most of the travelling is done by night.

Settling the accounts of our bearers, and dismissing them, occupied a whole day. The next day we were detained indoors examining and purchasing some of the various fancy articles manufactured at Poonah.

When we were at Poonah the number of troops in the station was considerably reduced by the Persian war. Among those still remaining was a regiment of irregular cavalry who had encamped opposite the dâk-bungalow. The irregular cavalry in the various Presidencies are volunteers in the fullest sense of the term. They find their own horses, enlist and retire from the service when they please, and each man is allowed to choose his own costume and arms. In this last respect, however, they do not avail themselves of their liberty, but wear a uniform native dress, and procure their arms through the colonel of the regiment. One of the best points in the equipment is the retaining of the native saddle, a cloth pad, which gives a much softer and firmer seat than the European "pig skin." Each regiment has only three European officers, who, like their men, wear the native costume. The discipline in these regiments is even less rigid than in the regular army; and they answer a very useful purpose by giving employment to that large class of natives, mostly Moosulmans, who have been deprived of occupation by the Company's government, and who, being too proud to work, would become dangerous and disorderly were not some such career offered to them.

CHAPTER XXXIII.

BOMBAY.

Khandála—The Ghât Mountains—Cave Temples—The Railway—Obstacles to its Construction—Situation of Bombay—The Fort—Native Town—Residences of Europeans—Growth of Eastern Cities—Commercial Ability of Natives—Commerce of Bombay and Calcutta—Variety of Nationalities represented in Bombay—Parsees—Their Costume, Religion, and Customs—Sir Jamsetjee Jeejeebhoy—Other Native Inhabitants—Hindooism in Bombay—Bóhoras and Portuguese—Peculiarities of English—Degeneracy of all other Nations in the East—The Hoolee—Nach at the House of Juggurnathjee Sunkurset—Anglomania in India—Old Hindoo Costume—Cave Temple of Elephanta.

On the afternoon of March 6th we left Poonah in a phaeton, and arrived at eight o'clock at the dâk-bungalow of Khandála, a place situated on the summit of the ghât of the same name. During the drive we saw constant marks of the railway which is being built to connect Bombay with the interior of the country.

The next morning we walked down the Khandála Ghât, which is three thousand feet high. It is one of that chain of mountains which runs parallel to the western shore of India, and separates the narrow strip of land known as the Malabar Coast, from the lofty table-land of the Dĕkkun. This whole range is called by Europeans the Western Ghaut Mountains. Near the southern extremity of the Peninsula they unite with another range, the Eastern Ghauts, which form the eastern boundary of the Dĕkkun, and separate it from the low plains of the Carnatic and the Coromandel Coast.

The scenery of the Khandála Ghât is very picturesque, and in many places the soft rock has been excavated into cave temples similar to those at Ellora. These, however, have long been abandoned as places of worship, and were occupied as temporary abodes by the workmen employed upon the railway, which is being conducted up the hill by a series of inclined planes and tunnels. The hill-side was entirely covered by the workmen employed in this undertaking, but the work was on so gigantic a scale that it was doubtful when it would be completed. Meanwhile they were going on with the line on the table-land above, and many additional miles were soon to be opened. This railway forms one of that series which has been planned, and is now being carried out, to connect all the principal coast towns of India with each other and the interior of the country. The progress in the construction of these roads has, however, been slow, the chief obstacle, as I understood, being that which is so universal a complaint in India, viz., the difficulty of obtaining efficient and honest overseers. It is therefore impossible to say when this vast scheme, which will have so important an effect on the productiveness of India, will be carried into practical operation.

At the foot of the hill we found the railway terminus, and getting on the train at two o'clock arrived in Bombay at seven —a distance of seventy miles. This may seem slow travelling, but appeared fast enough to us who had been used to doing the same distance in three days, by palkee.

Bombay, the capital of the smallest English Presidency, is a city of nearly 500,000 inhabitants. It is built upon an island, which is separated by a shallow strait from the larger island of Salsette. An arm of the sea, running north and south, separates both these islands, on their eastern side, from the mainland of India, but on the north the lines of water which divide them from each other, and from the continent, are so small that they might better be taken together and described as a triangular promontory projecting from the coast line of the continent.

The extremity of the island is occupied by the city proper, which is only about three quarters of a mile square, and being strongly fortified, is known as "Fort St. George." This was formerly the residence of the Europeans, but of late years they have preferred to occupy bungalows in the country, and the whole island is therefore covered with country seats, belonging to wealthy Europeans and natives. Even the Governor now lives in a house at Parell, a place several miles from the town. The houses in the fort, which were once occupied as residences, are now used almost entirely as places of business, and the greater part of the inhabitants of "the Fort" are natives. But the native town proper is built outside the walls of the fort, and contains much the largest part of the population of the island. The houses are generally very large and high, built either of pukka, or else with wooden frames filled in with brick-work, and faced with white stucco, in such a way as to leave the black wooden beams in sight.

Between the native town and the fort is a large and level plain, washed on two sides by the waters of the harbour. This is kept open and used as a parade-ground, and also for the evening drive of the Europeans and wealthy natives.

The country around Bombay, where are the residences of the Europeans, is very beautiful; the ground is well planted with trees, and the foliage has that rich *tropical* character of which one hears so much before going to India, and sees so little when he gets there.

The growth of Bombay is entirely due to its commerce, and has been marked by the same extraordinary increase which is seen in Calcutta. A century ago there were not fifty thousand inhabitants; now there are over half a million, and the population is still on the increase, having doubled in the last ten years. Calcutta, which was a mere village a hundred years ago, is now even much larger than Bombay. These instances of growth, which almost equal anything even in America, show with what rapidity an immense population will gather, in India, around any centre of trade and commerce. Indeed, the natives of India are naturally among the most acute and sagacious traders in the world, and yield to no other nation in their fondness for wealth.

The power of the "almighty dollar" in America, and the reverence shown to "pounds, shillings, and pence" in England, are bywords among the nations of the European continent, whose feelings are embodied in the sneering language of Napoleon, who called the English a nation of shopkeepers.

The Frenchman twits the Englishman with belonging to a nation of shopkeepers. The Englishman believes the American to be a slave of the "almighty dollar." But French, English, Americans, and, indeed, all European nations, unite in despising the Jew as the embodiment of the lowest and most absorbing form of avarice, as a man who would overreach his father in a bargain, and in dealing with whom the shrewdest Christian will probably find more than his match. And yet when brought into competition with the native of India, the Jew is absolutely "nowhere." In every department of business, great or small, high or low, legal or illegal, he is completely beaten out of the field, and it would be admitted in India that a Jew is as much at the mercy of the Hindoo bazár merchants, as a green Yankee is likely to be an easy prey of "my peoplesh" in Chatham street. If the Hindoo and other native traders had as much regard for their reputation as they have of other business qualities, no other nation could contend with them on their own ground, and trade with foreign countries would be entirely carried on by native houses. Even now, most of the European business is done with native capital, although largely managed by European firms. In Bombay, this is especially the case. Almost the whole wealth of the place is in the hands of natives, particularly Parsees; and of the business establishments much the larger part are conducted by natives, and many of the rest rely principally on native capital.

The foreign commerce of Bombay amounted, in the year 1853-54, to eight million four hundred and forty thousand pounds sterling of imports, and nine millions and a half exports. In the same year the foreign commerce of Calcutta amounted to seven million seven hundred thousand pounds sterling imports, and eleven millions and a half exports.* These figures show the remarkable fact that the business done in Bombay is but little inferior to that of Calcutta, and also that the discrepancy is chiefly in the amount of exports, Bombay taking nearly the same amount of foreign produce as Calcutta. It will be noticed that in both cases the exports much exceed the imports,

* These figures are from M. De Valbezen's work on India.

which accounts for the constant drain of silver in the direction of India. The trade of Bombay with England amounted, in the above-named year, to only three millions one hundred and fifty thousand pounds sterling of imports, and two millions six hundred thousand pounds sterling of exports. The remainder, or almost two-thirds of the whole commerce, was with other oriental countries, such as China and Arabia.

This commerce with oriental countries attracts to Bombay merchants of all the Eastern nations, and makes it the most cosmopolitan city of India. The streets are filled with Persians, Arabs, Copts, Afghans, Abyssinians and other Africans, Chinese, Jews, and members of almost every nation in India. The study of the characteristic peculiarities of these different nations adds not a little to a stranger's interest in Bombay, and makes it, for a traveller, much the most instructive city in India.

Of the native inhabitants, the Parsees, who number about twenty-five thousand, are the most remarkable class. Their name, which is merely the Hindoostanee word for "a Persian," indicates their origin. They are in fact the descendants of the old fire-worshippers of Persia, who were driven out of that country in the seventh century by the Mahommedan invasion, and taking refuge in India established their nation as a peculiar people, who, to the present day follow the precepts of Zoroaster and worship the eternal fire as Cyrus did. They still preserve their national characteristics, and have regular, and often finely-formed features, and complexions nearly as fair as those of Europeans.

Since this people have been in India they have adopted the Hindoo dress, altering it somewhat, as is customary with different nations and classes. They wear a high, flat turban of brown chintz, which looks so much like a mitre that some persons have supposed that it is the old Persian cap, or tiara, mentioned by Herodotus and Xenophon. This, however, is not the case—it is merely one of the many extraordinary forms which the turban assumes in Bombay. The present Persian head-covering, a very high, brimless hat of felt, in exactly the shape of a pointed sugar-loaf, is much more probably a continuation of the old tiara, and answers nearly to the description of it in the Greek writers. The Parsees are as particular about caste, as any other natives of India. It is not a part of their original system, but has been borrowed by them from the Hindoos, as also by the Moosulmans. Being fire-worshippers, they have a great reverence for that element, and will never employ it, except on necessary occasions, as in cooking food—however, the culinary operation is, I believe, with them, as with the Hindoos, a sort of sacramental act. For this reason, the Parsees never smoke, nor will they allow smoking in their presence. To this rule, however, there are exceptions, in the case of some of their merchants, who will allow English and Americans to puff cheroots in their counting-houses, and will even light a lucifer for them on occasion. It is said that, when a Parsee is dying, his relatives place him in an out-house surrounded by a wall of stones, and leave him there without food or drink until he dies. Mrs. Mackenzie tells an instance of this, where an English physician found one of his Parsee patients thus walled up, and only managed to get him out by threatening to enter a charge of murder against the whole family. He succeeded in restoring his patient, who lived for some weeks afterward. This strange people do not bury their dead, but expose the corpses in open stone towers, where the bodies are eaten by birds. Another of their peculiarities is a superstitious regard for dogs, a feeling which they carry to such an extent that, when the city government of Bombay, some years ago, ordered all stray dogs to be killed, the Parsees made such a riot that the military had to be called out to restore order. The Parsee women are kept in a retirement more strict than that of the Moosulman and Hindoo women. If any *accidents* occur, notwithstanding these precautions, the fair and frail one is brought before a council of five (panchayut), which is in India the general resort for settling all difficulties. If she is found guilty, she *disappears*. Of late years, however, there has been a disposition to admit the women to more public society, and now it is even sometimes customary to take them abroad in carriages, the blinds of which, however, are always drawn. This change, if made, will be an imitation of English custom, for the Parsees are the greatest Anglo-maniacs in India, and affect English usages as far as possible, some of them even wearing English trowsers and boots.

The Parsees are more enterprising, and generally much better informed, than any other class of natives. They carry on business, not only with England, but also with China and other Eastern ports, in all of which are found representatives of their nation. One of their number, Sir Jamsetjee Jeejeebhoy, has obtained a world-wide reputation by his extensive charities. His property, which is now estimated at three crors of rupees ($15,000,000), was accumulated entirely by his own exertions during a long life of nearly eighty years. His extensive and most useful charities, amounting to over a million and a half of dollars, obtained for him the honour of knighthood, and a subsequent elevation to the baronetcy. Both rewards were well deserved, and were most highly valued by himself and his whole nation, especially as it was the first instance of such a dignity being conferred upon a subject of her Majesty's Indian dominions.

Besides the Parsees, the native inhabitants of Bombay are composed of the Hindoos and various classes of Moosulmans. The former are a finer looking race than the natives of Northern India. I do not know whether they are taller, but they appeared stouter and more compact, and had much lighter skins. Their manners are also much more manly and independent than those of the Hindoostanee and Bengalee, and they do not use in conversation those phrases and attitudes of servile humility which prevail where the Moosulman influence has been predominant. Their dress is substantially the same that is seen elsewhere in India, but the chupkun is made short-waisted, and, on occasions of ceremony, is worn with an immensely full skirt, descending to the heels, and giving the wearer a decidedly womanish appearance. The turbans are generally very large, and made with great care, in various odd, and not always graceful shapes, which distinguish the different castes and trades. On the whole, I think there are a much larger number of Hindoos well and carefully dressed in Bombay than in any other city of India which I saw; and the style of costume, if not so gay and jaunty as in Northern India, is more effective and picturesque. The lower classes of Hindoos, of course, as elsewhere, have almost no clothing. In Bombay, the drapery is often limited to a strip of cotton, six inches wide, passing between the legs, and fastened in front and behind to a string tied around the waist.

It is a strange fact, that the Hindoo religion is much more powerful and vigourous in this part of India than in the North, which was its earliest cradle and still contains by far the greatest proportion of Brahmuns and high-caste people. In the Bombay Presidency, the temples are larger, finer, and more frequented than in the North. Almost every Hindoo is painted on his forehead with the mark of his god, a thing that is comparatively rare at the North; and, although they are great Anglo-maniacs in Bombay, and in many respects break through old native customs, yet there is not the least sign of such infidelity as is spreading in Calcutta, and no such disregard of their caste and religious rules as is fashionable among the wealthy Hindoos of that city.

Among the various sects of Moosulmans in Bombay, the only one which merits notice are the Bóhoras, a caste almost peculiar to that city. Their clothes are generally white, or of a shade between light yellow and drab, and they wear a raw-silk turban. They will not smoke, and are the only Indian Moosulmans who will engage in trade, or any other occupation than public or private service.

The Portuguese, as they are called, form another large class in Bombay. They come from Goa, and are darker in complexion than most of the natives. What little Portuguese blood there is left in their veins seems only to deteriorate the qualities which they derived from their native mothers, and their only occupation is as servants or small shopkeepers.

This one peculiarity distinguishes the English settlers abroad from all other nations. The English keep themselves separate and aloof from the natives. They preserve their old habits, manners, and morals, and consequently their character remains unchanged, and their pristine vigour unimpaired. In this way fifty thousand English have conquered and held in united strength an empire composed of 180,000,000 of men of all sorts of nations and languages. The Portuguese, on the other hand, and the French, seemed at once to coalesce with the natives whom they conquered. They assumed native dress and habits, married native wives, and eventually became degraded to the level of natives, and were absorbed by their overwhelming numbers. This metamorphosis is even more marked in the case of the Mahommedan conquerors of India, who, in a few years, became changed from brave and hardy Tartars or Afghans, into the weak, cringing, idle and luxurious Moosulmans of Hindoostan. At the present day they are scarcely at all distinguishable from Hindoos; they have universally adopted the Hindoo custom of caste, and in many places have almost lost their old faith and become idolaters. In fact, at the present time, they are inferior to many of the Hindoos in physical advantages; and as regards their mental qualities, are sunk even below the level of other natives. I have spoken before of the deterioration of the Portuguese in China, which is also a case in point. In fact, that very peculiarity of the English, which, I have heard said by Frenchmen and others, disqualified them from governing foreign countries, by shutting them off from all sympathy and common feeling with their subjects, is, I believe, the quality to which is to be attributed their unexampled success in India, where French and Portuguese in equal or greater numbers failed almost from the beginning, and where the Mahommedans, though more than a hundred times as numerous, never got so sure a footing, so united an empire, and so submissive an obedience.

During our stay at Bombay occurred the festival of the Hoolee, or Hindoo New-Year, which is celebrated throughout India, but more particularly in those parts that are thoroughly Hindoo. Besides the religious ceremonies observed, there are entertainments in the residences of the richer classes, and it is customary for the natives to pelt one another with red balls or a red liquid that stains the clothes and makes them look as if they were covered with blood. In some of the native courts elephants are trained to eject this liquid from their trunks. The aid of modern science has even been called in, and fire-engines are used to squirt the red liquid from the palace wall upon the Rajah's subjects below.

By the kindness of some Parsee friends we were invited to two of the largest entertainments given during the festival. The first was at the house of a wealthy Hindoo, Juggurnathjee Sunkurset. His residence is a large mansion, built and furnished in the English style. The rooms were lighted during the evening and thrown open for the inspection of visitors. The nach, however, was given in a temporary building of bamboo and canvass, erected for the occasion in the court-yard. The bamboo building formed one large room, about a hundred feet long by sixty broad; and the canvass walls were painted to represent Italian frescoes. On the floor was a Persian carpet, and along each side were parallel rows of sofas crowded with rich Hindoos and Parsees. At the upper end was a dais, on which sat our host and his more honoured guests, among whom were the Admiral of the Company's Navy and his family. At the lower end of the room were the nach girls, who were but little different from those of Delhi, except that they wore less voluminous dresses. At our entrance our entertainer rose to meet us, and sprinkled us with rose-water from a silver bottle, having a top perforated like a pepper-castor. We were also served with "pâns," which are some slices of areca-nut and fine chunam (lime) wrapped in a betel-leaf. These are much used for chewing by all classes of natives, and are always served to guests as coffee and pipes are in Ottoman countries. The taste is aromatic, and slightly astringent; and the juice, which is swallowed, is said to have a tonic effect on the stomach. The guests all sat on the sofas as naturally as possible, and also wore their shoes, which is an excess of Anglicism to which natives in Northern India have not yet attained. I heard in Calcutta that a few members of "Young Bengal" had attempted to wear their shoes at the Governor General's receptions, but his lordship told them decidedly that they must show some sign of respect either by uncovering the head as Europeans do, or by removing the shoes, as is the native custom.

We afterwards went to another nach at the house of a Hindoo physician. This entertainment was much smaller than the other, and those present all sat on the carpet in the native fashion. The doctor was a graduate of the University of Bombay, and had, as we understood, obtained a high position in his profession. He spoke excellent English, and was at great pains to entertain us. His dress was a chupkun, of the old fashion, with a skirt descending to the ankle, and formed of an infinite quantity of the finest white muslin gathered into an immense number of folds at the waist. On the following day, however, when we called on him, we found him without any clothing at all above the hips, which I fancy is his usual costume, at least when in the house.

The Hoolee lasted for several days, and during the whole time, these naches continued, and the streets were filled with gaily-dressed natives whose white dresses were liberally stained with the crimson marks of the season. At night the streets were brilliantly lighted, and even more crowded than during the day.

The greatest *sight* of Bombay is the cave temple in the island of Elephanta, which we visited in company with a member of the Parsee house of Dossabhoy, Merwanjee & Co., who were unremitting in their attentions during our stay.

We embarked in a "bunder-boat," a small native craft with a cabin, and sailed the seven miles to the island in about an hour's time, the wind being light. Long before reaching the shore our boat grounded, as the water is very shallow, and we were obliged to mount on the shoulders of some of the boatmen, who waded ashore with us on their backs.

The island is high, and richly covered with tropical trees and plants. A stone path, with several series of steps, leads up to the temple, which is over half a mile from the landing-place.

The temple is a large square room with a flat roof about twenty feet high, supported by several rows of massive pillars. The whole is carved out of the solid rock like the caves of Ellora, and in form and decorations much resembles some of them. At the further end is the principal idol, which is a colossal bust with three heads. This has been supposed to represent the Trĭmoortee, or Hindoo Trinity, but there are objections to this theory, and to all the other hypotheses which have been invented to explain its meaning. Several other statues decorate this apartment, and on each side is a smaller chamber, opening into the larger one, and also containing idols.

The antiquity of this temple has long furnished a subject of wonder for visitors to Bombay; and their fancy has had almost unlimited ground for conjecture as there is no inscription or other sign by which the antiquarian would be enabled to fix the age exactly. Late investigations, however, and particularly a comparison with similar caves the age of which is known, have combined to attribute to it a date more modern than the year 900 of our era. What adds to the probability of this conclusion is the fact that during the short time that it has been known to Europeans, although every care for its preservation has been taken by the authorities, it has sustained great injury from the weather, which makes it extremely improbable that so perishable a material as the soft stone from which it is excavated, could resist the power of the elements for many centuries.

The island of Elephanta was so named by the Portuguese. Its native name is Shahpooree. The Portuguese name is derived from a gigantic stone elephant, three times the size of life, which stands a short distance from the cave. This figure, however, like the cave itself, is very much defaced by the action of the weather, and the form of an animal, which it bears on its back, is now so disfigured that its distinctive peculiarities cannot be distinguished.

CHAPTER XXXIV.

BOMBAY TO CAIRO.

The "Ganges"—Our Fellow-passengers—The Crew—Life on the Steamer—Aden—Its Appearance—"Hell with the fires put out"—An Original Head-dress—Arabs—The Cantonments—The Fortifications—Importance of the City—Free Trade—A Footprint of Civilization—The "Gate of Tears"—The Red Sea—Its Heat—Suez—Transit across the Desert—Its Appearance—The Road—The Pyramids—The "City of Victory"—A Recommendation for Indian Travel.

WE remained at Bombay over a fortnight. On the eighteenth of March we bade good-bye to one of our party, Mr. Gibson, the English engineer, who went to England by ship. The rest of us took passages to Cairo, and on the evening of the nineteenth we went on board the Peninsular and Oriental Company's steamer Ganges, a vessel of 1200 tons, propelled by paddle-wheels. As these steamers are intended mostly for passengers, their accommodations are ample and very comfortable. Every provision is made for hot weather, and there are even punkahs over the tables.

Early on the morning of the twentieth we steamed out of the "beautiful bay,"* and by noon we had lost sight of land. Our fellow-passengers, who proved most agreeable companions, were about fifty in number. They were mostly officers of the army, from the Bombay and Madras Presidencies, although some of them had come from the Punjab and extreme North West, from which part of India the easiest way to reach England is by way of Mooltan, as there is a line of steamers between Kurrachee and Bombay, and steamboats run regularly on the Indus from Mooltan to Kurrachee. Among the passengers were eight or ten ladies and twice that number of children. The presence of the latter detracted almost as

* The name Bombay was given by the Portuguese, and is corrupted from two words in their language meaning "good bay."

much from our comfort as the society of the former added to it. The children were almost all attended by their native nurses, and few of them spoke any other language than Hindoostanee.

The crew were Lascars, except the secunnies, or steersmen, who were from Manilla. The duty of steering the ship was shared by the Chinese crew of the captain's gig. The servants were Parsees or Moosulmans, and the stokers were stalwart negroes from the African coast, the only men who can bear to work in the intense heat of the engine rooms, where the Scotch and English engineers sicken and often die, although they have no manual work to do, and are only required to expose themselves for a few hours each day. The officers were, of course, all British, and were most obliging and gentlemanly men. This great variety of nationalities gave the quarter-deck a very picturesque appearance on Sunday mornings when all hands were mustered, and appeared washed clean for the week, and each dressed in his national costume.

On Sunday we had divine service in the cabin, attended by all the Europeans. The natives, whose work was made as light as possible on that day, gathered around the deck in groups, listening to one of their number who read the Korán or some other book, and mending their tattered clothes.

On week-days, the regular amusement was single-stick for the officers and passengers, but it was generally so hot that most of us preferred to sit quietly and read or converse.

Most of the passengers slept on deck at night, as the staterooms below were too hot for comfortable repose. The only objection to this plan was that we were waked up soon after four o'clock by the washing and holystoning of the decks.

On the 27th of March we arrived at Aden,* which is situated on the southernmost point of Arabia the Happy, about a hundred miles east of the Straits of Bab-el-Mandeb, and perhaps a hundred and fifty miles from Mocha, which is within the straits. Aden is under the jurisdiction of the East India

* The accent of this word is on the last syllable, and it is pronounced exactly as the two English words *a den*.

Company, and is strongly fortified and garrisoned. It is considered one of the most important naval stations in the Eastern seas, from which circumstance, and its great strength, it has been called the "Gibraltar of the East."

If the rest of Araby the Blest looks like the country around Aden, the name must have been given in the bitterest irony. A more desolate scene it would be hard to find than that which met our eyes on awaking in the harbour. The shore was sand and rocks, the hills were steep ragged masses of cinders and scoriæ. Truly, as a former traveller has said, it looks like the "Region of the Demon of Desolation" in a melodrama. Another tourist declares, with scarcely less truth, that it is "Hell with the fires put out." At the harbour is the coaling station of the P. and O. Company. There is also an hotel where we took lunch, and some bungalows, the residences of officials connected with the Steamship Company, and of a few traders, among whom is an American who does quite a large business with the Arab and African ports.

The inhabitants are Sumalees and Arabs. The former are a wretched, half-starved and ill-formed race. Their skins are almost black, and they have a habit of covering the head with a thick coating of mud, which they keep wet as a protection against the heat. It is certainly an original head-covering, and converts the hair into a mass of tangled red bristles, the contrast of which, with their black skins, is considered by themselves as one of the most beautiful features in their appearance. They wear little or no clothing. The Arabs whom I saw were very dark-coloured, and quite an inferior race to those who live further north. They are all turned out of the town before night, a measure which is necessary to the safety of the place, and has been found considerably to reduce the number of murders and other crimes which were formerly of frequent occurrence. The defences of Aden are so strong as to afford entire protection from the surrounding tribes of Arabs, who are all hostile. Still it is not considered safe to venture many miles into the interior even in the daytime, and at night great vigilance has to be observed by the garrison.

As soon as breakfast was over, we all landed, and, mounting

upon horses or donkeys, proceeded to the cantonments, as the fortified town is called. The road was well macadamized, and led for a couple of miles along the beach. Then we turned inland, toward the steep hills, which the road ascended. We passed the ridge through an artificial cut, strongly defended by two massive gateways of great strength, which form part of the line of fortifications surrounding the town. Here we found on guard some Indian sepoys, several regiments of whom, and one of English soldiers, formed the garrison.

Further on, we came to the city, which has almost wholly sprung up since the occupation of this place by the British. It is now a town of over twenty thousand inhabitants, but contains no remarkable buildings. The larger part of the trade of Mocha and other Arab ports now centres in Aden, a result which is to be attributed not only to the greater security for life and property under the English rule, but is also largely due to its being a free port, so that the Arab merchant escapes the onerous duties of the Turkish Government, and the extortions of the customs' officials.

We remained but a short time at cantonments, where we found only a badly kept Parsee hotel. The landlord informed us that the only articles of food to be had in the vicinity are fish and oysters. Every thing else must be imported, and even the water has to be brought in boats for some distance, as that found in the place is scarcely drinkable.

The fortifications of Aden are of great extent, and have been perfected at an enormous expense. Bayard Taylor says of them: "The skill and genius exhibited in their design impressed me far more than the massive strength of Gibraltar. I never felt more forcibly the power of that civilization which follows the Anglo-Saxon race in all its conquests, and takes root in whatever corner of the earth that race sets foot. Here, on the furthest Arabian shore, facing the most savage and inhospitable regions of Africa, were law, order, security, freedom of conscience and of speech, and all the material advantages which are inseparable from them. Herein consists the true power and grandeur of the race, and the assurance of its final supremacy." I have taken the liberty of quoting these words, because they express so truly my feelings, and what I believe ought to be the feelings of every member of the Anglo-Saxon race, as he looks upon the progress of that mighty power which is spreading our laws, our liberty, our civilization, and our religion into the furthest bounds of the habitable world.

In the harbour of Aden were several English and Arab ships, filled with pilgims going to Mecca from Bombay, or on the homeward passage.

We went on board the Ganges at five o'clock, after taking dinner and playing a few games of billiards at the hotel near the harbour.

Before we arose next morning we had passed through the Straits of Bab-el-Mandeb, the "Gate of Tears," and were within the Red Sea.

We were five days running up the Red Sea. The land was seldom in sight, but a few islands which we saw were perfectly barren, and presented the appearance of volcanic rocks and ashes. The weather was comfortable, as there was a slight breeze ahead during the whole time. This was a most delightful disappointment, as we had been much frightened by what we had heard in India of the heat in the Red Sea, where the weather is so intensely hot at certain seasons that many ladies faint from its effects, and not a few invalids, returning from India with enfeebled constitutions, die from exhaustion.

Late on the evening of April 1st, we arrived at Suez, and bade good-bye with regret to the good ship Ganges, and her popular commander, Captain Bowen. The passage was as pleasant as any I ever made. We had had no rough weather, and no rain; the heat had not been excessive; every comfort and luxury was provided on the vessel; our fellow passengers formed a most agreeable society; and, altogether, I do not know that I ever passed ten days more pleasantly than on the steamer "Ganges."

We went ashore in boats, and as it was dark, of course saw nothing of the town. The hotel is a large but uncomfortable establishment. The first thing we noticed, on entering the sitting-room, was the want of the punkah, which hangs from the ceiling of every room in India.

From Suez to Cairo the distance is eighty-five miles across the desert. The transit is now effected by railway, but at that time passengers were carried in *vans*, which are two-wheeled omnibusses, each holding six persons rather closely packed. Not more than five vans start together. If there are more passengers, a second and a third batch are despatched at intervals of four hours. The baggage and freight are all carried on fast camels.

The preference of seats in these vehicles is determined by lot, on board the steamer. By good luck, our party got in the first batch, which is an advantage, as the horses are fresher, and it allows more time in Cairo.

At midnight we started, at the full speed of four fine Arab horses. We were in the first van, which was much the most comfortably fitted up, and which, from its position, escaped the dust which annoyed the passengers in the vans behind.

At four o'clock we stopped for twenty minutes at a square stone building, where we found a supper spread out. We were all, however, too sleepy to partake of it, though few of us had succeeded in actually sleeping, the jolting was so intolerable.

At eight next morning we stopped for another meal, and then mounting again in our close hot van advanced at a gallop toward Cairo.

The desert is sandy and rocky; but the surface is everywhere broken, and there are occasionally ravines of some depth. The vegetation consists solely of scrub bushes, but on the whole it looks quite as green and luxuriant as much of the country which I saw in Northern India; though the soil is in the one case arid sand, and in the other very fertile, and susceptible of high cultivation.

The road was broad, and had been once well macadamized, but when we crossed, it was suffered to fall into disrepair, on account of the building of the railway, and was gradually being obliterated by the drifting of the sand.

Every four hours we stopped for some time at a refreshment station, where we eat English dishes and drank Nile-water—all brought from Cairo; from which place all the food has to be carried even to Suez.

Once or twice during the day we saw the mirage, which did not deceive my eyes, but several of our party insisted that it was water, and would not be convinced of their error till we arrived at Cairo.

About two o'clock we came in sight of the dark green valley of the Nile. Soon afterwards some of us spied out the pyramids far to the left. Then we saw, in the low ground before us, the city of Victory, "Al Kahireh," its minarets rising above the masses of the trees. Soon we passed a very large white building which we were told was a new barrack for the Pasha's troops, and then passing abruptly from the white sands of the desert to the rich green plains of the river, the road wound among fertile fields and beautiful gardens. The houses, at first sparse, became thicker and thicker, the road was crowded with Arabs and other natives, occasionally we passed a European carriage, with fine blood horses, then (last evidence of approaching civilization) we met numbers of English people on donkeys, and finally, at four o'clock, we were set down in front of Shepherd's hotel, which looks on a large public garden.

This ends my travels in the East. I had to hurry on to Europe, and in three days more was steaming out of Alexandria in the *Pera*, having seen neither the pyramids nor any other sight at Cairo. This loss I hope to make up some day, but India I shall probably never see again. In fact, few countries repay a second visit, and India least of all. But I can confidently recommend it to that large and increasing class who are at a loss for a field in which to exercise the travelling propensities of our race. Europe has almost become cockney; Egypt and the Holy Land are fast descending to the same level. Everywhere you meet with people speaking your own language, which is of itself disagreeable; and what is worse, they are often not at all the sort of people you want to see. It is a bore to be disturbed, in a fit of enthusiasm over some remnant of antiquity, by a troop of ladies dressed in the last Paris fashions, and accompanied by papa, wearing a brown shooting jacket, and carrying in one hand a foot rule, in the other the ubiquitous "Murray." In fact, it may be set down for an axiom, that the moment Murray publishes a guide-book on a country, that country is no place for the truly enterprising traveller. He flies, like the Indian of America, from the haunts of the pale face.

To such a one India furnishes a refuge. There are so few English that all one need know of them are the comforts and conveniences which their government provides for his journey. The distance is nothing in these days of steam. One may go from America to Bombay in six weeks, and within a few years New York and Delhi will be not more than forty days apart. I have been that time in coming from Liverpool to New York. In India one can travel more luxuriously than in Europe, through countries where a white man's face is scarcely ever seen. The safety is far greater than in the streets of a great European or American city; and the expense will not exceed the cost of the same length of time spent in European travel.

CHAPTER XXXV.

CLIMATE AND HISTORY OF INDIA

Size of the Country—Not Thickly Settled—Rainy Season—Cold Season—Hot Season—Unfit for a Residence of Europeans—Effect on their Health—Origin of the Present Inhabitants of India—The Hindoo Conquest—Remnants of the Aborigines—The Four Castes--Changes in Them—Arguments in Favour of this Hypothesis—Mahommedan Invasions—Tamerlane—Foundation of Mogul Empire by Babur—Akbur—Shah Jehan—Aurungzeeb—Decay of the Empire—Revolts—Maharattas—Rajpoots—Death of Aurungzeeb—The Seekhs—Utter Disorganization—Nadur Shah's Invasion—Rise of the English—Conduct of the Company toward Conquered Princes—Annexation Contrary to the Company's Policy—Character of Native Dynasties—Government of Dependent States.

THE greater part of India is an immense plain. The whole extent of country, including all the dominions of the East India Company, is 1,457,000 square miles, of which more than one half is directly under English government, and the remainder is more or less subject to British influence. India is, therefore, as extensive as all the United States, not including the Territories. The population of India is now reckoned at 180,000,000, which gives 123 inhabitants to the square mile. It cannot, therefore, be considered a thickly settled country, while England supports over three hundred inhabitants to the square mile, and some states of Europe even more.

The climate is very hot, and the year is not divided, as in the temperate zones, into four seasons, but into three periods, each of which has its peculiar characteristics. The "rainy season," or monsoon, includes the months of June, July, August, and September. It is the season of production, and the yield of the land depends upon its regularity, and the amount of rain which falls. The quantity of rain is greatest and most equable upon the coast, and especially in the west; but in the great valley of the Ganges, and in the Dĕkkun, it happens sometimes that the rains are so slight as to be insufficient for the vegetation of the crops. Great droughts and famines were thus not of rare occurrence, particularly in the valley of the Ganges. The construction of the Ganges Canal by the East India Company, has, however, done much to remedy the uncertainty of the seasons, by providing for a vast system of artificial irrigation, which insures the productiveness of many millions of acres of land, the yield of which was formerly fearfully precarious. The disastrous results of a famine, or short crop, are much greater in India than in any other country, as the great mass of the people have no savings to rely upon; but, on the contrary, have usually pledged in advance the yield of each year, as security for money borrowed at the beginning of the season. The consideration of this fact places in very strong light the benefits conferred upon India by the Company in the construction of this canal and other great works of irrigation.

The "cold season" follows the rains, and continues during the months of October, November, December, January, and February. It is never very cold, to our ideas, since the mean temperature* of January in Calcutta is 67°; in Madras, 77°; and in Bombay, 78°. On the highlands in the southern part of India, and in Hindoostan, the average would be lower at this season, and for two or three months it generally freezes in the night. No rain falls during the cold season, or the hot weather which follows it.

The "hot season" begins toward the end of February, and lasts until the beginning of the rains in June. The average of the thermometer, in the month of May, when the heat is the greatest, is about 85° in Calcutta, Bombay, and Madras; while in New York, Philadelphia, and Boston, the mean temperature does not exceed 70° during the month of July, which is with us the hottest part of the year. The "rainy season" is also hot, but the heat is not so extreme as during the prevalence of the dry, hot winds from the desert, which blow during the hot season, properly so called.

As India extends over two thousand miles of latitude, the

* That is the mean of the temperature by day and night.

seasons, of course, vary somewhat. In the north, the cold weather lasts longer. On the western coast, the rains are more severe. In the south, the hot season occupies a greater part of the year. Still, the climate throughout India, except upon the mountain ranges, would unfit it for the permanent residence of a white race, even were the fevers of the country, which depend more on the soil than the climate, put out of consideration. Functional derangements of the liver attack almost every European resident; and abscess of that vital organ sweeps away large numbers of them yearly. No course of regimen, or precautions, however stringent, are found to give immunity from this disease, although over-indulgence in ardent spirits—a vice lamentably prevalent among the European soldiers, and principally occasioned by the monotony of their lives—certainly favours the development of this malady. On the other hand, total abstinence from stimulants so debilitates the constitution as to render it peculiarly liable to the fevers of the country, which are almost equally dangerous. The following facts appear by a table of the mortality among the European soldiers and officers in India, taken from official documents.

It is estimated that there are always, on the average, 129 men out of 1,000 in the hospital, and that the name of each soldier appears three times a year on the sick-list. As to the mortality, which is in England 1½ per cent., it is in Bengal 7 per cent. Those regiments, however, are fortunate, whose mortality remains within these limits, for there are others which see their entire force renewed within a few years. Thus, the 98th regiment, the effective force of which, on disembarkation, was as high as 718 men, had only 109 men of the original force remaining, after eight years' residence. Frightful as these figures are, they cannot be compared to the mortality among the children, of whom entire generations disappear, leaving only here and there a puny survivor. The following table, borrowed from official documents, and giving the mean of twenty years, will convey a tolerably exact idea of the annual mortality among the army of the three Presidencies.

	BENGAL.	MADRAS.	BOMBAY.
European Officers,	29 per mille.		
" Soldiers,	74 " "	39 per mille.	51 per mille.
Native Sepoys,	18 " "	21 " "	13 " "

It will be seen by this table that the Presidency of Madras is that in which European soldiers are least tried by the climate. In general, it is calculated that to replace the losses by natural causes alone, European soldiers in India must be recruited at the rate of 10 per cent. per annum.

The above figures give as accurate information as can be obtained with respect to the effect of the climate on Europeans; and they are even below the mark, since the European soldier is carefully looked after, and guarded from unnecessary exposure to the sun or weather; and when enfeebled by long residence on the plains, is removed to one of the sanitaria on the mountains, where the bracing air soon strengthens his constitution, and brings back to his cheek the ruddy glow of health. The best commentary upon the influence of the climate on Europeans is found in the fact that there is no such thing known as *a third generation of Europeans born in India*, and this fact alone would prove that India can never become extensively and permanently colonized by the English, but can only be, at best, a temporary sphere of action for their energy and enterprise.

The origin of the present inhabitants of India is involved in much obscurity. There is almost no authentic history before the time of the first Moosulman invasion, about A. D. 950. The natives of India differ too much in all respects, in the various parts of the country, for us to suppose that they have a common descent, while, at the same time, the universal diffusion of the Hindoo religion, and the Sanscrit element in most of the languages, would seem, at first sight, according to the principles of ethnography, to point to such a common origin. The theory which at present finds most favour among those who have given attention to the subject, is, that at a remote period, there was a great invasion from the North West, of a white, Sanscrit-speaking, *Hindoo* race, who found India peopled by various independent nations of blacks, speaking different languages, and having different religions. It is alsc believed that the barbarous races of the Bheels, Khonds, Kholees, &c., are the descendants of the original races, who have continued to the present day unmixed with Hindoo blood, and unaffected by Hindoo customs or religion. They are in a most degraded state, believe in a low form of paganism, and it is with the greatest difficulty that human sacrifices have been at length abolished among them by the exertions of the Company's agents.

The Hindoo or Caucasian conquerors were, it is supposed, divided into three castes: the Brahmuns, or Priests; the Kshatrias, or Warriors; and the Vaishyas, or Traders. After the subjugation of the country, the enslaved populations were formed into a fourth caste, the Soodras, or Slaves. The whole population was in subjection to the Brahmuns, for whose use and behoof, according to the Hindoo system, all things exist. The mass of the people, must (if the Institutes of Mĕnoo are allowed to be the code then in force) have been in a state of abject slavery, in comparison with which even the Mahommedan tyranny was freedom. By some means or other, in course of time, the two intermediate castes of Kshatrias and Vaishyas disappeared, and the Soodras came to play a much more important part in the political system; while at the same time the relative position of the Brahmuns was lowered, probably chiefly on account of intermarriage with lower castes. In fact, such an iron despotism as that described in the Institutes of Mĕnoo, could hardly have been supposed to continue unmitigated for the two thousand years during which the Hindoo system was probably in force. To support this theory, the following arguments are produced: First, the Sanscrit language puts it beyond doubt that some of the inhabitants of India must have come from the original seat of the Iranian races; but on the other hand the great number of races now found in India, the black skin, and other distinguishing marks of race, show equally clearly that the mass of the present population had not such an origin—while the debased and barbarous tribes of Khonds, &c., seem to present a type of the original people at the time of the invasion. Again, the number of distinct languages in India is, I think, thirteen. Of these, three or four, at least, are of different origin, one from the other, and their resemblance to Sanscrit is only on the surface—showing that the people who spoke them must have been of races distinct in their origin, and also pointing clearly, by the intermixture of Sanscrit, to the influence of the tongue spoken by the conquering people. Another very strong argument is, the great and universal corruption of the Hindoo religion, which, as expounded in the ancient Vedas, was comparatively pure, and, as some say, a monotheism. It is now a system of utter idolatry, and the deities who are worshipped are not such as would spring from the development or corruption of the original religion, but are, in many instances, evidently introduced from without. The vitality of the aboriginal religions, asserting their supremacy over the Brahmunical systems, is seen even more in the services by which these new gods are worshipped, and in the different classes of men whose privilege it is, in many parts of the country, to officiate in the temples—a privilege which, by the very essence of true Hindooism, is confined to the Brahmuns. So far have these changes been carried that, over a large part of India, but little of the early Hindoo religious system remains, excepting the general respect shown to Brahmuns, the Sanscrit services, and the institution of castes. Perhaps the strongest argument of all, however, is the degraded position which the Soodras, the mass of the population, occupied in the original Hindoo system. Their situation was one of such abject, utter degradation and slavery, that the only reasonable explanation of it we can give, is that it was imposed upon them by an irresistible force from without. In other words, that the present inhabitants of India, or at least the Hindoo portion of them, are not Caucasians, but the descendants of a number of black, aboriginal races who were overcome and reduced to bondage by the original Hindoo or Caucasian invaders; that these invaders were in numbers much inferior to the conquered races, and have, in time, become almost swallowed up in them —but not before the Brahmunical laws, worship and language had, if not supplanted, at least produced an ineffaceable impression upon the institutions of the country.

If the original conquerors of India were men of courage and patriotism, their numbers were so small that they failed to impress these characteristics upon the nation with which they eventually became amalgamated; and if under them India was united in one government, it certainly soon became broken up into a number of separate kingdoms, the want of union among which, added to the absence of national sympathy, and the cowardly character of the natives, made an invasion a matter of but little difficulty. Accordingly, from the time of the first establishment of Mahommedanism in Arabia and Persia, we find one force after another sweeping down upon the fertile plains of India, devastating, pillaging, and laying waste—and generally returning thereafter to the place whence they came. The first permanent establishment of the Moosulman supremacy was in the year 1206, under Kootub ood Deen. From this time forward various Mahommedan dynasties succeeded each other upon the throne of Delhi. The power of the Emperors was more or less extended according to their energy, and much of their time was occupied in crushing the rebellions of their own subordinates in distant provinces. Few of them died quietly in their beds; and usurpation was their general title to the imperial power. The most remarkable Mahommedan invasion was that of Tamerlane, A. D. 1398. He was a Mogul Tartar chieftain, who subdued Persia, and finally extended his conquests to India. After stripping that country of all the treasures and jewels he could find, massacreing hundreds of thousands in cold blood, burning Delhi under circumstances of the greatest cruelty and treachery, and overthrowing the existing Moosulman dynasty, he suddenly returned to Persia. His return was marked by the taking of Meeruth, on which occasion he put "every soul within it to the sword." His course homeward was distinguished by similar ravages; "he marked his way with fire and sword, leaving anarchy, famine and pestilence behind him."

After Tamerlane's invasion, there was no fixed government until, in 1526, Babur, his descendant of the sixth generation, who was the Sooltan of Cabool, again invaded India, and founded the dynasty which has been ever since on the throne. Under the Emperor Akbur, who ruled from 1556 to 1605, the Moosulman Empire in India reached its greatest extent. Akbur's sway extended over all that we now call India, and during his reign even the most remote provinces were submissive to the central authority at Delhi. Under the grandson of Akbur, Shah Jehan, whose reign began in 1627, the Empire attained its greatest glory, and it was by this monarch that many of the principal architectural remains of India were erected. Still the reign of Shah Jehan was far from peaceful and undisturbed. The fabric of Mahommedan supremacy gave evident tokens of how slight a foundation it possessed. The usual precautions which the Emperor had taken, on ascending the throne, by putting to death his brother and all the other members of the imperial family, except his own descendants, did not suffice to prevent attempts at usurpation. He passed several years in endeavouring to subdue conflicting rebellions organized by his sons, whom he had made viceroys. The third son, Aurungzeeb, after a double treachery to his father and to one of his revolted brothers, whose rebellion he had sworn to support, at length obtained the throne in 1658, and confined his father in a prison, where he dragged out the last years of his life. Aurungzeeb's reign lasted fifty years. Under him, the Empire, although outwardly as splendid as ever, became thoroughly pervaded by that incurable decay which, after his death, destroyed in a few years the vast and blood-cemented fabric of the Mogul power in India. Even during his lifetime disorganization was prevented only by his constant vigilance and the commanding power of his master-mind. After seizing the imperial power, Aurungzeeb was for some time annoyed by his brothers, who continued to support by arms their pretensions to the Musnud. Finally, however, he overcame all opposition, and rid himself of his troublesome relatives by summary executions.

It is during the reign of Aurungzeeb that we first hear of the Maharattas, who were then a warlike tribe of Hindoos dwelling in the highlands of the west of India, south of the

Nurbudda. Under the able command of a chieftain called Seewajee, they began that course which finally ended in the conquest of almost the whole of India, and the total prostration of the Mogul power. But the Maharattas were not the only enemies who troubled the peace of Aurungzeeb's reign. The Afghans revolted, set up a king, and coined money in his name. The Rajpoots, too, a nation of warriors occupying the country between the Jumna and Nurbudda, and that region which was afterwards erected by the British into the kingdom of Oude, organized a formidable insurrection. And to crown the misfortunes of the Emperor, his youngest son, Akbur, took advantage of the absence of his father from the capital, to assume the reins of government, and caused himself to be proclaimed sovereign. The young prince, however, did not long hold out, and was forced to take refuge among the Maharattas. The Rajpoot war, also, was concluded after some years. But the Maharatta power kept assuming more and more formidable proportions. Their original and ablest chieftain had died, his successor had been tortured and murdered at Delhi, but they found other leaders, and renewed their attacks in larger numbers and with greater strength. The government of Aurungzeeb had long lost much control over the Děkkun and southern India, which had consequently been broken up into numerous petty principalities. These became an easy prey to the Maharattas, whose power now assumed such threatening dimensions that the Emperor himself took the field against them, with an army, which, with its attendants, is said greatly to have exceeded one million of souls. The imperial force was, however, everywhere unfortunate, and the anxieties of Aurungzeeb were increased by renewed hostilities from the Rajpoots, and the revolt of a Hindoo tribe called *Jats*. The successes of the Maharattas continued in the Děkkun, into which country the Emperor had advanced to meet them, and the last act of Aurungzeeb's life was the successful conduct of a dangerous retreat to the city of Aurungabad, in what are now the territories of the Nizam. In the twelve years succeeding Aurungzeeb's death, five sovereigns held, one after another, the imperial power, now everywhere broken by the dissensions among the Mahommedan rulers, by the greatly extended ravages of the Maharattas, and by the rise, in the vicinity of Lahor, of a new and formidable tribe, that of the Seekhs. The formation of this body is due to a religious enthusiast called Nanik, who pretended to have received a new revelation, but the Seekhs first received a definite political system, and were expanded into the proportions of a nation, under a leader known as Gooroo Govind. Among them all distinctions of caste were abolished, and Moosulmans were placed in an equal position with Hindoos. All Seekhs were compelled constantly to go armed; they were not allowed to cut or shave the hair on the head or body, and were prohibited from wearing on the head any article which had been sewed. The superiority of the Brahmuns was still, however, preserved, and the cow retained all the sanctity attributed under the Hindoo system to that animal. The incursions of the Seekhs were marked by greater barbarity than even those of the Maharattas. The only object of the latter was booty. They tortured the inhabitants of cities to obtain a knowledge of their secret hiding places for property, and committed other ravages only that they might force the conquered countries to submit to their demand of the *chout*, or fourth part of the revenue. As long as this was punctually paid, it insured immunity. The Seekhs, however, never made any such compromises. Elphinstone says, "They destroyed the mosques, and butchered the moollahs; their rage was not restrained by any considerations of religion, or by any mercy for age or sex: whole towns were massacred with wanton barbarity; and even the bodies of the dead were dug up and thrown out to the beasts and birds of prey."

While the Empire was in this distracted condition, a new and more terrible invasion from without came to draw away men's attention from their internal difficulties, and to complete the destruction of the Mogul power.

Nadur Shah, one of the princes of Persia, had usurped the throne of that country, and put out the eyes of the former sovereign. He now directed his attention to India, and in 1738 began his march upon Delhi. The broken power of the

Emperor offered but slight opposition, and the imperial city was again in the hands of a foreign invader. His occupation of Delhi was attended by a general massacre of the inhabitants. The rich were put to torture to obtain their money, and the world-renowned treasures of the Mogul court were plundered and carried away by the conqueror. His stay was less than two months, and the amount of property which he took away with him is estimated at from £32,000,000 to £125,000,000.

The Mogul power was now completely broken. The subsequent history of India is one scene of invasions, revolts, and contests between the Afghans and the various warlike tribes whose origin has been spoken of above. The deputies and viceroys of the Emperor generally proclaimed their independence. The Maharattas were more than ever powerful, and extended their conquests over Hindoostan. All law and order disappeared, and the condition of the mass of the population must have been most wretched.

Affairs were in this condition when the British first appeared upon the field of action. Their conquests were directed against these revolted dependants of the Emperor; against robber chieftains who had made themselves the kings of a day; and against marauding bands like the Pindarrees, who came and were gone, not attempting to establish any government, but leaving smoking ruins, death and devastation wherever they had passed.

The throne of Delhi was entirely prostrate, and but for the efforts of the British would no doubt soon have been permanently abolished. It was, however, found more convenient to use the Emperor's name. For the advantage which that gave them, the Company must be allowed to have made an ample return in the restoration of the imperial dignity, and the enormous pension of £150,000 sterling, per annum, which has ever since been punctually paid.

The substantial power of the Padshah was never restored; in fact, such an act would have been equivalent to again plunging the unhappy countries over which his nominal rule extended, into all the miseries from which they had just escaped.

The power of the revolted wuzeers, and of the chieftains of the Maharattas and other tribes, was, however, confirmed by the Company. The Wuzeer of Oude, who had profited by the weakness of the last Emperors to proclaim his independence, under the title of Nawáb, was raised by the English to the royal dignity, with the view of opposing a strong and independent power against any attempts that might be made by the Emperor of Delhi to regain the position of supremacy once held by his house. The course of the Company in this instance is an example of what has always been their policy. Annexation, as being costly, hazardous, and likely to occasion protracted and expensive wars, has always been shunned. The Company has avoided war, when possible, knowing that peace is, in a commercial point of view, more desirable than any extension of their possessions. When, however, in the course of events, hostilities became necessary, either for self-preservation, or for the protection of their territories and subjects, no greater exhibition of force was resorted to than the necessities of each case absolutely required. Whenever it was possible, the ruler of a conquered country was left on the *gúddee*, and his power was put on a much firmer base than it had ever previously rested on. In many instances the rank and authority of conquered princes were raised and extended by the Honourable Company with a view of securing powerful allies against other native rulers, and at the same time avoiding the trouble, expense, and responsibility of administering the newly-conquered country. These princes, it should be remembered, were seldom of old dynasties. They were mostly adventurers, or the sons of adventurers.* They had attained their position by fraud and violence, and were liable at any moment to be deposed by similar means. When, therefore, their power became vested in the Company by the right of conquest, it would have been perfectly just and equitable had

* Like Hydur Ali, who was a common soldier; the original Gaikwar, who was a cow-herd; the first Peshwa, who was of equally humble origin; and those two powerful princes known as Sindia and Holkar, who were robber-chieftains of the Maharattas.

they been absolutely deposed and their country annexed to the other British dominions. This course would also have been much the most advantageous for the conquered countries, and has been, in fact, the recent policy of the Indian government. In the earlier years of the Company's rule, however, they were not aware of their own power, and sought, by a consistent course of concession, and the enlistment on their side of native interest, to strengthen a series of conquests so extensive and so rapid as to be bewildering. An additional motive against annexation was, that before the real relations between a native ruler and his subjects were understood, the latter were supposed to entertain toward their princes some sentiments of affection and loyalty, which, as well as their feelings of patriotism, would, it was thought, be shocked by a violent transfer of the sceptre. The wonderful success of the English, and the consolidation of their power which is the result of a wise and uniform administration, have removed the first objections to annexation. The discovery that a native prince governs as a brutal master tyrannising over cringing slaves, has dispelled any dread of opposition from the fidelity of the native population to their old masters; while the great development of those parts of the country which have been annexed, the rise in the value of property, the peace and prosperity which the subjects of the Company have enjoyed, when contrasted with the insecurity, anarchy, and misrule of all the native territories, point out annexation as the most profitable, if not the only truly lenient and benevolent policy.

A great deal of nonsense has been talked about these native princes, who have been treated with only too great clemency and consideration by the Honourable Company. In cases where it was deemed imprudent to intrust them with the management of their old dominions, they were always pensioned with the greatest liberality, and left at perfect liberty to live where and how they pleased, within certain limits of country—a treatment widely different from the trampling to death by elephants, the tortures, or the confinement in an iron cage which would have been their lot had their conquerors been natives. In cases where the old ruler was left in power, he was usually placed in an independent position. Tributes were sometimes imposed; sometimes not. The Company's government only retained the privilege of regulating the succession to the throne (a power which was generally exercised only to interfere in behalf of the regular successor against an attempted usurpation); and merely required that the native sovereign should govern with some justice, and maintain a certain amount of order; to secure which, and keep him in mind of his position, a British resident Agent, usually called simply "the Resident," was maintained at every native court. This officer had no power but such as resulted from his personal character and influence. The subject princes were also required to keep up a certain army, which was to be partly officered by Englishmen, and to the services of which the Company were, under certain circumstances, entitled. No terms could be more liberal than these, and they were always scrupulously observed by the Company. The right, which was of course inherent in the Honourable Company, to resume the sovereign power which had been once in their hands, in case of the non-performance by the native princes of their part of the agreement, was never enforced, except where, as in the case of Oude, the degradation of the court, the lawlessness of the capital, and the anarchy which prevailed throughout the country, were not only ruining the subject state itself, but threatened the peace and security of the adjacent territories of the Company. Even in such cases, the deposed monarchs were treated with a lavish liberality to which their previous merits gave them very little claim.

Never has there been a conquest more unwillingly made than was that of the English in India. The Company was at first exclusively mercantile, and trade was their only object. Every war was costly, diminished their revenue, and lowered their dividends. Accordingly we find the Board of Directors again and again commanding the Governors in India not to allow themselves to be dragged into war, and to endure anything in preference to taking up arms. But their wishes were overruled by Providence. The Indian government was forced*

* The wars in Afghanistan and Ṣindh, if exceptions to this rule, cannot be

into one contest after another, until, in less than one hundred years from their first great battle, under Lord Clive, at Plassey, they found themselves masters of the land from Cape Comorin to the Himalayas, and from Burmah to Afghanistan.

Henceforth India is delivered from tyranny, anarchy, and devastating invasions. The degrading sway of the Brahmuns, and the despotism of the Mahommedan rulers, are alike abolished. It is to be hoped that a few years will see the remains of the last native governments wiped away, and that India will be governed entirely by the beneficent rule of a Christian people; under whom alone civilization can be introduced, the immense resources of the country developed, and the Hindoos enjoy that peace and freedom to which they are entitled by centuries of oppression and suffering.

laid at the door of the Company. Like the annexation of Oude, they were forced upon the East India Company by the British Ministry through the Board of Control, and were entirely acts of the Home Government, although conducted in the name of the Company, and at its expense.

CHAPTER XXXVI.

ENGLISH GOVERNMENT IN INDIA.

Abolition of Company's Trading Privileges—Board of Control—Government of India Nominally in the Hands of the Directors, but really under the Control of the Ministry—Civil Servants Appointed by Examination—Objections to this System—Unfitness of Natives for Government Employ—Government in India—District Magistrates—Salaries—Character of the Civil Service—Native Employees—Uncovenanted Service—Universal Lying—Instances from Real Life—Rules of Testimony—Civil Law of India—Mild Criminal Code—Thugs—Dukoitee—Religious Murderers and Robbers—Infanticide and other Crimes—Suttee and Human Sacrifices—Poisoners—Peculiarities of Crime in India—Thieves—Stealing a Sheet from under a Man Sleeping—Precautions—Disregard of Capital Punishment—Black Water—Blowing from Guns—Model Prisons—Caste in Jail—Smoking—Licentiousness—Discourteous Manners of English to Native Gentlemen—What is a Gentleman?—Difficulties of Magistrates—Native Police—Their Corruption and Tyranny—Torture in India—Bribery and Corruption—The Remedy—Causes of the Moral Degradation of the Hindoos.

UP to 1833 the East India Company had continued to be a commercial company, ruling India in the name of the Great Mogul. At that time the Company's commercial power was taken away by the English Parliament, on the occasion of the renewal of their charter.* This measure was, commercially, of the greatest advantage to India, but conferred upon that country even greater benefits indirectly, by leaving the Company's servants free to devote their entire attention to gov-

* Under the charter of 1793, the first provision was made for private enterprise, and the Company were obliged to provide 6,000 tons of shipping every year for the accommodation of private traders. At the next renewal of the charter in 1814, the Company lost the *monopoly* of the Eastern trade, except that of tea. The unrestricted competition of private capital in the India trade soon took most of the business out of the hands of the Company, while the whole amount of business done was, by it, largely increased, as appears by this table:

	Exports by Company.	By Private Traders.	Total.
1814.	£826,558	£1,048,132	£1,874,690
1832.	£149,193	£3,601,093	£3,750,286

ernment, the development of the resources of the country, and internal improvements. The latter had been so much neglected that, in 1825, it is said, there did not exist twenty miles of carriage road in Bengal.

In the year 1833 the government of India was in fact taken out of the hands of the East India Company; or rather they remained the agents for its administration, but all the higher attributes of sovereignty were withdrawn from them. The royal Government assumed the responsibility of defraying the interest on the capital stock, guaranteeing to all stockholders 10½ per cent. annual dividend, and retaining the privilege of buying up all the stock, or what portions they pleased, at the rate of £200 for every £100 of stock.

In return for this assumption of responsibility, the king's Government exercised a controlling influence in the affairs of the Company. As early as 1784 a royal supervision had been exercised over the Indian government by means of a Board of Control. This Board has since acquired a supreme influence in all more important matters. The Board of Control consists of six members, appointed by the Crown, with a President, who is always a member of the Cabinet, and discharges the duties of Secretary of State for India. Every resolution or despatch of the Board of Directors must go for approval before the Board of Control, who have the power of sending the orders to India, or withholding them at will. In cases where the Board of Control and the Directors disagree as to what course it is proper to take under certain circumstances, it is the former who decide. In fact, the only unrestricted power left to the Directors by the last amendment to their charter in 1853, is that of appointing cadets to the army and a few of the higher officers of government in India. All orders and despatches continue to be in the name of the Board of Directors, but, in reality, for many years, the entire direction and responsibility of Indian policy has been in the hands of Parliament, by means of the Ministry, of whom the President of the Board of Control is one.* The

* The Ministry may send to India any despatch or order that they please, either in the name of the Board of Directors or of its Secret Committee. In

details of administration always, however, have continued to be principally entrusted to the Board of Directors, at least so far as they were matters for the consideration of the home authorities.

The whole appointment of the civil servants for India was formerly vested in the Directors, but this valuable privilege was taken away by the last charter, and they are now chosen according to the result of competitive examinations, to which all British subjects are admissible. The new system is an experiment, with respect to the success of which those who are best informed about India are most distrustful. Under the new system many men must be appointed whose antecedents are not well known, and who, when they arrive in India, and are placed in charge of large districts, far removed from all supervision and control, may fall a prey to those numerous temptations by which the Indian official is surrounded. Against these the most powerful barrier was the honour of his family, which every civilian appointed under the old system feels to be dependent on his conduct in a service, in the ranks of which he probably has more than one relation, and to many of the other members of which he is personally known.

Another great objection to the new arrangement is, that under it natives are eligible to high civil employs; and will probably obtain them, as they have generally quite ability enough to prepare themselves for passing any examination which may be appointed. It is a sad fact that the natives are wholly unfit for any position of responsibility in which they are not under constant European supervision. In connection with this I cannot express my own views, and those of all well-informed persons with whom I have conversed, more clearly than in the words of M. De Valbezen. After remarking upon the apparent injustice and abuse of power, in the systematic exclusion of natives from all high employs, he goes on to say: "Besides, the injustice is more apparent than

the former case the Directors must have seen the despatch or order, but cannot veto it; in the latter they need not even have seen it. By means of this extraordinary system, the Company has been made responsible to public opinion for many acts done in their name, but which were entirely opposed to their wishes and policy.

real: except infinitesimal exceptions, it must be acknowledged that it would be impossible to find natives capable of worthily filling the higher employs. Even had they the energy, the intellectual powers which are necessary, they would be destitute of that love of truth, that high respect for duty, that delicate sentiment of honour, which are as necessary to the magistrate as to the military officer. Whoever has the least experience of their character will grant this without hesitation." An American missionary, well known in another capacity among the religious community of this city, and whose views are in every way entitled to the highest respect, expresses even stronger opinions when speaking of the capacity of the Hindoos for self-government, and, by implication, of their fitness for being entrusted with the government of others. He says: "They are an ignorant, depraved, and heathen people; and yet both English and American writers speak of them as if they could be governed in the same way as British subjects or American citizens. A greater mistake it would be difficult to make; and our meaning will be clearer to most of our readers when we say that the coloured people of this country, free and bond, are a hundred-fold better prepared for self-government than are the great mass of the Hindoos."

At the head of the government in India is the Governor General, whose residence is at Calcutta, and who has the complete control of the whole administration. He is assisted by a council of four members, who compose, with him, the Indian Legislature. All their acts, however, are subject to the royal approval. Under the Governor General are the Lieutenant Governor of Bengal, the Lieutenant Governor of the North Western Provinces, who lives at Agra, and the Commissioners of the Punjab and Oude. The Governors of Madras and Bombay, though possessing legislative powers for their respective Presidencies, are also inferior to the Governor General.

The subordinate administrative duties are in the hands of the Magistrate and Collector of each district. In Bengal each magistrate has under his charge a district of three thousand two hundred square miles, and one million of souls, on the average. Within this district he has the entire care of the police, roads, &c., and also limited judicial powers. As this is quite as much as one man can attend to, he is assisted by a Collector, who regulates all the financial business of government, determines the assessment of land, restrains exactions of zĕmindars, and has the general fiscal charge of the district. In the smaller Presidencies, the duties of collector are exercised by the magistrate. Besides these officials, there are the judges, of whom there are, on the average, two to every three districts. Their principal occupation is to hear appeals from the native judicial officers, whose powers have lately been so much extended that almost all suits come before them in the first instance.

Both magistrates and collectors are aided by European deputies and assistants. The judges, however, except in Bombay, have only native subordinates. In addition to these officers, the civil service also comprehends the special departments of the customs, the salt excise, and the opium monopoly, which give employment to many Europeans.

The whole number of European employees of all sorts, in the civil service, properly so called, is under nine hundred. Their pay is on the most liberal scale. The salaries of magistrates and collectors range from $6,000 to $19,000 per annum, and those of the judges average $15,000. These amounts are found, however, not to be too large, and very few fortunes are made in the Company's service. In the earliest days of the British rule in India, the salaries were very low, and the Company's servants were too often tempted to neglect the interests of their masters for private speculations, by which immense fortunes were amassed, and to accept bribes in the discharge of the governmental duties with which they were entrusted. The Company soon, however, found it their interest to attract men of a higher class to their service, and, at the same time, to put them out of the reach of these temptations, by ample salaries. Accordingly, the salaries were fixed on a liberal scale, toward the end of the last century, and have continued almost the same since that time. The present civil servants are men of liberal education and high character; their labours are onerous and irksome; the difficulties they meet with in doing justice, almost insurmountable; the temptations to which they are exposed, great and continual; but since the time when the service was placed on its present footing, and men of standing were attracted into its ranks, probably no body of government officials in the world have ever been so entirely free from every taint of bribery or dishonourable conduct. The best testimony to the character of the European agents of government is found in the opinions of the natives themselves, who look upon an Englishman as a paragon of almost impossible uprightness and probity, and among whom a common expression for absolute truth is, "Ungleeze kee bat"—an Englishman's word. As their opinions, however, cannot be presented here, I take much pleasure in quoting the words of M. De Valbezen, who was intimately acquainted with his subject, and whose expressions are the more valuable, as the policy of England is, in many cases, far from meeting his approval. After remarking upon the very different life led by the present officials in India, from that luxurious existence enjoyed by their "old Indian" predecessors, he goes on to account for the fact, that, even with their present moderate style of living, their apparently ample salaries scarcely cover their expenses. He attributes this to the fact that now-a-days one of the first aims of every civilian is to get married, and that the great expenses of a family in India, the necessity for sending his wife and children to the Himalayas during the hot weather, the expense of sending the children to England to be educated, and the large establishment which a man of family has to keep up, amount to more than the sums which were formerly spent in costly wines, luxurious dinners, and gambling. He then goes on to say:—"The high salaries* of India, which have occasioned so many attacks, and caused so much envy, furnish doubtless the means of providing comfortably for the expenses of a family, but nothing beyond. They are, besides, the price of severe and incessant labour, and if all those who cry out against the am-

* The average salaries of the nine hundred civil servants are £1,000 per annum. This does not include the salary of the Governor General, or a few other of the highest magistrates.

ple pay of the civil service could see, close at hand, the life of the exile in an unhealthy climate, with its profound *ennui*, their envy for those who wear these gilded but heavy chains would doubtless be considerably diminished. We are not so extreme in our admiration of the Honourable Company's civil service, that we can see in it no defects. We do not doubt that its education can be made more perfect; that some of its members have given sad examples of corruption and incapacity, and that others affect the extravagant airs of the Grand Mogul. We only say, on the average, as a body, it is equal to its lofty mission; that never have more upright magistrates, more disinterested collectors, more independent judges presided over the destiny of the native population; that, in one word, the very great majority of the civil servants worthily represent in India one of those nations which march in the van of European civilization."

Beside the European civil servants, there are an immense number of native officials in the employ of the Honourable Company. They do pretty well as long as they are under the immediate eye of their European superiors, but unfortunately cannot be trusted further than they can be overlooked. As, however, it is impossible for the very limited number of European civilians to oversee all the minutiæ of administration, the natives have very considerable opportunities of oppression, extortion, and receiving bribes, and do not neglect them.

The total want of character among the native officials has caused the employment by government of numerous Europeans, mostly sprung from the humbler ranks, and many of them taken from the English troops in India. This branch of the administration is known as the "uncovenanted service," in opposition to the regular civil service described above, which is called the "covenanted service" on account of the regular agreement existing between each member of it and the government. The members of the uncovenanted service are generally employed to oversee the construction of the public works, inspect the roads, and superintend native contractors and workmen. They are a body daily growing in importance. Their pay is not regular, but each man makes the best bargain he can for himself.

The difficulties which the magistrates meet with in the administration of the government, from the unreliability of their native subordinates, are almost incredible; and the numerous acts of injustice, cruelty, and oppression committed in their name, which they know to exist, but can seldom redress, are a constant source of painful reflection.

The administration of justice meets with even greater obstacles from that total disregard of truth which characterises the native. In India, no disgrace attaches to untruth, and it is not uncommon to hear a man say, "I was lying," without ever suspecting that such an admission at all implicated his honour. In the courts of law, the most sacred oaths, on the Korán, Ganges water, or in whatever form they were supposed to be most binding on the conscience of the deponent, having proved totally ineffectual in securing the least regard to veracity, have been all abolished; which has this advantage, that it is now possible for witnesses to give testimony without perjuring themselves. In every bazár in the country, any number of men may be hired to testify to anything, for the small charge of two anas, (6 cents); and I was told by a magistrate who had held office for over fifteen years, that in all that time he did not believe he had ever heard a single deposition which was *entirely true*, and that such depositions as contained any large admixture of truth were the few exceptions in the great mass of evidence, which was *entirely false*. I was much amused by a conversation I had at Agra, with a high-caste Brahmun, whose occupation was that of moonshee, or native clerk understanding English. He was a very well informed person, and had most gentlemanly manners. We had been talking about the reverence shown to the cow in the Hindoo system, and he had been explaining to me by what process of reasoning he came to look upon the cow as his mother, and to regard the butchery of that animal as something worse than matricide. We then went on to speak of the native character generally, and I mentioned the habit of lying as, in my opinion, the "original sin," from which most of their other defects sprang. He denied that untruthfulness was as general as I supposed it to be. Whereupon, I asked him if there was any one whom he would believe rather than his father. He said there was not. On my inquiring which was the most sacred oath among the Hindoos, he said, an oath given with the hand in Ganges water. I then said, "Now suppose, Moonshee, your own father were to swear, with his hand in Ganges water, that a certain statement was true, with regard to which you knew it was his interest to deceive you, would you believe him?" The moonshee at first equivocated, and would not give a direct reply. On my pressing him, however, for a straightforward answer, he at last said: "I think, sir, I should wish for corroborative testimony." The following occurrence was brought to light in the Suddur Adawlut Court in Calcutta. "A *darogah* (native chief of police) had given information of a crime to the district magistrate, adding, that the most active researches had failed in putting him on the track of the perpetrators of the offence. The magistrate, who suspected the probity of his subordinate, announced to him that if in ten days the criminals were not discovered, he should be suspended from his functions. No result having been obtained after the fixed delay, the threat was put in execution, and the darogah was temporarily replaced by an inferior officer, whose zeal was stimulated by the promise of the late darogah's situation if he succeeded in discovering the guilty parties. The new functionary was not more lucky than his predecessor; but, rather than renounce the place promised to his ambition, he caused a reward of a hundred rupees ($50) to be offered to whoever would avow himself guilty of the murder in question. Two beings, in appearance human—in truth, I cannot call them two men—presented themselves to accept the terms offered; but, on account of the competition, the reward was diminished one-half. Hereupon, the police officer invented a narrative in harmony with the testimony of the witnesses. The two individuals made their avowals before the most considerable inhabitants of the village, and the report of the inquest was sent, together with the accused, before the magistrate, who in recompense appointed his faithless subordinate to the post of the deposed darogah. As it had been agreed, in the conditions of the bargain, that the accused should renew their confession before the magistrate, they related to him faithfully, anew, all the details of their imaginary crime; then, believing themselves to have honourably fulfilled all the terms of the contract, they retracted all their previous testimony, when examined before the district judge, denied their previous confessions, and declared that all they had done was to sign certain papers written by the head-man of the village, and that numerous witnesses could testify to their ignorance of the contents of the papers signed by them. These witnesses, whose favourable testimony had, no doubt, been bought by the accused beforehand, were summoned to the assizes; but, whether they were bribed or intimidated by the darogah, they only confirmed the facts elicited on the inquest; adding, that they had heard the avowal of the crime from the mouth of the accused. A condemnation to death terminated the trial. It was only then that the convicts avowed their agreement with the darogah, and were able, luckily for themselves, to bring witnesses to prove that they were in the district jail when the crime was committed." Again: "Some years ago, a rich farmer of the Dooab was accused of having killed a native in a quarrel. Twenty-five witnesses swore, in open court, that they had seen the accused strike the fatal blow; thirty others swore that at the time when the murder was committed, they had seen the accused at a village twenty-five miles off. So far, there is nothing extraordinary in the story—the same thing occurs every day, in every court in India. The amusing part of the occurrence was, that on both sides there was an equal amount of perjury and lying. The farmer had not committed the murder, but, on the other hand, he was not, at the time of its commission, in the village twenty-five miles off, but in his own dwelling, a few steps from the theatre of the crime." I forget the details of numerous other and similar occurrences which I heard of in India. Almost any one who has lived in that country has had many such cases brought to his notice, and he is lucky, indeed, if he is not made the victim of the hired perjurers whom the natives do not hesitate to employ in their legal affairs.

Notwithstanding this state of public morality, the rules of evidence in the courts of law are the same as in England, viz.: that *all testimony must be presumed true, until proved false.* The principal hardship of this rule is experienced when an Englishman is sued by a native, since the latter will bring as many witnesses as are necessary to prove his case, while the former is deprived of such facilities by conscientious scruples. The rigour of the English rule of testimony is, however, much modified by the discretionary power assumed by the magistrate, without which he would find it difficult to extract the few grains of truth from the mass of conflicting evidence daily presented to his notice.

The civil law has been left nearly as it was found at the conquest. The Korán is the rule for the Moosulmans; the Institutes of Mĕnoo form the ground-work of the Hindoo common law. The position of the other native communities, as Parsees and native Christians, has been recently settled, and they are subject to the English law only. The only changes of importance that have been made in the native civil law, are the following: First, a provision that a change in religion shall not affect a man's civil standing. By the old Hindoo law, a man lost caste on conversion to Mahommedanism or Christianity, and became civilly dead, his property going to his heirs. Second, the abolition of slavery, as a social status, recognised by the courts. Third, permission given to widows to marry. By the old Brahmunical law, a widow, though she might be (and many of them were) not over nine years old, could never marry again, but remained with her parents, the drudge of the household, a burden to the family, and treated contemptuously by all. A very large number of them became prostitutes. The evil of the old law can hardly be appreciated unless we remember that in India marriage is not an exceptional state, but *every man* is married, generally when a child; that a large proportion of these boy-husbands naturally die, leaving their widows virgins; and that there is not the same restraint, which in this and other

Christian countries operates by religion and public opinion to curb the indulgence of passion. The fourth, and last great change, is a late law forbidding native princes *to adopt* heirs to their dominions, where no natural heirs exist. This is one of the greatest measures of Lord Dalhousie's administration, and one which has called down the most reprehension in England. It must, however, be considered a great triumph of the highest principles of justice—since no one can contend that the feelings of an individual should be weighed for a moment against the substantial good of millions of human beings, who, as the law formerly stood, would have been banded over, on the demise of the last scion of one line, to a new generation of despots, and a fresh lease of misrule. All these changes were opposed to the principles of Hindooism, and have met with even more opposition in England than in India. Several of them have been the subjects of severe attacks by eminent members of Parliament. Still they are among the greatest benefits conferred by the English upon India, and a verdict upon them may be left with confidence to any number of well-informed philanthropic and Christian men, whose views are not biased by sitting on the "opposition benches."

The criminal code is based upon the "Regulations" published by Lord Cornwallis in 1793. The punishments prescribed are very mild. Sixteen years of prison is the heaviest penalty for Dukoitee (burglary), forgery, perjury, and counterfeiting. Murder is punished by transportation or death, and is the only capital crime. Every capital condemnation has to be forwarded to the Supreme Court for approval.

The evidence demanded by the English rules was found to interfere with the detection and punishment of the Thugs, as the witnesses, whose testimony was necessary for the conviction, were often living at points thousands of miles distant from the scene of the trial. This resulted from the habit which distinguished the Thugs, of never remaining long in one place; and also from most of their victims being travellers. It was, therefore, found necessary to establish a special department for the suppression of Thúggee. This department has agents all over India, employed to take the testimony of all essential witnesses wherever they may be found. The Thúggee department is also charged with the suppression of Dukoitee, a crime which consists in the robbing and burning of villages by armed bodies of men.

Both these crimes are fearfully common in India, and the former was conducted with so much secrecy that it was years before the British discovered the existence of a society whose whole occupation consisted in systematic murder, in honour of the detestable goddess Bhowánee, to whose service they had devoted themselves. After the appointment of the Thúggee Commission, 1,562 Thugs were arrested, tried, and condemned in one year. One of these murderers, Feringhee (who has been made an actor in Dumas' novel, "The Wandering Jew"), confessed having committed 779 murders, and regretted that a confinement of twelve years in prison had prevented his completing the thousand, which his ambition had led him to hope for.

The crime of Dukoitee, which has been mentioned above, is also very prevalent. It is also committed under the protection of Bhowánee, and, as in the case of Thúggee, religious services precede the commission of the crime. The Dukoits usually go in large bands, and attack a village. Their habit is to torture the principal inhabitants, until they confess the hiding places of their money. The tortures they employ are very various; but although there are several more severe, the most common, because the most convenient, is to tie the sufferer's hands together with tow soaked in oil, which is then lighted, and the fire fed with fresh oil until confession is extorted. After the village is robbed, it is not unusual to kill all the inhabitants and burn the houses. It is now a well ascertained fact that there is a caste of hereditary Dukoits. Still the profession is by no means confined to them, but is practised by a large number of amateurs—mostly Moosulmans.

Another crime, which is much commoner than has been supposed, is human sacrifice, which is practised among some of the aboriginal tribes. Dr. Allen states that in one small section of country, between three and four hundred victims were sacrificed in one year.

The powerful arm of government has done much for the repression of these three offences; and has entirely abolished the practice of Suttee, and other forms of voluntary religious suicide. There is one other offence, however, which, though it is known to be extensively prevalent, is yet practised so secretly, and is so entirely in consonance with the public opinion of the communities among whom it prevails, that all means of repression have hitherto been found ineffectual. I mean the crime of female infanticide, which prevails not only among the Khonds, and other aboriginal tribes who practise human sacrifice, but is also habitual among the Rajpoots—perhaps the finest Indian race.

All the public roads in India are infested by poisoners. They generally do business on a smaller scale than the Thugs, and are contented with less profit in proportion to the risks. Several times it has appeared, in judicial investigations, that whole families were poisoned for the sake of a few shillings, and Colonel Sleeman tells of one case where a man and his son were poisoned to obtain a coverlet worth twelve anas (thirty-six cents).

I have noticed these offences particularly, because some of them are peculiar to India, and all of them are practised as a regular business by certain classes in the community. The other crimes, which are also found in Europe, flourish under the Indian sun, and private enterprise is by no means driven out of the field by the competition of these organised bodies.

Several marked peculiarities distinguish crimes in the East from the same offences elsewhere. The first is, that, like other occupations, murder, robbery, stealing, and the like offences are hereditary in certain castes. The second is, the great cruelty which is often shown in the commission of crimes; but this is not so wonderful among a people whose very school punishments are tortures. A third peculiarity is the extreme youth of many of the malefactors. For instance, among the capital condemnations, we find the merest children who murdered their playmates for the sake of their gold and silver bangles. But the most remarkable feature of all, is the religious sanction which is given to some of the most detestable crimes. To quote the words of Lord Macaulay: "Through the whole Hindoo Pantheon you will look in vain for those beautiful and majestic forms which stood in the shrines of ancient Greece. All is hideous, grotesque, and ignoble. As this superstition is of all superstitions the most irrational, and of all superstitions the most inelegant, so is it of all superstitions the most immoral. Emblems of vice are the objects of public worship. Acts of vice are acts of public worship. The courtesans are as much a part of the establishment of the temple, as much ministers of the god, as are the priests. Crimes against life, and crimes against property, are not only permitted, but enjoined, by this odious theology. But for our interference, human victims would still be offered to the Ganges, and the widow would still be laid on the pile by the corpse of her husband, and burned alive by her children. It is by the command, and under the special protection, of one of the most powerful goddesses that the Thugs join themselves to the unsuspecting traveller, make friends with him, slip the noose round his neck, plunge their knives into his eyes, hide him in the earth, and divide his money and baggage. I have read many examinations of the Thugs, and I remember particularly an altercation which took place between two of these wretches in the presence of an English officer. One Thug reproached the other with having been so irreligious as to spare the life of a traveller when the omens indicated that their patroness required a victim. 'How could you let him go? How can you expect the goddess to protect us, if we disobey her commands? That is one of your North-Country heresies.'"

Thieving, as distinguished from robbery, is very common all over India, and is often practised upon Europeans. The Thugs and Dukoits, on the contrary, never venture to attack the English, for fear of occasioning disastrous investigations. The skill of the Indian thieves is almost incredible. My friend, Colonel Mowatt, told me of one instance within his knowledge, where an old resident of India made a bet with a recently arrived officer, that he would produce a man who, within a month, would steal from the latter the sheet on which he was sleeping. The bet was concluded—the only stipulations being that a month's time should be given for the performance of the feat, in order to prevent any extraordinary vigilance on the part of the officer, and that the latter should agree to take no more precautions than are usual in the way of locking his doors, &c. The end of the matter was that the officer woke up one morning and found no sheet under him. The mode in which the abstraction was accomplished was then explained. The thief entered the bedroom after the officer had retired, and concealed himself under the bed until he made sure, from the gentleman's breathing, that he was sound asleep. He then came out, and rolled up the sheet on each side of the sleeper, so that there remained only a narrow strip on which he lay. This done, he fanned the officer, that his rest might be perfectly sound, and then tickled him slightly on one cheek. The sleeper, of course, supposed the annoyance to arise from an insect, and attempted to brush it away with his hand. A constant repetition of this process, however, at last made him turn over in bed, leaving the sheet free. It now only remained for the thief to fan his unconscious victim into sound repose, to secure his booty, and make his exit as noiselessly as he had entered.

I heard afterwards, from another officer, of an equally authentic exploit, where a sheet was stolen from under two Europeans who were sleeping side by side. In this case, the thief actually lay down in the bed, between the two, and having, as before, put them into a sound sleep by fanning, he began to work them off the sheet by pushing against them alternately. Each of the officers supposed it to be the other, and moved a little to give him more room, until at length they were both entirely off the sheet, which the thief had, as in the previous case, rolled up close to their sides, so as to cover as little space as possible.

Indian thieves generally practise their trade stripped entirely naked, and having their bodies rubbed with oil, so that, even if detected, it is almost impossible to hold them. They dislike violence, but always have a naked knife in one hand, which they use with unerring certainty if their other precautions and great agility and suppleness fail in securing for them a safe retreat.

The precautions taken against discovery form one of the most remarkable features of crime in the East. It would seem that, as in Sparta, detection is considered the real offence. The Thugs, Dukoits, and Murderers, will wait patiently from month to month, and the former track their victims from place to place, until an opportunity arrives to perpetrate the crime in perfect safety. The booty is almost always buried or otherwise concealed, and they will suffer years to elapse, and all memory of the crime to disappear, before they enjoy the profits by disinterring the stolen articles. They are not, however, faithful to one another like the Chinese, who will not suffer the greatest torments to force from them the names of their accomplices. An Indian convict, when once condemned, shows the greatest alacrity in "peaching" upon his previous comrades. It was by taking advantage of this trait in their character that the "Thúggee Commission" made such rapid progress in suppressing that fearful association. A Thug would be detected and convicted in Hindoostan, and would then generally volunteer an account of himself, his exploits, and the gang to which he had belonged. They showed the most frightfully accurate recollection of details, and the Thuggee Committees found no difficulty in identifying the spots where murdered travellers had been buried, and the hiding places where their booty was concealed, from the indications forwarded to them by letter, though the localities might be in the Dĕkkun, a thousand miles from the part of the country where the Thug who gave the evidence had perhaps resided for years. A curious story is told of the way in which a band of thieves prevented the identification of one of their number. An attempt was made to rob the tent of an officer. He awoke, and succeeded in seizing the thief by his legs as he was creeping under the tent. A brief struggle then ensued, but the officer finally dragged his captive back, and was much shocked by discovering that the head of the unfortunate thief had been neatly amputated by his "pals" outside, to avoid the chance of recognition. These precautions, and the secrecy and mystery which surround all crimes, are among the principal obstacles to their detection and punishment.

I have already spoken of the penalties of crime when treating of the courts. A few details, however, may place the penal system in a clearer light. The death penalty is only used in case of murder, and is even then but rarely enforced, both on account of the necessity of the sentence being confirmed by the Supreme Court, and because the gallows is not an object of much dread to the native. It has not unfrequently happened that criminals have gone to the scaffold with flowers and music, surrounded by admiring friends, adjusted the noose with their own hands, and voluntarily taken the fatal leap. This was principally seen in the case of Moosulmans, whose execution by Kaffurs (infidels) was looked upon by the faithful as a martyrdom, who wore upon the scaffold the green dress of a martyr, and whose remains were worshipped as such by the Mahommedans. This latter abuse has, however, been stopped by a general order of government, requiring that the bodies of all executed convicts should be burned and their ashes scattered—a regulation as satisfactory to the Hindoos as it was distasteful to the Mahommedans. A penalty regarded in such a light could not of course prove very effectual in suppressing crime, and it has therefore happened that the severest punishment generally employed is transportation to one of the Company's convict establishments at Singapore, Moolmén, or Penang. To the Moosulman, transportation does not possess greater terrors than to the Christian, but it deprives him of the *éclat* attending a death upon the gallows. The penalty of transportation has, however, this advantage in the case of Hindoos, that it touches them in the only point in which they seem to feel punishment—their caste. Kala panee, or "black water," as deportation beyond the seas is called among the natives, takes away all caste not only from the criminals themselves, but also from their families, for several generations in ascending and descending lines. Blowing away from guns is the only form of the death penalty which has the same effect. It was a not unusual punishment under the old dynasties, but from its *apparent* barbarity was disused by the English government until the recent atrocities called for some speedy and efficacious means of discipline. I say its *apparent* barbarity; for of course the suffering is no greater than, or not so great as, in hanging, or execution by the military plan of shooting.

The lowest form of punishment is confinement in prison—all corporal penalties, as flogging or mutilation, which are prescribed by the old laws, having been abolished. The objection made to the "Model Prison," at Pentonville, that the prisoners were made more comfortable than they would be out of jail, used to apply with great force to the Indian prisons. So great regard was formerly paid to the feelings of the prisoners, that they were allowed to purchase and cook their own food; and a proposal to make them eat at a common table excited the greatest outcry among that class of persons who think the prejudices of the native are matters of so great importance that they should be suffered to interfere with the well-deserved punishment of the horrible crimes which they commit. Fortunately, however, economical considerations counterbalanced the opposition alluded to, and the food of the prisoners is now all cooked and served out to them in common. Smoking, too, which was formerly allowed, has been lately abolished. It may now be hoped that the prisons of India, while they continue to afford the convict every reasonable comfort, will be a "terror to evil doers" from the destruction of caste incurred by entering them, and from the deprivation of his habitual luxury, the hookah, to which the prisoner will henceforth be subjected.*

* It would appear from what Dr. Duff says, that the provisions above alluded to have not been thoroughly carried out. He gives an instance where an English clergyman visited one of the large jails about a year ago. "In one of the rooms was a large circular platform made of wood. On this platform two men were busily engaged in kneading bread. A little girl, one of the party, *accidentally touched this platform with her foot.* She did not touch the meal, or go within a yard of the men. But they at once became insolent,

I have now spoken of offences against life and property, and of one crime against morality, namely, lying. With respect to other offences against morality, and, in particular, the awful forms of licentiousness which are common, I cannot speak. They are such horrors as pollute the mind of him who only hears them mentioned. Bayard Taylor says of the Chinese: "Forms of vice which, in other countries, are barely named, are, in China, so common that they excite no comment among the natives. They constitute the surface-level, and below them there are deeps on deeps of depravity so shocking and horrible that their character cannot even be hinted. There are some dark shadows in human nature which we naturally shrink from penetrating, and I made no attempt to collect information of this kind, but there was enough in the things which I could not avoid seeing and hearing—which are brought almost daily to the notice of every Chinese resident—to inspire me with a powerful aversion to the Chinese race. Their touch is pollution," &c. From this Mr. Taylor concludes that "the Chinese are morally the most debased people on the face of the earth." Had he remained stationary as long in India as he did in China, he might have found reason to modify his opinion, and he would, no doubt, without "attempting to collect information," have become aware of facts which would have induced him to give to the natives of India the evil preeminence which he attributes to the Chinese, and he might even have concluded, as I did, that the Chinese were a moral race in comparison. It is quite impossible, without utter violation of decency, to give a full idea of the enormities which are common in India. If the reader can suppose the horrors of Sodom to be magnified and perfected by thousands of years during which they have been practised; if he can imagine that putrifying sore not to have been utterly consumed by the hot fires of an offended God, but to have been permitted by His long-suffering to pollute the earth, and to have gone on rotting and festering to the present time, then he may

refused to prepare the bread, and complained to the governor of the jail. The governor ordered all the meal to be thrown away and fresh to be given."

form some conception of the fearful excesses now daily practised in India.*

Officials in India are blamed for the tone assumed by them toward natives of education and position. It is alleged that too little consideration, too little respect is shown them. This allegation is unfounded. So far as regards courtesy in public, not only the orders of the government, but the gentlemanly feelings of the officers themselves, induce them to treat with every attention those natives of standing—native gentlemen they are called—with whom they are brought into connection, either officially or socially. But English officers cannot look upon these natives with any respect; they cannot look upon them as in any sense their equals, or worthy to mix in the society of themselves, and especially of their wives and families; and it is not very wonderful that the disgust, which courtesy forbids them to show in public, should be occasionally visible in the coldness of their manners, and that the utter contempt which the rough-mannered but honourable soldier feels for these whited sepulchres, these polished villains, should find an open and frequent expression in private. In fact, what a perversion of terms is it to apply to such men the name of gentleman—a term of which we are so justly proud, because no other language has for it an equivalent. What do we mean by a gentleman? We mean, in the first place, a man of position and of polished manners—these are possessed to the highest extent by those natives to whom the term is applied. But do we not mean something more? Do we not associate with the word the possession of those higher qualities, the respect for which has descended to us from the age of chivalry? Must not a gentleman be a man of *honour*, of *truth*, of *courage?* Must he not have a certain respect for what is weak and helpless; a detestation of all unfair advantage, a chivalrous respect for women; and must he not shrink from all that is mean, low, cowardly, and

* The lower classes, the mass of the population in India, are not, I think, as licentious as the same class in China. This frightful depravity is found developed in the higher orders, and especially among the Mahommedans, nearly all of whom, in all ranks, are more or less liable to the charge above named.

degrading? In fine, must not every gentleman be a man in the fullest and highest sense of the term? and will any amount of wealth, power, or refined manners, make up for the utter absence of truth, honour, and every ennobling moral quality? Now, when we consider that, in addition to all this treachery, lying, moral cowardice, and degradation, a native gentleman lives in the habitual practice of crimes so loathsome that no convict in our prisons would not shrink from the charge of them if made against himself, I am sure it will be a subject of wonder, not that all who know their character should despise them, but that any man who respects himself should be willing to mingle with them in society on terms of equality.

In ending this examination of crimes and their punishment, which is necessary to a right understanding of the native character, I must allude to the remarkable fact that convictions for various offences have undergone a progressive increase under the Company's government. In Bengal, for instance, there were in 1838 twenty-six thousand convictions, while in 1844 there were forty-five thousand. The only reasonable explanation is to be found in the greater perfection of the machinery of justice, which brought to light crimes that otherwise would have gone unpunished, and classes of offenders whose existence had not been suspected. English magistrates had administered justice for fifty years in India before they became aware of the wide-spread system of Thúggee, and it was only in 1842 that a large caste were found to be devoted by birth to the crime of Dukoitee. There is, unfortunately, in India, a wall of mystery, ruse, lying, and indifference to good and evil, which surrounds all the details of the inner life among native communities, and defies every effort made by the most active and intelligent magistrates. To this great obstacle may be added the unreliable and corrupt character of the native police, whose exactions and oppressions are so great as to deter the sufferers from applying to the authorities for protection. This last difficulty is the most formidable obstacle which the magistrate meets with in the discharge of his duty; and, what is worse, it is a difficulty to which no efficient remedy can be applied so long as the administration of justice involves the employment of native subordinates.

Of all the machinery of the Indian government, the police system certainly works worst. The police are of two kinds. First, the village police. This is an institution which has existed in India from time immemorial, under all sorts of governments, and has never been abolished by the Company. This is an indubitably native institution, and has existed from all time; and yet it is one of the most fatal curses that blight the prosperity of this unhappy country. The village police are the obedient and ready tools of every zĕmindar or rich native who will pay for their services. For money they will plunder the poor, will torture the obstinate, and will turn a blind eye to every offence, or will aid in the commission of any crime however atrocious. The outrages which they daily commit under the nominal authority of the law, either for their own purposes or in the interest of wealthy natives, are enough to draw down the execrations of the nation on any government, however well intentioned, which lends them the protection of their authority.

This is the first class, the old native police of the country, a thoroughly Hindoo institution. Besides these there are the government police, who number only about one-thirtieth of the first class. They are immediately under the authority of the magistrate, and are supposed to aid him in the administration of justice. In reality, however, they are but little better than the village police, and serve only to defeat the ends of justice, and protect the guilty, if rich.

The police connive at all sorts of villainy, and share the proceeds of the most horrible crimes. They take advantage of their position to blind the eyes of the European magistrate and divert his suspicions. When the crime of Thúggee was discovered, it was also found out that the police everywhere had long been aware of the existence of this crime, that in many places they were accomplices, and, in particular, the chief police magistrate of Delhi was actually a regular member of a band of Thugs. The same thing is true of Dukoitee and other crimes.

As for extortion, corrupting of witnesses, and intimidating prosecutors, their power in these respects is almost unlimited, and they have not hesitated in some instances to employ even torture to gain their ends. It is only of late years that the existence of "torture" under the English government has been discovered, though it has undoubtedly been continuously practised in secret, as it was the general and open custom of native governments, and remains in use in those native states which still exist. So much was this the case, that it has become recognised by the universal rule of right, namely, mamool (custom). A ryut once said to Mr. Lushington, an able servant of the Company: "I brought the money for my rent, but as no violence was used I did not pay it;" and it is well known that the villagers will often bring the whole amount of their dues, wrapped up in the folds of their clothing, and only pay as much as they are compelled to. A native looks upon all demands for money, whether just or unjust, in much the same light, and will generally only pay if he is forced to. This state of things would excuse torture in the eyes of the most enlightened and merciful native rulers, but would form no excuse for its employment under an English government. Accordingly, in the very thorough investigation which took place in India a few years ago, not one Englishman was implicated directly or indirectly. All the instances were found in places remote from the residences of European officials. In a few cases only it would appear that complaint had been made to the English magistrates. In most of such instances the offender had been summarily punished. The great mass of the magistrates had never even suspected the existence of such doings by their subordinates. The whole investigation proved two things. First, how entirely unreliable are native officials, and how unscrupulous they are in the employment of any means for their own advantage; secondly, how utterly insufficient is the number of European officials to exercise the necessary supervision over the actions of their subordinates. In Bengal, as I have said, each magistrate with his deputies, has, on the average, jurisdiction over a million of men. In Madras, where the abuses spoken of are the greatest, there is a district where there is only one European official to half a million of souls, and four other districts where the population averages over 300,000. How is it possible for a European to exercise an adequate supervision over so vast a territory? Even had he the most honest and efficient subordinates, it would be almost impossible to oversee their acts. But the case is infinitely worse, where, as in India, the magistrate is surrounded by subordinates universally venal, tyrannical, and directly interested in misgovernment, and in concealing the truth from their superior. With such agents as those, who can wonder if he fails in the government of a million of people, prone to vice, given to crimes unknown in Europe, and with powers of lying and deception which are absolutely unfathomable. Besides the executive government of this multitude, he is expected to administer justice in a foreign language, and according to codes the most various and contradictory, and the provisions of which are often absurd and unintelligible; and that too with a set of assistants who are every one of them venal rascals, from the door-keeper, who will exclude a witness for a bribe, and always demands a fee to admit a petitioner, to the magistrate's clerk, who takes down depositions and alters them as he is paid for it, or the interpreters of native law, who vary the readings for a consideration. Everybody bribes in these courts: those who are in the wrong that they may appear right; and those who are right, lest they should be made to appear wrong.

The magistrates are aware of this state of things, but they can do nothing. The work is such that they must have native assistants, and one man of this class is as bad as another. Bribing is the universal rule all over India. It is mamool—recognised custom; and if one set of corrupt subordinates are discharged, their successors will certainly be as bad, and may be worse. The only possible remedy is in a great increase of European officials. It is not too much to say that it would require a hundred men to perform thoroughly the work now assigned to a single magistrate. At present, the English government, though the magistrates are men of the highest character, and actuated by the best intentions, is quite inadequate to the thorough administration of justice and prevention of the abuses which spring up in frightful profusion and virulence wherever natives are left without supervision or control. The small quantity of European energy is lost in the immensity of native indifference and apathy, and the purity of the magistrate can do but little to remedy the corruption of his thousand abandoned subordinates.

If such is the state of things under English rule, one may imagine what it is under a native government, where the abuses of the inferiors are surpassed by the cruelty and extortion of the highest magistrates, where shameless bribery extends to all, and where truth and justice are systematically ignored, and any improvement is impossible, from the absolute corruption of the whole body politic, from the weakest member up to the very head itself.

In looking for an explanation of the low morality of the Hindoo character, we find its causes, first, in their religion, next in their education. The influence of the horrible superstitions of India has already been dwelt upon, and diffuses itself throughout the whole education of the child. As to the education, it is not only in the schools, where the ordinary reading-books are obscene legends of the various Hindoo deities, but much more in the family that the character is formed. Now what can be expected of a man, brought up from his youth to join in the foul ceremonies of the Hindoo religion; whose tongue was taught to lisp, as its first utterances, the impure hymns sung in the worship of the gods; who sees his mother considered as an upper servant, of infinitely less importance than himself; whose mind, from his earliest youth, was bent into the most abject reliance upon the Brahmuns, about whom it is said, "respect is due to a wicked Brahmun, but not to a Soodra, even if virtuous; is not a vicious cow better than an amiable cat?" and who practises as his religious devotions, the worship of the lowest animals —nay, even of the bench he sits on, or the spade with which he digs?

CHAPTER XXXVII.

THE ARMY OF INDIA.

Its Strength—Different Classes of Troops—English and Native Officers—Enlistment purely Voluntary—Pay—Madras Army—Bombay Army—Low-Caste Men—An Army of Gentlemen—Truckling to Caste—Tame Tigers—Salaries of Officers—Staff-Service.

THE army of India comprises troops of three classes: *First*, the Queen's army, consisting of royal regiments stationed in India, and paid, while there, by the Honourable Company. *Secondly*, the Company's European troops, comprising three regiments of infantry, and the European artillery. The whole European force probably never exceeded 30,000 men. *Thirdly*, the native soldiers, or sepoys, who were divided into three armies, belonging respectively to the three Presidencies, and having independent, though similar organizations. There is a commander-in-chief over the army of each Presidency; but the supreme command of the whole military force in India is vested in the commander-in-chief of the Bengal army, who must always be a general in the Queen's service. The entire strength of the native armies may be reckoned at 270,000, two-thirds of which belonged to the Presidency of Bengal. The aggregate number of troops in India, was, therefore, before the recent great mutiny, probably about 300,000.

The European troops were under English officers exclusively; but the sepoy forces were commanded partly by English officers, partly by natives. The colonel, lieutenant colonel, major, six captains, ten lieutenants, and five ensigns, compose the full complement of European officers for each sepoy regiment. The native commissioned officers are, ten soobahdárs, and ten jemadárs, who rank with captains and lieutenants respectively. All the non-commissioned officers are, of course, natives. Their titles are havildár and naik, answering to sergeant and corporal.

The army is recruited entirely by voluntary enlistment, and the advantages which it presents are so great that there has never been any necessity for establishing recruiting stations, or using any of the means found necessary, in England and this country, to encourage enlistment.

The pay of the sepoys varies from 7 to 9 rupees a month. Against this must be set off the cost of the uniform, and their food, both of which are furnished by government at fixed rates. These expenses amount on the average to about four rupees a month, so that most of the soldiers save thirty-six rupees a year, which they remit to their families through the hands of government. After fifteen years of service the sepoys retire with pensions of from four rupees upwards. The pay of the native officers is—the naik 12 rupees; the havildár 14 rupees; the jemadár, 40 rupees; the soobahdár, 60 rupees per month. The eagerness which the natives show to enter the Company's service is easily understood when we reflect that the lowest pay of a sepoy is nearly double what the same man could make at other occupations, and that, in the army, he is put beyond the reach of bad seasons, want of work, or any of the other eventualities which diminish or render uncertain the small wages of three or four rupees a month which is all that most kinds of labour can earn in India.

The Madras army is recruited among the inhabitants of that Presidency, and admits men of all castes, as does also the Bombay army. The soldiers for the latter, were, however, partly obtained in Oude, by means of recruiting agents. These low-caste men make much the best soldiers. Their caste does not prevent their serving beyond the seas; they can eat, if necessary, the food left cold from the day before; and they will not refuse any reasonable task. The only drawback is their appearance and height, which are not equal to those of the high-caste Rajpoots, who formed the Bengal army.

The army of Bengal was, in appearance, by far the best of the three: superior in stature, and equal in drill to most of the European services. The average height of the men is said to have been two inches greater than that of the British army ten years ago. They were exclusively composed of men of high caste, and many of the soldiers in each regiment were related to each other, as it was customary for the sepoys, when they visited their homes on leave, to bring back with them some of their brothers or cousins as recruits. The sepoys of the Bengal army always looked with the greatest disdain upon those of the two other Presidencies; and this pride was unfortunately encouraged by their officers and the government, who yielded to their wishes in forbidding the enlistment of low-caste men. The compliance with one demand occasioned others. They could not wear certain articles of clothing: the government changed the regulation uniform. They were of too noble birth to be flogged: flogging was abolished, and with it discipline gradually disappeared. They would not eat food prepared by others, or which remained from their yesterday's meal: ample time was allowed them each day to cook, and no officer could go near to inspect them during that operation. Their caste would be lost if they went on board ship: and after almost exciting a mutiny, the government yielded to this demand also, and sent to China and Burmah sepoys of the Madras army, at greatly increased expense, for those purposes. The cavalry were too fine gentlemen to groom their own horses, and the infantry thought it beneath them to pitch their own tents: the government went so far as to provide them with servants for these purposes. Lastly, they discovered that manual labour was degrading; and white soldiers were actually made to do their work in the trenches under the deadly rays of an Indian sun. The result of all this was, that while in the armies of the smaller Presidencies discipline was thoroughly kept up, in the Bengal army there was, during late years, the greatest want of it. The only substantial punishment which the officers could inflict, was dismissal from the service. The men became every day more arrogant and assuming; the officers, more compliant and yielding;* until,

* An extraordinary instance of truckling to caste has lately occurred. Du-

having had their pride, self-conceit, and opinion of their own importance raised to the highest point by the acts of the government, they became fit tools for the crafty agitators who worked upon their superstitious prejudices to bring about the recent terrible mutiny.

The English Government have now learned what they will never forget, that an Oriental is a very useful animal so long as you keep a tight rein, and let him see that you are the master; but that they are incapable of appreciating generosity or indulgence—qualities which they consider symptoms of weakness, and repay by ingratitude and treachery. In many towns of India, leopards may be seen, tied to bed-posts, in the open streets. They are perfectly harmless, tame, and docile, being kept so by the fear of a certain iron rod. I used often to think that each of these animals was a parable.

Promotion in the Indian army, whether among the native or European officers, is entirely by seniority. The former, (the native officers,) are no better than the men whom they command. They are mostly ignorant of reading and writing, without other education, and do not seem to be at all socially raised, in the estimation of the sepoys, by possessing a commission. Although, by the regulations of the army, they rank with the English captains and lieutenants, their duties are practically those of non-commissioned officers, and their only superiority over the common sepoys consists in their greater

ring the mutiny, the 70th regiment, stationed at Barrackpoor, were only kept from open revolt by the presence of British troops. At length, they condescended to proceed to China, in compliance with the request of government. Before they went on board ship, a commission of European officials was deputed to inspect the ship personally, and report whether the water-tanks and other arrangements were in accordance with the rules and usages of caste. On the way to Singapore, the scoundrels became noisy and impudent, and at length carried their insolence so far, that they requested, in the most offensive terms, *that the dinner should not be carried aft for the officers, as the steam or gravy from the dishes might touch them, and so take away their caste.* The commander of the transport, a bluff English sailor, expected to see such insolence at once put down with a strong hand. The officers of the regiment, however, temporized with their men, and soothed them; and actually asked the captain if the difficulty could not be remedied.

age, and their higher pay. The salaries of the European officers, which range from 200 rupees per month for the ensign, to 1,000 rupees for the colonel, are not found to be more than sufficient for the comfortable support of the officer, especially if he is married—so great are the necessary expenses of living in India; and it is rare to find an officer who lives upon his salary, and who has not involved himself more or less deeply in debt.

On account of the great difficulty, which has already been dwelt upon, of obtaining honest and able servants in the executive departments of government, the Company have been compelled to increase their administrative force at the expense of the army, by appointing officers to various civil employs. It is calculated that one quarter of the officers of the Bengal army were thus removed from their regiments. All these staff employs conferred a very considerable augmentation of pay, and did not remove the appointee from the line of promotion in his regiment, so that they became prizes eagerly sought after by the officers. Every "griffin" (cadet) on joining his regiment, set himself down to the task of acquiring the requisite amount of Persian and Hindoostanee, or whatever was required to pass the staff examination; and in this way the system did a great deal to improve the general character of the officers, by inducing them to spend their leisure hours in studying Persian and engineering, instead of idling away the day at billiards or whist. The system of conferring staff employs upon military men had the great disadvantage of removing the older officers from the regiment, and leaving the soldiers under the care of the younger and less experienced men. But on the whole, it probably did more good than harm, even in the regiments; and when considered with reference to the whole public service, it was perhaps the only expedient that could be adopted to remedy the great want of suitable administrative officials.

CHAPTER XXXVIII.

WEALTH AND REVENUE OF INDIA.

Undeveloped Condition of the Resources of India—Cotton—Obstacles to Development—Small Agriculturalists—Caste—Want of Capital among Agricultural Classes—Inferiority of Native Labour—Want of Roads—Railways—Ganges Canal—Want of European Capital and Energy—Obstacles to the Supply of this—Land-tax under Native Governments—Under the English—Lord Cornwallis's "Settlement"—The Madras System—The "Village System"—Its Advantages—To be made still more Liberal—Revenue and Expenses of the Indian Government—Low Taxation—*India a Poor Country*—Misapprehensions that have prevailed with regard to the Wealth of Oriental Nations.

The resources of India are in a wholly undeveloped condition. Vast tracts of fertile and valuable land are uncultivated; and even where cultivation exists, it is so rude, and the means of preparing the produce for market are so inferior, that many of the Indian products cannot compete in Europe with those which are also produced in other countries. The climate and soil of almost every part of India are adapted to the cultivation of some valuable crop. Cotton, rice, sugar, silk, and tea could all be grown in quantities sufficient to supply the native demand, and to take a very large, if not the largest place in the foreign consumption. Thus far, however, the fertile soil and cheap labour of India have not enabled it to compete successfully in these articles with the productions of other countries. For instance, that most important staple, cotton, which was first grown to any considerable extent in India, of which it has been calculated that three billions of pounds are still yearly raised, and with which India once supplied the markets of England and America, occupies in the English market a vastly inferior position compared with American cotton, and would scarcely be imported at all were it not for the limits of the supply derived from this country;

while manufactured cottons now hardly form an item in the list of exports from India, being entirely driven out of the market by the cheapness and excellent quality of the fabrics manufactured in England, which are now exported to India to the amount of over four millions and a half sterling yearly.

When we read that the cotton-plant is indigenous to India, and grows wild in many parts of the country; when we learn from the reports of American planters what immense tracts of land there are in India adapted by nature in every way for the growth of the best qualities of cotton; and when we hear that, four hundred miles from Bombay, cottons in no respect inferior to the finest grown in America* can be bought in the market for from 3 to 4 cents the pound, we are naturally at a loss to account for the fact that India does so little toward supplying the immense and increasing demand for this most important article of commerce.

It is true that the cotton of India, at least the largest part of it, and the whole of what is exported, is very inferior in length of staple to the American article. But this will by no means prove a satisfactory answer, when we reflect upon the greatly increased demand, far outrunning the means of supply; when we remember that even if inferior to American, the Indian cotton is still much the cheapest, and of great value to the manufacturer, and that supposing the article now produced in India were intrinsically useless, still the soil would offer every inducement to a planter who would bring with him American plants or seeds.

The real explanation of the undeveloped state of this and the other enormous productive powers of India, is to be found in a consideration of the following obstacles. In the first place, almost the whole agriculture of the country is in the hands of natives, each of whom cultivates only a small patch of land. This is of itself a most formidable check upon increased and improved cultivation, as no great improvements can be carried into operation without large tracts of land and considerable capital. Then, from those peculiar caste-prejudices which are

* M. De Valbezen.

20

the bane of India, agriculture is despised as a degrading occupation, and is left to the lowest class of the population who are too ignorant to be taught improvements and too stupid to put them in practice, and who, even if they could be persuaded to deviate from the system of cultivation which has come down to them unchanged since the days of Noah, are so far from possessing the smallest capital that most of them are mere slaves of the village bankers, to whom they are irretrievably in debt. The state of hopeless indebtedness of by far the larger part of the inhabitants of India, is not the least curious feature of that country. The ryut has no capital of his own, but receives advances from the banker or the zĕmindár, as the case may be, to plant his crops. For these advances he pays an exorbitant rate of interest, and to secure repayment hypothecates the crop. Besides the advances at the beginning of each season, he also has to borrow sums of money on the occasions of marriages, funerals, or lawsuits, which soon amount to so much that the profits of his whole crop each year are barely more than sufficient to repay the interest on his debts, and perhaps also those of his father, which have descended to him. Again, native labour is vastly inferior to that of Europeans or even of Chinese. For instance, a Lascar crew always has three or four times as many men in it as would be required if they were European sailors; and at Calcutta, where native skilled labour comes in competition with that of Chinese and Europeans, a native artisan does not earn more than from five to ten rupees a month, while his Chinese competitor will get as high as thirty or forty, and a European can obtain eighty or ninety at the same trade. I was told by the manager of one of the Company's large tea plantations that they found it quite impossible to entrust the picking of the tea-leaves or the manufacturing processes to natives, as they either had not enough skill or would not exercise the requisite care. They therefore found it necessary to employ Chinese labour, which was exceedingly expensive, as the Chinese would not come without their wives and families. Such, then, is the first great obstacle to the development of India—the intrinsic inferiority of native labour, and the want of capital embarked in agriculture. The next hindrance to development is found in the want of communication with the coast. Under the old native governments, India had not a single road by which goods could be conveyed from the interior to the sea-ports; the only medium of communication was by the dangerous and uncertain navigation of the rivers, or the slower conveyance by camels, rough carts, or bullocks-of-burden. Roads are not that matter of primary necessity in India which they are in other countries, since during the dry season the level plains are traversable by carts and armies; and during the rains, no communication between different parts of the country used to be attempted. This state of things remained almost unchanged in the earlier years of British rule, while their sway was still limited, their tenure of the country precarious, and their attention constantly occupied by commerce on the one hand and incessant wars on the other. Since the power of the English has been thoroughly established, a vast system of internal improvements has been begun, which includes roads and railways enough to open the whole country to commerce, and place every important point in ready communication with the coast. The most important road so far built is the Grand Trunk road from Calcutta to Pesháwur, which will be fifteen hundred miles long when completed, and will probably cost £900,000. It is already finished for three-quarters of its whole length, and has proved of immense benefit to the vast and fertile valley of the Ganges through which it extends. The whole of the Grand Trunk road is built and kept up as well as any highway in Europe, and there are beside over 2000 miles of similar first-class road either completed or under construction in Northern India alone. Besides these macadamized roads, four thousand miles of railway are now being constructed; only four hundred are complete, but 1861 is the latest date fixed for the completion of the remainder. In no respect, perhaps, has the Company been more blamed lately than for not hurrying the completion of these railways. As matters have turned out, that blame comes with the greatest weight, since there can be no doubt that many lives would have been saved and the duration of the mutiny much shortened by the convenience for sending troops up-country which they would have afforded. Still the benefits which would have been derived from them are probably exaggerated, as the first act of the mutineers would no doubt have been to tear up the rails. Again, it must be remembered that neither the Company, nor any of its agents, except Sir Charles Napier and one or two others, had any expectation of a general revolt, or the least suspicion of the possibility of such a movement. With regard to Sir Charles, his writings certainly read now very much like prophecies, but when they were written did not derive nearly as much support from facts as do now the disunion threats and prognostications made, not by one man, but by whole States in the southern part of our country; and yet no one here thinks it worth while to prepare for the eventuality of a dissolution of the Union. On the other hand, the Indian government have all along done everything to further the building of railways, except to take them actually into their own hands. They had no funds to spare for these gigantic undertakings, and preferred that they should be carried on by private capital; to encourage the investment of which they guaranteed a dividend of five per cent. besides offering other inducements. There is plenty of money among the native bankers and traders, but they have been found unwilling to divert their capital from its accustomed employment in money lending, to the untried field of vast enterprises such as railways. This the government could not foresee when they decided that it was better for the country that the railroads should be constructed by private enterprise and capital cheaply and rapidly (as it was supposed they would be), than that India should be burdened with a new debt, and the building of the roads left altogether in the hands of government agents, who would be probably as dilatory and as fond of jobs as the same class elsewhere.

So much for roads and railways, the want of which has heretofore proved so great an obstacle to the development of India. It is proper here to mention that the Ganges Canal will, when completed, play no small part in internal communication, as it is eighty feet wide, and, with its branches, nine hundred miles in length. When these roads, railways, and canals, are completed, they will do all that can be desired toward opening out the country, will remove what we have described as the second great obstacle to development, and will constitute, perhaps, the grandest series of internal improvements ever undertaken.

The third and last obstacle which we will consider, is the want of European settlers and cultivators. It is hardly too much to assert that the introduction of Europeans is absolutely necessary to the full development of a country where there is no capital among the ryuts—no agricultural enterprise among the native capitalists. Many things, however, have heretofore combined to prevent any extensive settlement by Europeans. The obstacles which we have already considered apply to them, as well as to natives. The inferiority of native labour, the unreliable character of the native subordinates which they must employ, and the tenure of land, which does not admit of freehold estates, are formidable impediments, but might be overcome by a man of capital, energy, and perseverance, were it not for the climate. This, apart from the numerous and fatal diseases to which it exposes the foreign settler, actually prevents his going into the open field during the daytime for a large part of the year, so that, however energetic he may be, he finds himself physically hindered from exercising that constant supervision so essential to the success of any enterprise, more particularly in India. This last obstacle, the great difficulties in the way of constant European superintendence, has had, I may here remark, the most unfortunate influence on every great undertaking in India, especially the government public works. Their progress has been delayed, and the perfection of their construction interfered with to an extent incredible to any one who does not appreciate the entire unreliability of native subordinates and contractors, and the absolute necessity for a constant, energetic, and minute supervision of whatever they do.

Having examined, to a small extent, the question of the development of India, we will now take a brief view of the land-tenure—a matter so important that it may be said to underlie the whole subject of agricultural improvement.

In India all land belongs to the government, to which the cultivators pay yearly a certain share of the crops, in lieu of all demands for rent and taxes. This has always been the case, the fee never having been alienated from the sovereign. The land-tax in India has always been very heavy, perhaps because the lower classes who cultivate the soil have always been in so utter a state of slavery to conquerors. In Turkey and Persia, where the same system prevails, the land-tax is said to vary from one-tenth to one-fifth of the crops. In India, it was fixed by the Hindoo law at one-sixth, exclusive of the tithes for the support of religion, which were no doubt oppressive. Under the Moosulman Emperors, the general principle obtained that all the property of infidels is forfeited to true believers, and the only limit to their rapacity was the fear of killing the goose which laid the golden eggs. Although this statement would seem to show that the ryuts were better off under the Hindoo law than when subject to the Mahommedan domination, yet it should be remembered that what they would gain by the moderation of the legal demand, they would lose by the rapacity of those charged with the execution of the law, so that their real situation was probably in both cases much the same. The Emperor Akbur, whose character was so much superior to that of the other Moosulman rulers, and whose philanthropic efforts form so bright an episode in the long tale of Mahommedan misrule, tried to introduce great and important reforms into the land assessment. The principle which he established was to take one-third of the average gross crops, as determined by a careful survey of the land. It is doubtful whether the benevolent intentions of the Emperor were of any advantage to the ryuts, since any diminution of the imperial demand would probably be a gain only to the collector of taxes. At any rate, Akbur's system perished with the fall of the Mogul Empire, and its division into numerous independent states, which occurred before the arrival of the English.

For a long time after the Company's power became established, they did not at all interfere with the native administration of the government and revenue system; but in 1793 Lord Cornwallis, who perceived with concern the oppressive exactions of those charged with the collection of the revenue, and who appreciated the great disadvantages of the system which subdivided all arable land among very small holders, devised a remedial system, which, after careful examination and much discussion, was applied to Lower Bengal. Under the new regulations, the zĕmindárs, who had been previously merely collectors of revenue, were erected into proprietors, the Company divesting itself in their favour of the fee vested in it, on condition of their paying yearly the same amount of revenue which they had previously furnished as tax-collectors, provided that, in case of failure in the payment, the land should revert to the Company. This was the only restriction on the arrangement, which has, therefore, been known as the "perpetual settlement." The hopes and expectations of Lord Cornwallis were, that the zĕmindárs, being thus erected into great and independent landholders similar to those in England, would find it their interest to give their chief attention to the improvement and development of their property, and that the condition of the ryuts would thus be bettered more expeditiously and effectually than could be done directly, while, at the same time, the zĕmindárs, being a numerous and wealthy body, with a great stake in public tranquillity, would be an important defence to the British power. Never were plans more hopelessly disappointed. Lord Cornwallis and his advisers had not taken into account the narrow-minded avarice of the native character, and were mortified by finding that zĕmindárs continued, as before, mere tax-gatherers and usurers, the only change in their position being that they had now acquired unlimited power of extortion, while the ryut was now without protection, or power of appeal, against those who had been elevated from tax-gatherers into landlords. This settlement, as before remarked, was, by its terms, perpetual, and, therefore, continues to the present day in operation in Bengal. The ameliorations which have been introduced are not very numerous, from the fact of government having so entirely divested itself of control over the zĕmindárs. The principal provisions are, to secure the careful education of all zĕmindárs, wards of government, during minority; to require every landlord to give each ryut a written agreement, specifying the amount of rent and conditions of tenure, and to make these agreements legally binding. The Bengal Zĕmindáree system must, however, be confessed a failure, and its worst feature is its permanent character. In all the later settlements of land, it has been taken, not as a guide, but as a warning. How much it is inferior to the system now employed in other parts of the country, appears from the fact that, when Cutták, which is in Bengal, but was not included in the "permanent settlement," was lately surveyed, and its land-tenure arranged on the "Village System," the value of the land at once rose from twenty-five to fifty per cent.

We have now described the Zĕmindáree system. We next come to the Ryutwáree system, introduced into Madras subsequently to the "permanent settlement" in Bengal. Sir Thomas Munro, its author, had been much struck with the wretched condition of the ryuts in Bengal, ground down by an unrestrained landlord who came between the actual cultivators and the government, and reaped all the profits of the arrangement. He therefore devised the Madras system, which allows of no middlemen. Under it the cultivator hires his land, each year, directly from government, paying according to the value of the soil, which was determined by a most careful survey, and fixed, in an ascending scale, from 7d to 70 shillings an acre per annum. Under this system, the actual cultivator, and not a great landlord, is looked upon as the proprietor of the soil, subject to the payment of his yearly tax. In the words of the last report of the Madras government, "the ryut has all the benefits of a perpetual lease, without its responsibilities, inasmuch as he can, at any moment, throw up his lands, but cannot be ejected so long as he pays his dues." The great evil of this system was the want of any permanence in the arrangement between the ryut and government, and the great intricacy and complexity of the plan for determining the annual rent. In the administration of it, all the details must be entrusted to native officials, since they are too numerous for the attention of any European collector; and the Ryutwáree system, in addition to its other disadvantages, is therefore peculiarly liable to all those abuses which prevail wherever native agency has to be employed. The principal improvements are the following: in the first years of the arrangement the rent of land was raised in proportion to the value of the crop cultivated; but since 1837 no increase of the rent is allowed, but the ryut reaps the full benefit of any more valuable crop than that provided for in his original rent which his land will produce. Formerly all improvements, such as wells, or irrigating machines, increased the rent after a certain number of years, during which the advantages derived from their use were calculated to repay the cost of construction. Now, the ryut has the undivided benefit of all his improvements. The last and greatest amelioration in the condition of the Madras ryuts, is the great reduction which has taken place in the rents. And this reduction, far from proving a sacrifice to government, has resulted in their advantage, from the impulse and extension it has given to agriculture.

Both of these systems, the Zĕmindáree, and the Ryutwáree, have their great disadvantages; they were both crude experiments, made by men with the best intentions, but ignorant of the customs of the people for whom they were legislating. It remains for us to discuss the "Village System," a modified form of which has always been the tenure in the Bombay Presidency, and which has been universally introduced into all the lately-acquired territory, the North Western Provinces, the Punjab, and Sind. The Zĕmindáree tenure assumed the proprietorship to be vested in the zĕmindárs, subject to government taxation; the Ryutwáree system assumed the same thing for the ryut. Longer experience, and a more careful study of native customs, showed both these views to be incorrect, and that the property in the soil throughout the greater part of India, resides neither in the zĕmindár nor in the ryut, but in the *village community*. The village communities all possess a regular organization, with hereditary municipal officers. They may be said to be the only Hindoo instition now existing, and have remained, probably, much in their present condition for hundreds, if not thousands of years. The surveys, preparatory to the settlement of the North Western Provinces, occupied ten years, ending in 1844, and cost £500,000 sterling. It is much the best system for collecting the land rent that has been tried, not only because it is the natural plan, and consonant with the policy of Hindoo law and the customs of the natives; but because in its administration a much broader view has been taken of the real advantages to government than that which prevailed at the time when the other land-tenures were fixed; and the policy followed in this assessment is to encourage cultivation by liberality, rather than to hinder the extension of agriculture by heavy rents. The practical operation of the "Village System" is as follows: the village, through its head men, makes a bargain with the government collector for a certain amount of land, which is subsequently subdivided among the several cultivators living in the village. The collector is assisted in determining the rent by the records of the survey, before mentioned, which includes the quality of the soil, &c. From these statistics, and the best information he can derive from the cultivators and on the spot, he fixes the average yield of the land. He then deducts from the average gross yield an amount representing the expenses of cultivation and the wages of the cultivators; or, in other words, allows for the capital and labour bestowed by the villagers upon the land. The remainder, or net yield of the land, gives what would be a fair rent to government, and may be stated at one quarter of the gross produce, being thus less than the amount fixed by the Emperor Akbur, which was considered a very low standard. When the net yield of the land is determined as above, two-thirds of it are fixed as the government demand for rent and taxes. The remaining third is a premium on extended cultivation. The land-tax is thus equal to about one-sixth of the produce of the soil—being lower than it ever was under any previous government. The assessment once fixed continues for thirty years. At the expiration of that time, if the net produce is found to have increased, the rent is raised, but in a proportion inferior to the ratio of increase in the value of the crops. This system is found to work most admirably. The condition of the ryuts, and the cultivation of the soil is improving, and a revenue of £4,000,000 sterling is collected without delay, and rarely by coercive processes. If any one is dissatisfied with the Company's government, and thinks it inferior to that of native princes, let him compare the condition of the people in the North Western Provinces with that of the inhabitants of the kingdom of Oude, which is the garden of India as regards natural advantages, but has been ruined by the misrule of ignorant, tyrannical, and profligate princes.

So great was the success of the village system in the North Western Provinces, that it was introduced into the Punjab immediately after the conquest of that territory. The main features of the original plan were left unchanged, but the details were carried out with somewhat more liberality, so that the proportion of the crops paid to government may be placed at from one-ninth to one-sixth of the gross yield. The whole amount of the land revenue has been diminished twenty-five per cent. since the Punjab came into the hands of the British, although the number of cultivators has increased; and the advantages arising to the ryuts from this change of masters, will be even more apparent when we consider the immense extortions which were practised upon them by the subordinates, charged with the collection of the revenue, under the former governments. The good results of this system are even more remarkable in the Punjab than elsewhere. This province now enjoys peace and security, instead of perpetual anarchy and war. A rapid increase has taken place in cultivation and production. Although a new territory, only acquired in 1849, and inhabited by the most warlike race in India, which formerly cherished the fiercest enmity against the British, yet so great was the general feeling of content, that the Punjab became the base of operations for the recovery of Hindoostan; and the Seekhs, so long and so lately in arms against the English, made an important part of the force employed in subduing the mutinous army of Bengal.

To sum up the comparison of the old native land-tenure, with the improved system in force under the English: it appears that, under the native governments, the rents were oppressive and variable, all improvements were overcharged in re-assessing the land, and the greatest extortion was exercised in the collection of the tax; under the new system, all rights and tenures are perfectly defined, the leases are sufficiently long to encourage improvements, which are not reckoned at their full value in re-assessment, and in every instance where large outstanding balances and increased difficulty of realization showed the rents to be excessive, they have been lowered. For a long time the oppressive taxes imposed by the former native rulers, remained unchanged under the Company's government; but experience showed the disadvantage of any tax so heavy as to check production, and the land-rents have, for years, been everywhere progressively diminished where they were formerly too large, within the older possessions of the Company. In the new territories, the village system has been everywhere introduced, the liberal features of which have been dwelt upon above. Moderate as is the demand of government under this system, it has been still further reduced lately, and in all territory, the land-tenure of which shall be hereafter settled, government will require only one half of the net produce, an amount equal on the average to one-eighth of the gross produce.

In reading this account of the various land-tenures in India, it may strike some persons that it would be advantageous if the fee of the soil were transferred to the actual cultivators. This plan, however, would be utterly impracticable. In the first place, the whole capital of the country is in the hands of the bankers, who would soon become proprietors of all the soil, and make infinitely worse landlords than any government. Secondly, even if this certain evil could be avoided, such a transfer would reduce the production of the country by diminishing those incentives to labour, which even now operate but feebly upon the indolent native of India.

The revenue of India is about twenty-four millions and a half sterling. Of this sum more than one half is drawn from the land-tax. The rest is raised by the customs, opium monopoly, and by the imposts on salt, tobacco, spirituous liquors, and other articles of luxury. The net product of the opium monopoly is two millions and a half sterling per annum. This may be considered a tax upon the Chinese, and so much gained by the Indian tax-payers.

The expenses of the government, in time of peace, nearly balance the receipts, but the wars into which the Company has been constantly forced, have necessitated repeated loans, the payment of the interest on which absorbs one-eighth of the revenue, and occasions a constant deficit in the budget.

The amount of the revenue, above mentioned, when divided by the number of inhabitants, gives only eighty-four cents for each person. This appears very light taxation, and will appear still lighter when it is recollected that more than one half of this sum represents, not taxes proper, but the rent of land, which, in any other country, would go into the pockets of private individuals. Yet the taxes are probably nearly as heavy as the country could bear under any other system; for *India is a poor country;* "*poorer*," in the words of Lord Macaulay, "*than the poorest countries in Europe.*" Notwithstanding the old, and almost inveterate, belief in the wealth of the Indies, it is well for us at the present day to recognise this fact. The mass of the population have no property at all. The soil is all in the hands of the sovereign; the disposable capital is held by a limited number of bankers and tradesmen. This concentration of all capital in the hands of a few persons enables them to make a show quite disproportioned to the general wealth of the country, and from this are derived the very erroneous impressions that have so extensively prevailed with regard to the great wealth of oriental nations.

CHAPTER XXXIX.

THE REVOLT.

Indian Rebellion not a matter of Surprise—Revolutions and Rebellions common under Native Governments—Rebellion did not originate among the People—Character of the old Native Governments—Nature of the English Conquest, and Character of their Rule—Evidence that the Rebellion was not a Movement of the People—The Rebellion was not in its Origin a Military Mutiny—The real Instigators were the Moosulman Princes—It was the dying Effort of Islamism—Character of the Mahommedan Population of India—Favourable Circumstances for the Rebel Leaders—Abortive Attempts of the Rebels to arouse the Mass of the Population—The Moosulman Character of the Movement evident in its Development—Atrocities—Noble Stand of the English—The Revolt in Oude—Sympathies of the Population of India—The Disaffected Classes—The probable Result of the Rebellion if it had not been restrained.

A REVOLUTION is no new thing in India. The whole history of that country under its native princes, before the establishment of the English power, is a narrative of usurpations, revolts and rebellions. The English government is the only power that has ever ruled for a hundred years without such attempts being made against its existence, and the fact of a rebellion having finally broken out against it, should not, therefore, be taken *a priori* as a proof of the injustice of its policy, or the tyranny of its administration. The student of Indian history will rather wonder that fifty thousand men, from a country situated on the other side of the world, should by any course of government, or any rule however wise, have maintained, for so long a time, an order before unknown, and exacted a universal obedience never before given to any sovereign in India; that they should have maintained this order and exacted this obedience from one hundred and eighty millions of people, differing from them and each other in language, religion, and every bond of sympathy, and comprising nations and classes whose whole employment and aggrandizement had, before their time, been derived from public conquest or private pillage.

The rebellion, however, is a fact, and as it has been considered in Europe, however unjustly, the *experimentum crucis* of English policy in India, it is interesting to investigate what were the real objects and aims of the movement. Before doing so, however, it will be well briefly to examine some opinions that have generally obtained credence, both in England and this country.

In the first place we are met by a theory that the revolt was a popular revolution, like the great movement which in the end of the last century, overthrew the Bourbon dynasty in France, or like the universal uprising in America which delivered our nation from transatlantic domination.

This theory, then, represents the rebellion as an attempt, on the part of the downtrodden masses, to throw off the oppressive and hated yoke of the stranger. That this should be believed, was, perhaps not unnatural, and yet this very belief shows what entire ignorance prevails with regard to India and its inhabitants. Any one who has read Indian history, knows that the natives have always been "under the yoke of the stranger;" that when it was heaviest, it never excited a murmur; and that no popular resistance has ever been called forth, even by the most grinding tyranny. The "rights of man" are abstractions which the oriental mind has never grasped. It looks upon tyranny as the normal manifestation of power, and the best evidence of a strength which it is dangerous to resist.

The people of India, then, the masses of the population, never could or would rebel; but even supposing that they had that consciousness of their rights, and that disposition to resist infringements upon them, which, even in Europe, only prevail in a very different condition of society, it is quite incredible that they should rebel under the English government, when they had endured, uncomplainingly, centuries of oppression from other rulers.

Some people, however, imagine that the real grievance has been annexation, and the substitution of the Company's government in place of native princes, for, say they, "After all the English are foreigners, and their rule, even if more lenient, must be as distasteful to the people, as foreign rulers always are. There can never be towards them the same sympathy as exists with native governments, which, even if harsher, are yet composed of men of the same race, who have ruled the country for centuries, and secured that popular allegiance which is never paid to any but an ancient dynasty."

This argument, which is advanced by the members of an influential party, proceeds upon assumptions quite as false as the first, though entirely different. The ancient native dynasties, ruling peacefully over millions of attached subjects, are a complete myth. India has always been a prey to adventurers of one kind or another, of whom the most successful occupied for the time, the seat of authority. Violence was their passport to the capital; violence, the policy of their government; and by violence, they were overthrown to give place to some other, who gained and abused his power in the same way.* The position of a native prince was thus very similar to that of the priest of Diana, at Aricia:

"The Priest who slew the slayer
And shall himself be slain."

* I may here cite an instance of this state of things from very recent history of the Punjab, a territory that has since, fortunately for itself, been annexed by the English. When Runjeet Singh died, he was succeeded by his son, Khurruk Singh, who was imbecile and poisoned by his son, Nao Mhal Singh, who, returning from his father's funeral pyre, was grievously, if not mortally wounded by a beam which fell upon him, perhaps by chance, in passing under a lofty gateway. When wounded, he was taken care of by the two Rajpoot brothers, whom that old tyrant Runjeet Singh had fallen in love with, and bought when they were slaves—Goolab Singh and Dhyan Singh. They suffered no one to enter his chamber until he was dead—a consummation in which they are supposed to have assisted. His mother, Ranee Kour Chand, then claimed the supreme power, which was contested by Sheer Singh a pseudo-son of Runjeet. The Ranee was beaten to death by her slave girls, who threw her body out of the window. Sheer Singh then became king, but was assassinated at a review by Sirdar Ajeet Singh, at the instigation of Dhyan Singh. His little son was also sought out and murdered. The two conspirators returned to the city together in a carriage, and Ajeet, having "his hand

It thus happened that almost all the native princes of India were different in nationality, and many of them in religion also, from the people whom they governed. Their rule was invariably tyrannous, oppressive, and extortionate. They treated their subjects as prisoners of war, and never expected any return of gratitude or devotion. A change of dynasty never excited the sympathy of the people, far less did it call forth any active efforts. They stood patient and motionless, and beheld one tyrant succeed another, without emotion and without interest.

When the East India Company commenced their career of conquest, they found the whole country under the control of the Maharattas, a nation of robbers, who had subjugated all India, and subdued the governors of the country, who were themselves mostly rebels against the once paramount authority of the Mogul Emperor, who, in turn, derived his power from the right of conquest only.

The efforts of the English were against the Maharattas, and when they had delivered the country from them, no one could expect that they would restore the booty to the previous set of robbers who had held it; and none would be more unwilling to consent to such an arrangement than the Hindoo population, who, while they had not the ability to govern themselves, or the resolution and pluck to choose and support any one set of masters, must still be supposed to have a preference for that government under which there was the least oppression and extortion. And this was actually the character of the English conquest of India. They took the sovereign power not from the people, or from a popular government, but from upstart tyrants who were mostly foreign to the soil

in," stabbed Dhyan Singh, as they passed under a gateway. He was pursued and killed by Hira Singh, the son of Dhyan. Ranee Chanda now brought forward Dhuleep Singh, as a son of Runjeet, but her brother, having caused the only real son of Runjeet then living, Peshora Singh, to be cut in pieces and cast down a wall at Attok, the troops became enraged and ordered him to come to a review. In vain he scattered gold and bangles among them, and entreated them to spare his life, in vain the Ranee accompanied him, and joined in his prayers; one volley missed him, the second brought him down.

which they governed. They gave the people what they had never before possessed; a permanent government which respected life and property; officials free from extortion and corruption, and untrained to oppression; and a mild and impartial system of law and taxation. They scrupulously respected national religion, and even went so far as to support, in a few instances, the idolatrous worship of its subjects. The civil laws of the country founded on the religious codes, were left unchanged, although in every respect conflicting and unwieldly, in order not to offend national prejudice. The criminal code was so modified as to become simple in administration, and lenient, instead of ferociously cruel in its punishments. Every effort, every sacrifice was made to secure the attachment of the people, and the policy of the Company was to develope peacefully the resources of the country, and thus indirectly benefit themselves, rather than to seek aggrandizement and wealth by an indiscriminate system of cruel extortion and oppression, as had been the custom of all previous conquerors.

The native does not ask for liberty, or desire it. He has no spirit of independence, and when without a master will voluntarily choose one. All that he asks of government is, that they should respect his religious prejudices, that justice should be equally administered, and the taxes not oppressive. It is, perhaps, too much to say that this is what they *ask;* for they do not ask or expect anything but that he who has the power will use it to the uttermost for his advantage, as any one of themselves would do in his place. But the whole amount of what they pray for is, that they should be respected in their superstitions, and, if possible, in their property also.

It cannot be denied that the English government was despotic and oppressive. It was despotic, because the people can be ruled in no other way. It was oppressive, because there was a necessity for employing native subordinates who cannot be prevented from abusing the power with which they are entrusted. But it was incomparably better in every respect than any previous rule. India is no longer desolated by the Maharattas laying waste towns and villages with fire and sword. The natives are no longer ruined by the systematic and grinding oppression of their Moosulman rulers. The villagers are no longer exposed to murder and pillage by periodical inroads of robber bands, as they were under the old system of anarchy and misrule. Every man's head is now safe on his shoulders, and every man's property is secure from the violence of government or individuals.

It might thus be concluded, purely from *a priori* reasoning:

(1st.) That, judging from the whole past history of India, no conceivable tyranny or disregard of their rights could arouse resistance, or excite an insurrection among the cultivators of the soil and other industrious classes, who form by far the greatest mass of the population; and therefore that a *popular rebellion*, in the proper sense of the words, would be in the highest degree improbable, if not impossible.

(2d.) That, even granting that circumstances might arise which would cause a general popular rising, there were no such causes to account for this rebellion.

So much for the *a priori* reasoning, which, after all, is always more or less liable to error. But when we come to the *a posteriori* proof it is no longer possible to doubt. If it was a popular movement, why did it extend over only one-third of India? Why did it arise in that very part of the country where the administration was most perfect, and why was the Madras Presidency, the worst governed part of the British dominions, the most tranquil throughout the disturbances? If the movement was occasioned by annexation, why were Nagpoor, and the Punjab, with its warlike inhabitants, tranquil, while Oude was in flames? Why has nearly the whole revenue been paid punctually, when there was no power to enforce it? and why have the English army, wherever they went, been as well provided with transport and provisions as if they were in a settled and peaceful country?

In all its outward manifestations, and especially at the beginning, the revolt has been purely military. When we heard of an outbreak, it was not the revolt of a district, but the mutiny of a regiment. When the mutineers departed, all was again quiet and orderly. The enemies which the English troops have had to fight had been regularly-organized regiments, many of them dressed in the English uniform, not vast and ill-disciplined bodies of populace. The mutineers, whereever they passed, have robbed the property of the shop-keepers and rich men, and mercilessly levied contributions on the miserable cultivators. The disturbed districts were the military stations, and wherever there were no mutinous soldiers things went on as if nothing was occurring elsewhere.

As for the assertion that, although the revolt was purely military, it was yet a real popular movement, since the army was the only body that had the power to offer resistance to government, and in doing so they were representatives of the nation at large; such an explanation is quite inadmissible, as the mutiny was confined to the Bengal army, and did not extend to the troops of Bombay or Madras, or to the Punjab forces, which were all certainly quite as much representatives of their respective parts of the country. Besides which, we should in such a case expect to find the populace sympathising openly with their valiant defenders; and it shows an entire misconception of the sepoy character to suppose that they care for any rights, privileges, and interests, except their own.

Was the revolt, then, purely military, that is, did it originate in the army? and has it been entirely confined to them? This has been the view of many persons, though not in India, and is quite as wrong as the theory that the rebellion originated among the people, though it is not so absurd, and does not show such ignorance of the country. In the first place, it is quite clear that the revolt has not been confined to those who were soldiers of the Company when the disturbances began. New levies have been raised to supply the losses of war, and have been disciplined and organized into regiments on the European plan. This, to be sure, does not divest the mutiny of its military character, as the new recruits came from the same soldier castes that furnished the original revolters, and were brothers and friends of the mutinous sepoys. This explanation, however, will not reach the case of Oude and other districts, where the feudal chiefs have risen with their followers and gone to swell the ranks of the rebels. Moreover, it is not to be concealed that India is filled with classes discontented with British rule, and longing for a restoration of the anarchy on which they or their ancestors grew fat, and if the rebellion had been a little more successful in the beginning, it is probable that the whole peninsula would, before now, have been plunged in universal revolt. Still, it is quite clear that all these movements on the part of the non-military classes did not precede, but followed the mutiny of the army, which was their cause and occasion. The first part of the question is, therefore, still unanswered—did the rebellion originate in the army? To this we may now answer certainly, no ; the developments and disclosures that have lately taken place have shown that the real instigators and ringleaders were not in the ranks of the army, but were the same individuals upon whom public suspicion in India has all along been fixed. All who knew the character of the sepoys felt sure that they never could have conceived, or carried out unitedly, so vast a scheme. They were too ignorant, too inactive, too submissive, and too distrustful of each other. Beside which, they were nearly the only class in all India who had no reasonable pretext for discontent. In fact, they had been ruined by too much pay and petting. The whole Bengal army was demoralized. They were in a fit condition to lend themselves readily to the plots of their seducers, who promised them as large pay, and as luxurious living, as those of their English officers and governors.

There is now no doubt that the rebellion was set on foot by the deposed Mahommedan princes, pensioners on the Company's bounty, and the movement may be looked on as the expiring effort of Islamism to regain its lost supremacy in India. The evidence given on the trial of the King of Delhi shows that the rebellion was a concerted movement of the Moosulman princes; that the plan was communicated to the Shah of Persia, and perhaps also to the Sultan of Turkey; and that the occupation of Herat by the former, an act which occasioned the Persian war, was really only a feint to draw away British troops from India, the scene of the main action. In this plot nearly all the Moosulman princes were implicated, and especially Ali Nakhi Khan, the prime minister of the late King of Oude, is pointed out as having taken a most active part, and is by many suspected of being the originator of the whole thing. With such consummate skill, however, has he woven the threads and meshes of the plot that not a trace remains to mark where he has passed. Almost the same may be said of many of the other conspirators. Though the evidence against them amounts to a moral certainty, it is to be feared that it will not be sufficient to secure any legal punishment. There is too much secrecy around every action of a native for the true details of the conspiracy and the real agents ever to become thoroughly known. So little confidence have natives in each other that it is probable that the real extent and aims of the movement, and even the day on which it was to break out, were, until the last moment, known only to a very few, if they were not concealed in the breast of a single individual.

This rebellion, originated by Mahommedan princes, called out the religious and natural sympathies of all the Moosulmans in India. They are a very numerous class, forming from one-twelfth to one-tenth of the population, and numbering, therefore, from 15 to 18 millions. They had been for centuries the dominant race, masters of the soil and people, and naturally felt disgusted at being placed by the English on a level with the despised Hindoo. They have always hoped and prayed for the restoration of Islam, and the recovery of that position of superiority of which they had been so largely deprived. As to their origin, they are mostly descendants of the off-scouring and camp-followers of the various invading armies that have at different times ravaged and depopulated India. They do not, however, retain any of the manly qualities of their Afghan or Tartar ancestors, but by constant inter-marriages with the Hindoos have assimilated to them in all respects, even adopting the absurd and burdensome restrictions of caste. Low as is the moral character of the Hindoos, that of the Moosulmans is still lower. They are more licentious, if possible more treacherous, and possess besides indomitable pride of nationality and unreasoning fanaticism—two qualities not found in the Hindoo. The Mahommedans in India have always looked upon themselves as a superior race. They call themselves the sipahee-log, or warrior people, and hold that the Empire should be in their hands by the right of descent and religion. Their pride prevents their earning a livelihood by manual labour, and consequently the only means of support open to them are private service, enlistment in the army, or situations under government. The last employment has always been considered the best, both as being the most honourable and as giving great opportunities of extortion and plunder, though in this respect their gains were diminished by the vigilance of their English superiors.

The diminution of the number of government servants, which took place under English rule; the appointment of great numbers of Hindoos to office; and the general prevalence of peace, and disbanding of the irregular soldiery which had sprung up under the anarchy of native rule, threw out of employment a large number of this proud, lazy, fawning, unscrupulous and crafty population; and the mutiny of the Bengal army was a grand scheme to turn the military establishment of the English against themselves, and to restore the supremacy of the Mahommedan religion and the Moosulman nation. In this scheme the indolent and simple sepoys were merely the catspaws of others, and would have been discarded when no longer needed.

No circumstances could appear more favourable for the rebel leaders than the condition of India at the time of the outbreak. The whole Mahommedan population would certainly lend their sympathies and most of them would give active coöperation. The sepoy army of Bengal, with their tremendous pride of caste, and the opinion of their own power, exalted by years of petting and indulgence, and the disuse of all punishment, furnished a ready and powerful means of beginning the disturbance. Besides them there were immense classes, such as the predatory chiefs, the warlike tribes, and the robber castes of India, who had been dormant under English rule, but would at once emerge into activity when order was disturbed, and thus indirectly aid the plans of the Moosulman agitators by diverting the efforts of their opponents.

To resist all these immensely powerful and numerous enemies, there were not over twenty thousand English soldiers, and those not concentrated upon any one point, but scattered here and there in little bodies over thousands of miles, each separate company in the midst of thousands of the mutinous or disaffected classes. With such odds it is not wonderful that the mutiny spread as it did. The only matter of surprise is that a single Englishman was left alive in all the North-country; and if the population could only have been induced to join, it would have been impossible for one man to escape.

The plan employed by the Moosulman leaders for exciting the army to mutiny, was also used by them with the view of arousing the sympathies of the general population. In both cases they appealed to the only sentiment of the Hindoo, on which they could rely for the purpose—namely, the prejudices of caste. In the case of the army, who were only looking for an excuse to revolt, this device succeeded perfectly. With the people, who ask for nothing but quiet, it totally failed. The proclamations of the rebel leaders are certainly remarkable productions; but the most curious feature of them is that they never say one word about the injustice of annexation, or the misgovernment of the English, knowing that such charges, even if true, would have no effect on the native population, who would look on such acts as the most natural way of using power. The whole tenor of the proclamations, where-ever issued, consists of appeals to religion and caste, and the only charges against the English are based upon assumed intentions to interfere with these institutions.

In the explosion of the mutiny, its Moosulman character became clearly manifest. The plan was to exterminate the English at every station, and then unite all the rebel forces at Delhi, the sacred city of Indian Mahommedans, and the seat of the old Mogul Emperors, the last descendant of whom was recognized as the new sovereign. In the fearful atrocities*

* The fiendish acts committed by the mutineers perhaps excited even more

which accompanied the work of extermination, the Mahommedan cavalry, who had for years been a by-word and jest for their arrant cowardice, showed themselves the cruellest and most merciless. Wherever there was a Moosulman city, there the spirit of revolt was most virulent. Even in places beyond the actual circle of revolt, like the city of Poonah, in the Dĕkkun, this feeling was unmistakeably evident. On the other hand, the mass of the population who are Hindoos, and the Hindoo rajahs, over two hundred in number, were faithful almost to a man. Too much stress, however, must not be laid on this fidelity of the rajahs, as it may be attributed more to a dislike of a Moosulman sovereign than to any loyalty to the English; and if the Moosulmans had succeeded in overcoming the English, the Hindoo princes would probably have begun war on their own account.

There is no prouder page in the History of England than the subjugation of this rebellion. The English were a mere handful of men in comparison with the hordes of mutineers and the millions of disaffected classes by whom they were surrounded. They were far away from all help; while their adversaries were on their own ground, abundantly supplied with

astonishment than horror in Europe. People could not believe that such unsparing cruelty and brutal capacity for enjoying the tortures of their enemies, existed at the present day, in any members of the human family, however degraded. They seem to have forgotten that the sepoys were heathens, of whom it is said that "their tender mercies are cruel;" and that they are quite ignorant of those mitigations which Christianity alone has introduced into war. In fact, cruelty and torture have always been features of Oriental warfare, and atrocities even greater than those of Meeruth, Delhi and Cawnpoor, were daily occurrences in the revenue-collections of native states; and have always been practised in the predatory excursions of the feudal chiefs and robber-tribes. Even in Bengal such outrages were ordinary accompaniments of a dukoitee robbery. It is scarce three hundred years since Rome was taken by Bourbon, when the inhabitants were treated with nearly as much brutality. The pillage of the "chateaux" during the French revolution will furnish cases of almost as much horror, and the sack of various cities by the Israelites, as narrated in the Bible, shows the same pitiless extermination of old and young, though I believe no mention is made of tortures. If such things could be done by Jews and Christians, we should at least not be surprised at them in heathens.

arms and ammunition, and defended by fortifications of great strength; and yet they did not even stand upon the defensive, but at once began an aggressive warfare. They not only met unshaken the overwhelming tide of revolt, but actually drove it back; and before a single British soldier could come to the rescue from England they had checked the insurrection at its head, had taken the Imperial city, captured the rebel Emperor, and saved India from a general rebellion; for there can be little doubt that had the movement succeeded in the north, the whole Peninsula would soon have been in flames.

From Delhi the mutineers retreated to Lucknow, which is the second great Mahommedan city of India, where their forces were swelled by fresh levies, and their strength increased by the assistance of the Talookdars, Zĕmindars, and other feudal chieftains.

The conduct of these men is a type of what would have been the course of the whole class to which they belong, if more success had attended the first rising. The Talookdars and Zĕmindars of Oude were feudal chieftains, who had grown rich by the anarchy which prevailed during the old government. Their estates were obtained by violence and fraud; they lived by plunder and cruelty; acknowledged no law or authority, and never paid taxes to the king without standing a regular siege. To maintain this life they were surrounded by armed followers, who were generally the greatest rascals in the country. Indeed, a usual method of recruiting was to break open the nearest jail and enlist the convicts. The offence of the English government in the eyes of these barons, was not the abstract wrong of annexing Oude, for few people care less for wrong or right, abstract or concrete; but that they had introduced a system which did not recognize their usurped titles to land, which established order and extinguished violence, and under which the tax-gatherer could not safely be resisted.

Now the class to which these zĕmindars belong exists all over India, and they have everywhere the same grievance. In other parts of the country they have been so long reduced to order and compelled to live respectable lives that their swords have grown rusty; but if there had been any probability of success attending their efforts, they would have risen from one end of India to the other, and would have found no difficulty in obtaining followers among the *dangerous*, that is, the unemployed classes, who form so large a part of the native population.

The only class who have sympathized with the English during the disturbances are the bankers and capitalists, who would dread nothing so much as a restoration of native rule. The great mass of the population have been decidedly neutral, as they always have been under all changes. On the other hand all the disorderly classes have been inimical to the English—some of them openly, like the zĕmindars of Oude, and the immense numbers of convicts whom it was the first care of the mutineers to release from jail; others secretly, among whom have been all the Moosulmans, most of the native princes, the old feudal chieftains, the predatory tribes generally, and all the robbers, murderers and thieves, whether by caste or profession.

If there had been force enough to crush the mutiny at Delhi, we should probably never have heard any more of it. If, on the other hand, there had not been force enough to check it there, all these classes would at once have broken into insurrection. What would have been evolved out of the chaos it is hard to see, but certainly it is very unlikely that the result would have been a restoration of the Mahommedan empire. The Indian Moosulmans are not what their ancestors were when they planted their feet so easily on the necks of the Hindoos. The Maharattas tore down the green flag of Islamism once, and would not see it again unfurled without a struggle for supremacy. The larger part of the military classes of India are Hindoos, and they would not be likely now to submit to a Mahommedan yoke which their fathers always wore uneasily and often resisted successfully. The end would probably have been the establishment of a great number of small sovereigns; not the old hereditary dynasties, for they are all effete and would soon disappear in the confusion. An era of anarchy would then be inaugurated, such as existed when the country was first conquered by the English, and India would be again thrown back a century in her infinitely slow progress toward civilization, and would again be ripe for another name to be added to the long list of those who have conquered her.

APPENDIX.

"Tazu ba tazu, Now ba now!"

PERSIAN SONG OF THE NACH GIRLS.

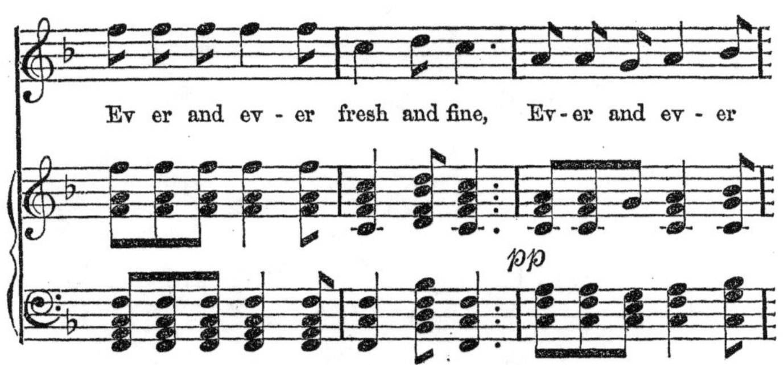
Ev er and ev - er fresh and fine, Ev - er and ev - er
pp

Verse.
fresh and fine. Here, with a heart - al - lur - ing lass,
f

Mer - ri - ly let the moments pass, Kissing her red lips
pp

while I may, Ev - er and ev - er fresh and gay.

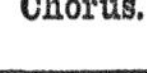
Chorus.

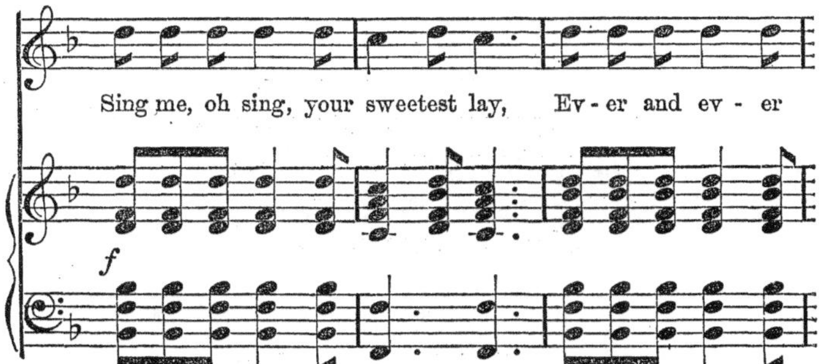
Sing me, oh sing, your sweetest lay, Ev - er and ev - er
f

fresh and gay; Bring me the joy - in - spir - ing wine,

2.

Lost is my heart, oh lady fair,
Lost in your jet black locks of hair,
Heavy with perfume, as is meet,
Ever and ever new and sweet.
Chorus. Sing me, &c.

3.

Still will I drink the cup I love,
Happier here than saints above;
The blessed in heaven long for wine
Ever and ever fresh and fine.
Chorus. Sing me, &c.

4.

Listen, oh breezes! as you move
Close by the dwelling of my love,
Softly my words and song repeat,
Ever and ever new and sweet.
Chorus. Sing me, &c.

A LIST

OF

NEW WORKS

IN GENERAL LITERATURE,

PUBLISHED BY

D. APPLETON & COMPANY,

346 & 348 Broadway.

**** Complete Catalogues, containing full descriptions, to be had on application to the Publishers.*

Agriculture and Rural Aff[illegible]rs.

Boussingault's Rural Economy,	1 25
The Poultry Book, illustrated,	5 00
Waring's Elements of Agriculture,	75

Arts, Manufactures, and [illegible]rchitecture.

Appleton's Dictionary of Mechanics vols.	12 00
" Mechanics' Magazine. vols. each,	3 50
Allen's Philosophy of Mechanics,	3 50
Arnot's Gothic Architecture,	4 00
Bassnett's Theory of Storms,	1 00
Bourne on the Steam Engine,	75
Byrne on Logarithms,	1 00
Chapman on the American Rifle,	1 25
Coming's Preservation of Health,	75
Cullum on Military Bridges,	2 00
Downing's Country Houses,	4 00
Field's City Architecture,	2 00
Griffith's Marine Architecture,	10 00
Gillespie's Treatise on Surveying,	
Haupt's Theory of Bridge Construction,	3 00
Henck's Field-Book for R. Road Engineers,	1 75
Hoblyn's Dictionary of Scientific Terms,	1 50
Huff's Manual of Electro-Physiology,	1 25
Jeffers' Practice of Naval Gunnery,	2 50
Knapen's Mechanics' Assistant,	1 00
Lafever's Modern Architecture,	4 00
Lyell's Manual of Geology,	1 75
" Principles of Geology,	2 25
Reynold's Treatise on Handrailing,	2 00
Templeton's Mechanic's Companion,	1 00
Ure's Dict'ry of Arts, Manufactures, &c. 2 vols.	5 00
Youmans' Class-Book of Chemistry,	75
" Atlas of Chemistry. cloth,	2 00
" Alcohol,	50

Biography.

Arnold's Life and Correspondence,	2 00
Capt. Canot, or Twenty Years of a Slaver,	1 25
Cousin's De Longueville,	1 00
Croswell's Memoirs,	2 00
Evelyn's Life of Godolphin,	50
Garland's Life of Randolph,	1 50
Gilfillan's Gallery of Portraits. 2d Series,	1 00
Hernan Cortez's Life,	38
Hull's Civil and Military Life,	2 00
Life and Adventures of Daniel Boone,	38
Life of Henry Hudson,	38
Life of Capt. John Smith,	38
Moore's Life of George Castriot,	1 00
Napoleon's Memoirs. By Duchess D'Abrantes,	4 00
Napoleon. By Laurent L'Ardèche,	3 00
Pinkney (W.) Life. By his Nephew,	2 00
Party Leaders: Lives of Jefferson, &c.	1 00
Southey's Life of Oliver Cromwell,	38
Wynne's Lives of Eminent Men,	1 00
Webster's Life and Memorials. 2 vols.	1 00

Books of General Utility.

Appletons' Southern and Western Guide,	1 00
" Northern and Eastern Guide,	1 25
Appletons' Complete U. S. Guide,	00
" Map of N. Y. City,	25
American Practical Cook Book,	
A Treatise on Artificial Fish-Breeding,	75
Chemistry of Common Life. 2 vols. 12mo.	
Cooley's Book of Useful Knowledge,	25
Cust's Invalid's Own Book,	50
Delisser's Interest Tables,	4 00
The English Cyclopaedia, per vol.	2 50
Miles on the Horse's Foot,	25
The Nursery Basket. A Book for Young Mothers,	38
Pell's Guide for the Young,	38
Reid's New English Dictionary,	1 00
Stewart's Stable Economy,	1 00
Spalding's Hist. of English Literature,	1 00
Soyer's Modern Cookery,	1 00
The Successful Merchant,	1 00
Thomson on Food of Animals,	50

Commerce and Mercantile Affairs.

Anderson's Mercantile Correspondence,	1 00
Delisser's Interest Tables,	4 00
Merchants' Reference Book,	4 00
Oates' (Geo.) Interest Tables at 6 Per Cent. per Annum. 8vo.	2 00
" " Do. do. Abridged edition,	1 25
" " 7 Per Cent. Interest Tables,	2 00
" " Abridged,	1 25
Smith's Mercantile Law,	4 00

Geography and Atlases.

Appleton's Modern Atlas. 34 Maps,	3 50
" Complete Atlas. 61 Maps,	9 00
Atlas of the Middle Ages. By Kœppen,	4 50
Black's General Atlas. 71 Maps,	12 00
Cornell's Primary Geography,	50
" Intermediate Geography,	
High School Geography,	

History.

Arnold's History of Rome,	3 00
" Later Commonwealth,	2 50
" Lectures on Modern History,	1 25
Dew's Ancient and Modern History,	2 00
Koeppen's History of the Middle Ages. 2 vols.	2 50
" The same, folio, with Maps,	4 50
Kohlrausch's History of Germany,	1 50
Mahon's (Lord) History of England, 2 vols.	4 00
Michelet's History of France, 2 vols.	3 50
" History of the Roman Republic,	1 00
Rowan's History of the French Revolution,	63
Sprague's History of the Florida War,	2 50
Taylor's Manual of Ancient History,	1 25
" Manual of Modern History,	1 50
" Manual of History. 1 vol. complete,	2 50
Thiers' French Revolution. 4 vols. Illustrated,	5 00

Illustrated Works for Presents

Bryant's Poems. 16 Illustrations. 8vo. cloth,	50
" " " cloth, gilt,	50
" " " mor. antique,	00

Gems of British Art. 30 Engravings. 1 vol. 4to. morocco, ... 18 00
Gray's Elegy. Illustrated. 8vo. 1 50
Goldsmith's Deserted Village, ... 1 50
The Homes of American Authors. With Illustrations, cloth, ... 4 00
" " " cloth, gilt, 5 00
" " " mor. antqe. 7 00
The Holy Gospels. With 40 Designs by Overbeck. 1 vol. folio. Antique mor. . . 20 00
The Land of Bondage. By J. M. Wainwright, D. D. Morocco, ... 6 00
The Queens of England. By Agnes Strickland. With 29 Portraits. Antique mor. . . 10 00
The Ornaments of Memory. With 18 Illustrations. 4to. cloth, gilt, ... 6 00
" " Morocco, . . 10 00
Royal Gems from the Galleries of Europe. 40 Engravings, ... 25 00
The Republican Court; or, American Society in the Days of Washington. 21 Portraits. Antique mor. 12 00
The Vernon Gallery. 67 Engrav'gs. 4to. Ant. 25 00
The Women of the Bible. With 18 Engravings. Mor. antique, ... 10 00
Wilkie Gallery. Containing 60 Splendid Engravings. 4to. Antique mor. . . . 25 00
A Winter Wreath of Summer Flowers. By S. G. Goodrich. Illustrated. Cloth, gilt, . 3 00

Juvenile Books.

A Poetry Book for Children, ... 75
Aunt Fanny's Christmas Stories, ... 50
American Historical Tales, ... 75

UNCLE AMEREL'S STORY BOOKS.

The Little Gift Book. 18mo. cloth, . . . 25
The Child's Story Book. Illust. 18mo. cloth, 25
Summer Holidays. 18mo. cloth, ... 25
Winter Holidays. Illustrated. 18mo. cloth, . 25
George's Adventures in the Country. Illustrated. 18mo. cloth, ... 25
Christmas Stories. Illustrated. 18mo. cloth, . 25

Book of Trades, ... 50
Boys at Home. By the Author of Edgar Clifton, 75
Child's Cheerful Companion, ... 50
Child's Picture and Verse Book. 100 Engs. . 50

COUSIN ALICE'S WORKS.

All's Not Gold that Glitters, ... 75
Contentment Better than Wealth, ... 63
Nothing Venture, Nothing Have, ... 63
No such Word as Fail, ... 63
Patient Waiting No Loss, ... 63

Dashwood Priory. By the Author of Edgar Clifton, ... 75
Edgar Clifton; or Right and Wrong, . . . 75
Fireside Fairies. By Susan Pindar, . . . 63
Good in Every Thing. By Mrs. Barwell, . . 50
Leisure Moments Improved, ... 75
Life of Punchinello, ... 75

LIBRARY FOR MY YOUNG COUNTRYMEN.

Adventures of Capt. John Smith. By the Author of Uncle Philip, ... 38
Adventures of Daniel Boone. By do. . . 38
Dawnings of Genius. By Anne Pratt, . . 38
Life and Adventures of Henry Hudson. By the Author of Uncle Philip, ... 38
Life and Adventures of Hernan Cortez. By do. 38
Philip Randolph. A Tale of Virginia. By Mary Gertrude, ... 38
Rowan's History of the French Revolution. 2 vols. 75
Southey's Life of Oliver Cromwell, . . . 38

Louis' School-Days. By E. J. May, ... 75
Louise; or, The Beauty of Integrity, . . . 25
Maryatt's Settlers in Canada, ... 62
" Masterman Ready, ... 63
" Scenes in Africa, ... 62
Midsummer Fays. By Susan Pindar, . . . 63

MISS McINTOSH'S WORKS.

Aunt Kitty's Tales, 12mo. 75
Blind Alice; A Tale for Good Children, . . 38
Ellen Leslie; or, The Reward of Self-Control, 38
Florence Arnott; or, Is She Generous? . . 38
Grace and Clara; or, Be Just as well as Generous, ... 38
Jessie Graham; or, Friends Dear, but Truth Dearer, ... 38
Emily Herbert; or, The Happy Home, . . . 37
Rose and Lillie Stanhope, ... 37

Mamma's Story Book, ... 75
Pebbles from the Sea-Shore, ... 37
Puss in Boots. Illustrated. By Otto Specter, . 25

PETER PARLEY'S WORKS.

Faggots for the Fireside, ... 1 13
Parley's Present for all Seasons, . . . 1 00
Wanderers by Sea and Land, ... 1 13
Winter Wreath of Summer Flowers, . . . 3 00

TALES FOR THE PEOPLE AND THEIR CHILDREN.

Alice Franklin. By Mary Howitt, ... 38
Crofton Boys (The). By Harriet Martineau, . 38
Dangers of Dining Out. By Mrs. Ellis, . . 38
Domestic Tales. By Hannah More. 2 vols. . 75
Early Friendship. By Mrs. Copley, . . . 38
Farmer's Daughter (The). By Mrs. Cameron, 38
First Impressions. By Mrs. Ellis, ... 38
Hope On, Hope Ever! By Mary Howitt, . . 38
Little Coin, Much Care. By do. 38
Looking-Glass for the Mind. Many plates, . 38
Love and Money. By Mary Howitt, . . . 38
Minister's Family. By Mrs. Ellis, ... 38
My Own Story. By Mary Howitt, ... 38
My Uncle, the Clockmaker. By do. . . . 38
No Sense Like Common Sense. By do. . . 38
Peasant and the Prince. By H. Martineau, . 28
Poplar Grove. By Mrs. Copley, ... 38
Somerville Hall. By Mrs. Ellis, ... 38
Sowing and Reaping. By Mary Howitt, . . 38
Story of a Genius. 38
Strive and Thrive. By do. 38
The Two Apprentices. By do. 38
Tired of Housekeeping. By T. S. Arthur, . 38
Twin Sisters (The). By Mrs. Sandham, . . 38
Which is the Wiser? By Mary Howitt, . . 38
Who Shall be Greatest? By do. 38
Work and Wages. By do. 38

SECOND SERIES.

Chances and Changes. By Charles Burdett, . 38
Goldmaker's Village. By H. Zschokke, . . 38
Never Too Late. By Charles Burdett, . . 38
Ocean Work, Ancient and Modern. By J. H. Wright, ... 38

Picture Pleasure Book, 1st Series, . . . 1 25
" " " 2d Series, . . . 1 25
Robinson Crusoe. 300 Plates, ... 1 50
Susan Pindar's Story Book, ... 75
Sunshine of Greystone, ... 75
Travels of Bob the Squirrel, ... 37
Wonderful Story Book, ... 50
Willy's First Present, ... 75
Week's Delight; or, Games and Stories for the Parlor, ... 75
William Tell, the Hero of Switzerland, . . 50
Young Student. By Madame Guizot, . . 75

Miscellaneous and General Literature.

An Attic Philosopher in Paris, 25
Appletons' Library Manual, 1 25
Agnell's Book of Chess, 1 25
Arnold's Miscellaneous Works, 2 00
Arthur. The Successful Merchant, 75
A Book for Summer Time in the Country, 50
Baldwin's Flush Times in Alabama, 1 25
Calhoun (J. C.), Works of. 4 vols. publ., each, 2 00
Clark's (W. G.) Knick-Knacks, 1 25
Cornwall's Music as it Was, and as it Is, 63
Essays from the London Times. 1st & 2d Series, each, 50
Ewbanks' World in a Workshop, 75
Ellis' Women of England, 50
" Hearts and Homes, 1 50
" Prevention Better than Cure, 75
Foster's Essays on Christian Morals, 50
Goldsmith's Vicar of Wakefield, 75
Grant's Memoirs of an American Lady, 75
Gaieties and Gravities. By Horace Smith, 50
Guizot's History of Civilization, 1 00
Hearth-Stone. By Rev. S. Osgood, 1 00
Hobson. My Uncle and I, 75
Ingoldsby Legends, 50
Isham's Mud Cabin, 1 00
Johnson's Meaning of Words, 1 00
Kavanagh's Women of Christianity, 75
Leger's Animal Magnetism, 1 00
Life's Discipline. A Tale of Hungary, 63
Letters from Rome. A. D. 138, 1 00
Margaret Maitland, 75
Maiden and Married Life of Mary Powell, 50
Morton Montague; or a Young Christian's Choice, 75
Macaulay's Miscellanies. 5 vols. 5 00
Maxims of Washington. By J. F. Schroeder, 1 00
Mile Stones in our Life Journey, 1 00

MINIATURE CLASSICAL LIBRARY.

Poetic Lacon; or, Aphorisms from the Poets, 38
Bond's Golden Maxims, 31
Clarke's Scripture Promises. Complete, 38
Elizabeth; or, The Exiles of Siberia, 31
Goldsmith's Vicar of Wakefield, 38
" Essays, 38
Gems from American Poets, 38
Hannah More's Private Devotions, 31
" " Practical Piety. 2 vols. 75
Hemans' Domestic Affections, 31
Hoffman's Lays of the Hudson, &c. 38
Johnson's History of Rasselas, 38
Manual of Matrimony, 31
Moore's Lalla Rookh, 38
" Melodies. Complete, 38
Paul and Virginia, 31
Pollok's Course of Time, 38
Pure Gold from the Rivers of Wisdom, 38
Thomson's Seasons, 38
Token of the Heart. Do. of Affection. Do. of Remembrance. Do. of Friendship. Do. of Love. Each, 31
Useful Letter-Writer, 38
Wilson's Sacra Privata, 31
Young's Night Thoughts, 38

Little Pedlington and the Pedlingtonians, 50
Prismatics. Tales and Poems, 1 25
Papers from the Quarterly Review, 50
Republic of the United States. Its Duties, &c 1 00
Preservation of Health and Prevention of Disease, 75
School for Politics. By Chas. Gayerre, 75
Select Italian Comedies. Translated, 75
Shakespeare's Scholar. By R. G. White, 2 50
Spectator (The). New ed. 6 vols. cloth, 9 00
Swett's Treatise on Diseases of the Chest, 3 00
Stories from Blackwood, 50

THACKERAY'S WORKS.

The Book of Snobs, 50
Mr. Browne's Letters, 50
The Confessions of Fitzboodle, 50
The Fat Contributor, 50
Jeames' Diary. A Legend of the Rhine, 50
The Luck of Barry Lyndon, 1 00
Men's Wives, 50
The Paris Sketch Book. 2 vols. 1 00
The Shabby Genteel Story, 50
The Yellowplush Papers. 1 vol. 16mo. 50
Thackeray's Works. 6 vols. bound in cloth, 6 00

Trescott's Diplomacy of the Revolution, 75
Tuckerman's Artist Life, 75
Up Country Letters, 75
Ward's Letters from Three Continents, 1 00
" English Items, 1 00
Warner's Rudimental Lessons in Music, 50
Woman's Worth, 38

Philosophical Works.

Cousin's Course of Modern Philosophy, 00
" Philosophy of the Beautiful, 62
" on the True, Beautiful, and Good, 1 50
Comte's Positive Philosophy. 2 vols. 4 00
Hamilton's Philosophy. 1 vol. 8vo. 1 50

Poetry and the Drama.

Amelia's Poems. 1 vol. 12mo. 1 25
Brownell's Poems. 12mo. 75
Bryant's Poems. 1 vol. 8vo. Illustrated, 3 50
" " Antique mor. 6 00
" " 2 vols. 12mo. cloth, 2 00
" " 1 vol. 18mo. 63
Byron's Poetical Works. 1 vol. cloth, 3 00
" " " Antique mor. 6 00
Burns' Poetical Works. Cloth, 1 00
Butler's Hudibras. Cloth, 1 00
Campbell's Poetical Works. Cloth, 1 00
Coleridge's Poetical Works. Cloth, 1 25
Cowper's Poetical Works, 1 00
Chaucer's Canterbury Tales, 1 00
Dante's Poems. Cloth, 1 00
Dryden's Poetical Works. Cloth, 1 00
Fay (J. S.), Ulric; or, The Voices, 75
Goethe's Iphigenia in Tauris. Translated, 75
Gilfillan's Edition of the British Poets. 12 vols. published. Price per vol. cloth, 1 00
Do. do. Calf, per vol. 2 50
Griffith's (Mattie) Poems, 75
Hemans' Poetical Works. 2 vols. 16mo. 2 00
Herbert's Poetical Works. 16mo. cloth, 1 00
Keats' Poetical Works. Cloth, 12mo. 1 25
Kirke White's Poetical Works. Cloth, 1 00
Lord's Poems. 1 vol. 12mo. 75
" Christ in Hades. 12mo. 75
Milton's Paradise Lost. 18mo. 38
" Complete Poetical Works, 1 00
Moore's Poetical Works. 8vo. Illustrated, 3 00
" " " Mor. extra, 6 00
Montgomery's Sacred Poems. 1 vol. 12mo. 75
Pope's Poetical Works. 1 vol. 16mo. 1 00
Southey's Poetical Works. 1 vol. 3 00
Spenser's Faerie Queene. 1 vol. cloth, 1 00
Scott's Poetical Works. 1 vol. 1 00
" Lady of the Lake. 16mo. 38
" Marmion, 37
" Lay of the Last Minstrel, 25
Shakspeare's Dramatic Works, 2 00
Tasso's Jerusalem Delivered. 1 vol. 16mo. 1 00
Wordsworth (W.). The Prelude, 1 00

Religious Works.

Arnold's Rugby School Sermons, 50
Anthon's Catechism on the Homilies, 06
" Early Catechism for Children 06
Burnet's History of the Reformation. 3 vols. 2 50
" Thirty-Nine Articles, 2 00

Bradley's Family and Parish Sermons, . . . 2 00
Cotter's Mass and Rubrics, ... 38
Coit's Puritanism, ... 1 00
Evans' Rectory of Valehead, ... 50
Grayson's True Theory of Christianity, . . 1 00
Gresley on Preaching, ... 1 25
Griffin's Gospel its Own Advocate, . . . 1 00
Hecker's Book of the Soul, . . .
Hooker's Complete Works. 2 vols. . . 4 00
James' Happiness, ... 25
James on the Nature of Evil, ... 1 00
Jarvis' Reply to Milner, ... 75
Kingsley's Sacred Choir, ... 75
Keble's Christian Year, ... 37
Layman's Letters to a Bishop, ... 25
Logan's Sermons and Expository Lectures, . 1 13
Lyra Apostolica, ... 50
Marshall's Notes on Episcopacy, . . . 1 00
Newman's Sermons and Subjects of the Day, 1 00
" Essay on Christian Doctrine, . . 75
Ogilby on Lay Baptism, ... 50
Pearson on the Creed, ... 2 00
Pulpit Cyclopædia and Ministers' Companion, 2 50
Sewell's Reading Preparatory to Confirmation, 75
Southard's Mystery of Godliness, . . . 75
Sketches and Skeletons of Sermons, . . 2 50
Spencer's Christian Instructed, . . . 1 00
Sherlock's Practical Christian, . . . 75
Sutton's Disce Vivere—Learn to Live, . . 75
Swartz's Letters to my Godchild, . . . 38
Trench's Notes on the Parables, . . . 1 75
" Notes on the Miracles. . . . 1 75
Taylor's Holy Living and Dying, . . . 1 00
" Episcopacy Asserted and Maintained, 75
Tyng's Family Commentary, . . . 2 00
Walker's Sermons on Practical Subjects, . 2 00
Watson on Confirmation, ... 06
Wilberforce's Manual for Communicants, . 38
Wilson's Lectures on Colossians, . . . 75
Wyatt's Christian Altar, ... 38

Voyages and Travels.

Africa and the American Flag, . . . 1 25
Appletons' Southern and Western Guide, . 1 00
" Northern and Eastern Guide, . 1 25
" Complete U. S. Guide Book, . . 2 00
" N. Y. City Map, ... 25
Bartlett's New Mexico, &c. 2 vols. Illustrated, 5 00
Burnet's N. Western Territory, . . . 2 00
Bryant's What I Saw in California, . . 1 25
Coggeshall's Voyages. 2 vols. . . . 2 50
Dix's Winter in Madeira, ... 1 00
Huc's Travels in Tartary and Thibet. 2 vols. 1 00
Layard's Nineveh. 1 vol. 8vo. . . . 1 25
Notes of a Theological Student. 12mo. . . 1 00
Oliphant's Journey to Katmundu, . . . 50
Parkyns' Abyssinia. 2 vols. 2 50
Russia as it Is. By Gurowski, . . . 1 00
" By Count de Custine, ... 1 25
Squier's Nicaragua. 2 vols. 5 00
Tappan's Step from the New World to the Old, 1 75
Wanderings and Fortunes of Germ. Emigrants, 75
Williams' Isthmus of Tehuantepec. 2 vols. 8vo. 3 50

Works of Fiction.

GRACE AGUILAR'S WORKS.

The Days of Bruce. 2 vols. 12mo. . . . 1 50
Home Scenes and Heart Studies. 12mo. . 75
The Mother's Recompense. 12mo. . . 75
Woman's Friendship. 12mo. 75
Women of Israel. 2 vols. 12mo. . . . 1 50

Basil. A Story of Modern Life. 12mo. . . 75
Brace's Fawn of the Pale Faces. 12mo. . 75
Busy Moments of an Idle Woman. . . 75
Chestnut Wood. A Tale. 2 vols. . . . 1 75
Don Quixotte, Translated. Illustrated, . 1 25
Drury (A. H.). Light and Shade, . . . 75
Dupuy (A. E.). The Conspirator, . . . 75
Ellen Parry; or, Trials of the Heart, . . 63

MRS. ELLIS' WORKS.

Hearts and Homes; or, Social Distinctions, . 1 50
Prevention Better than Cure, . . . 75
Women of England, ... 50

Emmanuel Phillibert. By Dumas, . . . 1 25
Farmingdale. By Caroline Thomas, . . 1 00
Fullerton (Lady G.). Ellen Middleton, . 75
" " Grantley Manor. 1 vol. 12mo. 75
" " Lady Bird. 1 vol. 12mo. 75
The Foresters. By Alex. Dumas, . . . 75
Gore (Mrs.). The Dean's Daughter. 1 vol. 12mo. 75
Goldsmith's Vicar of Wakefield. 12mo. . 75
Gil Blas. With 500 Engravings. Cloth, gt. edg. 2 50
Harry Muir. A Tale of Scottish Life, . . 75
Hearts Unveiled; or, I Knew You Would Like Him, ... 75
Heartsease; or, My Brother's Wife. 2 vols. 1 50
Heir of Redclyffe. 2 vols. cloth, . . . 1 50
Heloise; or, The Unrevealed Secret. 12mo. . 75
Hobson. My Uncle and I. 12mo. . . . 75
Holmes' Tempest and Sunshine. 12mo. . . 1 00
Home is Home. A Domestic Story, . . 75
Howitt (Mary). The Heir of West Wayland, 50
Io. A Tale of the Ancient Fane. 12mo. . 75
The Iron Cousin. By Mary Cowden Clarke, . 1 25
James (G. P. R.). Adrian; or, Clouds of the Mind, ... 75
John; or, Is a Cousin in the Hand Worth Two in the Bush, ... 25

JULIA KAVANAGH'S WORKS.

Nathalie. A Tale. 12mo. . . . 1 00
Madeline. 12mo. 75
Daisy Burns. 12mo. 1 00

Life's Discipline. A Tale of Hungary, . . 63
Lone Dove (The). A Legend, ... 75
Linny Lockwood. By Catherine Crowe, . 50

MISS McINTOSH'S WORKS.

Two Lives; or, To Seem and To Be. 12mo. 75
Aunt Kitty's Tales. 12mo. 75
Charms and Counter-Charms. 12mo. . . 1 00
Evenings at Donaldson Manor, . . . 75
The Lofty and the Lowly. 2 vols. . . 1 50

Margaret's Home. By Cousin Alice, . .
Marie Louise; or, The Opposite Neighbors, . 50
Maiden Aunt (The). A Story, . . . 75
Manzoni. The Betrothed Lovers. 2 vols. . 1 50
Margaret Cecil; or, I Can Because I Ought, 75
Morton Montague; or, The Christian's Choice, 75
Norman Leslie. By G. C. H. 75
Prismatics. Tales and Poems. By Haywarde, 1 25
Roe (A. S.). James Montjoy. 12mo. . . 75
" To Love and to Be Loved. 12mo. 75
" Time and Tide. 12mo. . 75
Reuben Medlicott; or, The Coming Man, . 75
Rose Douglass. By S. R. W. 75

MISS SEWELL'S WORKS.

Amy Herbert. A Tale. 12mo. . . . 75
Experience of Life. 12mo. 75
Gertrude. A Tale. 12mo. 75
Katherine Ashton. 2 vols. 12mo. . . . 1 50
Laneton Parsonage. A Tale. 3 vols. 12mo. . 2 25
Margaret Percival. 2 vols. 1 50
Walter Lorimer, and Other Tales. 12mo. . 75
A Journal Kept for Children of a Village School, 1 00

Sunbeams and Shadows. Cloth, . . . 75
Thorpe's Hive of the Bee Hunter, . . . 1 00
Thackeray's Works. 6 vols. 12mo. . . 6 00
The Virginia Comedians. 2 vols. 12mo. . 1 50
Use of Sunshine. By S. M. 12mo. . . . 75
Wight's Romance of Abelard & Heloise. 12mo. 75

www.ingramcontent.com/pod-product-compliance
Lightning Source LLC
LaVergne TN
LVHW020915110826
845150LV00004B/680